THE DIFFICULTIES OF **Modernism**

THE DIFFICULTIES OF Modernism

Leonard Diepeveen

Routledge
New York and London

Published in 2003 by
Routledge
29 West 35th Street
New York, New York 10001

Published in Great Britain by
Routledge
11 New Fetter Lane
London EC4P 4EE

Copyright © 2003 by Taylor & Francis Books, Inc.

Routledge is an imprint of the Taylor & Francis Group.

Printed in the United States of America on acid-free paper.

All rights reserved. No part of this book may be reprinted or reproduced or utilized in any form or by any electronic, mechanical, or other means, now known or hereafter invented, including photocopying and recording, or in any information storage or retrieval system, without permission in writing from the publishers.

Library of Congress Cataloging-in-Publication Data

Diepeveen, Leonard, 1959–
   The difficulties of modernism / by Leonard Diepeveen.
      p. cm.
   Includes bibiographical references and index.
     ISBN 0-415-94068-0 (hardcover : alk. paper) — ISBN 0-415-94069-9 (softcover : alk. paper)
     1. Modernism (Literature) 2. Literature—20th century—History and criticism.
I. Title.
   PN56.M54 D54 2002
   809'.9112—dc21

2002007371

For Susan

Contents

Preface ix

Acknowledgments xvii

CHAPTER 1
Difficulty as Fashion 1

CHAPTER 2
Articulating Anxiety: A Theory of Difficulty 43

CHAPTER 3
Professional Romanticism: Defending Difficulty 87

CHAPTER 4
Difficulty, Vigor, and Pleasure 145

CHAPTER 5
Simplicity and the Modern Canon 178

CONCLUSION
Modern Difficulty's Inheritance 221

Notes 245

Works Cited 277

Index 309

Preface

Speaking at Harvard in the early 1950s, the poet Randall Jarrell noted that he had been asked to talk about the "Obscurity of the Poet." Jarrell commented that his assigned topic did not mean that he was to talk about a timeless quality of art, but was instead to speak on something that had come to prominence in the first half of the century. Its outlines could be sketched with precision:

> That the poetry of the first half of this century *was* too difficult—just as the poetry of the eighteenth century *was* full of antitheses, that of the metaphysicals full of conceits, that of the Elizabethan dramatists full of rant and quibbles—is a truism that it would be absurd to deny. How our poetry got this way—how romanticism was purified and exaggerated and "corrected" into modernism; how poets carried all possible tendencies to their limits, with more than scientific zeal; how the dramatic monologue, which once had depended for its effect upon being a departure from the norm of poetry, now became in one form or another the norm; how poet and public stared at each other with righteous indignation, till the poet said: "Since you won't read me, I'll make sure you can't"—is one of the most complicated and interesting of stories. (Jarrell 1953a, 12)

Jarrell's take on modern difficulty is a complex of shorthand arguments. When he insisted that difficulty *was* modern poetry's central characteristic, Jarrell also asserted that modernism was no longer in flux, that modernism had been accomplished, and that its difficulty was central to this completion. The details of this accomplishment were a matter of record; with his assertion that "romanticism was purified and exaggerated and 'corrected' into modernism," Jarrell suggested that difficulty had a publicly recognized discourse. Jarrell's sense of difficulty as public discourse was part of his characterization of "difficulty" as a story; moreover, it was a story that his listeners needed to understand as a social phenomenon, one in which poets and readers had consciously played out their roles, playing them out to some degree as melodrama. This story, Jarrell believed, had important consequences, not the least of which was a loss of audience for poetry.

Now, Jarrell knew he was being polemical, arguing for a particular way of understanding modernism's difficulty. But many of his ideas about difficulty would have been beyond argument to almost anyone in his audience. In particular, he did not need to convince his audience that modernism was commonly seen as difficult, or that this difficulty needed to be understood as a social phenomenon, or that everyone involved in the difficulty debate claimed the ethical high ground—or that difficulty had triumphed. All that could be assumed.

However, fifty years later, this "most complicated and interesting of stories" remains untold. *The Difficulties of Modernism* narrates this story and considers its effects. It does so with the understanding that difficulty is an experience familiar to everyone with some knowledge of twentieth-century high culture. Readers even mildly interested in twentieth-century high art can connect difficulty to modernism, often by referring to one of modernism's famous stories—the scandal of the Armory Show, perhaps, or the riot at the Paris premiere of the *Sacre du printemps*. They might be familiar with the critical wisdom that while Joyce wrote a difficult but worthwhile book in *Ulysses*, in *Finnegans Wake* he went several steps too far. And while every reader of this book will have some personal experience of the exhilaration that can accompany a successful struggle with difficult art, more memorable perhaps are the *failed* struggles with it: perhaps the memory of fumbling through *The Waste Land* or *Mrs. Dalloway* in college (an acquaintance, on hearing me describe this book, remarked of *The Waste Land*: "I didn't even understand the notes"); or of glumly listening to a perplexing piece of twentieth-century music that filled the second half of a symphony concert; or of walking into a contemporary art gallery and staring blankly at the neat rectangle of firebricks Carl Andre had arranged in the center of the gallery floor.

The Difficulties of Modernism, from its definitions on up, stays close to this sense of difficulty as an experience. It defines difficulty in terms of how modern readers understood and used it: as a barrier to what one normally expected to receive from a text, such as its logical meaning, its emotional expression, or its pleasure. For modern readers, difficulty was the experience of having one's desires for comprehension blocked, an experience provoked by a wide variety of works of art ("comprehension" is here defined broadly). Without dealing with this barrier in some way—and such dealings were not restricted to *understanding* or decoding the syntax of the difficult moment—it was impossible to interact significantly with the text. Difficulty thus drove its readers forward, for they realized that their bafflement was an inadequate response. Further, until they removed or contained their bafflement, readers overwhelmingly reacted with anxiety. Modernism's difficulty, then, is not merely a classifiable set of techniques. To discuss difficulty solely as the property of texts is to impoverish it and miss how difficulty became an integral part of high culture. Difficulty must be understood in terms of a reading process, and it manifests itself socially; modernism begins with a typical interaction between art and its audience. Difficulty, this book argues, is that recurring *relationship* that came into being between modernist works and their audiences.

Two central claims about difficulty shaped its social articulation. First, literary modernism's first readers often asserted that difficulty's prevalence was unique to modernism, frequently commenting that difficulty currently was, as one reader grumbled, "running rampant in literature" ("Flat Prose" [1914] 1986, 38). Difficulty, in fact, was the most noted characteristic of what became the canonical texts of high modernism; it dramatically shaped the reception of Faulkner, Joyce, Stein, Moore, Eliot, Pound, and Woolf, just to name those who early were considered to be central modernist writers. Now, it's not that people thought difficulty had never before surfaced in literature. However, there was a general sense that this was the first time in history that difficulty was so widespread, and that modernism was unique in that its difficulty was seen as being central to art's *direction*. Second, modern difficulty made big claims for itself. T. S. Eliot, for example, would claim that "it appears likely that poets in our civilization, as it exists at present, must be *difficult*. Our civilization comprehends great variety and complexity, and this variety and complexity, playing upon a refined sensibility, must produce various and complex results" (Eliot [1921] 1975b, 65).

Difficulty thus was central to people's sense that modernism was a sea change—not just in the properties of art works, but in the default and most useful ways of talking about and interacting with art. Modernism's difficulty set up the terms and protocols by which readers read and gained access to modernist texts, and it became a litmus test: one could predict both a given reader's response to modernism by his or her reaction to difficulty, and a writer's place in the canon by the difficulty of his or her work. Modern difficulty was a powerful aesthetic, then. It also continues to be one, for aesthetic difficulty retains its legitimizing force today. Modern difficulty has profoundly shaped the entire twentieth century; one's ability to move in high culture continues to depend, in large part, on how one reacts to difficulty.

Focusing primarily on literature, this book examines what followed from the moment when modernism's readers began to comment that difficulty was everywhere. Why did difficult writing produce such anxiety? In what ways did difficult works contest traditional understandings of pleasure? How did the argument over difficulty shape what became the high modern canon? How much of literary professional activity is bound up with difficulty? How much do modern understandings of difficulty shape contemporary culture? Answering these questions is crucial to understanding not only difficult literature, but the relationship between all forms of high art and culture in the past century, for the major arguments about literary difficulty travel unchanged to other arts, using the same rhetorical tropes, describing the same kind of experiences.

Difficulty's movement in culture is not only widespread, it is routinized, doing its work quietly, using presuppositions that most often "go without saying." As a result, in answering the above questions, this book attempts to defamiliarize difficulty, to make it look strange. It does so by examining the routine ways in which difficulty functions, questioning whether these activities serve culture best by working unexamined in the background.

To make my generalizations about modern difficulty accurate, I have made my research broad. This book examines the initial response to the work of Pound, Eliot, Joyce, Woolf, Stein, Faulkner, and Moore, as well as the reception histories of Robert Frost and Willa Cather. In addition, it turns to early thumbnail arguments about the modern canon, found in the introductions to over one hundred anthologies of modern poetry, as well as the first generation of books on modernism (ca. 1927 to 1935), particularly those on modern poetry. It works with the essays of Eliot, Pound, and Moore; with the editorials of J. C. Squire at the *London Mercury* and those of Harriet Monroe at *Poetry*; and, of course, little magazines such as *The Little Review* and *transition*. To broaden my evidence, I have collected representative arguments from the visual arts and music. To get a sense of the hold of modern difficulty on contemporary high culture, I have also researched contemporary responses to difficulty and difficulty's role in the culture wars. This has given me a base of more than 1,500 books, reviews, articles, and anthologies from which I make my generalizations.

Early on, my research revealed the basic characteristics of difficulty's movements; as I continued, the broadness of my research revealed those basic characteristics to be present everywhere. Probably the most important aspect of the difficulty argument—one that shaped the theoretical approach I found most useful—was that developed theoretical arguments did not drive the conversation about difficult modernism. There is no well-reasoned argument by someone like, say, Pound that established a theoretical basis for difficulty. What primarily drove the discussion were comments like Eliot's. The most frequently quoted comment on difficulty in twentieth-century Anglo-American literary culture, Eliot's remark is shaped more like an epigram than an argument. That casualness typifies modern comments on difficulty. A lot of the difficulty argument was carried out as shorthand, almost as rhetorical tropes. (Perhaps some of this was because difficulty was central to *public* discourse about modernism and had the generalizing that characterizes such discourse.) Further, there is no evidence that modernist readers were silently using more sophisticated arguments on which to base their ad hoc comments. The argument about difficulty can more profitably be understood as a kind of game, a game with a limited number of rhetorical counters but a great variety of combinations. This book reveals what those counters were, the standard ways in which they were moved, and their consequences. *The Difficulties of Modernism* thus is, in a sense, a social rhetoric of difficulty: "rhetoric," because it is concerned with recurrent linguistic strategies, and "social" because these strategies occurred within a social domain and were profoundly implicated in it.

The sketchiness yet preponderance of arguments about difficulty, the stylized reactions to it, along with the breadth of my research have led me to analyze the work performed by *typical* descriptions of difficulty. I do not give pride of place to those discussions that are the most theoretically sophisticated or that "get it right," for such an approach would not adequately portray difficulty's extraordinary activities. Making sense of modern difficulty necessitates looking at how it typically functioned in its culture.

Since what is typical in modernism drives my argument, modernism's understandings of difficulty set the agenda for how I discuss accounts of difficulty from before the twentieth century (not that I believe that modernism's understandings were always right). As a consequence, though there are many moments in the book where I point to earlier understandings of difficulty, *The Difficulties of Modernism* does not give a time line. It does not begin with Aristotle, move through Dante, Kant, and Hegel, and then onward toward early modernism. It is not that these earlier moments are irrelevant to modernism's difficulty, but a writer like Aristotle shows up where he impinges most clearly on modernism's peculiar difficulties; this book addresses how difficult modernism put Aristotle to use.

This book limits its attention to Anglo-American culture during the years 1910 to 1950, setting the parameters of analysis at the beginning of the twentieth century and at midcentury. The chronological range is pragmatic: beginning in the second decade of the twentieth century one starts to hear the complaint that difficulty is everywhere. Earlier, and in the previous century (except, possibly, in painting), comments about difficulty are directed at individuals, such as George Meredith or Joseph Conrad. Around 1915 difficulty starts to be discussed as a *movement*, and a large movement indeed, for readers begin to comment on how difficulty had overtaken *all* the arts. By

1950, a fairly impermeable canon of high modernism had been established in the university curriculum. And that general sense of modernism is the one that functions as my definition. It is the idea of modernism that typically was promoted in English departments from the mid-1940s to the mid-1970s, modernism with a capital *M*: portentous, asserting a unity for itself, and claiming privileged status to speak about early twentieth-century culture.

To have stretched this history to the end of the twentieth century would have resulted either in a monstrously large book or one too full of demurrals and throat-clearings as it tried to separate the beginning from the end of the century. On the other hand, my research reveals that contemporary difficulty has an enormously weighty inheritance from high modernism. Postmodernism may present some new forms of difficulty, but the *reflexes* about difficulty haven't changed. Thus, although this is not primarily a book about contemporary difficulty, there are obvious homologies that I point out in notes, text boxes, and some of the anecdotes that start or conclude chapters. But I do not give an extended argument about them; this is not an exhaustive argument, but a suggestion of how modern difficulty continues to have its hold on us.

The same desire to create a tellable narrative has limited my focus by and large to Anglo-American culture. This is not to say I was oblivious to the allure of wandering outside this linguistic cultural situation, given the connection many high modern writers had with various continental aesthetic communities. Moreover, many of the arguments from other cultures about difficulty not only contain the same basic logic, they use the same tropes and demonstrate the same social and physiological responses (chapter 2 begins to point out why this similarity might be the case). Yet while I sometimes point to those highly suggestive similarities, my interest in telling a relatively complete story prompted me to use a culturally more uniform and stable body of evidence.

The Difficulties of Modernism begins by noting the perceived preponderance of high modern difficulty and examining how that preponderance shaped modern culture. As well, it considers how modern understandings of earlier difficulty helped form the high modern canon. Chapter 2 turns to examine the powerful affective responses to difficulty. In the formation of the modern canon, difficulty did its work in a highly charged atmosphere, for difficulty is always accompanied by evaluation and often gives rise to powerful affective responses. Difficulty is an odd aesthetic experience; using their whole bodies, people react viscerally to difficulty, often with anxiety, anger, and ridicule. The public debate about difficulty and its scandalousness, then, was much more than a story of elitism and middle-class anti-intellectualism. It was also a story of anger, of pleasure, and of the body. Moreover, those affective responses are enmeshed in the standard ways of conceptualizing difficulty and profoundly influence how difficulty shaped modern culture.

Not surprisingly, given their highly charged responses, people thought difficulty was important. High modernism's skeptics thought it was destroying literature, even civilization; while modernism's apologists made big claims for difficulty, arguing that difficulty had important things to say about modern culture or human psychology. Chapter 3 examines those standard arguments for difficulty and looks at the kinds of work they did in forming the high modern canon. It considers the arguments that difficulty is the inevitable domain of the professional, that difficulty accurately portrays the human mind or modern culture, that difficulty is an agent for social change, that all new works are difficult and that difficulty will disappear as the difficult work becomes a classic, that the apparently difficult is actually simple, or that difficulty is essential to all great art. (These arguments, as this and chapters 4 and 5 indicate, did not march along in a triumph of efficient logic. Instead, they were driven by an inner conflict, a conflict that on the one hand grounded difficulty in a professionalist/classicist ethos, and on the other hand kept nervously reaching back to romanticist ideals of aesthetic expression, including the sublime.) Chapters 4 and 5 look at several instinctive attitudes in high modernism, attitudes that were key to difficulty's triumph: the relationship between modernism's moralistic sense of machismo and its distrust of both pleasure and simplicity. In doing so, these chapters posit that these attitudes are entangled with the visceral attitudes delineated in chapter 2.

The Difficulties of Modernism also continues the current examination into the social context of modernism. What modernism's defenders did not clearly acknowledge, but which is central to understanding how difficulty worked in modern culture, is that difficulty had an important social function as a cultural gatekeeper. Knowing how to respond properly to difficult art became a way of indicating one's membership in high culture. High culture eventually accepted this social function so completely that it was possible for it to do its work in the background. This acceptance has everything to do with how we got where we are today, and *where* that "where we are" actually is. Modernism was formed on an aesthetics of difficulty; since that time high culture has been living off of a modernist inheritance. Unless we reexamine that allegiance and the ways in which it continues to control contemporary culture, we are doomed to accept its benefits and its costs.

Finally, a note on the vexing question of terminology. Most of the time I have tried to indicate specific aspects of early twentieth-century literature by referring to "high modernists" or "difficult modernists" as a way of indicating those who generally supported difficult modernism. Those who were skeptical of difficulty I typically refer to as "traditionalists," or "difficulty's skeptics." At times when it is clear that I am referring to difficulty, I occasionally use the plain term "modernism." I realize that the terminology may dichotomize early twentieth-century culture more than it at times deserves, that some interesting variegations exist (for instance, a conservative like Harriet Monroe represented herself as more modern than Ezra Pound). But difficulty *was* a highly charged debate, with almost no one occupying a middle ground, and my terminological shorthand does keep the book from grinding to a halt every time I use these terms. Context on each of these occasions should make it clear in which direction my terminology is pointing.

Acknowledgments

The Research Development Fund at Dalhousie University and the Social Sciences and Humanities Research Council of Canada awarded grants that made this project possible. They also provided funds for an efficient team of graduate assistants, including Natalie Collins, Natalie Crocker, Nate Dorward, Sharon Hamilton, Mark Silverberg, and Sheilah Wilson. I owe them much for their generosity and proficiency. The Department of English at the University of Illinois was also extremely generous in lending me office space and resources during a sabbatical.

I would additionally like to thank the many people who pointed me to resources along the way, including Bruce Barber, Gregory Colomb, John Xiros Cooper, and Brian Johnson. As well, colleagues at Dalhousie University have been a great help in their willingness to prod me along: I think especially of John Barnstead, Melissa Furrow, and Trevor Ross. I have also received useful readings of versions of this book from Mary Ann Gillies, Gail McDonald, Tim Newcomb, Lawrence Rainey, and as well as two readers for Routledge (the helpfulness and dispatch of editors at Routledge ought to be legendary). Nick Lolordo and Vernon Shetley have been particularly generous in their time. My greatest intellectual debt is to Timothy Van Laar, whose advice and patience during hours of conversing on this topic were invaluable. Susan, and our children, Benjamin and Annelies, deserve commendation for continuing to tolerate me when this project and I became especially difficult.

Permissions

Excerpt from "Burnt Norton" from *Four Quartets* from *Collected Poems 1909–1962* by T. S. Eliot, and in *Four Quartets* by T. S. Eliot, copyright 1936 by Harcourt, Inc. and renewed 1964 by T. S. Eliot, reprinted by permission of the publisher. "Poem (As the cat)" by William Carlos Williams, from *Collected Poems 1909–1939*, Volume I, copyright ©1938 by New Directions Publishing Corp. Reprinted by permission of New Directions Publishing Corp. and Carcanet Press Limited. "The Connoisseur" printed by permission of the Norman Rockwell Family Agency. Copyright ©1962 the Norman Rockwell Family Agency. From "Difficult Listening Hour" by Laurie Anderson ©1985 *Difficult Music*. "Box of God," a poem by Lew Sarett. From *Box of God*, copyright © 1922 by Lew Sarett. Used by permission of Lloyd Sarett Stockdale. The copyright holder for "Romance," by W. J. Turner, could not be traced.

CHAPTER 1

Difficulty as Fashion

> Poets in our civilization, as it exists at present, must be *difficult*.
> —T. S. Eliot

> The trick of incomprehensibility is the best trick that has ever been invented for the benefit of writers who, if they can feel or think, do not know how to translate their thoughts and feelings into the language of art.
> —J. C. Squire

If the literary history of the early twentieth century teaches anything, it teaches that modern writers liked nothing better than a good fight. Literary enemies were useful; they allowed one to heighten the rhetoric, to draw in one's arguments with decisive strokes, and to point out the clear direction literature, if it was to have any integrity at all, must follow. In retrospect the polemics may seem overdone; early twentieth-century writers drew the demerits of their opponents' claims (and the virtues of their own) more like cartoons than like subtle portraits. But these histrionics were useful; indeed, it is likely that the institution we now know as high modernism could not have been created without such melodrama.

High modernism, then, was built with clumsy but efficient arguments. Of these arguments, difficulty was central. Difficulty, one of the early twentieth century's great cultural debates, had big consequences—as everyone in the literary community then was aware. Everybody had something to say about modern literary difficulty, and they often did not rest there; those who argued about difficulty and modern literature extended their claims to *all* modern art forms and beyond—to *all* literature, and to *all* art. Anything but equivocal, early twentieth-century readers made grandiose assertions, claiming that *all* good literature was difficult, or that *all* good literature was simple. Further, all those embroiled in the difficulty argument referred to themselves as the underdog, a strategy that created the necessary sense of crisis and imbued their writing with polemical urgency.[1]

While that dichotomizing made for robust assertions, it did not allow for much maneuvering room. By magnifying their claims to *all* literature, and by demonizing their opponents, early twentieth-century writers made literature into a zero-sum game, a game that acknowledged neither ties nor stalemates, a game that would end only when the competitors had been separated into the victors and the vanquished. Modern readers thus did not discuss literature in terms of a variety of honorable strategies, of which difficulty was but one option among many. The difficulty argument did not open up literature to a variety of strategies; rather, it assembled a canon of like-minded literary works. Further, difficulty was made to carry more weight than it could support—difficulty became not just an argument about comprehension, it became an argument about professionalization, about pleasure, about the meaning of twentieth-century culture. Difficulty took in a huge chunk of the aesthetic landscape, and it seemed that the winners of the difficulty argument would walk away with a very large prize.

Difficulty, then, was the early twentieth century's central tool for arguing about what literature is and who should control it. However, whatever gains modern difficulty produced came with a price. By making the stakes so high (something that, as chapter 2 argues, was perhaps unavoidable), modern readers forfeited diversity and flexibility. This loss made two things inevitable: difficulty's apparently seamless end product (a product that by the 1950s was known unproblematically as modernism), and the dominant ways of reading that product.[2]

In modernism's cantankerous setting an exceptionally resonant voice was that of J. C. Squire, editor of the *London Mercury*. In the pages of his monthly, from which he coolly surveyed contemporary culture, Squire often grumbled about the difficulty of modern literature, painting, and music. Even so, the issue of June 1924 was something special. To be sure, it followed its usual agenda; as it did every month since its first issue in 1919, the magazine commented on a wide range of books and cultural events. For the edification of its ten thousand readers the *London Mercury* meditated on contemporary theater and the Wembley Exhibition; it indulged in some literary chat and ruminated on the virtues of the now-forgotten poet Herbert Trench; and its lengthy review section assessed contemporary poetry, fiction, music, belles lettres, literary history, and biography. But the June issue's short story, Squire's "The Man Who Wrote Free Verse" (1924, 127–37), contained Squire's most sustained attack on modern difficulty to date. Giving a forum for Squire's métier—parody and satire—the story not only puts into play the basic rhetorical strategies that writers used to oppose difficult modernism, it

> Apollo through the woods came down
> Furred like a merchant fine,
> And sate with a sailor at an Inn
> Sharing a jug of wine.
>
> Had sun-rays, spilled out of a storm,
> Thither the God conveyed?
> Or some green and floating cloudlet caught
> On the fringes of a glade?
> —Opening lines of Herbert Trench's 1907 *New Poems*

also illustrates the social stresses that brought the modern canon into being, and it serves as a primer for the concerns of *The Difficulties of Modernism*.

The story begins on a hot summer day at the country home of Lady Muriel, who is hosting several guests for the weekend, including two young men, Adrian Roberts and Reggie Twyford. Resting after lunch, Reggie, languidly thumbing through Lady Muriel's collection of currently fashionable authors, drops his book to complain that Lady Muriel's books "seem even more ridiculous here than they do in town" (121). Adrian, taking on the role of cynic that he wears throughout the story, cannot see why Reggie wastes his time on such trash. However, with the air of someone who sees it as his painful duty to know avant-garde high culture, Reggie responds with a lament for the state into which contemporary literature has drifted: "I can't quite ignore it all as you do. It's the poetry I was thinking of most. I confess I can't make head or tail of three-quarters of it, but I can't help thinking I may be wrong. Why should they be writing what seems to us cacophonous gibberish? It isn't only Muriel, you know. Lots of people seem to admire it, and it's happening all over Europe and America" (128). As Reggie sees it, the incomprehensible writing found in Muriel's books (particularly the poetry) raises two issues that don't mesh very well: the problem of motivation (the question of why "they" would write "cacophonous gibberish"), and the problem of fashion (not only the fact that "lots of people seem to admire it," but also that so much is being written, that "it's happening all over Europe and America"). These two observations, coupled with his own incomprehension, shape Reggie's anxiety.

Adrian, on the other hand, doesn't share Reggie's apprehension. He sees difficult writing as not much more than a publicity stunt: "We hear a good deal about it and the papers we read seem to think it all ought to be taken seriously. In point of fact these creatures are scarcely read by each other." He follows this dismissal with a startling attack: "It's a kind of hideous little underworld; the sort of thing you see when you lift up a large stone and see disgusting insects, beetles and centipedes, scuttling about. They dislike the daylight too. It's all the most awful nonsense. The second-rate have discovered the trick of incomprehensibility in our own time; the trick of bogus audacity has always been known" (128). According to Adrian, difficult contemporary writers have the marketing techniques and moral probity of snake-oil salesmen.

In response, Reggie, "still generously resolute to put a case against which all his instincts revolted," wonders if there "may be something genuine in all this movement." When asked which movement, he replies airily: "Oh, the whole of it. The general mix-up. All these isms and experiments." The twentieth century seems to be a unique time, Reggie muses, and perhaps its uniqueness demands new forms of writing: "Scientific and social conceptions can't alter without modifying art; music changes and poetry may change; and I can conceive new things being said in a new way." Reggie, arguing that perhaps the fashion for difficult writing may be "important and symptomatic," presses his case and asks, "Doesn't it seem to you significant that when the Bolshevists got into power in Russia they made all the Cubists and things official artists?" (128).

Adrian's response is swift: "'I'm sure that highly elaborate nonsense means nothing whatever to the proletariat. To their leaders it meant only one more annoyance to the bourgeoisie; though perhaps they naturally felt a kind of affinity for the rape of language and the murder of ideas.' His eyes strayed to the far landscape. 'The confiscation of the comma,' he murmured, as it were for his own benefit" (128).

Adrian then hatches a plot. Asserting that nothing is easier than to write difficult art, he claims that Reggie too could write "all this bosh" easily, and he suggests that Reggie "start a career as an advanced poet" (129). Having far too much time on their hands, the two conspire to expose contemporary poetry's cheap and deliberate obscurity. Under the assumed name of Sidney Twyford (ostensibly his black sheep cousin), Reggie will write intentionally incomprehensible verse, which, since the times are ripe, everyone will praise. Following that success, Reggie will unmask himself and expose the fraudulence of contemporary avant-garde writing.

Taking on the role of manager, Adrian instructs Reggie in the easy process of writing difficult poetry: "You must begin . . . by emptying your mind completely and recording only disconnected impressions. You can work in the rebellion and work out the verbs later" (129). So, Reggie bends to his task. He writes the first piece under the deadline of a lobster luncheon, and the pressure shows:

> The chimney-cowls
> Gyrate
> In the wind
> There is a blot of ink
> On my paper.
> I am going to have lunch
> Before long
> And I am glad there is
> A
> Lobster. (130)

This work gets Adrian's measured approval. As a start, he comments, this is not bad. But, he continues, the "faults" of the above piece are that "the sentences are quite ordinary." Also, Adrian says, "you actually express, in one place, a genuine emotion: I mean when you refer to the lobster" (130).

Dutifully returning to work, Reggie produces the following, more constricted version:

> Gyrating cowls.
> Ink.
> Oh God! A Lobster! (130)

That is more like it, Adrian comments, and, his surrogate ambition swelling, he instructs Reggie in the various forms of twentieth-century obscurity: "Don't forget the classical one and don't forget the one which is allowed to rhyme, by way of compensation for its especially polysyllabic obscurity" (130). Writing in response a poem that he describes as "fearfully obscure," Reggie produces what many readers of the *London Mercury* would have recognized as a parody of T. S. Eliot's quatrain poems, particularly his "Sweeney among the Nightingales:"

> Apocalyptic chimney cowls
> Squeak at the sergeant's velvet hat
> Donkeys and other paper fowls
> Disgorge decretals at the cat.
>
> The lead archdeacon eats her cheese
> Corrupting their connubial bliss
> And Mary on her six black knees
> Refuses Christopher a kiss.
>
> Autumnal abscesses relent
> The twilight of ancestral days
> But, smiling at the parsnip's scent,
> The Nubian girl undoes her stays! (131)

> Apeneck Sweeney spreads his knees
> Letting his arms hang down to laugh,
> The zebra stripes along his jaw
> Swelling to maculate giraffe.
>
> The circles of the stormy moon
> Slide westward toward the River Plate,
> Death and the Raven drift above
> And Sweeney guards the hornèd gate.
>
> Gloomy Orion and the Dog
> Are veiled; and hushed the shrunken seas;
> The person in the Spanish cape
> Tries to sit on Sweeney's knees
>
> —Opening lines of Eliot's "Sweeney among the Nightingales," 1920

The work relentlessly goes on. Musing whether his next poem "is quite obscure enough," Reggie produces the following parody of American expatriate H. D.:

> O Phoibos Albanios
> The white limbs
> Of the nymphs
> On Hymettos
> Io Pan, the honey
> Acrid
> In the nostrils
> Io, the purple
> Of the vats of Herakles
> On the cliffs
> By Akrokeraunia
> Hard and bitter
> The shells
> But the flesh
> Ah Zeus!
> Ah good! (132)

Adrian sees this piece as "absolutely perfect," and he is proven correct.

The career of Sidney Twyford takes off, his first public affirmation occurring a month after the above poems were written. Reggie is again invited by

Muriel, this time to luncheon at her London home. There, he meets what Adrian called the "hideous little underworld" of fashionable literary society: "There was a company of twelve in the jazz dining-room: six young men and six middle-aged women. The women, at a glance, seemed all to have white faces and red hair; the young men had white faces and either no hair or too much; tortoise-shell spectacles were generally worn; voices were pitched high; and any little indecency was welcomed by titters of appreciation" (134). Squire's audience would have recognized at least some of the resemblance to such contemporary literary figures as T. S. Eliot, Ezra Pound, Lady Ottoline Morrell and Edith, Osbert, and Sacheverell Sitwell. Reggie does his best to keep up with their conversation, but finds himself at a disadvantage: "He knew very few of the names of the latest and most devastating Franco-Brazilian painters, and pornography, owing to some strange inhibition, he always shrank from discussing in mixed company. But he met his companions halfway and, now and then, when he inadvertently slipped into seriousness, sense, or the disclosure of an acquaintance with the major artists of the past, he delighted them with the surprise of a fresh point of view. The time might come, he reflected, when they might think morality too charming and agree to turn to it for an entirely novel sensation" (134).

These are the kind of people and the kind of setting where difficulty is embraced, and discussion soon turns to the new poet, Sidney Twyford, in whose work many of the guests "revel." They agree that while Twyford "had not yet found a definite direction," his lack of a single purpose was a sign of vitality and ambition: "Even Cubism and Futurism, it was agreed, had been too narrow. Sidney Twyford comprehended these and more: he was at once Electrist, Early Victorian, Deliquescent, Sadist, Universalist, Psychoanalyst and Communist; and he could equal each of the most advanced poets on his own ground. Words like reality, metaphysics, complex, impression, release, significance, dull, sentimental and priapic began to swarm in the air like swallows preparing for migration" (135). Reggie's deliberately obscure writing fares well in this setting. A "myopic youth" argues that Twyford's work is much superior to another fashionable poet's poem, entitled *Convulsions in Blue Flat Minor*, which, although Muriel describes it as "delicious," is ultimately dismissed as "*vieux jeu.*" Twyford's work, the guests agree, has gone "much farther" (135). Eventually the party breaks up, and on the way home Reggie, still feeling a bit at sea in this avant-garde circle, asks a female guest "whether she could explain the *Mammon Fox-Trot* to him, or indeed throw the slightest hint of its meaning to him." Although she cannot articulate the poem's meaning, her response is emphatic. Fashion, according to her, is never wrong, and Reggie needs to get on board: "'Reggie,' she said, 'I wish you wouldn't be so obstinate. *All* the amusing young men are doing it, and they *must* be right'" (135).

Time goes on, and the narrator notes that Reggie "managed his career with great acumen." Some of the poems that seal his success are made up entirely of lines like the following:

i—i—iii—iii—ii—oksz
P.?..... NWVQ (135)

Reggie even publishes some of his "own" poems, work written before he became Sidney, work which the narrator describes as those "seriously pretty poems of his regenerate days." These poems cause his ascendant reputation to rise even higher: "his disciples rejoiced that their hero could do that sort of thing on his head, and the earnest seekers after truth argued still more earnestly that the fault, as concerned his darker works, must obviously lie with the reader and not with the poet" (136). Reggie's vogue grows "in all the advanced circles of England and America." His book of poetry, *Ourang-Outang*, gets a tumultuous reception, and an American bookseller offers £5,000 for the manuscript. Reggie's career is further boosted not by his accepting this offer, but by rejecting it (even the bookseller prospers, for he uses Reggie's rejection as advertising). Reggie is seen as a heroic artist "who not merely declined all personal publicity but had stated that he did not approve of the factitious making of money by the sale of manuscripts" (136). Thus, Adrian's original prediction about Reggie's success is proven right: it is not chance that so much contemporary work should be both difficult *and* fashionable; rather, a work's difficulty *ensures* that it will be fashionable. Reggie's readers value his poetry *because* they cannot understand it.

Squire's story, having discharged its load of gags, ends with "the great British Bolshevik Revolution." St. Paul's and Westminster are burned, and refugees flee to Russia, which over the years has been transformed into "the safest and most prosperous monarchist country remaining" (136). Reggie, on the other hand, is awakened in his bedroom by "three dirty and hirsute men with pistols who announced themselves as the heads of the British Soviet, Abramovitch, Macalister and Evans" (136). They snap to attention and their "harsh voices" chime "We greet the Poet of the Revolution." Although Reggie protests that he is not Sidney, the leader of the group, Abramovitch, replies: "'Zere is,' he said, 'no further need for deception, gomrade. Ve haf spied on you and your letters for a year. You haf done your work; you must now haf your revard.'" The reward is not auspicious: taken outside, Reggie is greeted by the "roar of a multitude" who are the first crowd ever to "invade" the "cloisters" where Reggie lives. As Poet Laureate of the Revolution, Reggie gets to keep one of his rooms, and is paid with "a million paper pounds a day" and a yearly barrel of beer (137).

Although his living conditions have sagged considerably from what they were at the beginning of the story, Reggie is stoic, since his employers attach easy conditions to his employment. The narrator notes that "so long as [Reggie] could not be understood they were quite satisfied with him." After some time, Reggie dies, a casualty "of boredom and intellectual starvation." But he dies a hero; the narrator reports that "half the army and millions of the proletariat" attend his funeral, followed by his burial in the "National Pantheon in Villiers Street, Strand" (137).

J. C. Squire and Modernism

"The Man Who Wrote Free Verse" apparently pleased Squire, who reprinted it in a collection of his stories later that year. The story's satire, of course, exaggerates reality, but in order for his gags to work, Squire depended on people recognizing the ways in which difficulty—accompanied by its social nuances—permeated modern culture. Modern difficulty, in fact, was a parodist's dream. One did not have to agree with Squire's take on difficulty to recognize that his satire was pointing to the real world. While not everyone agreed, for example, that modernism was decadent or that it reveled in scandalizing the general public, everyone recognized that questions about scandal, decadence, marketing, and elitism shaped the public debate about modernism's difficulty. Many of Squire's readers would further agree with Squire that these questions shaped modernism so profoundly, in fact, that they had destabilized literary production, creating the social conditions that made a successful hoax plausible.

Squire's story has more ambition than its light tone suggests. In using difficulty as its springboard, "The Man Who Wrote Free Verse" not only pillories aspects of modernism that the *London Mercury*'s readers recognized, in doing so it addresses the social and textual conditions that in fact were central to modernism's formation. Squire's story shows that one can recognize difficulty not just by looking at a text's properties, but also by looking at what *accompanies* those properties, how those properties enter social discourse. Difficulty is a social situation: it is produced by certain kinds of people and received favorably by other identifiable groups. Turning to the "advanced circles" that produce and celebrate difficulty, Squire repeatedly jabs at the kinds of people professionalism attracts, as well as central presuppositions of aesthetic professionalism: its belief that a work's aesthetic value depends upon its importance or its status as a development of some aesthetic concern, as well as the idea that art should reflect the radical newness of modern life. And, while Squire ridicules difficulty as the latest literary fashion, the equivalent of wide (or, perhaps, narrow) neckties, he also implies that it is more insidious than a change in clothes, for, as Eliot's epigraph to this chapter shows, difficulty makes big claims for itself. Squire notes these big claims by repeatedly referring to those who write and value difficulty as being "advanced" and through quoting their jargon. Squire also attacks the professionalized elitism of modern literature (an elitism different from Reggie and Adrian's class-based elitism, which is a social snobbery the story also lampoons, though with a lighter touch). He satirizes how this coterie of professionals is self-serving and self-congratulatory, and how it ignores, or worse, abuses, the common reader. The story repeatedly claims an entangled relationship between modern writing and politics, not only through its potshots at Marxism (which near the story's end are accompanied by a startling whiff of anti-Semitism), but also with the American bookseller's capitalist venture. Through his portrayal of the radical elite and its mania for the latest literary fashion, Squire lampoons what he sees as modernism's decadence, a decadence brought to life by modernism's acrid mixture of pseudo-intellectualism, effete unnaturalness, and overbearing women.

Thus, the great crime of modernism, according to Squire, is that it is self-serving and driven by social forces such as fashion, publicity, and marketing. But Squire's story goes further; it suggests that understanding how difficulty works, and knowing what attitude to adopt when confronted with difficult work, is a ticket of entry into high culture. If you don't know what to do with *Mammon Fox-Trot*, you don't get invited to the luncheon. In asserting this, Squire also recognizes that a primary effect of difficulty is anxiety for the uninitiated. All this, according to Squire, shapes the context and texts of modernism, and all of this is what's wrong with it. Squire's story, then, contains almost all the major issues that accompanied or even drove the construction of modernism. But what is striking about this list is that Squire chooses *difficulty* as the vehicle to foreground these issues. Difficulty does a lot of work in "The Man Who Wrote Free Verse,"—as it did in modernism itself.

Squire was well-positioned both to make these assertions and to have his audience understand them. Not only was the difficulty to which he referred well known, so was Squire himself; most readers of the *London Mercury* could have predicted the aim of "The Man Who Wrote Free Verse" just by knowing that Squire wrote it. By the time he published "The Man Who Wrote Free Verse," Squire had been involved in literary journalism for fifteen years (during the first ten he wrote for the *New Age* and for the *New Statesman*, of which he was literary editor). He was known as an excellent parodist, and the twenty-two books (including poetry, essays, and collections of reviews) he published between 1907 and 1922 received serious reviews. Literary types took Squire seriously; in his 1922 anthology of contemporary English poetry, J. E. Wetherell claimed of J. C. Squire that "no living poet has a wider influence on the literary views and tendencies of his age" (36).

His editorship of the successful *London Mercury* allowed Squire to amplify his opinions; soon after it began publishing in 1919, the circulation of the

London Mercury approached ten thousand (Howarth 1963, 136).[3] The journal quickly signaled its aesthetic preferences; its opening editorial claimed a disinterested universality, arguing that the magazine would not be accused either of "attempting to make universal the shibboleths of some coterie or school, or of carrying some technical 'stunt' through the country as if it were a fiery cross" (Squire 1919, 2). Wielding the whimsy which brought him his readers, Squire pronounced: "As convenient descriptions we do not object (save sometimes on grounds of euphony) to the terms Futurist, Vorticist, Expressionist, post-Impressionist, Cubist, Unanimist, Imagist: but we suspect them as banners and battle-cries, for where they are used as such it is probable that fundamentals are being forgotten" (3). Rather, he argued, the magazine would be above such behavior: "Our aim will be, as critics, to state and reiterate what are the motives, and what must be the dominant elements, of all good art" (3).

That insistence upon universal values, according to Squire, put him at odds with a lot of new writing and art. Characterizing the art of the past few years as "an orgy of undirected abnormality" (4), Squire made his stance clear: "We have had 'styles' which were mere protests and revulsions against other styles; 'styles' which were no more than flamboyant attempts at advertisement akin to the shifting lights of the electric night signs; authors who have forgotten their true selves in the desperate search for remarkable selves; artists who have refused to keep their eyes upon the object because it has been seen before; musicians who have made, for novelty's sake, noises, and painters who have made, for effect's sake, spectacles, which invited the attention of those who make it their business to suppress public nuisances" (3). It was pretty clear which writers Squire had in mind. Of Joyce's *Ulysses*, Squire wrote in 1923 that it "sunk a shaft down into the welter of nonsense which lies at the bottom of the mind, pumped up this stuff and presented it as criticism of life" (Squire [Affable Hawk] 1923, 775). And, in a review of Eliot's *The Waste Land* a few months later, Squire argued: "I read Mr. Eliot's poem several times when it first appeared; I have now read it several times more; I am still unable to make head or tail of it. Passages might easily be extracted from it which would make it look like one of those wantonly affected productions which are written by persons whose one hope of imposing on the credulous lies in the cultivation of a deliberate singularity" (1923, 655). With the deictic "those" (in the phrase "one of those wantonly affected productions"), Squire directed his readers' assent that there was a particular kind of difficulty written by particular kinds of people. Difficulty went beyond *The Waste Land* and had generally infected contemporary society. In Squire's mind, at least, T. S. Eliot's *The Waste Land* and Reggie Twyford's *Ourang-Outang* were kissing cousins.

His acerbic public statements made Squire a favorite target of high modern writers. Virginia Woolf wrote that Squire was "more repulsive than words can express, and malignant into the bargain" (quoted in Pearson 1978, 147). Using the pages of *The Dial*, for which he was the London correspondent, Eliot attacked Squire repeatedly, at one point describing him as a critic "whose solemn trifling fascinates multitudes" (Eliot 1921a, 690). Writing to John Quinn a few years before Squire's review of his poem, Eliot noted the imminent publication of Squire's *London Mercury*, hoping that it would "fail in a few years' time." Eliot thought that the forces of traditionalism assembled in that magazine were a "small clique of bad writers" (among whom were some then-illustrious, now-forgotten names: Walter de la Mare, Laurence Binyon, Robert Lynd, Edmund Gosse, Edward Shanks, and John Freeman). Eliot feared that Squire would prevail, but not by his virtues as either critic or poet. Squire, Eliot snorted, "knows nothing about poetry; but he is the cleverest journalist in London." However, Eliot also acknowledged that Squire wielded a lot of power; because of Squire's skill as a journalist, his success would be modernism's disaster. Eliot wrote: "If he succeeds, it will be impossible to get anything good published" (Eliot [25 January 1920] 1988, 358).

The charged context of early twentieth-century literary culture spread beyond Eliot and Squire's rivalry, of course. Consider as a typical example the *Georgian Poetry* anthologies, the cause célèbre of many conservatives. As many literary historians have observed, one tool moderns used to draw the line was the work of those who published and represented the values of the relatively traditional work published in Harold Monro's Georgian anthologies. The critic Arthur Waugh (father of Evelyn), for example, after he had denounced the *Catholic Anthology* (which contained Eliot's "The Love Song of J. Alfred Prufrock") as a collection of "unmetrical, incoherent banalities" composed by "literary 'Cubists,'" argued that "the humour, commonsense, and artistic judgment of the best of the new 'Georgians'" would save contemporary letters (Waugh 1919, 39). Directly opposing these kinds of sentiments was John Middleton Murry, husband of Katherine Mansfield and editor of the journal *Athenaeum*, in whose pages he regularly attacked Georgian writing. After attending a lecture by Eliot, Murry, undoubtedly agreeing with Pound's description of Waugh's writing as "senile slobber" (Pound [1917] 1922, 77), exultingly described the two encamped armies that had gathered at the talk: "The anti-*Athenaeums*—Munro [sic], Jack Squire etc—present in force. There's no doubt it's a fight to finish between us & Them—them is the 'Georgians' *en masse*. It's a queer feeling I begin to have now: that we're making literary history. But I believe we are going to. More than that, in spite of the *London Mercury* and all its money and réclame, I believe we've got them on the run. They're afraid" (Murry [29 October 1919] 1983, 199).

> *Romance*
> When I was but thirteen or so
> I went into a golden land,
> Chimborazo, Cotopaxi
> Took me by the hand.
>
> My father died, my brother too,
> They passed like fleeting dreams,
> I stood where Popocatapetl
> In the sunlight gleams.
>
> —Opening lines of the first poem in the 1917 edition of Georgian Poetry. Written by W. J. Turner, who, among other activities, reviewed literature for the *London Mercury*

Murry's dramatization may be overdone, but it is typical. For many involved in forming the modern canon, the issues were sharply defined, and there clearly was a public battle going on. It was a battle between those who saw themselves as serious artists, who realized that the unique conditions of modern life demanded cultural artifacts uniquely shaped by those conditions—represented by the proponents of difficult modernism—on one side. On the other side were those who considered themselves as the defenders of tradition, who thought that modern art had abandoned the universal qualities of great art—represented by Squire and others. It was a battle with high stakes, a battle in which difficulty, wielded more like a broad-ax than a scalpel, was the main weapon.[4]

Writers Are "Doing It" This Season

This argument was launched by a simple observation, repeatedly made, an observation that simultaneously managed to be a polemical assertion: difficulty is everywhere in modernism. Along with Reggie and Adrian, many early twentieth-century readers noted that difficulty was everywhere; in fact, they often argued that the rapid proliferation of difficulty was an immediately noticeable characteristic of modernism, at times even going so far as to claim that difficulty, because of its preponderance, *defined* modernism. Although initially those *opposed* to modernism made these claims most often, modernism's opponents may have adopted a self-defeating strategy. By arguing that "difficulty is everywhere" they tacitly conceded that there was a movement (eventually called "modernism"), and that this movement could be understood through its stylistic properties and social positioning ("difficulty"). "Difficulty" and "modernism," two terms whose dubious status was often signaled by quotation marks, were linked, and that linkage eventually served modernist interests. For now, though, it is enough to note that the repeated claim (that difficulty was everywhere in modernism) had immediate and enormous consequences.

It is hard to exaggerate how often modern readers claimed that difficulty was everywhere. Arguing about their difficulty, in fact, is the dominant initial response to modernism's texts. Comments on the prevalence of difficulty dominate responses to *all* those writers who became the high moderns. And, these comments show up in a wide variety of sources—from anthologies, to newspapers, little magazines, scholarly books, private correspondence, and even advertisements. Difficulty, for those even slightly connected to modern art, could not be missed.[5]

Consider the following exemplary moments. In its inaugural issue, March 3, 1923, *Time* magazine published an article titled "Shantih, Shantih, Shantih: Has the Reader Any Rights before the Bar of Literature?" This article, reviewing the publication of both *The Waste Land* and *Ulysses*, opened with the following quip: "There is a new kind of literature abroad in the land, whose only obvious fault is that no one can understand it." *Time*'s reviewer went on to describe the effect of this kind of literature on the common reader: "To the uninitiated it appeared that Mr. Joyce had taken some half million assorted words—many such as are not ordinarily heard in reputable circles—shaken them up in a colossal hat, laid them end to end." As for Eliot's *The Waste Land*, the reviewer closed with an observation that could have been made of Twyford's *Ourang-Outang*: "It is rumored that *The Waste Land* was written as a hoax. Several of its supporters explain that that is immaterial, literature being concerned not with intentions but results."

Two years earlier, while composing his celebrated poem, Eliot had reviewed a collection of seventeenth-century poetry for the *Times Literary Supplement*. In it, as in many of Eliot's essays, a digression is what stayed in most readers' minds. Here, in an aside, Eliot claims that "it appears likely that poets in our civilization, as it exists at present, must be *difficult*. Our civilization comprehends great variety and complexity, and this variety and complexity, playing upon a refined sensibility, must produce various and complex results" (Eliot [1921] 1975b, 65). Certainly this stands out as a polemical assertion of difficulty's necessity and, consequently, its value. But Eliot's digression is more than that, for, while not all of modernism's readers agreed that modern difficulty was necessary, all would have agreed with Eliot's claim that difficulty was one of modernism's central characteristics.

Claims like those of *Time* and Eliot were frequent, and they were typically made casually, without rigorous substantiation: the appeal was to readers'

> Take a newspaper.
> Take some scissors.
> Choose from this paper an article of the length you want to make your poem.
> Cut out the article.
> Next carefully cut out each of the words that make up this article and put them all in a bag.
> Shake gently.
> Next take out each cutting one after the other.
> Copy conscientiously in the order in which they left the bag.
> The poem will resemble you.
> And there you are—an infinitely original author of charming sensibility, even though unappreciated by the vulgar herd.
>
> —Tristan Tzara, "To Make a Dadaist Poem," 1924

general sense of the literary landscape. In 1918, for example, Dorothy Dudley, reviewing William Carlos Williams for *Poetry* magazine, commented that Williams "has resorted to the obscure and the cryptic." Dudley continued, "This refuge of course has just now the virtue or the vice, as one looks at it, of being distinctly the fashion. Writers are 'doing it' this season" ([1918] 1980, 56).

If Dudley was predicting a temporary seasonal increase in difficulty, to be followed by a less rigorous off-season, she got it wrong. More than twenty years later, in *Modern Poetry and the Tradition*, Cleanth Brooks's influential attempt to establish a modern canon, difficulty was still seen as central to modern writing. Brooks begins his book with the following observation: "Many readers find modern poetry difficult, and difficult in a special sense. [The modern educated reader] is apt to find the modern English and American poets bewildering, and his knowledge of nineteenth-century poetry ... actually seems to constitute a positive handicap" (1939, 1). But Brooks has modulated how Dudley understood difficulty: he does not present difficulty as a temporary *fashion*, but as the established *property* of what had become canonical texts (I will later explore why Brooks insisted that one see this difficulty as radically different from the writing immediately preceding it).

In the twenty years between Dudley and Brooks, dozens of other writers commented that difficulty was everywhere in modernism, while hundreds more discussed the difficulty of a given writer or of modernism in general. Over the course of those years, difficulty became central to the canon. Not surprisingly, *all* the major early promoters of modernism (to cite a few: T. S.

> And whom shall we call on, pray, to heed and to hurry our message,
> But opera-chairs, limousines, and their occupants,
> Women who earnestly nod over nonsense,
> Heavy academies canting
> And coteries wearing soft collars,
> The elite and the slums of illusion!
> —From "Lines to W.B.," by Witter Bynner,
> co-author of the hoax anthology
> *Spectra*, 1913

Eliot, Allen Tate, Edmund Wilson, John Crowe Ransom, F. R. Leavis, William Empson, I. A. Richards, Yvor Winters) wrote about difficulty. These critics are central to what the modern canon came to look like. Brooks, for example, is the author of the critical and pedagogical classics *The Well Wrought Urn* (1947) and, with Robert Penn Warren, *Understanding Poetry* (1938)—works central to the formation of the modern canon, to the establishment of the modern canon in university curricula, and to making close reading the standard professional activity of several generations of literary scholars. Eliot's statement also shaped modernism. Cited as often as his pronouncement on the disassociation of sensibility, it was and continues to be the most frequently quoted comment on difficulty in twentieth-century Anglo-American literary culture.[6]

But it is not just those who promoted high modernism who made difficulty a central part of their critical rituals. Those suspicious of high modernism had their own high profile intellectuals, who also asserted that its widespread difficulty radically separated early twentieth-century culture from what had preceded it. Realizing that high moderns asserted that difficulty came with an "ought," that difficulty was not just the expression of an individual, but a matter of cultural and aesthetic *necessity*, modernism's skeptics also sensed that difficulty had designs on the literary canon—though for them, difficulty's proposed canon was formed on shakier principles than necessity or aesthetic excellence. Calling high modernism a "plague of unintelligibility," leading Marxist intellectual Max Eastman grumbled that there had been a "veritable international conquest of power by the Cult of Unintelligibility" (1931a, 110, 113). Eastman's comments are paralleled by Elizabeth Atkins (author of the first book on Edna St. Vincent Millay), J. C. Squire, Louis Untermeyer, and many others not as well known today as are high modernism's promoters.

Thus, across the spectrum of literary opinion, what unites the canonical writers of high modernism (e.g., Gertrude Stein, T. S. Eliot, James Joyce,

William Faulkner, Ezra Pound, and Virginia Woolf) is that their first readers found their writing difficult. While *Time* employed what would become a standard middlebrow attack on high culture, and Cleanth Brooks does not share its skepticism about difficult modernism, Brooks does share *Time*'s analysis that difficulty is everywhere, and that it has big consequences for twentieth-century culture. During the years 1910 to 1950, years that saw the formation of the Anglo-American modernist canon and the establishing of these texts and writers in the university curriculum, readers overwhelmingly sensed that difficulty was central to what was beginning to be called modernism.[7] Difficulty was the most common frame for readers' discussions of what was *different* and new about modernism. Further, when they noted modernism's difficulty, readers did not just direct their comments at a single figure (as in the nineteenth century, for example, readers had grumbled about the difficulty of George Meredith's *The Egoist*), or even just at a group of texts, but at these difficult texts, their authors, readers, and the processes by which texts were canonized. The simultaneous appearance of modernism and the discussion about difficulty was not coincidental: difficulty allowed modernism to rise, and it was central to how modernism shaped the canon not only of twentieth-century literature but of the literature that preceded it.

This difficult modern canon was bigger than just literature. It was modernism writ large, for people commonly perceived that modern music and visual art as well were radically more difficult than their predecessors. Moreover, writers used the same arguments for these arts as they employed to discuss literary difficulty. The 1910 London post-Impressionism exhibit, the scandal that erupted at the premiere of Stravinsky's *Sacre du printemps*, the furor over the 1913 Armory Show—all these events, to a large degree, galvanized the public because of their difficulty.[8] This difficulty of modernism's arts was commonly recognized. The Chicago *Record-Herald* was employing an instantly recognizable public discourse when it announced the arrival of the Armory Show in Chicago with the headline "Cubist Art Is Here: As Clear As Mud." Aaron Copland, adding a chapter on modern music to the revised edition of his 1939 *What to Listen for in Music*, began it with the observation that "Over and over again the question arises as to why it is that so many music lovers feel disoriented when they listen to contemporary music. They seem to accept with equanimity the notion that the work of the present-day composer is not for them. Why? Because 'they just don't understand it'" ([1939] 1957, 146).

Further, participants on both sides of the difficulty debate believed that the difficulty in these various arts was part of a single package. It was common to explain the difficulty of a given work by turning to the difficulty of another art form. Thus, in an issue of *Arts and Decorations* that had been designed to accompany and comment on the Armory Show, Mabel Dodge

([1913] 1986) turned to Picasso to explain and promote Stein's difficulty, while in the comparatively sedate *Boston Evening Transcript* a more skeptical reviewer of Stein turned for illumination to an even more broadly defined artistic climate: "Boston has seen some of the paintings of Matisse and Picasso, the sculptures of Brancusi, which created such a stir of amazement and contempt last spring. It has heard too, perhaps, of the new symphonies, wild sounds produced on new and unmusical instruments, which originated lately in Italy. Boston has pretended to try not to understand them, nor to admit that there is anything to understand, not even the point of view of the perpetrators" (Rogers [1914] 1986, 31).[9]

Moreover, as these reactions to modernism suggest (and as Squire pointed out in his story), difficulty produced a response that was more intense than the response to other aesthetic qualities. An immediately noticeable reaction accompanying difficulty (noticeable both for its extremity and its frequency) is an unsettled emotional response, a response of anxiety, or laughter, or anger (chapter 2 will explore this response in some detail). For example, a reviewer of *Ulysses* claimed that "As a work of art we can compare it with nothing but that picture which provoked laughter in the galleries a few years ago, 'Nude Descending a Staircase,' in which there was neither nude nor staircase and where art was the only thing that was descending" (H.S.C. [1934] 1970, 244). After claiming that difficulty "is running rampant in literature," an anonymous reviewer of Stein's *Tender Buttons* fumed "After a hundred lines of this I wish to scream, I wish to burn the book, I am in agony.... Some one has applied an egg beater to my brain" ("Flat Prose" [1914] 1986, 38–39).[10] While difficulty would have been noticeable just for its frequent mention, such extreme reactions made the experience of difficulty an even more visible and spectacular part of modernism.

Thus, early twentieth-century culture, for all its inconsistencies and fractures, saw overwhelming agreement on this one point: difficulty, which produces anxiety in many readers, was a common feature of "modernism." Those who commented on difficulty did so with the understanding that modernism's difficulty was part of most readers' casual knowledge, a knowledge that allowed for both clarity and shorthand in public discussions. When Max Eastman, irritated with the prevalence of difficulty, titled his famous 1929 *Harper's* essay "The Cult of Unintelligibility," he could count on his readers to know exactly the cultural phenomenon to which he was referring, and what his position would be.

The Cult of Difficulty

Difficulty's preponderance demanded an answer; readers found it necessary to *do* something with the assertion that difficulty was everywhere (even today the question is not just about "difficulty," but why *so much* difficulty). The belief that difficulty was everywhere raised the question of *ought*, a question whether its omnipresence meant that difficulty was in some sense necessary, inevitable. Modern readers most frequently answered this question by examining the relationship of modernist difficulty to literary history. Often, modernism's skeptics found few, if any, historical correlatives, and provided a negative assessment: modern difficulty was unique, and in a trivial way, for difficulty was *fashionable*. Despite the big claims made for it, readers argued, difficulty was an inconsequential and passing shift in literary taste. A second, more long-term view was that, whether it was or was not trivial, modern difficulty could be understood, for good or for ill, by looking at earlier instances of aesthetic difficulty. It is to these two responses that I now turn.

Often the opening gambit of a strategy to curtail incipient modernism, the observation that difficulty was everywhere allowed for other, more loaded claims: modernism's skeptics did not just claim that difficulty was everywhere, they thought its sudden prevalence to be at odds with literary history. For such readers, difficulty's prevalence was the sign of a particular, socially nuanced phenomenon: difficulty was *fashionable*.[11] This nuance allowed difficulty's omnipresence to become the major argument against difficulty, for if difficulty was fashionable, it wasn't intrinsic to literature. The fashion for difficulty was thus not something that Squire would have called "fundamental" to all good art. If difficulty was fashionable, it necessarily was deliberate, calculated, rhetorical. In fact, by embracing fashion, what was coming to be known as "modernist" literature and its difficulty opposed great art, and threw contemporary literature into a crisis.

Conservatives articulated this crisis in terms of three entangled ideas: that difficulty was the product (1) of a clearly defined school, (2) of deliberate strategies, and (3) of weak writers. Armed with these three ideas, skeptical readers asserted that difficulty needed to be understood not just as a formal property of some texts, but as a complex social situation—difficulty functioned in society in specific ways and was rearranging how art interacted with its audience. The fact that one *noticed* these social aspects of high modernism was in itself an indicator of difficulty's weakness.

The first thing suspicious readers noted was that while difficulty might be fashionable in *modernism*, it was not a characteristic of *all* twentieth-century writing. Rather, they commented, difficulty was prevalent in certain circles; there was a "movement" out there; difficulty was a school, a coterie, or perhaps even, as Eastman and others suggested, a cult.[12] Membership in this cult was indicated not only by the difficulty of a given writer's writing, but by difficulty's corollaries: difficult writers' publishing venues, the city in which they chose to live, or even by their physical appearance. (Squire, remember, was able to mock difficult writers by generalizing about their hair, their glasses, and their complexions.) One of the reasons high modernism's detractors disliked difficulty was because they believed that difficult writers were not honest and lonely artists, creating splendid, pure works of self-expression; difficult writers were part of a *movement*.

Second, when antimodern readers argued that difficulty was fashionable, they did not suggest that modern difficulty was an incidental (though perhaps necessary) by-product of a work of art. There was too much difficulty for that to be plausible. The more plausible explanation was that modernist writers *set out* to make difficult art; difficulty was modernism's *conscious product*.[13] Arthur Waugh argued that many "young poets" had a "determination to surprise and even to puzzle at all costs" (1919, 36). Readers like Waugh believed that effects deliberately aimed for were not the province of real art, and *difficulty* deliberately aimed for was doubly damning. For these readers, the narrative of Reggie Twyford's deliberate difficulty (including its cynicism) was no mere fable; it was the real thing.

Finally, the fashion for difficulty suggested to many readers that difficult writers, like members of cults everywhere, were just not very smart or talented. Because they sought refuge in a group, difficult writers were, as Adrian Roberts pointed out to Reggie, "second-rate." In an argument whose contours were so familiar that it worked more like a rhetorical trope than like logical analysis, poet and critic Humbert Wolfe grumbled about "the excesses of Eliot's imitators and those who seek in obscurity a disguise for poetic inability" (1931, 227–28).[14] As Squire's story shows, when weak writers get together and use deliberate strategies to create art, the resultant work is shoddy. For many, modern difficulty was the product of a technique, a stunt, a formal game, and because it was easy, it had no aesthetic value. Squire summed up modernism with the complaint that "The second-rate have discovered the trick of incomprehensibility in our own time" (1924, 242–43). One anthologist inveighed against "the more eccentric examples of the crossword puzzle school" and the "vociferous clique of literary snobs who grew like mushrooms in the ambiguous shade of T. S. Eliot's reputation" (Mégroz 1936, ix, viii).[15]

A Modernist History of Difficulty

That is one way to use literary history: to assert that modernism's difficulty is a temporary fashion, extrinsic to the real concerns of art, the ephemeral product of dubious forces. A second way is to search literary history for a useful comparison with which to judge the uniqueness of contemporary writing. Everyone involved in the difficulty debate found this turn to history to be polemically useful, and all could find historical examples of *good* difficulty; few claimed that *every* instance of difficulty was necessarily bad. Further, readers from across the spectrum occasionally found moments of harmony with one another, for few claimed that modernism *invented* difficulty, and

> Arthur Waugh, more than a little nervous about his sixteen-year-old son Evelyn's flirtation with modernism, began his 1919 collection of reviews (which included his famous attack on Eliot's "Prufrock") with a dedicatory epistle to Evelyn. It begins with the father's elegy on the memories contained in Evelyn's old nursery. The elder Waugh then pauses with a look at the wall Evelyn had "frescoed with strange Cubist pictures," pictures that had functioned as his "private temple of the most modern school of art." Shaking his (presumably gray) beard at these Cubist works, Waugh dedicated *Tradition and Change* to his son, accompanied by the following hope: "You are born into an era of many changes; and, if I know you at all, you will be swayed and troubled by many of them. But you are not yet so wedded to what is new that you seem likely to despise what is old. You may copy the Cubist in your living room, but an Old Master hangs above your bed" (vii–viii). There is no record of how Evelyn immediately responded, but his 1945 classic *Brideshead Revisited* portrays the coming to Oxford of modernism, most memorably indicated by Anthony Blanche's standing on a balcony to recite *The Waste Land*, through a megaphone, to a "sweatered and muffled throng that was on its way to the river."

most agreed that modernism—for whatever reasons—marked a turn from the nineteenth century, signaled most dramatically by the huge increase in difficult writing. And, all agreed that this turn marked a crisis.

Yet much depended on how one understood difficulty's increase *as literary history*—whether one thought that difficult modernism marked a triumphant return to writing that the nineteenth century had abandoned, or that modern difficulty's parallels could be found only in equally dubious moments. Negative readers occasionally found startling parallels to modern difficulty. Consider F. L. Lucas, literary critic and Fellow of King's College, Cambridge. His review in the *New Statesman* of *The Waste Land*, quoted here at some length, reaches back to the third century B.C. in order to describe a social context analogous to modern difficulty:

> Among the maggots that breed in the corruption of poetry one of the commonest is the bookworm. When Athens had decayed and Alexandria sprawled, the new giant-city, across the Egyptian sands; when the Greek world was filling with libraries and emptying of poets, growing in erudition as its genius expired, then first appeared, as pompous as Herod and as worm-eaten, that *Professorenpoesie* which finds in literature the inspiration that life gives no more, which replaces depth by muddiness, beauty by echoes, passion by necrophily. The fashionable verse of Alexandria grew out of the polite leisure of its librarians, its Homeric scholars, its literary critics.

Indeed, the learning of that age had solved the economic problem of living by taking in each others' dirty washing, and the "Alexandra" of Lycophron, which its learned author made so obscure that other learned authors could make their fortunes by explaining what it meant, still survives for the curious as the first case of this disease and the first really bad poem in Greek. The malady reappears at Rome in the work of Catullus' friend Cinna (the same whom with a justice doubly poetic the crowd in "Julius Caesar" "tears for his bad verses"), and in the gloomy pedantry that mars so much of Propertius; it has recurred at intervals ever since. Disconnected and ill-knit, loaded with echo and allusion, fantastic and crude, obscure and obscurantist—such is the typical style of Alexandrianism. ([1923] 1982, 195)

Predictably, Eliot's famous poem becomes Lucas's most recent example of Alexandrianism. History here serves the present: Lucas tells the story of Alexandria not to fill in a gap in his readers' knowledge about the past, but to demonstrate the kinds of cultural forces that had unleashed Eliot's poem. And, while Lucas's visceral language may seem over the top (and similar to Adrian Roberts's reference to modern avant-garde culture as made up of "disgusting insects, beetles and centipedes"), the values Lucas brings up are not unusual for modernism's readers. Lucas presents Alexandrian difficulty as a cultural situation analogous to modernism, as a relationship among poets, their culture, and their readers. In Lucas's history, difficulty is unhealthy and parasitic, its excesses a deliberate product of professionalism. This one moment in literary history, Lucas asserts, teaches all these things about modernism.[16]

A History of Difficult Writers
The way in which modern readers used this history tells much about the formation of the high modern canon—and how difficulty functions in high culture today. Given the ferocity of the difficulty debate, modern readers had a surprising consensus about what might be the salient points in a history of difficult writing, though there was predictably less agreement about the uses to which they might be put. Thus, readers went to certain places if their point was about an audience initially bewildered by difficulty (a point that attracted comments about romanticism and Tennyson). They turned to other places, equally predictable, if their point was about the dubious technique of difficulty (which attracted comments about Alexandrianism and Euphuism); to others if they wished to discuss hermetically private difficulty (which brought forward comments about French Symbolism and Blake); or to yet other places if they wished to illustrate something about the defensible difficulty of the genius (an argument that attracted discussion of Dante and Shakespeare).

 The basic stopping points are as follows: although modernism's skeptics might begin with the Alexandrian poets, defenders of modern difficulty were more likely to begin with Dante (as Eliot did), whom *all* readers agreed presented legitimate difficulty, although they might differ on its causes and social function. For those who distrusted modernism, Dante's work was the difficulty of the genius whose work could yet speak to a wide audience. For modernism's supporters, Dante's difficulty was the difficulty of all good art, an art produced without bowing to the social forces of an external audience. Standard historical references to difficulty also turned to Shakespeare and the Elizabethans, whose difficulty was typically described as arising from their idiosyncratic uses of language.[17]

The high spot in the history of difficulty (because of its generally agreed-upon link to modernism) was metaphysical poetry, of which Donne was either the chief hero or culprit, depending on one's view of modernism. Romanticism again takes up the argument about metaphysical difficulty, and twentieth-century readers put this romantic discussion to two distinct uses. Modernism's apologists turn to Coleridge's aesthetic theory to find a justification for Donne's kind of difficulty. (They also noted, with the obligatory register of incredulity, how even the romantic poets were initially seen as difficult.) But of course, it was also plausible to use the romantics to defend simplicity, either to romanticism's credit or discredit. (In this use, Wordsworth replaces Coleridge as the chief romantic, and Blake's difficulty goes unmentioned.) After the romantics, the immediate predecessors of modern difficulty were seen to be Browning and (to a lesser degree) Meredith, and, across the channel, the French symbolists, followed by Gerard Manley Hopkins and Henry James.[18]

My argument will first consider how readers used these historical references *against* modern difficulty. For the most part, those who used history to distinguish between bad and good difficulty distrusted modernism. These readers claimed that there used to be good difficult writing, but modern difficulty wasn't it, for it was too extreme, or it was the wrong kind—perhaps it was deliberate, professionally crafted difficulty instead of the inevitable difficulty of the sublime, or of the genius, or even of the new. Harold Monro, owner of the Poetry Bookshop and the generally conservative publisher of *The Chapbook* and of the *Georgian Poetry* anthologies, complained in 1920 that Pound's poetry had "the obscurity without the wit or natural intelligence of a Browning" (1920b, 92), and novelist and poet Elinor Wylie, reviewing *The Waste Land* for the *New York Evening Post Literary Review*, made a similar contrast. While granting that Eliot was no more obscure than Donne or Yeats, she asserted that Eliot's poem had neither the "incomparable wit" of Donne nor the "incomparable magic" of Yeats, who was an older and at that time more established poet than Eliot ([1923] 1982, 154).[19]

For jaundiced readers, literary history also revealed a lot of bad difficulty, frequently perpetrated by those who took another writer's stylistic idiosyncrasy and exaggerated it, transforming an accidental secondary characteristic into a raison d'être. For example, in his introduction to an anthology whose

> He lived amidst th'untrodden ways
> To Rydal Lake that lead:—
> A bard whom there were none to praise
> And very few to read.
>
> Behind a cloud his mystic sense,
> Deep hidden, who can spy?
> Bright as the night, when not a star
> Is shining in the sky.
>
> Unread his works—his "Milk white Doe"
> With dust is dark and dim;
> It's still in Longman's shop, and Oh!
> The difference to him!
>
> —Hartley Coleridge, "He Lived Amidst Th'Untrodden Ways," 1827

purpose was to revive eighteenth-century poetry, J. C. Squire argued that Dryden's clear, rational writing "was a necessary corrective when Elizabethan luxuriance had run to seed in extravagant tropes, and, when largely under Donne's influence, ruggedness and obscurity had been cultivated to a point at which they threatened the complete ruin of poetry" (1922, xiii).[20]

Not surprisingly, some argued that most modern difficult writers were lesser imitators of a modern to whom one might concede a measure of greatness. Louis Untermeyer, who had initially called *The Waste Land* "a pompous parade of erudition" ([1923] 1982, 151), and whose anthologies of modern poetry were reluctant to admit Eliot as an important poet, reached the following compromise in 1930: "most of those so strongly influenced by Eliot—and by Eliot's influences—captured nothing except his (and Jules Laforgue's) idiom. His abrupt allusiveness, his style at once coarse and subtle, his emotional acuteness, could be imitated but not captured; his unacknowledged disciples merely parodied the trick of disassociation, the erudition without Eliot's wisdom, the gesture without (if I may misquote) emotion" (1930, 28).

Two important things are going on here. First, Untermeyer employs a defense of difficulty that argued for the virtues of the inarticulable aspects of Eliot (his emotion and wisdom) over Eliot's technique and method. In doing so, Untermeyer was typical of modernism's skeptics. But in its reliance on emotional expression over a professionalist sense of aesthetic development,

Untermeyer's defense turned Eliot's poetry in a direction different from the one apparently posited by the Eliot of the objective correlative. Second, and more central to the sense of how literary history was understood, when Untermeyer argued that lesser writers "parodied" Eliot, he took a typical line for skeptical modern readers: bad forms of difficulty take good difficulty and exaggerate it, take it too far. Such exaggeration rippled back to the originating writer; difficulty's excesses limited Eliot's greatness by showing what his writing led to.[21] Herbert Gorman, participating in a 1929 *Modern Quarterly* symposium on the "revolution of the word" manifesto, which *transition* had announced as its editorial policy, noticed a similar trajectory with respect to Joyce's recent writing: "The revolutionized word suffers from the 'lunatic fringe' that surrounds all nascent movements. It has been victimized by fools and meddlers and half-baked undergraduates and lazy fellows who regard the changed word for its own sake, and tuppenny imitators of James Joyce and spiritual sots and moronic iconoclasts and piddling poetasters and sempiternal jackasses. A pox on such whoreson knaves!" (1929, 293).

Negative readers thus argued that history showed that lazy difficult writers kept the outer form of difficulty (the tricks) without bringing along the central aspects of great art: wisdom, emotion, and pleasure, all of which can't be achieved by imitating a technique. Modernism's technical difficulty typically derived its energy from a single individual, who discovered something and made it fashionable, but who also made it so easily duplicable that this writer had lesser followers. In these situations difficulty is just fashion, produced in mechanical imitation—not the product of a solitary genius, who might occasionally produce difficulty as an accidental effect of creating great art.[22]

But other readers used history to difficult modernism's *advantage*. Modernism's promoters retrieved analogs from literary history to make points about the actual status of modern difficulty: to question whether a given modern work actually *was* difficult, or (particularly later on) whether perhaps *all* literature was difficult. Pressing home the former, some argued that modern literature's difficulty was not inherent, but was caused by readers' bad habits. In his 1940 article "Understanding Modern Poetry," Allen Tate grumbled that for some readers it was not just modern poetry that was difficult; difficulty extended to writers like Marvell and Donne and Sidney. Twentieth-century readers found difficult "a poetry that requires of the reader the fullest co-operation of all his intellectual resources, all his knowledge of the world, and all the persistence and alertness that he now thinks only of giving to scientific studies." Tate argued that many contemporary readers wanted to be more passive than this ([1940] 1959, 122–23). Richard Aldington similarly commented: "Now the charge of 'obscurity' may be just, for all verse which on analysis proves to have no intellectual or emotional content is 'obscure'; obscure because it pretends to possess a meaning which

> About 300 years ago there lived in Spain a poet whose name was Gongora. He came trailing along in the wake of the Golden Age of letters and lived during a transition period when the creative spirit had simmered down to fitful, meager burning; and because he himself had little enough to say, he took to inventing new ways to say old truths. His obsession became form, and he amused, and no doubt kidded himself, by experimenting with form. I don't know how deeply the old boy believed in himself and the poems he wrote. I do know he wrote verses strangely similar to the unintelligible typographical contortions of today. He suggests Cummings, William Carlos Williams in his earlier manifestation, James Joyce when he is patently thumbing his nose at himself and his readers, Gertrude Stein, hypnotized by repetitive sound.
>
> Gongora, you see, endeavoured to hide the weakness of his imagination by overdoing the tricks his fancy could handle. He was a decadent; a writer who wrote in handsprings because that was the best he could do.
>
> Far be it from me to suggest that modern experimenters are without significance; far be it from me to insist that all they write is incomprehensible and somehow useless. They are merely tiresome; their rhetorical and printers' gymnastics require too much effort to be comprehended in this day of many books. There just isn't time to worry over them and their literary convictions.
>
> —Walter Yust, reviewing *The Sound and the Fury*, 1929

it has not. But the obscurity of Mr. Eliot is as much a myth of lazy people as the obscurity of Browning. Indeed, Mr. Eliot's verse never makes the heavy demands on a reader that were made by 'Sordello.' But this subtlety of mind which makes necessary an effort for full comprehension is not something invented by Browning, but goes far beyond him to the so-called metaphysical poets, to Donne and Davies and Chapman" (1924, 188).

While the attack on ordinary reading habits had its attractions, a more popular reappraisal of modern difficulty's actual status (an appraisal perhaps designed to win over some of these lazy readers) assembled figures from literary history in order to demonstrate that works that initially seem difficult eventually become easier to understand. Unlike the argument that distinguishes between kinds of difficult writing (which those suspicious of difficult modernism used as a major argument, while those supportive of modernism used it as a concession), arguments about the transitory nature of difficulty were a major strategy of those amenable to difficult writing and a minor concession by those suspicious of it.

The most frequently used example of transitory difficulty was romantic poetry, whose initial difficulty augured well for modernism. For example, Edith Sitwell, spoofed by Squire in "The Man Who Wrote Free Verse," began her 1926 defense of difficult poetry, *Poetry and Criticism*, with several pages that demonstrate that the major romantics, when first read, were thought to be difficult (8–10). In his 1934 *ABC of Reading*, Ezra Pound also argued (with the de rigeur expression of bafflement) that "Incredible as it now seems, the bad critics of Keats' time found his writing 'obscure', which meant that they couldn't understand WHY Keats wrote" (64). Eliot made the same point with more precision: "difficulty may be due just to novelty: we know the ridicule accorded in turn to Wordsworth, Shelley and Keats, Tennyson and Browning" ([1933] 1964, 150).

Modernism's defenders also turned to literary history to bolster their claims that *all* good or new writing was difficult, an argument that sits uneasily with the claim that difficulty would pass. Many, defying contradiction, often held both positions at the same time.[23] Mark Van Doren illustrates how one could bring these two assertions together. In his introduction to a 1930 anthology of prize-winning poetry, Van Doren addressed the following comment to readers "who find themselves a bit bewildered among modern poets": "Poetry which is both new and good is also difficult to read. In a sense all good poetry is difficult to read, but we are not aware of the fact when we are considering the classics, which centuries of human experience have taught us how to read" (10). The history of literature, then, reveals that difficulty is universal—but, because we have learned to read earlier difficulty, difficulty just doesn't *feel* universal. This point is illustrated through many examples, sometimes surprising ones, as when Donald Stauffer proposes to select "three poems by Pope, Herrick, and Burns for their apparent simplicity, and study . . . their actual poetic complexity" (1946, 160).[24]

Inevitably, the argument that all good writing is difficult summoned Shakespeare's ghost, for if Shakespeare is difficult, *all* good writing is difficult. Eliot, for example, commented that "some of the poetry to which I am most devoted is poetry which I did not understand at first reading; some is poetry which I am not sure I understand yet; for instance, Shakespeare's" ([1933] 1964, 151). Preserving for Shakespeare both his difficulty and his ability to be understood by common readers, Elizabeth Drew, in one of the first books on modern poetry, argued that "There have always been 'difficult' poets. Shakespeare is the most difficult of all, and it is only because he appeals at so many different levels to so many different types of audience and reader[s] that his difficulty has escaped much comment" (1933, 82).

For many modern readers, such as Hugh Ross Williamson, poetry was always difficult because *language* (and communication in general) is difficult. Dire consequences follow from not recognizing difficulty's universality:

The refusal to recognize this elementary fact is the fallacy at the root of a third objection to Eliot's poetry—objection to its "difficulty." It is popularly assumed that great art is always "simple"—that is to say, immediately intelligible to everybody. (So Democracy flatters itself. The truth is rather in Stendhal's remark that it takes eighty years for anything to reach the general public.) But art is never simple in that sense, and the belief that it is based on the curious dogma of the infallibility of language.... no one acquainted, even superficially, with poetry would really wish to sustain the thesis that "difficulty" denotes inferiority. (1933, 51–53)

As Eliot would write, secure in his status as the century's dominant poet:

> Words strain,
> Crack and sometimes break, under the burden,
> Under the tension, slip, slide, perish,
> Decay with imprecision, will not stay in place,
> Will not stay still. ("Burnt Norton," in *Complete Poems* [1935] 1969, 175)

If one grants that a proper use of language reveals and explores language's inherent difficulty, the shape of the English literary canon (as it was generally understood at the turn of the century) changes to reveal the "real" tradition of literature, in which the nineteenth century is devalued, and Donne and other writers who clearly are difficult are valorized. As many critics have pointed out, this redrawing of history is central to modernism. Such redrawing is seen in William Van O'Connor's *Sense and Sensibility in Modern Poetry*, which argues that those who dislike modern difficulty are using "only eighteenth- or nineteenth-century poetry as the norm, forgetting that Elizabethan and Jacobean poetry tend to be obscure and forgetting, further, that the nature of poetic language invites obscurity" (1948, 227). For many of modernism's apologists, because eighteenth- and nineteenth-century writing resists the natural function of language, it is neither particularly good nor normative. Cleanth Brooks makes just that point, setting aside Johnson, Addison, and the romantics, and valorizing metaphysical and renaissance writers, who, Brooks argues, would not have balked at being considered difficult: "their practice would indicate that they did not fear being censured as too prosaic, or difficult, or daring, or fanciful, or 'unpoetic.' Whatever their positive standards, they were free from the negative inhibitions carefully cultivated from Dryden's time onward and now long established in the traditional account as orthodox criteria" (1939, 11). According to modern difficulty's apologists, the proper role of the difficult writer was to abandon the deliberate cultivation of simplicity, realize the inevitable difficulty of poetic language, and make it central to one's writing.

The devaluing of two centuries of literary expression could not lie on the shoulders of a lightweight. The figure on whom the weight of this change rested was John Donne, whose upsurge in popularity was seen as closely tied to modernist difficulty. Public awareness of Donne's importance to modernism was so great, in fact, that the modern fashion for his difficulty became a sound bite. In 1945, novelist Sinclair Lewis, writing to a mass audience in *Esquire* magazine, commented on the Donne phenomenon. Reviewing a book of poetry by Marguerite Young, Lewis argued that Young "displays obscurity at its most irritating," and he termed Young as one of "the new Metaphysical poets, whose gods are T. S. Eliot and John Donne" (1945, 51). F. L. Lucas, who compared *The Waste Land* to Alexandrian writing, noted with disapproval the kinds of writers who had turned to Donne. In his *Decline and Fall of the Romantic Ideal* he argued that such writers used Donne not for his limited merits, but because they admired his difficulty, the questionable writing of "Donne the human corkscrew" (1936, 217).

For proponents of difficult modernism, though, Donne's difficulty was the central sign of his value. During the 1931 tercentenary of Donne's death, the *Bookman* devoted an issue to Donne, featuring essays by Hugh l'Anson Fausset (who would later edit a collection of Donne's poems) and F. R. Leavis (who was the first Cambridge academic to teach the canonical works of high modernism), and closing with an appended essay on *T. S. Eliot* by Hugh Ross Williamson (who in 1933 would publish the first major book-length study of Eliot).[25] In his essay, Fausset claims that the upsurge in interest in Donne suggests "not only a taste for mental subtleties, but also a hunger for a kind of vital consciousness which the Victorian, like the Augustan, compromise denied" (341).[26]

This reshuffling of the canon put into play a temptation many could not avoid: to argue that works that were good and difficult were also, in an important way, *modern*. Though skeptical of much modern difficulty, Christopher Morley, commenting on the clear "revival of interest in Donne," argued that "In such brilliant poets as Elinor Wylie and John Crowe Ransom I seem to observe a voice that the Dean would have understood. It is plain that there is something in Donne that speaks to our present time" (1926, 206). Selden Rodman made the equation more specific, arguing in 1938 that "Whitman and Dickinson are modern to be sure—but so are Blake and Marvell and Donne" (22). Close companions, metaphysical and modern writers stood shoulder to brawny shoulder against the debilitating effect of much of the literary tradition; Cleanth Brooks claimed that Donne was popular because "the metaphysical poets and the modernists stand opposed to both the neoclassic and Romantic poets on the issue of metaphor" (1939, 11). Surveying the Donne craze from the perspective of 1945, Douglas Bush argued that in the years 1920 to 1925 Donne "became the idol and shibboleth of intellectual poets, critics, and undergraduates." Bush argued that this fashion found its impetus in a recognition of Donne's "unique quality," but also because of qualities that were similar to the central concerns of modernist writers:

Donne's rejection of "'poetical'" writing and his unified sensibility. Perhaps most important was "Donne's supposed modernity of outlook," which, "especially when half-misapprehended, harmonized perfectly with the mood of what used to be called the post-war world." Bush concluded that "[s]uch reasons, good and less good, combined to exalt Donne to a place beside Shakespeare" (135). For many of modernism's most ardent supporters, then, Donne and Shakespeare existed on an equal level in the canon, and they both (though in different ways) demonstrated that all good writing is difficult.[27]

A History of Audiences for Difficult Writing

As the preceding section has intimated, the history of difficulty was not just a history of individual writers and their texts; it was also a social history of *audiences*. Moderns used the response to romanticism, for example, to demonstrate how wrong an initial audience could be. These anecdotes about audiences have a weightier function than many other historical anecdotes, for they are the occasion for some pointed polemics about the *social* function of difficulty; modernism's apologists and critics used these anecdotes about audiences to illustrate how difficulty enters a culture.

Whenever the evaluation of difficult writing became contentious, not only did readers frequently refer to historical audiences, but they also delineated different *kinds* of audiences from one another. The audience most often idealized was the general audience, which typically was imagined to be made up both of common readers and of a tonier, hazy group (made up of critics, publishers, and other writers) more closely involved in how writing gets produced. Not surprisingly, the common readers in this bifurcated audience were frequently invoked to display the shortcomings of modern difficulty. Robert Nichols, whose poetry Harold Monro published in the Georgian anthologies, complained that Ezra Pound's *Three Cantos* was not a masterpiece, "for masterpieces have a habit of being both readable and understandable. 'The Three Cantos' are barely one and hardly the other." Nichols grumbled that common readers could not understand Pound's work, for it lacked comprehensibility, the central feature of all great art: "Comprehensibility is a virtue. The greater masters knew this; hence Molière and his valet, Cervantes and his groom. These artists did not necessarily write down; they *wrote into* the comprehension of slower mortals" ([1920] 1972, 166). Unlike Pound's *Cantos*, the real masterpiece is accessible to a wide audience.

While many high modernists agreed with their skeptics that modern literature was not reaching a wide audience, not everyone worried about this constriction. Ezra Pound, corresponding with *Poetry* editor Harriet Monroe, scolded her about *Poetry*'s motto (a phrase borrowed from Whitman: "To have great poets there must be great audiences too"). Warming to his task, Pound queried:

Had Dante the popular voice? He had his youthful companionship with Guido, and the correspondence with a man from Pistoja and with the latinist De Virgilio.

Must we restrict this questions to poets? I ask the efficient man in any department of life. Can we have no great inventors without a great audience for inventors? Had Curie a great audience? Had Ehrlich for his bacilli? Can we have no great financier without a great audience? Had the savior of the world a great audience? Did he work on the magazine public? (1914, 30)

The general audience, according to Pound and others, provided a much less reliable guide to a work's quality than did the judgments of fellow professionals.[28] (That alternate form of evaluation, a later chapter will show, indicates that Pound, like all moderns, did not completely reject mass culture. One of the things he borrowed from it was its attraction to professionalism, wielding professionalism as a set of publicly understood protocols to validate his discussions of aesthetic worth and production.)

While this negative assessment of the general audience undeniably held a lot of weight among high modernists, readers more sympathetic to the common reader thought that history furnished a different lesson. For them, difficult writing, addressed to a self-serving coterie, was a diminished thing. In the introduction to his anthology *100 Modern Poems*, Selden Rodman commented that Donne, Coleridge, Blake, and Hopkins "had already chosen the narrower path, electing to limit their audience, if not to poets, then at most to connoisseurs of poetry." The resulting problem? These writers "retreated from the 'real' world of [their] time into an 'ideal' world of personal fantasy, and in so doing widened still further the gap between the artist and his public" (Rodman 1949, viii).[29] And, so the argument went, when a writer no longer desires to reach a large audience, literature is trivialized. Gorham Munson in 1924 described Eliot's writing as "dandyism" because Eliot "does not want to communicate . . . to the general reader." Munson then articulated the consequences of Eliot's wish to be "incomprehensible": "In his desire to make his suffering inscrutable to all but a chosen coterie of his similars, he is affecting what is commonly called a romantic mannerism, a mannerism that cannot be credited, however, to the great romantics" (207). Many readers noted that difficult writing, addressed to a specialized audience, was not only limited in scope, it was unambitious; it was a "mannerism," an empty gesture, lacking the power of real art.

A History of Difficulty Theories

In addition to sketching histories of difficult literature and its audiences, modern readers also provided a utilitarian history of *theories* about difficulty. Although some readers ranged as far back as Aristotle, this history of theory had but two major stopping points: Samuel Johnson and Samuel Taylor Coleridge, both of whose theories were almost always presented in light of

John Donne's poetry.[30] In discussing Johnson, readers agreed: he was the person who, for good or ill, had buried John Donne and put simplicity near the top of desired aesthetic effects.

The modernist use of Johnson on the metaphysicals is straightforward. Hugh l'Anson Fausset, in the 1931 *Bookman* issue on Donne, commented on Johnson's dislike of Donne, particularly Donne's use of metaphor in a poem like "A Valediction: Forbidding Mourning." Fausset recounted how Johnson described this compass metaphor in particular as "'improper or vicious' because it deviated 'from nature in pursuit of something new and strange.'" Fausset, pushing a modernist agenda, argued that Johnson "failed altogether to feel the intense pulse of feeling beating within the delicate nerves of a poem which was too real to be elegant and too unique to be normal" (341). Fausset's last phrase articulates values central to modern difficulty (such as crudity, intensity, and authenticity), values that Johnson was apparently unable to appreciate. The values modernists thought Johnson *did* promote are articulated by Cleanth Brooks. After quoting Johnson's preference for "the grandeur of generality" over "a scrupulous enumeration" (i.e., too much detail), Brooks argues that Johnson, like the romantics, "is anxious to preserve a certain sublimity which he feels is injured by too much show of ingenuity or the use of undignified and prosaic diction" (1939, 7–8).

Of course, one could also enlist Johnson to attack modern difficulty. John Freeman, reviewing Eliot's *Homage to John Dryden* for Squire's *London Mercury*, mused whether Eliot had "himself in mind" when he wrote his famous phrase that "poets in our civilisation, as it exists at present, must be *difficult*." Freeman went on to ask: "is it not odd to find Mr. Eliot concluding with a sharp reminder of Johnson on the metaphysicals—Johnson, 'a dangerous person to disagree with'? He is indeed, and especially if disagreement with him should mean agreement with future writers who find it necessary to dislocate language into meaning" (1924, 664).

As my discussion shows, critics generally agreed about *what* Johnson had to say about Donne and difficulty, though they might disagree on the *value* of Johnson's opinions. Samuel Taylor Coleridge had a more problematic place in modernist literary history (as indeed does romanticism in general).[31] In marshaling Coleridge to defend difficulty, modern readers went to two places. The first is Coleridge's assertion that "Poetry gives most pleasure when only generally and not perfectly understood" (1895, 5), a remark approvingly echoed by I. A. Richards ([1935] 1960, 214) and T. S. Eliot ([1933] 1964, 138). The second place readers went to, a place central to the establishment of Donne in modernist literary history, is Coleridge's famous statement on the imagination. Coleridge argues that the imagination "reveals itself in the balance or reconciliation of opposite or discordant qualities," a balance

> Our two soules therefore, which are one,
>   Though I must goe, endure not yet
> A breach, but an expansion,
>   Like gold to ayery thinnesse beate.
>
> If they be two, they are two so
>   As stiffe twin compasses are two,
> Thy soule the fixt foot, makes no show
> To move, but doth, if the'other doe.
>
> And though it in the center sit,
>   Yet when the other far doth rome,
> It leanes, and hearkens after it,
>   And growes erect, as that comes home.
>
> —From John Donne, "A Valediction: Forbidding Mourning"

that includes a reconciliation of several qualities essential to modern difficulty: "the sense of novelty and freshness, with old and familiar objects; ... a more than usual state of emotion, with more than usual order; ... [and] judgement ever awake and steady self-possession, with enthusiasm and feeling profound and vehement" ([1817] 1983, 16–17). Such an understanding of the imagination was congenial to the disjunctive and allusive difficulty of high modernism.

But many modern readers believed that Coleridge was *not* to be distinguished from a typical romantic, the sort of person who distrusted the intellect and favored simplicity. Cleanth Brooks, for example, believed that Coleridge was just another Wordsworth, naively wallowing in simple pleasures. In establishing this claim, Brooks disapprovingly quoted the following passage from Wordsworth: "In the higher poetry, an enlightened Critic chiefly looks for a reflection of the wisdom of the heart and the grandeur of the imagination. Wherever these appear, simplicity accompanies them; Magnificence herself, when legitimate, depending upon a simplicity of her own, to regulate her ornaments" (1939, 6). It was not startling, then, when F. R. Leavis (who in a series of books during the 1930s was the first academic to make modernism an object of serious literary study) argued that romantic and nineteenth-century presuppositions about poetry had a "malign strength" and that "the nineteenth century tradition was disastrous" (1931, 346).[32]

Implications of the History of Difficulty

This fragmented literary history carries some weighty implications. Certainly, the modern histories of difficulty indicate who modern writers and readers believed were difficulty's central proponents: Donne, Johnson, Coleridge, Blake, and the nineteenth-century French poets. But they also indicate which writers were in the main tradition, for in the first half of the twentieth century one's position on difficulty was central to one's canonical status. Further, all modern histories of difficulty assert that early twentieth-century high culture was in a state of crisis. They differed, of course, on the source of this crisis. Modernism's skeptics claimed the crisis came about because of the fashion for difficulty, while modernism's apologists claimed that the real crisis lay in what the nineteenth century had done to literature, in its turning away from difficulty.

Early twentieth-century readers' uses of history also had some side effects. When modernism's readers told the history of difficulty, only certain kinds of works were considered: works that aspired to the status and reading conditions of high art (and therefore, particularly before the late nineteenth century, of all the genres of literature, poetry was the best example of what high art looked like). Folk art and the popular novel do not enter the difficulty discussion; there is only a history of difficult works of *high* art. Thus, while difficulty is not a necessary feature of high art, it is a feature that modern readers found only in high art. It consequently became easy to take this idiosyncrasy and argue that it was one of high art's defining qualities; in the minds of some readers, an accidental feature of art became its necessary condition. No difficulty, no high art.

Because these were *polemical* histories, difficulty was always *attached* to something: to reading practices, to individual poets, and, most important, to value judgments. In all of these attachments, difficulty was never presented as something by itself, alone, ready to submit to analysis of its own qualities, unalloyed by other considerations. It was always better or worse than some other aesthetic quality. Further, distinctions between forms of difficulty (an activity that some critics reveled in) came down to distinctions between good and bad difficulty. And *that* distinction, for all, was quite simple: good difficulty provided some meaning; bad difficulty either provided none, or whatever meaning it provided was trivial, since the difficulty sprang from conscious, and therefore impure, motives. The consequences for modernism were that difficulty always was an argument, often the central argument, about modernism's *value*.

Finally, these polemical references to literary history were the only occasions on which a history of difficulty reached a general public. As a result, the general history of difficulty was defined by the parameters of a peculiarly *modernist* discussion that never strayed far from such issues as elitism, originality, professionalism, and the strenuous nature of good art. And wherever in the modernist history of literature (and, consequently, in the formation of the modern canon) elitism, originality, professionalism, and strenuousness signaled a work's value, difficulty (as the prime indicator of these qualities) also became a sign. As this book will argue in later chapters, contemporary culture has inherited both the terms of modernism's argument over history and its lack of finesse. And one side of the modern argument has clearly won the day. Although critics fight over the forms of difficulty, contemporary high culture has generally accepted the claim that all good art is in some way difficult. Indeed, the claim that all literature is difficult has been institutionalized into a reading practice. The modern discussion still goes on, and on modern terms.

The Hoax

At this point it is profitable to turn once more to difficulty's detractors' first step in their argument against modernism, the observation that there just seemed to be *so much* modern difficulty. The prevalence of difficulty provoked questions about modernism's aesthetic merits, its readership, and its producers. Difficulty, in short, produced a crisis in aesthetic evaluation that made inevitable discussions as to whether a given work might be a hoax. For readers like J. C. Squire, the times seemed right: modern difficulty used techniques that were deliberately and consciously produced, that defied standard evaluative criteria, exploited a gullible readership, and attracted young writers of unexceptional ability. Moreover, the melodramatic context in which modern difficulty circulated contributed to this crisis. It's not just that a successful hoax shows that people can imitate the formal features of difficulty. Rather, things that are *distinctive* are imitable, and in modernism, those distinctive things included the social context that produced difficulty: Reggie's Sidney Twyford did not just have to write difficult art, he had to engage in some of the behaviors of difficulty. In his story, Squire implicitly argued that since difficulty is founded upon imitable features, and not on the *je ne sais quoi* of great art, it is possible to duplicate these features and create lesser art, or even a hoax. The range of this accusation was broad: accusations of fraud were directed at such high modern classics as *Tender Buttons, Finnegans Wake, Ulysses, The Waste Land,* "The Love Song of J. Alfred Prufrock," and *Absalom, Absalom!* They also surfaced in public reactions to the 1913 Armory Show and to Stravinsky's *Sacre du printemps*. The more visceral the reaction to a particular work of difficult modernism, the more likely it was that it would be accused of fraud.

Naturally, the hoax discussion was carried out by those opposed to difficult modernism, who argued that difficult writers were either faking the work, or that the general public was faking its understanding, or—more insidiously—that literary professionals (critics, other writers, and reviewers) collectively were faking their understanding and taking everyone else along for the ride.[33] Thus, John Sparrow in his 1934 *Sense and Poetry* (a book which Robert Lynd cited in 1939 as one of the four most important books on modern poetry), turned his attention to F. R. Leavis's reading of Pound's *Hugh Selwyn Mauberley*. Citing Leavis's favorable pronouncements on the poem in *New Bearings in English Poetry*, Sparrow retorts: "One of the most admired of modern critics is here appraising the *chef d'oeuvre* of one of the most successful of modern poets; and yet it sounds much as if an imposter had duped a clever fool into writing high-sounding nonsense" (131). In his *The Literary Mind*, Max Eastman tore into "the part played by the admiring critic in promoting the Cult of Unintelligibility." Describing the critical mentality as "childlike," Eastman argued that "he may actually believe that he understands, and go round puffing out his cheeks and telling us with a swagger that the new methods of writing are merely 'direct and vivid,' and that all the talk about not being able to understand them come[s] from 'trying to judge them by standards other than their own, etc., etc.' I am quoting from John Dos Passos, but I might be quoting from any one of a hundred men of alert fancy who mistake a stimulation of their own gifts for communication from another" (1931a, 120–21).

To modernism's detractors, the hoax was irritating (because of its successful wielding of illegitimate power) or amusing (because of its pathetic *attempts* to exercise such power), but, if there were any justice in the world, the voices of reason and practicality should laugh the hoax of difficulty off the stage. A discussion of Faulkner's *The Sound and the Fury* ends with the inevitable comparison: "One has the feeling that all the grandeur of Faulkner's style—his Mississippi baroque—all his grotesqueries and posturing, all his high-flown bombast are attempts to wrest from his material a profound meaning which has persistently eluded him. It is high time that someone pointed out that the emperor has no clothes" (Nichols [1954] 1995, 361). And, if reason and ridicule did not work, the fraud, fueled by the whims of fashion, would eventually run out of steam. Three years before he would trash *The Waste Land*, Squire optimistically predicted that "we have noticed that most of these dealers in chaos soon tire. Those who have something in them (and any young man is liable to be infected by a current fashion) get through, none the worse: those who have not flag and stop" (1920, 388).

The exposé of the hoax, always done with the moral fervor of the undeceived, was both a pessimistic and an optimistic act. On one hand, there was dismay that contemporary culture would take such fraudulent work seriously. On the other hand, there was the optimism of the undeceived writer, who, for one, would not be taken in, and whose exposé should—if there were

> D is for Duchamp, the Deep-Dyed Deceiver,
>   Who, drawing accordeons, labels them stairs,
> With a lady that must have been done in a fever,—
>   His model won't see her, we trust, it would grieve her!—
>   (Should the stairway collapse, Cubie's good at repairs.)
> —D is for Duchamp, the Deep-Dyed Deceiver.
>
>   —Mary Mills Lyall, *The Cubies' ABC*, 1913

any fairness in the world at all—bring the fraud to justice. Squire's "The Man Who Wrote Free Verse," then, was darkly pessimistic: according to Reggie, after running for some time the hoax was to be unveiled and end the current fashion for difficulty. But in the story—and in the real world—difficulty had accumulated too much steam to be stopped so easily.

Central to these discussions was not just difficulty's prevalence and its imitable features, but a crisis in how to *evaluate* this work. Conservative readers argued that it was possible for a difficult work to be an elaborate hoax not only because its central features were so easy to point to and parody, but because literature's stable evaluative criteria had lost the force they used to have. And certainly, several grand and vague evaluative criteria—emotional expression, the directness of pleasure, and authentic communication—were clearly put under stress by difficult writing. With traditional values thus undermined, it became hard to tell what was *good*, and it became impossible to discern the real from the sham. In a 1928 verse editorial, Squire playfully protested to the muse of contemporary poetry for allowing the current "spate of senseless and amorphous verse" (337):

> What can have happened to you, Muse?
> Time was you never held such views.
> You used to sing like a canary
> With quite a small vocabulary
> Of trees and grass, the sun, the moon,
> Which then you always rhymed with swoon,
> So simply, with such innocence,
> And such a lack of deeper sense
> That any passer-by could tell
> If you were singing ill or well.
> 'Twas usually ill, no doubt,
> But you were easily found out.
> Now you bewilder me: how could
> I tell if that were bad or good,
> That gnomic stuff you sang just now,
> That cacophonic senseless row. (342–43)

With the disappearance of traditional aesthetic standards, Squire argues, there is nothing in modernism that could give one a purchase on whether it is any good. Since no such fulcrum exists, any claims of quality on the part of modernism's apologists must, of necessity, be fraudulent. And the social context of modernism encouraged such claims, for if it is impossible to tell what is good, then it is inevitable that there also be absurdly high estimations of value. According to Squire, critics, bowled over by "The spate of senseless and amorphous verse," find that they "really don't know what to say," and find themselves with their backs to the wall:

> Fearing that if they do say what they think
> Their names may, later on, be made to stink,
> Because their crassness failed to recognise
> The fire of Shelley in a Snooks's eyes— (1928, 337)

Further, modernism's skeptics claimed, difficulty's fraud was evident not just from these works' formal properties nor from the evaluative criteria brought to bear on these works. The evidence for fraud also lay in the social conditions that allowed these evaluative criteria to be blurred or made irrelevant. Often modernism's skeptics revealed these social conditions by imagining the artist's thoughts as he or she composed the difficult work, as did Squire in this *London Mercury* editorial, where he commented on the influence of the Italian futurists:

> But Signor Marinetti and his congeners—we had been gently acclimatised to great obscurity by artists like Mallarme—provided these poets with a priceless gift. Let rhythm go, let sense go: put down in barbarous sequence any incongruous images that come into your head: even, if you like, put down sheer gibberish: if possible, deceive yourself, and you will deceive others. Produce a work so opaque that it cannot be seen through. The innocents will either wildly protest against these dangerous revolutionaries—a much more pleasing role to find oneself in than that of harmless mediocrity—or else they will knit their brows with the reflection "if this young man expresses himself in thoughts too deep for me, why what a very, very very deep young man this deep young man must be." (1920, 388)

That step back to the author's motivations implied that hoaxes were made possible by their social context. Negative readers thus always paid attention to the social conditions that produced the hoax, and they implicitly argued that the obviousness of these social conditions clearly showed that such work was not great art. According to Squire and others, modernism was ripe for a hoax; difficult writing was able to seize center stage because modern high culture was in a state of decay. The increased cultural influence of women and effete men were the harbingers of decay, as were the values they brought with them, such as professionalism and publicity. As many conservative read-

> If you're anxious for to shine in the high aesthetic line as a man of culture rare,
> You must get up all the germs of the transcendental terms, and plant them everywhere.
> You must lie upon the daisies and discourse in novel phrases of your complicated state of mind.
> The meaning doesn't matter if it's only idle chatter of a transcendental kind.
> And everyone will say,
> As you walk your mystic way,
> "If this young man expresses himself in terms too deep for *me*,
> Why, what a very singularly deep young man this deep young man must be!"
>
> —W. S. Gilbert, "Patience," 1881

ers lamented, modernism was not a time of *individuals*, removed from the stresses of contemporary society; rather, artists were parts of schools and coteries; they were too immersed in society, and wanted to produce what was in fashion. Literature, music, art—even all of society—was in crisis. And difficulty fueled that crisis.

Norman Rockwell Tackles Jackson Pollock

Modernism's lessons were thoroughly learned. Consider Norman Rockwell, the most successful illustrator of his time, who built his career on painting relentlessly cheerful illustrations of American values, illustrations whose attitudes were instantly readable by his public. Yet although he grinned all the way to the bank, Rockwell was aware of his lack of status in high culture. In his biography he comments on his desire for popularity and his relationship to art critics: "I have always wanted everybody to like my work. I could never be satisfied with just the approval of the critics (and, boy, I've certainly had to be satisfied without it) or a small group of kindred souls. So I have painted pictures that didn't disturb anybody, that I knew everyone would understand and like" (1960, 44–45). Rockwell always fulfilled his wish to be universally understood. His cover for the January 13, 1962, *Saturday Evening Post* is no exception, a classic Rockwell, as instantly readable as Squire's "The Man Who Wrote Free Verse." For that issue Rockwell painted *The Connoisseur* (figure 1.1), a depiction of a lone figure contemplating what the *Post*'s readers would instantly have recognized as a generic Jackson Pollock.[34]

40   The Difficulties of Modernism

Figure 1.1
Norman Rockwell, *The Connoisseur*, 1962

Rockwell built this illustration around an enigma of sorts. Unlike most of Rockwell's illustrations, here the central person is faceless. What we get instead is just a stance, but one that speaks volumes. The viewer is aging, but dapper, and has suffered no loss of power. What is left of his hair is well, even fussily, combed. An erect stance, a good suit, recently shined shoes, a white fedora, white gloves—this is a person of leisure who has time to read about art, as indicated by the book or magazine he holds. A nice umbrella, too, but perhaps too obviously a sign of capitalist power. A bit of prosperity protrudes above his collar, in the neck flesh, which is a bit thicker than the collar. Hands behind his back, he gazes at the painting in a stance of authoritative ease. The faceless viewer is clearly in a setting where he belongs. This is an expensive place, one with walls high enough to hang the massive painting, and one with expensive, well-maintained flooring, as its shine indicates. This is not the linoleum of Rockwell's working-class barbershops.

There is an attitude that goes with these details: the ersatz Pollock is big, and like most large paintings, it demands serious attention. Standing within a foot and a half of the large work, so close that it covers his entire field of vision, Rockwell's man gives it that attention. By placing the viewer so close, Rockwell encouraged the *Post*'s readers to speculate irreverently on what about the painting could provoke a viewer to give it such close attention. After all, the work doesn't seem to be one in which details matter—there are no details in a blob. The viewer apparently sees *details* where the *Post*'s reader doesn't; Rockwell heightens this by using the faceless viewer's head to block whatever it is that he is so closely examining. Rapt with attention, the viewer has taken off his fedora, a gesture of respect (but also, with the removed gloves and the magazine, a suggestion that this is a liminal place where the powerful can experience leisure and relief from the pressures of the world). These are the protocols of difficulty, and Rockwell's viewer, unlike Squire's heroes, has learned them well. Erect but at ease, he gazes at the emperor's new clothes.

In one of its standard comments on the present issue's cover, the *Post*, loading on the heavy-handed whimsy for which it was famous, writes:

> Is that prosperous-looking art collector about to reach for his checkbook to buy a prize-winning work titled "The Insubstance of Infinity?" Or is he simply imagining his teen-age daughter calling it "Strictly from Blobsville?" Cover artist Norman Rockwell won't say. "If I were young now I might paint that way myself," he explains. "Recently I attended some classes in modern-art techniques. I learned a lot and loved it." He had fun, too, "painting" this abstraction. When he got tired of waving a dripping brush, he invited a man painting the windows of his studio to help. From the top of his ladder the fellow obligingly dumped a can of white paint onto the canvas spread out on the floor. "I wish," Rockwell says, "I'd had those lessons before I did this cover." ("The Cover," 1962, 3)

That last statement is, of course, fatuous. After all, Rockwell put his signature on the gallery wall, not on the Pollock. Yet, for all his smugness, Rockwell really didn't want or need those lessons: he understood some aspects of difficulty perfectly. Difficulty is about power and about knowing the protocols to maneuver through it. Further, Rockwell's illustration is painted from the viewpoint of an invisible third person, one who looks not only at the work, but at the man looking at the work, at a social situation. Rockwell understood that modernism is not just a set of formal strategies; it is a way of interacting with art. Choosing to make this *Post* cover an illustration of a painting *and* a viewer, Rockwell understood that difficulty is not just a property of some works of art—it is a cultural *situation*, the smooth management of which gains a person entry into high culture.

CHAPTER 2

Articulating Anxiety: A Theory of Difficulty

> The Cubists are entitled to the serious attention of all who find enjoyment in the colored puzzle pictures of the Sunday newspapers.
> —Theodore Roosevelt

> Present day geniuses can no more help doing what they are doing than you can help not understanding it, but if you think we do it for effect and to make a sensation, you're crazy. It's not our idea of fun to work for thirty or forty years on a medium of expression and have ourselves ridiculed. —Gertrude Stein

Texts like "The Man Who Wrote Free Verse," the reviews of *The Waste Land* and of *Ulysses*, Graves and Riding's *A Survey of Modernist Poetry*, Brooks's *Modern Poetry and the Tradition*, and the introductions to dozens of anthologies show how difficulty's prevalence energized debate both about how to evaluate art and about the social conditions that gave rise to and shaped this evaluation. But modern difficulty received its energy not just from these moments, or from the contingencies of modern fashion or literary history. It also took on its large place in modernist history because of the peculiar shape it had as a theory, the shared ways in which that theory was articulated, and the common ways in which difficulty was *experienced*. Putting aside for a moment the more developed arguments for or against difficulty, this chapter looks at how difficulty was conceptually and experientially organized, and how, on the strength of this organization, difficulty seized the aesthetic agenda of the twentieth century.

Difficulty's place in modernism was driven by shared understandings of what difficulty was, understandings that routinely allowed localized instances of difficulty to stand in for all of modern culture. Even more striking, modern understandings of difficulty revealed what was *inherent* to the experience of difficulty—though modern readers' understandings of this inherence were, at best, vague, and the commonality in their understandings of difficulty was unstated, provisional, ad hoc. Yet, together these understandings and the visceral experiences that gave rise to them explain how the moments described in the opening chapter and the rest of this book make sense as a *theory* about difficulty.

To introduce the issues involved, I first turn, briefly, to what is inherent about the *experience* of difficulty, by looking at the work of French theorist Michel Foucault. But I do not turn to the Foucault whose chilly olympian writing reveals how all cultures are gripped by social forces of which they are unaware. Rather, I turn to Foucault the *person*, and a minor byway in his work. In an uncharacteristic moment of self-revelation during an interview, Foucault claims "Personally I am rather haunted by the existence of discourse," and a few moments later narrates the following anecdote: "A nightmare has pursued me since childhood: I have under my eyes a text that I can't read, or of which only a tiny part can be deciphered; I pretend to read it, but I know that I'm inventing; then the text suddenly blurs completely, I can no longer read anything or even invent, my throat constricts and I wake up" ([1967] 1989, 27). Despite its unusually personal flavor, Foucault's story has a resonance typical of his writing: when he asserts that this dream has "haunted" him since childhood, Foucault attempts to master the event by giving it a recurring status, one capable of being framed by a larger discourse and turned into a parable. This mastery leads him to follow this anecdote with a standard modern defense of difficulty, the idea that difficulty is an inherent property of language. Nervous about how his own idiosyncrasies might be flavoring this nightmare, Foucault attempts to universalize: "I don't know what there can be of the personal in this obsession with language, which exists everywhere and escapes us in its very survival. It survives by turning its look away from us, its face inclined toward a night of which we know nothing" (25–26). Yet for my purposes Foucault's theoretical divagation on the dream is forgettable, and so I turn not to the impersonality and mastery (or difficulty) that readers expect from Foucault. Rather, I turn to the subjectivity and anxiety that shape this incident, an anxiety hinted at in the Gallic melodrama of his theorizing—the face of language turned "toward a night of which we know nothing." It is not Foucault's theoretical stance that is striking about this passage, and that tells us much about cultural life in this century; rather, it is his physical state, his personal response to not being able to understand, a response that reveals him to be quite an ordinary human being: his determinedly pretending to read even when he knows he is inventing, the panicky tightening of his throat, his abrupt losing of any sense at all as the text "suddenly blurs completely," and his escape from the problem into consciousness.

Foucault's experience is the classic encounter with difficulty, a visceral, anxiety-filled encounter that gave high modernism its energy, morality, and power. Concomitantly, Foucault's nightmare suggests that difficulty's universality does not reside in a set of formal strategies that make a work difficult, formal strategies that characterize either all great or all shoddy art. Rather, difficulty's universality arises from the extreme responses it elicits, provoking people to anxiety, laughter, or anger. The public reactions to the post-Impressionist show, the initial performance of Stravinsky's *Sacre du printemps*, and the 1913 Armory Show are instances of such responses, as are many reviews of writers like Gertrude Stein and James Joyce. Initially, the viscerality of such responses makes each one seem highly personal and extremely unreliable as a moment where one might discover something universal about art. Seen together, however, these moments look more like a stylized dance or a liturgy. And it is when they are looked at together that the function of difficulty in modernism becomes clearer.

The awkwardness, though, was that moderns on all sides of the difficulty argument didn't know what to *do* with these extreme responses. Though such responses were very common, readers did not think of them as being normative responses to aesthetic objects. For difficult modernism's supporters, laughter and anger were stupid responses, the mark of philistinism. For modernism's skeptics, while laughter and anger were morally justified, they were not the responses one would have to *real* art. Both sides did not recognize that the anger and laughter were inevitable, and, for the formation of the modern canon, highly instrumental. Though odd and highly charged, these common visceral responses, riding alongside the unrigorous ways in which modern readers talked about difficulty, shaped both the modern canon and how audiences interacted with it. Indeed, knowing how to interact with difficult art became—and remains—the ticket of admission to high culture.

Conceptualizing Difficulty

These visceral responses to difficulty (which I will set to the side for the moment) operated in a linguistic context that, on several levels, did not encourage rigorous analysis. That context is shaped by an odd, quiet phenomenon. Many critics who wished to make a point about modern difficulty put its two most common terms, "difficulty" and "obscurity," in quotation marks. In his 1934 ambivalent reading of modernist difficulty, for example, John Sparrow wrote that what unified readers' responses to writers such as Proust, Joyce, Eliot, and Woolf was that "each of these writers have been found 'difficult' by many readers" (43). Sparrow is paralleled by Hugh Ross Williamson, who in defense of Eliot's difficulty claimed that he wrote his book for "the lover of poetry who is puzzled by Mr. Eliot's 'difficulty'" (1933,

> The "dominant impression" conveyed upon the uninitiated viewer in viewing M. Henry Kahnwiller's [sic] "The Woman and the Pot of Mustard" may be an agonizing toothache that gives him a violent impulse to recommend a one-minute cure to the sufferer.
>
> —Herman Landon, "Hark! Hark! The Critics Bark! The Cubists Are Coming," Chicago *Record-Herald*, 1913

10); and Laura Riding, who in the preface to her *Collected Poems* grumbled that she had "been persistently accused of 'difficulty'" ([1933] 1980, 406).

Whatever is going on here, it is not simply a wish for accurate documentation, for modern readers quote in a very odd way. They quote merely one undistinguished word; further, they never identify a single person as its source (indeed, the source is never given or only vaguely identified). Rather, with their single-word quotations modern readers signal that they are quoting from a group or a mindset, and they are quoting not so much the term itself as the term *as evidence* of sloppy thinking. The single-word quotation suggests that the quoting writer is apologizing for the sloppiness of the term, and that he would use a clearer term but for the term's typical user, and the general public, who are most familiar with and habitually use the messy forms. The quotation marks suggest that the people who typically use this term, although they are responsible for its wide circulation, do not think clearly about it. Careful thought, by contrast, recognizes the problematic nature of the term. Putting "difficulty" and "understanding" in quotation marks not only indicated that one was aware of how messy these terms were, and that one used this term for lack of a better word. It also fastidiously insinuated that it was beneath one's dignity to use unproblematically the awkward, unrigorous term of one's opponents. The quotation marks raised the question whether difficulty, as it was typically understood, was a serious issue—even, at times, questioning whether the supposed barrier of difficulty was illusory. Quotation marks silently announced these concerns to one's readers, who, by recognizing how the quotation functioned, implicitly accepted the quoter's shorthand analysis.[1]

While the recurrent quotation marks show that difficulty was under some contestation, the quoting was also a part of a recognizable polemic, for the fact that one could use quotation marks silently also demonstrated that one's readers knew what was going on. Further, the polemic tended to move in one direction: those who contested difficulty's public meanings by putting one of its terms in quotation marks are almost invariably those who were arguing for the virtues of the supposed difficulty of modernism.[2] This suggests that difficulty, as it was used in the first half of the twentieth century, was by default a negative term; moreover, according to modernism's apologists those who used the term unproblematically had a simplistic idea of what difficulty was, what its values were, and who were the difficult writers. As they often do when used as a hedge, quotation marks early in the twentieth century signaled an attack on this unproblematic use of difficulty as a concept. Louise Morgan, for example, in her review of Eliot's *Poems 1909–1925* for *Outlook*, argued for the validity of Eliot's juxtapositions, referring to them as "sincere and simple effects which because they do not understand them are labeled 'obscure' and 'merely clever' by the worldly-wise critics" ([1925] 1982, 221). Bracketing her key terms with quotation marks, Morgan implied that these terms had been corrupted by "worldly-wise critics." Richard Aldington made a similar connection in his evaluation of Eliot, identifying the source of his quotation as "lazy people": "Now the charge of 'obscurity' may be just, for all verse which on analysis proves to have no intellectual or emotional content is 'obscure'; obscure because it pretends to possess a meaning which it has not. But the obscurity of Mr. Eliot is as much a myth of lazy people as the obscurity of Browning" (1924, 188).[3]

Of course, a solution to this sloppiness immediately presents itself: after putting difficulty in quotation marks one could go on to clarify it or employ a better term. After all, quotation marks reassert control over the term's use—and allow one to look more theoretically sophisticated in the process. But that theoretical clarification doesn't often happen. Quotation marks do not presage the coming of theoretically rigorous behavior; critics do not go on to define difficulty more precisely, but continue to use the sloppy term, with or without quotation marks. This nervous use of quotation marks, and the unwillingness to argue in detail why it was necessary to use them, indicates how omnipresent, but also how casual and imprecise, the difficulty discussion was (and continues to be).

This casualness was abetted by an accompanying lack of clarity in difficulty's lexicon. A slippery concept, *difficulty* at times lexically surfaced as "erudition," at other times as "obscurity" or "complexity," and at still other times as "nonsense."[4] The list could be extended. And although writers could direct individual terms such as "erudition" at an individual text with some precision, these terms were not part of a systematic taxonomy and were rarely subjected to careful semantic scrutiny. In the first half of the past century, there was no discussion in which a complicated terminology precisely set out the agenda for public discussion. Even when descriptions of difficulty accumulate in one place, as they do in reviews of *The Waste Land*, critics show little agreement about which term to use: at different points *The Waste Land* is called "difficult," "complicated," "esoteric," "obscure," "Alexandrian," "cryptic," "unintelligible," and "a puzzle." These readings of *The Waste Land* show the same terminological disparities as do reactions to such widely differing texts as Joyce's *Ulysses*, Stein's *The Making of Americans*, and Faulkner's *As I Lay Dying*. There are neither clearly stated agreements on how *difficulty* might be defined, nor clearly drawn boundaries on disagreements over its definition—the opposite of terms usually thought of as important.

The context of remarks about difficulty goes a long way to explaining their lack of terminological rigor. Talk about difficulty—casual, imprecise, unrigorous—most often appeared in ephemeral sources (such as reviews and anthology prefaces) and was consequently pressed into serving local agendas, such as a defense of one's anthology selections, or praise for a certain writer, or, in the case of Eliot on metaphysical writing, a defense of an unjustly neglected moment in literary history. Eliot's claim for the necessity of difficulty, the most famous argument for modernist difficulty—his claim that "poets in our civilization, as it exists at present, must be *difficult*"—appeared in a review of an anthology of metaphysical poetry. Further, Eliot's claim is not a detailed argument; the claim itself is just a three-sentence series of propositions that twice, through the use of the word "must," makes an assertion that receives no supporting evidence. While his use of *must* implies a theory that lies waiting in the shadows, Eliot never spells out *why* difficulty must move from a condition evident in the general culture into a characteristic of art. He does not argue the point; he asserts it.[5] The epigrammatic shape of Eliot's argument is typical of modern comments on difficulty. While difficulty appears often, there are few *developed* arguments about difficulty. For the most part, writers just volley assertions back and forth, and the missing steps in argumentation perform their work unnoticed. Assertions about difficulty's omnipresence (like all modern arguments about difficulty) more often function like a rhetorical trope than careful thought: readers present assertions with evidence that is at best sketchy. Difficulty floats around, apparently untethered to rigorous analysis.

Its quotation marks, imprecise terms, and casual discussion indicate that in modern discussions "difficulty" as a concept was not subject to rigorous scrutiny. *Difficulty* was neither theorized nor part of a systematic taxonomy. *Difficulty* was instead a *naturally* occurring category, constructed casually, for the most part unknowingly, and without the rigor of, say, the category of the sestina. For some, such literary chat may seem too sloppy to be useful, background noise to the real work of modernism. However, this plethora of terms and lack of theoretical rigor does not suggest that difficulty was unimportant for the creation of modernism; indeed, just the opposite is true. Difficulty gained its massive place in shaping twentieth-century high culture precisely *because* it was so sloppy.[6]

Difficulty as a concept was assumed to be commonly understood, an assumption that allowed difficulty to work in many ways as if it were entrenched, such as (but on a more modest scale) the Western concept of time as linear—omnipresent, central to many daily activities, yet powerful *because* it typically goes without saying.[7] As Lakoff and Turner point out, such basic, unexamined categories have power: "Anything we rely on constantly, unconsciously, and automatically is so much part of us that it cannot be easily resisted, in large measure because it is barely even noticed" (1989, 63). Difficulty's superstructure is unnoticed, and because it is unnoticed it has a silent power. If one had to unpack its theoretical presuppositions each time one used an entrenched concept like difficulty, the concept would not be as effortless to use; the activities performed by it would begin to look culture-bound, strange, less "natural."

Its casual nature and entrenchment have consequences for how one might employ the swirling mass of ideas about difficulty. It suggests, first, that one *not* approach these different terms as pointing to radically differing understandings of difficulty. Now, scholars tend to reach instinctively for this option, and would be predisposed to explore difficulty's particular differences in different contexts. But difficulty's use in anthologies, advertisements, and reviews and the reception of texts like *The Waste Land* actually pushes toward an opposing strategy, the idea that these different terms all point to roughly the same textual reality, and perhaps even the same conceptualizing of that reality. In this reading, modernism's unsystematic understanding of difficulty disguises one loose and baggy monster. Fundamentally, the vagaries that eddy around discussions of difficulty—even the differences occasionally articulated for different forms of difficulty—all do the same work. (Indeed, even the distinctions between good and bad difficulty more often *make* for a single subject than fragment it.) This similarity is essential to understanding modernism's cultural triumph.

In their casual use of its central terms, modern readers generally presented difficulty as a property of a text, a property that had immediate consequences for the reading process, for it stymied the strategies one typically used to generate meaning from a text, and it demanded to be addressed first in order for one to have a significant interaction with that text. According to standard modern uses of "difficulty" and its allied terms, readers could receive pleasure or interact with the difficult text significantly only by coming to terms with those aspects of it that they considered difficult. Without some way of dealing with the difficulty (which presented itself immediately to readers), it was impossible to interact significantly with the work of art. Different terms for difficulty stressed different aspects and manifestations of this definition.[8]

How did readers understand the shape of this impasse? First of all, difficulty did not stand alone; it was always conceived in terms of its opposite, the process that the difficult text impeded. Difficulty produced an impasse, a *failure* of comprehension, and therefore modernism's ad hoc understanding of difficulty is elucidated by what modern readers generally meant by "meaning" and "understand." Further, difficulty's opposite was considered primary, basic, a conceptualizing that made difficulty into a *marked* category, a category that in its definition, linguistic form, or appearance points to another, more basic category ("woman" is a marked category, "man" is not). The unmarked thus has some kind of silent primacy that can be understood in various ways, from the chronological, to the conceptual, to the ethical. Thus, there are significant conceptual (even political) consequences that are motivated by markedness, most of which stem from the fact that the marked term is defined by the unmarked, and that the marked has more work to do than the unmarked. Many linguistic forms for difficulty indicate this dependent markedness: the etymology of its most basic term, "difficulty," means "not easy"; "obscure" has its source in the Latin "*obscurus*" (meaning "dark"), whose root in Sanskrit means "sky," and whose prefix, "ob," means "not" (Glare 1990, 1210, 1220).

Modernism's skeptics, through their parodies of high modern difficulty, give a clear account of the dominant ways in which high culture at that point understood "meaning" and the ways in which difficult modernism attacked such notions. I turn to these parodies not only for their occasional hilarity, but also because the characteristics that they stretch and parody, in order to work, must be both imitable and instantly recognizable to the culture at large. The parodies thus provide a taxonomy of the kinds of art that modern readers as a group found difficult to understand. When they talked about the difficulty of a text, modernism's skeptics often worked with a model of art in which a text was "meaningful" if its assertions could be understood. "Assertions" must be understood in various ways here, as not just being a text's logical propositions, but also the metaphoric or literal status of its concrete language, its presentation of a speaker with clear psychological characteristics, and even its presentation of itself *as* a work of art and not, say, a guidebook description of a Nantucket bed and breakfast.

Most basically, understanding a text's assertions meant being able to comprehend its logic. Thus, in his 1931 *Cinder Thursday*, a parody of Eliot, Herbert Palmer wrote the following:

> Let the Law of indisciplined Association of Ideas take leading control,
> that everything go leaping and whirling,
> As it is in the brains of lunatics
> and little children.
> Ouranga, wanga, stanga. (15–16)

Palmer uses the phrase "Ouranga, wanga, stanga," which appears as a refrain in his poem, as his particularly outrageous parody of modernist difficulty. In this case, the poem is difficult because it is hard to discover what the words themselves mean, and doubly difficult to discover what they mean in relation to the preceding lines, which present, presumably, the principles that the refrain then responds to or illustrates.

But the assertions of a work of art were also thought of in terms other than their logical sense. Some modern works were difficult because one needed to look up what certain of its words meant. This, a problem based on knowledge, is what George Steiner refers to as "contingent" difficulty (1978, 18–33). For one of his verse editorials, Squire composed "Piebald Unicorn," a parody that in part reads:

> Under the hyperthyroid moon
> Seated, I shall eat caviar with a spoon,
> While Mr. Nokes, that melancholy man,
> Will cool my heated features with his fan
> The ghost of sainted Elagabalus
> Will sometimes come to drink his tea with us (1928, 342)

While there are certainly other forms of difficulty here, Squire's major target is the modernist propensity to use arcane references, some highly private ("Mr. Nokes"); others, more public but obscure ("sainted Elagabalus"). Knowledge-based difficulty was forgivable if either the poet was great enough (such as Dante) or if the knowledge wasn't trivial. Most often, though, modernism's skeptics scoffed at what novelist Sinclair Lewis called "the coy snootiness of obscurity, of taking a weak little newborn thought and dressing it up like a mikado." Lewis was pointed in his description of this attitude: "It is particularly to be noted in the poets whose attitude is 'If you're such an illiterate that you do not immediately see, when I speak of "Dora," that I am really referring to *doryphora*, which is, as I have just this minute learned from the dictionary, the Latin scientific word for the potato bug, why then I can't be bothered by your silly, senile and probably Fascist opinion'" (51).[9]

Other difficult works were thought to be obscure because they were not clear about the status of their assertions, whether (and how) they were to be understood literally or metaphorically. When Squire had Reggie write "Gyrating cowls. Ink. Oh God! A Lobster!" as a poem (1924, 130), he was spoofing modern difficulty's propensity to put forward statements that could make aesthetic sense only if they were understood metaphorically, but that were difficult because the tenor of the metaphor was so private that it had no accessible public understanding. In 1935 Louis Untermeyer produced this kind of difficulty in his parody "Einstein among the Coffee-Cups," whose author, he noted, was "T.S. Eli-t":

> Deflective rhythm under seas
>   Where Sappho tuned the snarling air;
> A shifting of the spectral lines
>   Grown red with gravity and wear.

52 The Difficulties of Modernism

> New systems of coördinates
>   Disturb the Sunday tablecloth.
> Celestine yawns. Sir Oliver
>   Hints of the jaguar and sloth.
>
> A chord of the eleventh shrieks
>   And slips beyond the portico.
> The night contracts. A warp in space
>   Has rumors of Correggio.
>
> Lights. Mrs. Blumenthal expands;
>   Calories beyond control.
> The rector brightens. Tea is served;
>   Euclid supplanted by the sole. (363)

In the phrase "the warp in space has rumors of Correggio," at least either the "warp" or the "rumors" (or perhaps both) must be functioning on some level metaphorically, both here and in Eliot's quatrain poems, where similar lines appear. Failing that, Untermeyer implies, the phrase is pretentious nonsense.

But modernism also had difficult texts whose syntax and logic were perfectly understandable and did not obviously present problems of metaphor. Such texts attacked normal ideas of understanding on a different level. In them, meaning went beyond one's understanding logical or metaphoric assertions, to understanding the psyche of the mind that produced that art work, that spoke it; and further, to understanding a work's assertions about its own status as an art object. Thus, in the work of writers like William Carlos Williams and Gertrude Stein, in the visual art of Marcel Duchamp, and in the music of Stravinsky, people had trouble understanding the work's basic proposition: why is this object, or collection of words or sounds, presenting itself as a work of art? These are issues of what George Steiner calls "modal" difficulty (1978, 27–29). Michael Roberts, in the introduction to the 1936 edition of *The Faber Book of Modern Verse*, noted the "active animosity" aroused by work that ordinary readers believe "is not poetry at all" (1). Harriet Monroe, in a *Poetry* symposium on the work of Marianne Moore, remarked of Moore's recently published *Poems*, "If one were to accept the challenge of the title, and of the geometrical verse-designs which frame these cryptic observations, one might be led straight to the ancient and rather futile enquiry, What is poetry?" (1922, 208). This is the difficulty that shaped one writer's renaming of Marcel's Duchamp *Nude Descending a Staircase*, the cause célèbre of the 1913 Armory Show, as "an explosion in a shingle factory." It also shapes the following quatrain from the Chicago *Tribune* of February 8, 1913, written at the time that the Armory Show came to town:

> Morning stirs the feet and hands
> (Nausicaa and Polypheme).
> Gesture of orang-outang
> Rises from the sheets in steam.
>
> —From T. S. Eliot, "Sweeney Erect"

> I called the canvas Cow with cud
> And hung it on the line,
> Altho' to me 'twas vague as mud,
> 'Twas clear to Gertrude Stein.
> ("A line o' type or two," quoted in Brown 1963, 111)

As soon as one asked of a given work, "Is it art?" one indicated that the work's central assertion was unclear, that the work was either difficult or a fraud.

According to standard thinking, all these differing senses of "understanding" were normally a given to aesthetic reading practices, and they consequently allowed a reader to experience the text's pleasure (an aspect of the text that went *beyond* its meaning). By blocking an artwork's assertions, difficulty, in its common understandings, not only created a crisis in evaluation, it was not "normal." As the next chapter will show, how to find tools for evaluation, and how to either overturn or rework such notions of "meaning," became some of modernism's central tasks.

Difficulty as a Category

In addition to its implicit notions of "understanding" and "meaning," difficulty's linguistic manifestations ("obscurity," "opacity," "complexity") work as a single understanding in two other ways: as a category and through these terms' implied logic and conceptual metaphors. Both the categorization and the conceptual metaphors nestled within them exemplify standard ways of understanding the difficult experience. Equally important, the ways in which this category and its conceptual metaphors were employed do much to explain the peculiar force that difficulty had in shaping modernism (including the highly visceral responses directed at difficult texts and works of art).

I will first examine these different terms as members of a single category of aesthetic experience and the various shapes they took on within that category. What I mean by "category" deserves some elucidation, and here my argument, drawing on cognitive linguistic understanding of categories, gets technical.[10] A category is a conceptual structure that unites disparate entities, ideas, emotions, and actions. As such, it is a basic tool for structuring and understanding experience. In the early twentieth century, those disparate terms that readers used to talk about *difficulty*—"erudition," "esotericism," "obscurity," and so on—were all employed as members of the same category.

Because certain of its terms are more central than others, modern difficulty is a peculiar kind of category, however. While some categories are based simply on members with different specific characteristics all sharing certain general characteristics (e.g., all amphibians have a gill-breathing and a lung-breathing stage), many categories are more awkward than that. These categories can have members of different statuses, with some members being better examples of the category than others. Research shows, for example, that people think a robin is a better example of a bird than an ostrich or an owl, and that focal red is a better example of red than maroon (Lakoff 1987, 24–30). According to George Lakoff in his *Women, Fire, and Dangerous Things*, many such categories have a radial structure. A radial category is an organization of experience that contains both a central subcategory and non-central extensions of it, extensions "which are not specialized instances of the central subcategory, but rather are variants of it" (1987, 91). *Difficulty* is that kind of category, and as a radial category *difficulty* has a center and periphery. As the members of this category are typically used, the lexical term "difficulty" and its typical content is at the center, with "obscurity" only slightly off to the side, but with terms such as "erudition" and "esotericism" clearly nearer the edges.[11] A term such as "incoherence," because (unlike more central terms) it doesn't promise a "real" meaning lurking somewhere within the difficult work, is even more peripheral.

There are some characteristics that place "difficulty" (and, to a lesser degree, "obscurity") nearest the center of this radial category. First, although readers' distinctions among lexical terms are overwhelmingly unsystematic, they turn to "difficulty" and "obscurity" more often than any other term—more than twice as often as the next most frequently used term.[12] This favoring of one or two terms is not the result of sophisticated logical scrutiny: the lexical term "difficulty" in particular is central to the category partly because it is easy to use. It is a simple name—it is the first to enter most readers' lexicons, ahead of terms such as "obscurity," "erudite," and "esoteric," and it contains the most common attributes of category members. "Difficulty" is also the most contextually neutral term, and it is the term that has the greatest cultural significance—it applies to the greatest number of human activities. With a sweep that is missing from its related terms, "difficulty" extends beyond artistic or even primarily intellectual activities—a forkball may be a difficult pitch to throw, but it is not an obscure or erudite one. Of all the terms used to delineate the *category difficulty*, the *term* "difficulty" is capable of carrying the biggest load (not surprisingly, its etymological origin is wonderfully bland, from the Latin *facultas* or *facilis*, meaning, with the prefix:

"not easy").[13] "Difficulty" is also turned to so frequently because difficulty's typically implied content does work that is central to *difficulty* as a category. For modern readers, the term "difficulty" typically suggested that the difficult text had a real meaning somewhere, and that the text's features (not the reader's abilities) were responsible for that meaning not being available.

"Obscurity," a term turned to almost as often as was "difficulty," shares many of "difficulty's" qualities. Like "difficulty," it did not suggest that the difficult text was meaningless. And, unlike a term such as "erudition" or "esotericism," it did not specifically point to the exact *causes* of the difficulty. While it doesn't have the complete portability that "difficulty" has (it's hard to think of a particular climb up El Capitan being an "obscure" route), "obscurity" is in some ways more useful in that its etymological origins clearly tie it in to the dominant conceptual metaphor for difficulty.

The remaining, peripheral terms—used less frequently than "obscurity" and "difficulty"—are brought into play (motivated) and organized by several principles that had a big impact on how moderns argued about difficult texts. Two prominent principles are excess and lack, both of which were almost always used negatively and indicated that the difficult text had crossed a boundary of sorts. Many of the terms that readers used to describe difficult art employ some notion that the difficult work is excessive, that it overloads viewers and readers, as when John Crowe Ransom speculated that Eliot's intention in *The Waste Land* "is evidently to present a wilderness in which both he and the reader may be bewildered, in which one is never to see the wood for the trees" ([1923] 1982, 177). "Excess" is found in the content implied by such terms as "erudition" and "esoteric," "dense" and "opaque" writing, and it is either an excess of knowledge that the text demands and the reader does not have, or it is an excess of information and sensory data that the text presents and the reader has inadequate resources to manage. The difficult work puts up too much stuff between it and the lucid pleasures of the text. Many terms and arguments that use an idea of excess imply an authorial intentionality that is either perverse, or that needs to be dealt with in some way if the text is to be understood, and they suggest that the excesses of the difficult text eliminated the possibility of a single principle being able to control it. Difficult, excessive texts were not *unified* texts. Shane Leslie, reviewing Joyce's *Ulysses* for the *Quarterly Review*, speculated that "Pages without punctuation or paragraph show an attempt to beat up a sustained and overwhelming orchestral effect. French and possibly American critics will utter their chorus of praise in proportion to their failure to understand" ([1922] 1970, 211).

Terms (and their implicit arguments) that used some idea of excess suggested that modern difficulty, in its very form, violated a model of reading that many held dear. It was a model in which readers best enjoyed the pleasures of the text in a transparent reading process, in which the claims of the real world faded away, in which the formal characteristics of the text did not draw attention to themselves, and which did not call on readers to overtly use (or find) some specialized knowledge. All of these things should dissolve and allow one to communicate with the literary work directly. This model of reading was central to readers suspicious of modern difficulty. As Squire argued in "The Man Who Wrote Free Verse," one shouldn't have to pay attention to how the literary work was produced; literature ought to be *above* the social. Writing about Joyce's *Work in Progress* (which would eventually become *Finnegans Wake*), G. W. Stonier grumbled about its formal excesses: "Most of the failures of Mr. Joyce's new prose come from too much distortion and the introduction of patterns and allusions which merely bewilder the reader with irrelevant deftness" (1930, 410).

This understanding of excess had considerable cultural force. It was, for example, a standard device in reviewing *The Waste Land* simply to give a list of the knowledge the poem required and to have that list silently damn the poem's excesses. Consider Gorham Munson: "To win a complete understanding of 'The Waste Land,' the reader must scan eleven pages of notes, he must have a considerable learning in letters or be willing to look up references in Milton, Ovid, Middleton, Webster, Spenser, Verlaine, St. Augustine, etc., etc., in order to associate them with their first context, he must read Latin, Greek, French and German, he must know Frazer's 'Golden Bough' and steep himself in the legend of the Holy Grail, studying in particular Miss Weston's 'From Ritual to Romance'" ([1924] 1982, 206). As the repeated use of "must" indicates, the text's excesses *demand* a response from the very beginning. And, for conservative readers, those demands, issuing from an insane *Wunderkammer*, were unreasonable and counterproductive. The excesses of the difficult text, then, were typically not a sign of its richness or inexhaustibility or depth. They were a sign of the text's overwhelming its readers. The payoff that accrued from these excesses, according to modernism's skeptics, was rarely worth it. After listing *The Waste Land*'s excesses, Munson went on to argue: "The texture of 'The Waste Land' is excessively heavy with literary allusions which the reader of good will, knowing that it is not unjust to make severe requisitions upon his knowledge, will diligently track down. But our reader of good will is entitled, I think, to turn sour when he discovers that after all his research he has not penetrated into some strange uncharted region of experience but has only fathomed the cipher of a quite ordinary and easily understandable state of mind" (206).

Other lexical terms, however, characterized the difficult text in exactly the opposite manner. Some of difficulty's terms describe the difficult work as fundamentally lacking something. It just has too *little*. Terms such as "lack of clarity," "compression," "meaninglessness," "obscurity," "nonsense," and "incoherence" all use some form of this idea. Thus, Morton Dauwen Zabel mentioned the "reader who was once mystified by the frugal concision" of Yvor Winters's poetry (1931, 226), and Kenneth Burke argued that a central problem of Gertrude Stein's writing was its method of "subtraction" ([1923] 1986, 43). Louis Kronenberger claimed that the ending section of Virginia Woolf's *To the Lighthouse* was "obscure, a matter of arcs, of fractions, of uncoordinated notes. By comparison with the rest this final portion seems pale and weak" ([1927] 1975, 196). The difficult work, according to these terms, missed something that was usually thought of as essential to art. Neither rich, nor inexhaustible, nor deep, the difficult text was impoverished.

This understanding of difficulty as a lack did not go uncontested. Difficult modernism's promoters, arguing that modernism was a necessary corrective in literary tradition, postulated that sometimes in its compression difficult work had just cut out the flab that padded lesser art (particularly nineteenth-century art). Now, the story of modernism's compression has been told often. But while histories of modernism regularly note its concision, it is much less common to place modernism's concision within a history of difficulty and the peculiar values such difficulty set into play. These values are central to understanding high modernism's rise to cultural dominance. Thus, while acknowledging that *The Waste Land*'s "compression and the methods it entails do make the poem difficult reading at first," F. R. Leavis argued that this compression was essential: "By means of such references and quotations Mr Eliot attains a compression, otherwise unattainable, that is essential to his aim; a compression approaching simultaneity—the co-presence in the mind of a number of different orientations, fundamental attitudes, orders of experience" ([1932] 1960, 107).

Finally, while the principles of excess and lack shaped many of the terms and arguments that modern readers used to describe difficult art, difficulty was also organized by how members of the category implicitly referred to either the formal structure or the logic of a text. Terms such as "lack of clarity," "incoherence," and "complexity" move away from "difficulty" as a term to point specifically to missing, hidden, or excessively complicated structuring principles. "Lack of clarity" and "incoherence" can *also* be extended from the center of the category in a different direction—to the "content" half of this form-content split—and join such terms as "incomprehension," "erudition," and "unintelligibility." These terms then point to the difficult work's missing or overcomplicated content. And, of course, many terms can refer to either or both simultaneously, terms like "tangled," "perplexing," "opaque," and "obscure." It is to many of these terms, and their underlying logic, that I now turn.

Difficulty's Conceptual Metaphors

The terms used to describe difficult texts have curious etymological kinships, which are based on visual and spatial understandings of difficulty. When Louis Kronenberger commented that he found the last section of *To The Lighthouse* to be particularly "perplexing" ([1927] 1975, 196), he was using a term with cognates in other words for difficulty. "Perplexing" has its etymological source in the Latin term for plaiting (*plexus*), which is the same source for "complex," while its synonymous term, "complicated," has its source in Latin's *plicare*, meaning "to fold," and yet another term, "confusing," has its source in the Latin *confusus*, meaning "mixed up." Other terms for difficult works, such as "contorted" and "tangled," use the same conceptualizing, though with their metaphoric structure (and, as will be discussed later, their ideas of health and naturalness) more clearly showing. Writers not only found these terms ready to hand, they effortlessly extended the logic of these terms' connotations of entanglement and twisting, extending these terms' connotations to metaphorical descriptions of difficult texts. Such extension is seen in Ted Robinson's remark in the Cleveland *Plain Dealer* that in *The Sound and the Fury*, Faulkner "mixed events of a year ago, ten years ago, his infancy, with the happenings of today and yesterday; and the reader had to disentangle this skein. This made the book difficult, but none the less fascinating" ([1930] 1995, 46). Louis Untermeyer, in his anthology *American Poetry Since 1900*, used a more typical, negative understanding of this entanglement when he complained that "Simplicity is more foreign to Eliot than the mountains of the moon. His recondite euphuisms twist their length through tortuous lines" (1924, 352).

A second major grouping of semantic kinships clusters around the sense of sight. John Gould Fletcher, writing in the *Freeman*, argued that the poet Wallace Stevens, though he was obscure, as were "internationally famous writers" like Eliot, Paul Valéry, and the Sitwells, was "head and shoulders above them all" because "his obscurity comes from a wealth of meaning and allusion which are unavoidable; and his intention, when we finally do fathom it, is far clearer and more earnestly pursued than theirs" ([1923] 1985, 47). "Obscurity," from the Latin *obscurus*, meaning "dark," has similarities to "recondite" (from the Latin *reconditus*, a form of "to hide") and to "opaque" (from the Latin *opacus*, meaning "dark," or "shady").[14]

And, of course, as befits the ad hoc argument that is modern difficulty, writers could combine entanglement with darkness. Thus, Edward Thomas, reviewing the early work of Ezra Pound, noted that "doubtless no ordinary man could or would write like Mr. Pound. But having allowed the turbulent opacity of his peculiarities to sink down we believe that we see very nearly nothing at all" ([1909] 1972, 61). Edwin Muir wrote of Woolf's *To the*

> Let the poet's dreams be mixed or telescoped.
> Let him pilfer and echo and intermingle without scruple.
> Let the consciousness of life be garnered from broken, twisted phrases and images,
> As it is in real dreams,
> As it is in sleep.
> Let the Law of indisciplined Association of Ideas take leading control,
> that everything go leaping and whirling,
> As it is in the brains of lunatics
> and little children.
> Ouranga, wanga, stanga.
> Therefore also
> Let some things be upside down, and some of the epithets be unnatural.
> Let the tentacles of nightmare visitations strangle all alabaster comeliness of repose
> As well as grammar and punctuation.
> And with all that let, oh let
> Let the most incomprehensible language of Blake be parodied into the language of despair
> And contempt and disillusion. Ceres! let them triumph.
> Although, although, although with it all
> The miracle of the sudden oasis shall arise to dazzle the eyes and tempt the admiration,
> While a strange hypnotic power permeates the universe.
>
> Thus shall the Waste Land be born out of a man's brain
> And the disillusioned and desiccated get their High Song.
>
> —Herbert Palmer, in his 1931 *Cinder Thursday*,
> an answer to Eliot's recent "Ash Wednesday"

Lighthouse: "The symbolism is plain enough; but in the novel, so entangled is it with other matters, interesting enough in themselves, that it becomes obscured" ([1927] 1975, 209).

These terms for difficulty and their interrelationships are neither remarkable nor surprising, for they took modern readers (and us) to familiar conceptual places in which difficulty and understanding were thought of as visual and spatial phenomena. Of course, to think of difficulty (and understanding) as a visual or a spatial phenomenon is to think metaphorically. But these terms are not merely ways of decorating an abstract truth, of pinning on a linguistic corsage; they are ways of conceptualizing what difficulty means and what it does—it is hard to think about difficulty without thinking, at a very basic level, metaphorically. These metaphors are about *thought*, not just about accidental features of language. They *conceptualize* difficulty; they imply certain consequences. These terms, then, embody shorthand propositions about what makes for difficulty, and they all tend to claim the same kinds of things: difficult works have an unseeable depth, an entangled structure, an obscured and ungraspable surface.

Consider, as an example, John Crowe Ransom's assessment of *The Waste Land*, quoted earlier. The passage shows not only a standard conceptual metaphor in its central term for difficulty; as well, the logic and phrases of the passage as a whole work within the same conceptual system. Ransom claims that Eliot's "intention is evidently to present a wilderness in which both he and the reader may be bewildered, in which one is never to see the wood for the trees" ([1923] 1982, 177). Clearly, Ransom's point depends upon a metaphoric understanding of the poem's difficulty. His clichéd phrase has a funny direction, but one every reader is able to negotiate: the phrase "never to see the wood for the trees" is directed not just to the maker of the poem, but also to its reader. It's not just an instance of Eliot being unable to generalize and being lost in specificity, but also his *reader* being completely lost in details. That sense of being lost and having one's vision blocked gives more specificity to, and expands the metaphor of, Ransom's idea of the poem as a "wilderness." It is a wilderness that readers are to understand in terms of their wishes being blocked: they can't see the forest, the general plan. That ties in well to how "wilderness" has been understood as a concept. The *Oxford English Dictionary* gives one of its primary meanings as "something figured as a region of a wild or desolate character, or in which one wanders or loses one's way." So, the cliché and the wilderness fit together. But it is not just the sense of indistinguishable flora that links parts of Ransom's assertion; the term "bewildered" links this semantic field even more closely. The *OED* lists the etymology of "bewilder" as "to lead one astray"; it presents the word's literal meaning as "to lose in pathless places," and its figurative meaning as "to confuse in mental perception." So, not just because of the poem's topographical title, "bewildered" was a particularly apt term for describing the difficulty of *The Waste Land*.

It makes sense to call these linguistic details of Ransom's cliché a metaphor. But the specific words of his phrase also instantiate a more general metaphor in which we think of understanding as seeing, as following a path, and of difficulty as not being able to see and getting lost. Ransom and his readers rely on what linguist George Lakoff calls a *conceptual* metaphor, a metaphor that underlies and structures how cultures think about a given aspect of reality. Conceptual metaphors have some heft; arguing that such metaphors are "not a matter of mere word play," Lakoff and Turner assert that such thinking "is endemically conceptual in nature. It is indispensable to comprehending and reasoning about concepts like life, death, and time" (1989, 50). Without these metaphors it would be hard to think about abstract concepts like difficulty at all.

Conceptual metaphors proceed by mapping one terrain onto another (Lakoff and Turner 1989, 107). In the case of difficulty, it is a mapping of "seeing" onto ideas of "understanding." This kind of mapping is standard human behavior (some argue that it is essential to *all* thought); as well, an individual metaphor (such as UNDERSTANDING IS SEEING) can be omnipresent in daily life. Because of these two qualities, specific metaphors about difficulty are instantly understandable, for they participate in the more general conceptual metaphor: few readers had to pause over Ransom's words to figure out what he meant. Thus, when Ransom moved beyond the individual terms for difficulty, and used phrases to describe difficult art, his metaphoric language was consistent with the basic terms for difficulty, their etymologies, and difficulty's conceptual metaphors.

To understand how these metaphors work, consider the following example. Much Western literature relies on the conceptual metaphor DEATH IS DEPARTURE.[15] It is seen at work in the following stanza from Emily Dickinson:

> Because I could not stop for Death—
> He kindly stopped for me—
> The Carriage held but just Ourselves—
> And Immortality. (1999, 219)

It structures the concluding couplet of Shakespeare's sonnet "That Time of Year Thou Mayst in Me Behold," in which each quatrain enumerates the signs of the poet's coming death. The poem concludes: "This thou perceiv'st, which makes thy love more strong, / To love that well which thou must leave ere long." And finally, it is seen in Dickens's *David Copperfield*, when the narrator, having tantalized readers for hundreds of pages with the imminent death of his wife, Dora, finally begins to lay her in her coffin with the following rhetorical question: "Do I know, now, that my child-wife will soon leave me?" (1981, 656). While all three writers expand and complicate the metaphors in linguistically specific and aesthetically unique ways (and the levels at which they stretch these metaphors is typically seen as a sign of their greatness), this expansion and complication is understandable because the basic conceptual metaphor, DEATH IS DEPARTURE, is so common.

Conceptual metaphors also structure talk about difficulty, which is based on the conceptual metaphor UNDERSTANDING IS SEEING. A secondary metaphor, less frequently used but more visceral than the previous, is

UNDERSTANDING IS GRASPING; the third major metaphor is UNDERSTANDING IS FOLLOWING (Lakoff and Turner 94, 129).[16] Difficulty is the opposite of these, when activities are hindered, when one can not see, grasp, or follow the work one is reading, listening to, or viewing. Things you see, grasp, and follow have dimensions, and difficulty's conceptual metaphors think of the poem, the work of art, and the piece of music as three-dimensional structures. As in life, the basic ways in which one apprehends such structures are through the senses of sight and touch. In this model, then, understanding a work of art is like the sensual perception of objects—three-dimensional structures, structures that are bounded, typically with an exterior and an interior. Thus, modern readers argued whether there was a meaning at the difficult work's "core" or whether there was a meaning "below" the obvious meaning; that one "gropes" for the meaning of a work (Tietjens 1923a, 151; Aiken [1919] 1980, 57; Eliot, [1931] 1964, 151).

Readers *argued* about difficult art using these metaphors. First, some argued that the difficult work directed one's vision improperly, that it was visually confusing. Readers claimed that the difficult text was one whose meaning was difficult to "see" or whose sense was "blurred"—in this sense the text has a visible outline that is obscured. Or, the difficult text put too much stuff in the way of seeing properly, so that seeing became refracted, indirect, distorted. Many knowledge-based terms use this conceptual metaphor by arguing that the difficult text is beyond reach, it is over our heads.[17] Or, readers argued that the difficult work did not allow one to see through to the work's depth. Thus, Edith Sitwell, grumbling about the "younger poets" who did not have the genius of their immediate predecessors, Eliot and Pound, noted: "All, or nearly all, of these poets present surface difficulties, because they suppress intermediary processes of thought, or else they give so many that the reader is bewildered. This surface difficulty gives the average person the impression that the poems conceal great depths. But this is rarely so" (1934, 231). Such metaphors about meaning and incomprehension (and their implicit logic) cannot be avoided; they structure my own descriptions in this book. In the opening pages of this chapter, for example, I mentioned an "illuminating place to begin understanding" difficulty's inherence, I announced that I would "turn" to Foucault, that "difficulty's universality is not seen in a set of formal strategies," that it is "necessary to take a look at" an aspect of difficulty, and that readers rarely "clarify" their quoted terms.[18]

The conceptual model of difficulty, based on the apprehension of a three-dimensional structure, entailed that difficulty was understood as a *relationship* between a person and a thing. Difficulty's conceptual metaphors, then, suggest that it is an experience; difficulty does not inhere in the properties of a text, or in the skills of a reader, but in the failure of the two to correspond with each other. Modern readers, although they often used syntax that suggested that they thought of difficulty as a property of a work of art, were never very far from addressing its effects on a reader. Subjectivity thus is central to discussions of difficulty—again and again, readers mention their *experience* of the difficult text. Not surprisingly, many of the terms used to describe difficulty are affective, describing what difficulty does to *readers*: "bewildering," "confusing," "baffling," "perplexing," and "challenging." Difficulty, then, first shapes itself as an *experience*, and though the structures that give rise to difficulty are various, the experience is quite unitary.

A further correlative emerges from the conceptual metaphor UNDERSTANDING IS SEEING: the more one sees, the more complete one's understanding is. There is a sense in which seeing (as in UNDERSTANDING IS SEEING) is infinitely expandable and the great text is inexhaustible—just look more closely or focus more sharply. Or, dig deeper—the spatial metaphors for understanding worked with three dimensions and represented works of art as having a surface and a depth. The difficult text is "dense," in reading it one needs to go "beneath the surface." Note, however, that the difficult text is infinitely expandable only in terms of its depth, not in terms of its surface. The metaphors suggest that its surface is consequently of lesser value than the depth of a work, as is clear in Conrad Aiken's reading of William Carlos Williams: "Mr. Williams too seldom goes below the surface. He restricts his observations almost entirely to the sensory plane.... We get the impression from these poems that his world is a world of plane surfaces, bizarrely coloured, and cunningly arranged so as to give an effect of depth and solidity; but we do not get depth itself. When occasionally this is not true, when Mr. Williams takes the plunge into the profounder stream of consciousness, he appears always to pick out the shallows, and to plunge gingerly" ([1919] 1980, 57–58). For conservative modern readers, the surface was usually a given, something that one needed to get past; what lay underneath that surface was what art was about. In this conceptualizing, one's understanding can be understood as a surface understanding (i.e., insignificant, incomplete) or, at the other extreme, a deep understanding (i.e., complete, profound).

As a consequence of using these metaphors, no matter where they stood on difficulty, all modern readers subscribed to the same hierarchy of value, preferring depth over surface. Each argued that the central aspect of their rivals' understanding was merely on the surface, while their own sense of understanding was deep. Thus, for those suspicious of modernism the tricks of difficulty were surface tricks, while for modernism's proponents the simple poem was all surface. Modernism's skeptics asserted that the simple text went to the heart of human experience, while its supporters countered that the difficult text went beyond the surface simplicities of life. Skeptical readers complained that difficult work put up too much stuff between it and the deeper pleasures of the text, while high modern supporters of Frost claimed that behind his surface simplicity was a rewarding, deeper complexity.

But in getting below the surface of the difficult text one needed both the right lens and a cooperative object. And difficult texts, according to the most common negatively used terms (such as "convoluted," "baffling," "impenetrable"), were emphatically *not* cooperative (indeed, the peculiar force of modernism's difficulty was that it was uncooperative from the very outset of one's reading experience, so that a crisis immediately ensued). Marjorie Seiffert would write in Chicago's *Poetry* magazine of Stevens's *Harmonium* that "His emotion lurks behind design. We must peer through thickets to catch a glimpse of that shy wary bird as it flits into obscurity" (1923, 160). The difficult text, then, was not seen by its detractors as an inexhaustible text, leading the patient reader to ever more rich interpretations. As such, it operated against the usual way of seeing a text as inexhaustible. The difficult text was a *resistant* text, and modernism's proponents needed to make this resistance an inherent part not just of the difficult text at hand, but of aesthetic experience in general. To accomplish this, they needed to create the right kind of lens, to move readers away from the kind of reading to which they had been accustomed.[19]

Laughter and Anger

In modernism, these shared understandings of difficulty—silent, untheorized, casually constructed—worked in tandem with their more showy partner, those spectacular responses to difficult art. Consider how the lexicon of difficulty points to that relationship. While some of difficulty's terms seem neutral presentations of a text's properties—"incoherent," "opaque," "obscure," "difficult"—other terms less clearly describe the difficult text than they describe readers' *experiences* of these texts. And these experiences are remarkably similar. All of these affective terms—"bewildering," "confusing," "baffling," "perplexing," and "challenging"—indicate readers' high level of uncertainty as to how to proceed. These affective terms not only attest to one's lack of confidence in being able to solve the difficulty, the resistance of the work of art. They also indicate an anxious uncertainty as to how one might overcome this resistance. And this radical uncertainty makes the anxiety, rage, and laughter surrounding difficulty very common.

Based on anxiety, these terms and reactions, of course, are overwhelmingly of those who found modern difficulty to be a negative thing. They show that readers' resistances to difficulty are peculiar, for they are not just intellectual, they also are highly emotional. This anonymous reader of Gertrude Stein's *Tender Buttons* is perhaps more extravagant than some who expressed their "irritation" or "annoyance," at difficult art, but he or she is not atypical: "After a hundred lines of this I wish to scream, I wish to burn the book, I am in agony. It is not because I know that words *cannot* be torn loose from their meanings without insulting the intellect. It is not because I see that this is a prime example of the 'confusion of the arts.' No, my feeling is purely physical. Some one has applied an egg beater to my brain" ("Flat Prose" [1914] 1986, 38–39).

As reader after reader shows, the difficult text is not a comfortable text, arousing nervously grandiose claims on the part of its proponents, and, more startlingly, anxiety, anger, and laughter on the part of its detractors. These visceral reactions are also very common. About one in ten of my sources that comment on some aspect of modern difficulty explicitly mention or demonstrate the anger and ridicule that such works often incurred—Rockwell was using the terms of a widespread anxiety when he wrote, "I have painted pictures that didn't disturb anybody, that I knew everyone would understand and like" (1960, 44–45). Further, the general public and artists alike recognized that laughter and rage were related, and that they arose, explosively, from difficult art. Their extremity and their prevalence made it common to talk about anger and laughter in the same breath. Writing in *The Chapbook*, Harold Monro commented on the London critic who dismissed Eliot's *The Waste Land* as an "'obscure but amusing poem. . . . Obscure it is, and amusing it can be too; but neither quite in the way he seems to have meant. They who have only one definition for the word poem may gnash their teeth, or smile" ([1923] 1982, 164).

In fact, stories about audiences reacting with anger or ridicule to difficult art are central to the founding of modernism as a movement. The premiere performance of Stravinsky's *Sacre du printemps*, on May 29, 1913, is just one of several famous examples. The story is well known: the work debuted in front of a Paris audience that was primed for controversy, that was ready to see the performance as a battle between the forces of modernity and the forces of tradition. The company that danced that evening, the Ballet Russes, had already scandalized Europe with its performances and on this night they did not disappoint expectations. Employing one of the premier languages of difficulty, that of crudity, the dancers' base position was knees together, toes pointing inward—the grotesque antithesis of classical ballet. The music, forceful, driving, percussive, assaulted its audience. And the audience responded viscerally. Carl Van Vechten, novelist and supporter of Gertrude Stein, reported:

> Cat-calls and hisses succeeded the playing of the first few bars, and then ensued a battery of screams, countered by a foil of applause. We warred over art (some of us thought it was and some thought it wasn't). . . . Some forty of the protestants were forced out of the theater but that did not quell the disturbance. The lights in the auditorium were fully turned on but the noise continued and I remember Mlle. Piltz executing her strange dance of religious hysteria on a stage dimmed by the blazing

light in the auditorium, seemingly to the accompaniment of the disjointed ravings of a mob of angry men and women. (1914, 34)

Valentine Gross noted that "there was slapping and even punching," and claimed to have seen the composers "Maurice Delage, beetroot-red with indignation, little Maurice Ravel truculent as a fighting cock and [the poet] Léon-Paul Fargue spitting out crushing remarks at the hissing boxes. I cannot think how it was possible for this ballet, which the public of 1913 found so difficult, to be danced through to the end in such an uproar" (quoted in Buckle 1971, 300). Others reported that members of the audience spit at each other, and that a duel was fought the next morning. One critic, unable to resist the pun staring him in the face, referred to the work as "Le Massacre du Printemps" (Buckle 1971, 299–304).[20]

Anger and laughter were not strangers to difficult visual art either. Two examples come to mind. The first is the 1910 post-Impressionist exhibition, an exhibition that, like the *Sacre*, was quickly seen as a battle for control of the aesthetic landscape. (As the reception of this exhibit and of Stravinsky's work suggests, difficult works were routinely seen as both aggressive and ambitious by their antagonists.) Organized by Roger Fry, the exhibition gave the London public its first major look at such artists as Cézanne and Matisse. The painter Walter Sickert described the exhibit as a "rumpus" (quoted in Dunlop 1972, 120), responding, no doubt to the spectacle of some viewers shaking with rage, others bent double with laughter. Bloomsburyian Desmond McCarthy, the secretary for the show, noted that "the big rooms echoed with explosions of laughter and indignation," and commented on "a stout, elderly man of good appearance, led in by a young woman, who went into such convulsions of laughter on catching sight of Cézanne's portrait of his wife in the first little room that his companions had to take him out and walk him up and down in the fresh air" (1945, 124). Public satire soon followed, including this cartoon for the *Illustrated London News*, which provided readers with an instantly recognizable taxonomy of visceral responses to difficulty (figure 2.1).

The New York Armory Show is yet another famous instance of the visceral response that modern difficulty elicited. Bringing to America what for most viewers was their first look at Cézanne, Matisse, Duchamp, and others, the show became *the* place to be in early 1913. The enormous crowds did not file silently in and out of the armory. William Zorach, an exhibitor in the show, recalled that Theodore Roosevelt "waved his arms and stomped through the Galleries pointing at pictures and saying 'That's not art!' 'That's not art!'" (Munson-Williams-Proctor Institute 1963, 94). Enrico Caruso attended and "thrilled the crowds by doing caricatures of the paintings on Armory Show post cards and distributing them as souvenirs." One of the standard gags

Figure 2.1
Frank Reynolds, "Post-Impressionist Expressions," *Illustrated London News*, December 3, 1910

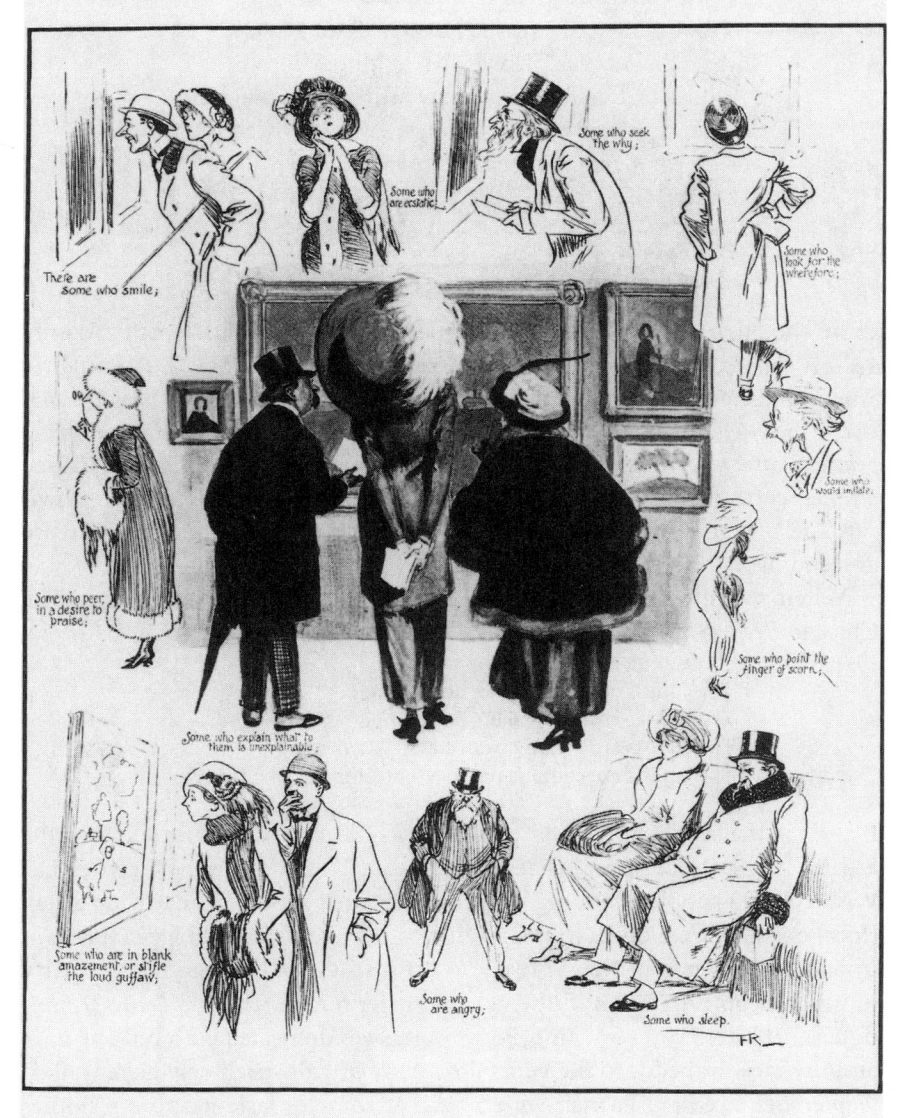

> G is for Gertrude Stein's limpid lucidity
>   (Eloquent scribe of the Futurist Soul,)
> Cubies devour each word with avidity:
> "*Alone* words lack sense!" they affirm with placidity
>   But *how* wise we'll be when we've swallowed the whole."
> —G is for Gertrude Stein's lucid limpidity.
>
> —Mary Mills Lyall, *The Cubies' ABC*, 1913

about the show was that "It is a long step from Ingres to Matisse, but it is only a short one from Matisse to anger." In response to the show, G. P. Putnam's Sons published a parodic children's book, *The Cubies' ABC* (Brown 1963, 112, 115, 117). Various wits described Marcel Duchamp's *Nude Descending a Staircase*, the show's cause célèbre, as an "elevated railroad stairway in ruins after an earthquake," a "dynamited suit of Japanese armor," a "pack of brown cards in a nightmare," "an explosion in a shingle factory," and "a staircase descending a nude" (quoted in Brown 1963, 110).

When the show transferred to Chicago, its publicity preceded it. The Chicago *Record-Herald* composed the following lines:

> The cubists are coming, ho, ho, ho, ho;
> The cubists are coming, ho, ho, ho, ho;
> The cubists are coming from stately Manhattan;
> The cubists are coming, ho ho. ("Director French" 1913, 1)

It also ran the headline "Cubist Art Is Here: As Clear As Mud," and subtitled the article "If You Don't Know What It Is Just Read This and Never Worry Again." With 200,000 people attending the show, the furor soon modulated up a step (local boosters were quick to point out that the show made a bigger splash in Chicago than it had in New York). The Art Institute of Chicago threw a party in which people dressed as futurists. A reporter for the Chicago *Daily Tribune* noted that "Here you saw Mme. Pogany, her eyes decorated with bulging gogs and her face draped into the general contour of an ostrich egg. Here walked 'September Evening.' A man with a bale of shingles fastened to his clothes danced with a girl whose face represented a spider web, or a map of a railroad yard on a foggy night" ("Artists Give Cubist Play" 1913, 1). Students of the Art Institute built a fictional character, Henri Hairmatress, and put him on trial for a large number of crimes. Summarily convicted, Hairmatress was placed on the terrace of the Art Institute and then "stabbed, pummeled, and dragged about the terrace to the edification of a large crowd on Michigan Avenue." The

> Cubist Art—The portrayal in one perfectly stationary picture of about 5,000 feet of motion pictures; a "woozy" attempt to express the fourth dimension.
>
> Futurist Art—Same as the former, only more so, with primeval instincts thrown in. Cubism carried to the extreme or fifth dimension.
>
> Post-Impressionism—The other two thrown together.
>
> How To Appreciate It—Eat three welsh rarebits, smoke two pipefuls of "hop" and sniff cocaine until every street car looks like a goldfish and the Masonic Temple resembles a tiny white mouse.
>
> —Chicago *Record-Herald*, 1913

students then set to work on the art itself, and burned imitations of Matisse's *Luxury* and *The Blue Lady* (Brown 1963, 178–79).

These stories have been told often and have become part of modernism's mythology. But they need to be understood as something more than quirky responses, anecdotes that are ad hoc, entertaining, but ultimately insubstantial. They need to be recognized as having identifiable intellectual content; they need to be taken seriously as a response to art, for they are more than just a story of bourgeois philistinism. Consider the cartoon of the post-Impressionist exhibit once again (figure 2.1). The artist, Frank Reynolds, by noting that "all London" was going to the Grafton galleries, registers the delicious scandal of difficulty. Further, with his catalogue of responses (ponderously set up as a catalogue by the recurring "Some who"), Reynolds documents *types* of responses; these reactions are predictable and stylized. Some responses, such as those portrayed by the center illustration ("Some who explain what to them is inexplainable"), the swooning woman ("Some who are ecstatic"), and the gullible artist ("Some who would imitate"), refer to the ability of difficulty, in the right setting, to perpetuate a hoax. But a number of them point to the more extreme responses that difficulty generates, such as ridicule or laughter ("There are some who smile," "Some who stare in blank amazement, or stifle the loud guffaw") and anger ("Some who point the finger of scorn," "Some who are angry"). Reynolds presents these as *patterns* of behavior, *recognizable* responses—indeed, Reynolds depended on their being recognizable for his livelihood. And he was right, for as the century moved on, the histrionics depicted in the cartoon were repeated in the reception of all the classics of high modernism; indeed, they helped set high modernism in motion.

> What we cannot understand, it is very common, and indeed a very natural thing, for us to undervalue; and it may be suspected that some of the merriest witticisms which have been uttered against Mr Wordsworth, have had their origins in the pettishness and dissatisfaction of minds, unaccustomed and unwilling to make, either to others or to themselves, any confession of incapacity.
>
> —J. G. Lockhart writing in *Blackwood's* in 1800s, quoted as an epigraph by F. R. Leavis in *New Bearings in English Poetry*, his 1932 defense of difficult modernism

Although they recognized these responses as an almost ritual display, modernism's readers and audiences from all points on the spectrum didn't think there was much aesthetic analysis and intellectual content to them. For modernism's apologists, laughter and anger were inane responses; for its skeptics, laughter and anger might be morally justified reactions, but they were not the stuff of profound aesthetic responses. This sense that such viscerality missed the aesthetic continued to be the standard reading of difficult art at the end of the twentieth century. Music critic Samuel Lipman, after attending a 1982 concert of contemporary composer Roger Sessions, commented in the *New Criterion* that the educated audience that attended, from whom one might have expected "comprehension," instead reacted with a "palpable air of hostility and irritation." Lipman's dismissive response: "What they evidently wanted was Puccini. It is to this pass that musical sophistication—even among professionals—now appears to have come" (1982, 59). On the other hand, Harold Fromm, writing in the *Massachusetts Review* in 1987, grumbling about the self-servingness of difficult art and criticism, ended his article with the following harrumph: "But critics have an obligation to ask themselves who and what it is they are really serving by means of their professional skills. If such skills in fact serve to reduce the audience for the arts to a handful of the self-chosen who respond only to the right party shibboleths, then these self-absorbed Laputans with eyes turned inward or upward need to be recalled from their narcissistic afflatus by periodic Swiftian slaps in the face" (29). There is righteousness here, but there is not serious art criticism. According to Fromm, by not being *art* these works and their critics engender and deserve a response from a different domain of human life—the moral.

As Fromm's response suggests, those who ridiculed difficult art thought they knew the principles that had produced it, an understanding most succinctly expressed in their jokes. About a month after the London post-

Impressionist exhibit, Floyd Dell reviewed Ezra Pound's *Provença* for the Chicago *Evening Post*. Dell compared Pound to the "Neo-Impressionists," noting that both were "open to misunderstanding, and even to ridicule": "People are saying that one of the Neo-Impressionist pictures was secured by tying a paint brush to a donkey's tail and backing the animal up to the canvas. A jocose story like that might be invented to explain one of Mr. Pound's poems" ([1911] 1972, 70). The content of the joke explains the origins of the work; the fact that it can be given as a joke provides the rationale for dismissing it. The difficult artist's motivations were explainable, even if they were as simple as Sherwood Anderson's attempt, in his defense of Gertrude Stein's writing, to characterize skeptical reaction to her work. For Anderson, skeptics believed that in *Tender Buttons* Stein had succeeded in "'putting something across'—the meaning being that she had, by a strange freakish performance, managed to attract attention to herself, get herself discussed in the newspapers, become for a time a figure in our hurried, harried lives" (Anderson [1922] 1986, 40). Laughter, then, was most often dismissive laughter, as in this *Carnegie* magazine summation of *Ulysses*:

> How absurd then it is to say, as some of the reviewers are extravagantly saying, and as the author himself encourages them in saying, that this book is a tour de force in literature, a profound study in philosophy, a presentation of life that is mysterious and recondite, an achievement that reaches up into the very stratosphere of thought, a transcendental portraiture that goes beyond the average limit of human understanding and, like a new Einstein Theory, can be comprehended by only twelve men in the world! There is nothing at all of any of these qualities about it. As a work of art we can compare it with nothing but that picture which provoked laughter in the galleries a few years ago, "Nude Descending a Staircase," in which there was neither nude nor staircase and where art was the only thing that was descending. (H. S. C., [1934] 1970, 244)

Not surprisingly, those who laughed in this way at difficult work did not often acknowledge that this work was difficult. For such readers, presumably, *real* difficulty would have required a more serious response; they dismissed both the work's value *and* its difficulty. As such, dismissive laughter was closely tied to the claim that the difficult work was a hoax: both refused to acknowledge the difficulty and reached for another explanation that moved the difficulty into the social realm (as shoddiness, as charlatanism, or as a hoax), and consequently away from the realm of real art, the realm in which the social had no part to play—the realm in which art is not *explainable*.

While angry responses, like those of laughter, also claimed to understand the principles by which difficult works were produced, they were more likely to acknowledge the work as difficult, and to do so through affect-loaded terms. The Reverend Cyril Alington, headmaster of Eton College, argued in the *English Review* that modernist poems "leave an old-fashioned reader in a bewilderment which alternates between humility and indignation" (1923, 547). And, unlike laughter, the anger was not dismissive; for angry readers, difficulty was a real threat, something that deserved strong reactions. Max Eastman, in his well-known attack on modernism, *The Literary Mind: Its Place in an Age of Science*, argued that the only useful response to "the whole tribe" of the "doctors of Unintelligibility" (by which he meant high modern literary critics) was to "bundle them into a well-rotted ship and shove them out to sea." As were many others, Eastman was angry at difficult modernism for its illegitimate use of power; Eastman went on, "We should no doubt long ago have adopted this mode of mitigating the plague of unintelligibility, were it not for the fact that a majority of these critics are poets too" (1931a, 122).

Their dismissiveness, intellectual disdain, and moral self-righteousness notwithstanding, these responses should figure in an intellectual history of the twentieth century. In their ubiquity, stylization, and physicality these responses point to essential aspects of the experience of difficulty, aspects that have profoundly shaped twentieth-century arguments about difficulty's value. Despite their different ways of engaging with the difficult (both in what the response looked like and its actual acknowledging whether the difficulty even existed), there is a central unity to the responses of anger and laughter. They are both visceral responses. When the anonymous reviewer of Gertrude Stein describes himself as being "in agony" because "some one has applied an egg beater to my brain," he indicates that unfavorable responses to difficult art involve not just the intellect, but one's emotions, and the whole body.[21] In *The Shock of the New* Ian Dunlop describes the post-Impressionist exhibition gallery as being filled with "excited, gesticulating people"; and he reports that Duncan Grant, the painter, recalled "visitors expressing their anger by shaking their umbrellas at the paintings" (1972, 120). Similarly, Harold Child, reviewing Ezra Pound's *Ripostes* in 1912 for the *Times Literary Supplement*, noted the relation of its difficulty to the response generated by the post-Impressionist exhibition: "At the Post-Impressionist exhibition some spectators may be seen dancing with fury, others quaking with laughter, others indiscriminately worshipping and a few using their brains coolly. Mr. Ezra Pound's book will have the same effect, no doubt, upon its readers" ([1912] 1972, 94).

These visceral responses, so common in high modern culture, are not a phenomenon peculiar to the late nineteenth and the twentieth centuries. Neither are they responses that surface only in aesthetic experience. They are larger than that; they are *inherent* to the experience of difficulty in general. After making that ambitious assertion, I will admit that my claims for inherence are circumscribed, for not everyone who read, heard, or saw difficult modernism demonstrated these reactions of anxiety or anger, of course. But, for those who did not find an adequate way to deal with the difficulty of a

> **The Post-Discretionists**
> "Those pictures," Ernest Penwell said,
> "They knock me all kerflummick,
> For some of them upset my head,
> The rest upset my stomach."
> —"A Line-O' Type or Two," Chicago *Daily Tribune*, 1913

given work (as for any experience that one perceives as being too difficult), these highly emotional reactions were typical. Some version of these responses were inevitable for those who found a work or an activity to be too difficult, when it had crossed a boundary, when in a sudden moment of panic, as one reviewer claimed of new readers of Joyce's *Work in Progress*, they "throw up their hands in horror" ("*Ulysses* Lands" 1934, 50).[22]

This response to difficulty is inherently visceral and emotional because, once they decide that a given object is an artwork (or a book, or a piece of music, or any other work of art), human beings have an instinctive and restless drive to make it mean. Indeed, meaning-making in general is a very strong drive, one that compels humans, if they are attentive to something, to try to make it *mean* something. All attentive perception is goal-directed, an idea given early expression by William James, who argued that "The pursuance of future ends and the choice of means for their attainment are thus the mark and criterion of the presence of mentality in a phenomenon" (quoted in Gardner 1985, 108). Since James, research in comprehension has at times worked with differing ideas on what drives that search for meaning, but the basic premise—that there is an inherent search for meaning—is well established.[23] In their interactions with the world, and their attempts to comprehend it, people attempt to achieve goals, and many of these goals are ones that an individual routinely *expects* to achieve.

This drive for meaning patterned not only the way comprehension and difficulty were conceptualized, it also shaped the *experience* of them. Subverting expectations, modern difficulty instilled uncertainty, and a resultant anxiety, in the aesthetic experience of its audience. Thus, when Harold Monro argued that readers of *The Waste Land* who had "only one definition for the word poem may gnash their teeth, or smile" ([1923] 1982, 164), he was pointing to the major reason for the visceral response to difficulty: unfulfilled expectations, an uncertainty as to how to proceed, an uncertainty that leads to anxiety. As Paul Jordan Smith wrote in 1934 of Joyce, "But the average novel reader expects a work of fiction to be simple, straightforward prose. No amount of talk about expressionism, dadaism, or the subconscious mind, can reconcile him to the unintelligibility of Joyce's unpunctuated pages. He is outraged. Where he expected to find a story of love and ambition and struggle, he finds a bewildering crossword puzzle" ([1934] 1969, 15).[24] (Smith was no stranger to moral outrage. Three years earlier, suspicious of the contemporary art scene, in which he claimed, "critics would praise anything unintelligible," Smith painted a few deliberately crude, Fauve-like works and founded the "Disumbrationist" school. Under the name Pavel Jerdanowitch, Smith successfully spun out this hoax for three years, enjoying a growing reputation, and finally confessing the ruse in 1927 to a reporter for the Los Angeles *Examiner* [MacDougall 1940, 267–68].)

Those unfulfilled expectations are completely enmeshed in high modernism and its difficulty. First, consider difficulty's most common conceptual metaphors, that understanding a work is like seeing or touching a three-dimensional structure. Apprehension according to these terms seems natural—of course, under normal conditions, one ought to be able to see and touch a three-dimensional structure. This metaphor posits as its "default" setting the assertion that seeing (i.e., understanding) is supposed to be unproblematic (indeed, given how necessary seeing and touching are to survival, it's hard to imagine how it could be otherwise).[25] Linguistically, at least, from its etymologies to its conceptual metaphors, there is a great investment in having comprehension be normative, while difficulty is typically presented as an abnormal state of affairs.

In high modernism, unproblematic apprehension bumped up against the recalcitrant text. There, the nature of human desires to create meaning exacerbated problems, for these were desires that, for many readers, were totally unused to being impeded. When those expectations were suddenly thwarted, the reactions were like reactions to other nonproblematic activities, such as balance, of which one loses control. There is anxiety, you feel powerless, and you react instinctively, with anger or its close relative, laughter—ways of both expressing anxiety and reasserting control over the difficult work. Modernism's difficulty destabilized entrenched modes of perception, and that destabilizing, cognitive linguists have shown, is an unsettling, high-stakes activity. Disturbances of normative activities, unless they are comprehended and domesticated in some way, are not just intellectually, but also emotionally resisted. In this context, being unable to perform these actions, being unable to make something *mean*, is a threat. The emotion is a response to that threat. In fact, the common experience of difficulty is a classic "fight or flight" reaction, in which laughter and rage are related not just because they are both extreme responses. They are different ways of embodying the same response, a response that deals with, finds a way to articulate, extreme anxiety.

The basic cognitive activity that takes place as this anxiety arises is outlined by Constance Perin. In her analysis of difficult visual art, Perin, drawing on work in cognitive dissonance, reports that the experience of difficulty is like a "freezing and flight" response, in which the mind reacts violently to difficulty as a way to "keep clear what is already clear to us," by "keeping ambiguity and its uncertainties at bay." Such responses are unavoidable; as Perin claims, "Neurophysiologically, these responses are as autonomous as breathing" (1994, 178). Jeffrey Gray, in his seminal *The Psychology of Fear and Stress* (1971), notes that the mind is limited in its capacities to absorb newness and ambiguity, and that once a threshold is crossed, one sees the classically visceral responses to difficulty a point reiterated, with modifications, by Nico Frijda (1986, 263–77; 350). (Of course, what counts as a limit for newness or ambiguity varies from person to person.) Keith Oatley, pursuing the problem from a slightly different direction, argues that anger typically arises from a situation in which a person construes that there has been an impediment placed between him or herself and his or her goals (1992, 98–103).[26]

The goals that difficulty disrupts, then, are quite basic; with difficult art you get such an anxious reaction because comprehension is necessary for survival. The inherent viscerality comes about not just because in these contexts we are accustomed to having comprehension happen, but because, more generally, comprehension is necessary for life.[27] Rooting the response to difficulty in the human body also accounts for how the reaction to difficulty can be so similar across the arts. (Note, however, that the universalism has some limits. I am not claiming that members of other cultures would inevitably have these kinds of reactions to, say, *Nude Descending a Staircase*. But they would have these kinds of reactions to an usually unproblematic task that they suddenly found too difficult.)

The visceral response also shows that difficult modernism was not engaged in trivial experimentation, as its detractors at times claimed. It was assaulting fundamental strategies of meaning. Difficulty's ambition extends in multiple directions, though; there was a real seriousness both to what modernism was doing *and* to the highly charged responses to it. The stories of the Armory and post-Impressionism shows and of *Sacre du printemps* are impoverished if they are understood merely as stories of bourgeois philistinism. Modernism was about bigger things than that. Difficult modernism, working at a primal level, thwarted basic desires for meaning through its confusing assertions about its status as an artwork, to a confusion between the literal and metaphoric, to an uncertainty about logic and syntax itself—a series of difficult strategies compounded by their often being the *first* thing audiences noted about these works. As Maxwell Bodenheim noted of Pound's *Cantos* in 1922, "At a first reading, even a careful one, they are apt to appear obscure, and they will be ignored and derided by those who approach poetry for mental and emotional caresses, and quick affirmations of judgement, and not for extremes in mental exercise" ([1922] 1972, 206). That kind of ambition on the part of high modernism's proponents has been known and explored. But if we consider the moral aspect of Bodenheim's comment, holding to the side its dismissive tone, a further aspect of difficulty's ambition becomes clear. More fundamentally, difficulty prodded at a new aspect of art's relationships among meaning, morality, and anxiety. The connections, given modernism's difficulty, were inextricable. Arguing that works of art "try to make us see the world differently" (1997, 247), David Novitz notes more generally that challenges to one's basic beliefs create the kind of reactions I have been describing: "Any challenge to one's deep convictions is likely to be met with an emotional response. One may be upset, outraged, bewildered, shocked, and sometimes, when it is all too much, one may be irritated beyond words or else reduced to helpless laughter" (246). The reactions to moral and aesthetic disturbances are similar; modernism is that powerful moment when the two converge. That moment needs to be analyzed generously from the perspectives of all of modernism's readers, and not just its proponents.

While survival dictates that people be able to figure things out and creates stress when they can't, there is a reading response that avoids the common extreme reactions: flight—or, its equivalent in modernism—boredom, the reaction of the sleeping figures in the lower righthand corner of the Reynolds cartoon. Holbrook Jackson, reviewing *Ulysses* for *To-Day*, reported that "The very format of the book is an affront. Bloom could have been drawn effectively in a quarter the words. There are the deadliest of Dead Seas in this ocean of prose. You get becalmed in them—bored, drowsed, bewildered" ([1922] 1970, 199). Readers can shut down the anxious response to a difficult text by refusing to engage it. This reaction of flight—avoidance—is a reaction that for obvious reasons is the least commonly articulated reaction to difficulty during the formative years of high modernism. Unless compelled to, people tend not to write about boring art. But also, in the opening decades of the twentieth century so few seem to have been bored by difficult modernism because readers were unprepared for it. How to negotiate around modernism's difficulty was not something readers were used to doing, and readers sensed there was a lot at stake in these difficult texts. (However, as modernism moved along, modernism's skeptics increasingly referred to difficulty as the cause of an apparent loss of audience for high art, particularly for poetry and music.)

Understood in the ways I have outlined, difficulty's anxiety also has important connections to aesthetic pleasure, connections with immense social consequences for the reception of difficult art. Particularly helpful in this regard is D. E. Berlyne's *Aesthetics and Psychobiology*, and research based on that ground-breaking study. Berlyne's work examines the relationships among complexity, novelty, and pleasure, an examination that sheds light on

> If one opens *Ulysses* at random almost anywhere, one will confront passages meaningless on the surface, and decipherable only after concentrated study.... The book is a treasure-trove, to be sure; but its riches are so well hidden in the grottoes of recondite learning, of classical allusions, of literary and scientific profundities, that the average seeker—blindly groping about in the surrounding maze—soon tires of the venture and turns back.
>
> —Defense lawyer Max Ernst, arguing in the 1934 trial that its difficulty made *Ulysses* too boring to be obscene

how difficulty's anxiety functions and how one might describe the moment when anxiety overwhelms one. Berlyne posits that people experience pleasure when the right degree of novelty and complexity is present. As novelty and complexity increase in an aesthetic experience, there is a rising curve of pleasure/arousal (the two states frequently, but not necessarily, occur together). The curve's maximum height represents what Berlyne terms an experience's greatest "hedonic" value, followed by a rapidly declining experience of pleasure (1971, 75–95).[28] Once the maximum has been reached, the curve drops away quickly; the visceral responses to difficult modernism show that, in these cases, readers have gone over the edge of maximal pleasure. When pleasure drops because there is too much novelty and complexity, anxiety kicks in. Ibsch continues, "information which is very different from what a person knows already, generates the feeling of threat" (1986, 45).[29] As the rapidly dropping curve suggests, it is a continuum that, in its social manifestations, looks like a dichotomy because of the effect of there *suddenly* being too much difficulty. It seems to "click" on, rather than gradually make its presence felt.

While the general shape of this curve does not change from person to person, where that curve reaches it highest point is something individually determined. As Elrud Ibsch argues, tolerance for difficulty increases with the increasing expertise of a given person in a given field and moves from left to right along the complexity axis as one's experience increases (1986, 45).[30] As well, habituation toward a given stimulus or artwork results in one's decreased reaction to it; the point where maximum arousal/pleasure values are reached can shift over time (Martindale 1990, 45). Not surprisingly, professionalism and the rise of literary criticism, social structures that increase one's tolerance for difficult aesthetic experiences, occur contemporaneously with the rise of difficult modernism.[31]

> I had an old uncle whose thinking was always to the point. One day he stopped me on the street and asked, "Do you know how the devil tortures the souls in hell?" When I said no, he declared, "He keeps them waiting." And with that he walked away. This remark occurred to me when I was ploughing through *Ulysses* for the first time. Every sentence raises an expectation which is not fulfilled; finally, out of sheer resignation, you come to expect nothing any longer. Then bit by bit, again to your horror, it dawns on you that in all truth you have hit the nail on the head. It is actual fact that nothing happens and nothing comes of it, and yet a secret expectation at war with hopeless resignation drags the reader from page to page.... You read and read and read and you pretend to understand what you read. Occasionally you drop through an air pocket into another sentence, but when once the proper degree of resignation has been reached you accustom yourself to anything. So I, too, read to page one hundred and thirty-five with despair in my heart, falling asleep twice on the way. The incredible multifariousness of Joyce's style has a monotonous and hypnotic effect. Nothing comes to the reader; everything turns away from him and leaves him to gape after it.
>
> —Psychologist Carl Jung on reading *Ulysses*, 1932

When difficult modernism is understood in this way, as inextricable from pleasure, anxiety, panic, and anger, it becomes clearer why the reaction against (and for) difficulty was frequently couched in moral terms, often strenuously so. In Chicago, people didn't just quibble with Matisse, perhaps setting up a panel discussion on his merits; they burned his work and dragged, beat, and stabbed him in effigy. At the 1910 post-Impressionist exhibit an academician warned Oliver Brown, director of the Leicester Gallery: "Don't go in, young man, it will do you harm. The pictures are evil" (quoted in Dunlop 1972, 120). The morality of difficulty was often attacked, and, for modernism's detractors, the moral issues at stake justified the extreme responses. Modern difficulty was not just low quality art, as the following 1934 monograph on Joyce's *Ulysses* makes clear. In it Paul Jordan Smith, in an otherwise deferential analysis of Joyce, turns with startling venom on Joyce's unnamed followers: "The influence of Joyce became immediately apparent in the writing of crack-brained, ill-informed moronettes, who, paying the tribute that mediocrity is said to yield to genius, aped the superficial mannerisms of their master, and thought to ride Pegasus without a bridle. Modernity came at a bound to mean poor spelling, no capitals, and

> Famous Cubists' Collection Here
> Talked of "Freak" Paintings Reach Institute for Exhibition Next Week.
> MAGAZINE RAKES GROUP
> Art Critics Refer to Post-Impressionist Views as "Crime Against Nature."
> —Headline in *Chicago Tribune* for March 22, 1913

the complete absence of punctuation;—bedlam in a psychopathic ward. One spits on the result" ([1934] 1969, 59–60). Righteous indignation was a wonderful and inevitable tool. For readers like Smith, the violent reaction was not over the top; it could be defended in the name of morality. There was a crisis, and extreme situations called for extreme responses. This reaction lines up with the preponderance of negative terms for difficulty that use some idea of twisting and entanglement. Such terms convey both that the norm is for straightness and that this twisted difficulty is negative. "Knotty," "twisted," "perplexing," "contorted," "tangled"—these terms belong to the same semantic field as distortion and perversion.

Modernism had antecedents for its linkage between difficulty and morality, antecedents most clearly seen in responses to John Donne, whose difficulty was often presented as unnatural. Comparisons between the simplicity of nature and the unnaturalness of his difficulty dominate Donne criticism from the late 1600s to the end of the nineteenth century. The argument is straightforward: because difficulty does not represent nature (which is simple), difficulty is unnatural. That nexus of beliefs about Donne's difficulty, mimesis, and nature is drawn together by William Mason, who wrote in 1793 in a note that Donne was the archetype of the metaphysicals, writers who "thought it a test of excellence to combine true and natural images in a forced, a false, and unnatural manner" ([1793] 1975, 202). Samuel Johnson, in his life of Cowley, argued that the work of the metaphysicals was composed of "thoughts so far-fetched as to be not only unexpected but unnatural," and he speculated that readers wonder "by what perverseness of industry they were ever found" (Johnson [1779–81] 1967, 20, 24). In 1841 Evert Duyckinck claimed that Donne, along with "the other perverse writers of his times ... mistook the true laws of poetry, for they failed in universality of style, nature's own simplicity, by which Homer and Shakespeare are to be intelligible forever" (Duyckinck [1841] 1975, 384).[32] George Gilfillan in 1860 asserted that in Donne's poetry "Every second line, indeed, is either bad, or unintelligible, or twisted into unnatural distortion" (Gilfillan [1860] 1975, 423).[33]

Skeptical reactions to high modernism work with the heritage of these comments, which posit a relationship between entanglement, health, naturalness, and morality. One early reviewer of Ezra Pound, after quoting from the poetry, exclaimed:

> No! Chinese word-puzzles do not convey emotion!
> As I have said, Mr. Pound has the poet in him; but he will never do anything worth preserving till he abandons his eccentricities. A genius should not covet the brain-twists, and their productions, of the lunatic! (Granville [1911] 1972, 80)

These connections to morality were at times extended. Many angry moral reactions implicated difficulty in modernism's celebrated obscenity. This is clearly seen in the reception of James Joyce, where obscenity and difficulty routinely appeared together.[34] Writing in the *New York Times Book Review*, Joseph Collins claimed "A few intuitive, sensitive visionaries may understand and comprehend *Ulysses*, James Joyce's new and mammoth volume, without going through a course of training or instruction, but the average intelligent reader will glean little or nothing from it—even from careful perusal, one might properly say study, of it—save bewilderment and a sense of disgust" ([1922] 1970, 222).[35] The linkage between obscenity and difficulty was underscored by the strong connection between difficulty and other marked concepts, such as unnaturalness and ill health (difficulty and obscenity both being an indication of unnaturalness and ill health). Consider Clifton Fadiman's response to Djuna Barnes's *Nightwood*, which had been published with a laudatory preface by T. S. Eliot:

> One hopes devoutly that Djuna Barnes's "Nightwood" may not be visited with a *succès de snobisme* or served up as a caviar to the general. The portents, however, are dire: it arrives upborne on the rare incense of such intellectual English critics as Edwin Muir and T. S. Eliot; its pitiless concision may make it seem obscure, and therefore destined only for the lofty-browed; its language is on occasion scatological; the central character is a homosexual, and the three chief female characters are dominantly sapphic. Only by a miracle, it would seem, can "Nightwood" escape the affectionate, destroying hands of some twittering literary cult. (1937, 83)

While Fadiman's linkage between mental morality, health and difficulty was somewhat speculative, and shaped by his belief that the "obscurities" of the book were "not willful but imposed by the weird materials of the story" (83), another reviewer linked unnaturalness and difficulty more closely, with one causing the other. In the *New Masses* Philip Rahv claimed that Barnes had "merely exploited perversion to create an atmosphere of general mystification and psychic disorder that will permit her to transcend reality and make plausible a certain modernist attitude whose essence is a tragic pose and a learned metaphysical sneer" (1937, 33).

> Cubist Art Called Lewd: Investigator for Senate Vice Commission Fears Immoral Effect on Artists
> Art must answer to the Illinois Senate White Slave Committee. Futurist and Cubistic art are indicted.
> —Headline in the Chicago *America*, after the arrival of the 1913 Armory Show
>
> Preparations are being made to care for additional patients at Dunning.
> —Mental asylum apparently readies itself for arrival of Armory Show, Chicago *Record-Herald*, March 20, 1913

Similarly, a reviewer of Joyce's *Work in Progress* claimed that the "technical difficulties" of the work "have given rise in certain quarters to an expression of humorous despair and to doubts concerning the author's sanity" (Schlauch [1939] 1970, 722); a reader of Stein argued that "the first thing to say" about the author of *Tender Buttons* is that "the woman is either a colossal charlatan or mad" (Rogers [1914] 1986, 32).[36]

The Consequences of Rage and Laughter

This way of understanding the responses to modern difficulty accounts for the stylized shape of modern difficulty, for its viscerality, its riots and ridicule, its boredom. It helps explain why the viscerality is so omnipresent and not just an occasional aberration. The viscerality of the difficult response also signals that the experience has gone outside the contingencies of a particular culture, and into a more shared experience. However, though the reactions to difficulty are predictable and shared, it is a shared instability. Difficult work set in motion an uncontrollable reaction on the part of those who did not have the cultural literacy (or the will) to put this difficulty within manageable bounds. Once the threshold of acceptable difficulty had been crossed, it was close to impossible to respond moderately. The anxious response to modern difficulty was inevitable, but it was more like an explosion than a controlled burn.

The emotive responses to difficulty had other consequences for modernism as well. First, difficulty became a cultural gatekeeper, and one's anger or laughter at difficult work was a sign that one hadn't made it through the gate. This was recognized early on. Consider this example from Arnold Bennett, who although pilloried by Virginia Woolf for his novels, was very much on the side of visual modernism. In an article for the *New Age* on the post-Impressionist exhibition, Bennett noted:

> The exhibition of the so-called "Neo-Impressionists" over which the culture of London is now laughing, has an interest which is perhaps not confined to the art of painting. For me, personally, it has a slight, vague repercussion upon literature. The attitude of the culture of London towards it is of course humiliating to any Englishman who has made any effort to cure himself of insularity.... The mild tragedy of the thing is that London is infinitely too self-complacent even to suspect that it is London and not the exhibition which is making itself ridiculous.... London may be unaware that the value of the best work of this new school is permanently and definitely settled—outside London. So much the worse for London. For the movement has not only got past the guffawing stage; it has got past the arguing stage. Its authenticity is admitted by all those who have kept themselves fully awake. And in twenty years London will be signing an apology for its guffaw. (1910, 135)

Difficulty is a problematic gatekeeper, though. While laughter or anger often indicate a lack of cultural expertise, it is not the case that those who belong to high culture (who do not get angry or laugh at difficult art) and those who don't are having the same kind of experience. The sense that something is "too difficult" (with its accompanying anxiety) is individually determined. "Real" (unresolved) difficulty produces anxiety, rage, or laughter; those who claim that they are experiencing difficulty but do not show these responses are not really having the same level of difficult experience as those who do (the inverse is also true: those who get angry or ridicule difficult art should not assume that those who claim pleasure from it are dishonest).[37] That individuality of response makes the moral claims of difficulty's proponents hard to support. One could argue, I suppose, that Eliot, in his ability to enjoy difficult literature, was a more courageous reader and writer than J. C. Squire. But that claim is in itself hard to figure out, since it probably was the case that for Eliot the difficulty hadn't crossed a boundary. Even more problematic, often the difficulty argument was made on behalf of *groups*, such as the common reader, the bourgeoisie, or intellectuals, as when Edith Sitwell grumbled about "people who want comfort and not the truth" (1926, 22). While it was common to claim that one group was less courageous than another, it makes more sense to base differences in reactions to difficulty on the claim that one group is less likely to have the cultural competency that other groups have.

Visceral responses to difficulty also tended to make the stakes quite high; difficulty inherently provoked large claims, being seen by all involved in the debate about modernism as both aggressive and ambitious. The benefits of this strenuousness are mixed: while high modernism showed that the realm of real art also involves our viscera, the rage and laughter that inevitably accompanied difficulty meant that modern difficulty attracted dichotomies and did not lend itself to moderate judgments. The argument was structured so that the winner would take all.

This lack of moderate judgments manifested itself not only in the spectacular responses to difficulty, but also in the more measured statements made about difficulty. Modernism's difficulty was never a value-free topic: it was inevitably put side by side with arguments about why it was necessary or useful. No one just asserted that a text was difficult and, after perhaps giving evidence for that difficulty, silently moved on to other, separate issues. Readers always tied difficulty to something else—either to a judgment about its value or to a reason for its existence. For example, Elizabeth Atkins, in her 1936 *Edna St. Vincent Millay and Her Times* (a book that attempted to place Millay centrally into the modern canon in place of Eliot, who according to Atkins "was leading a flock of followers straight on into the desert of nihilism"), put both the generalizing and value judgments into play when she grumbled about "the obscurantist cult of the day" (93, 108). Atkins was not alone; during the first half of the twentieth century arguments about difficult modern texts were also almost always arguments about the shape and value either of difficulty or of the modern canon in general.

Further, a peculiar kind of focus resulted when readers did attempt to finesse difficulty's territory through distinguishing between good and bad forms of difficulty. For modern readers, good difficulty was held within limits and was necessary, while bad difficulty was excessive and deliberate. As Clive Bell, speaking from the heights of Bloomsbury, argued, "I respect the man who admits that he finds Eliot's poetry stiff; him who from its obscurity argues insincerity and mystification I take for an ass" ([1923] 1982, 190). Bell, contrasting legitimate and illegitimate difficulty, makes his distinction according to such criteria as sincerity and deliberateness. And his judgment, like all such judgments, is overwhelmingly centered on a very simple distinction: good difficulty ultimately has ascertainable meaning behind it, while bad deliberately does not (or, more accurately: good difficulty is not *too* difficult; good difficulty does not cross a given reader's threshold of tolerance).[38] Thus, the distinctions made between different lexical items were *always* value-driven. The two most-cited opponents of modern difficulty, Max Eastman and John Sparrow, are cases in point. In 1939 Eastman argued that the difficult poet must learn to "distinguish obscurity from unintelligibility" (xv), while five years earlier (using "unintelligibility" in an opposite sense) Sparrow contrasted "unintelligibility" with "incoherence" (1934, 52), to the latter term's disfavor. Richard Aldington's defense of Eliot, quoted earlier, goes on to make the following defense of modernism: "Is it not certain that this feigned obscurity is no obscurity, but simply density of thought" (1924, 188)?[39]

> X is for Xit, Xtremely alluring
> When Cubies invite us to study their Art;
> And the Xquisite pain we are sadly enduring
> The while they protest, with an air reassuring:
> "Of course this is merely a diffident *start!*"
> —X is for Xit, Xtremely alluring.
>
> —Mary Mills Lyall, *The Cubies' ABC*, 1913

When they distinguished between forms of difficulty, modernism's readers typically expanded their address beyond the text at hand to evaluate different forms of difficulty in general. This expansion does not confine itself to distinctions between forms of difficulty. While most arguments about difficulty were sparked by the difficulties of a specific text or writer under discussion, readers were quick to comment on modernist difficulty in general, and they consequently made generalizations central to their comments about difficulty. As a result, when readers comment about difficulty they not only judge the idiosyncrasies of the difficult text at hand, but they take on difficulty in general—either modernist difficulty or *all* difficulty, regardless of historical context. Thus, in arguments about difficulty the stakes were always higher than just the text at hand.

High modernism, then, was constructed around the inevitable presence of anxiety and its consequences, a universal and physical reaction. The task for modernism and its difficulty was complex but clear: it needed to configure this anxiety into a useful aesthetic property. Given these visceral responses that resulted from difficult modernism, its apologists needed to show that modern difficulty wasn't entangled and that it was healthy. They needed to transform its marked status into the *norm* for aesthetic experience and to find strategies that for most readers would shift the Berlyne curve to the right. As later chapters will show, modernism's apologists kept returning to some basic approaches. Difficulty was typically introduced by modernism's proponents with a gesture toward higher principles that made this difficulty necessary, or useful, or perhaps even nonexistent (i.e., works that seem difficult are actually simple). Modernism turned to these defenses with some profound ambivalence about this anxiety. On the one hand, it was easy to argue that the most spectacular manifestations of this anxiety—anger and laughter—were a sign of being on the outside of high culture, a sign of one's aesthetic illiteracy. On the other hand, there was also a fascination on the part of modernism's insiders with their own anxiety with difficulty, an anxiety that they often presented as a sign of their own aesthetic vigor and heroism.

Buying *Voice of Fire*

Visceral responses to difficulty, and the litany that arises from them, are not confined to the first half of the twentieth century. Modernism's rituals continue, unchanged. In 1990 the National Gallery of Canada purchased Barnett Newman's 1967 *Voice of Fire*, a large canvas (5.4 meters high by 2.4 meters wide) consisting of two vertical blue stripes on either side of a central red stripe. After the gallery announced to the press the purchase price of U.S. $1.5 million, politicians, editorial cartoonists, and many members of the public erupted.[40] The nastiest voice in the furore belonged to the editor of the Kamloops *Daily News*, who began: "The experts say it's worth it, the general public is bound to disagree." Going on, the editorialist made it clear that the *Daily News* was with the public, against the experts:

> The work of—uhm—art, *Voice of Fire*, is a giant striped panel. It looks pretty simplistic, but for those in the know, it's no doubt a significant piece of art.
> Most Canadians, however, aren't in the artistic know.... They will look at that 5.4 metre-high by 2.4 metre-wide red stripe on a blue background and think of P. T. Barnum, "There's a sucker born every minute and they saw us coming." (57)

The editor's hedge, "uhm," more heavy-handed than scare quotes, let readers know that this was to be a battle about what made art *art*. Many saw the painting, whose dimensions and two colors were all the description necessary for most editorialists, as too reductive to be art. The Ottawa *Sun*, characterizing National Gallery director Shirley Thomson as believing that in *Voices of Fire* "the simplicity is deceptive," set up a phone line, urging people to phone in: "You don't have to know anything about art—as long as you know what you like—and what you like paying for" (59). Many people followed these editorialists and directed their anger and ridicule at the work's austerity. A cartoon in the Toronto *Globe and Mail* showed a woman complaining to a man who has just hung the painting: "What are you, blind? You hung it upside down!" A house painter near Ottawa painted a copy of the Newman, titled it *Voice of the Taxpayer*, and offered it for sale at $400 (the cost of his supplies, plus his usual hourly rate for labor). Behind the ridicule there was, of course, real anger. Many insisted that the National Gallery had exceeded its mandate, and that its directors should be fired. Inevitably, the National Gallery was called to defend its purchase before a panel of politicians, in this case the House of Commons culture committee, chaired by MP Felix Holtmann, who had said, "It looks like two cans of paint and two rollers and about ten minutes would do the trick" (58).

Before this committee and in other venues, the public anger about the purchase of *Voice of Fire* was responded to in two ways. The first was a professionalist defense, that the work was an important work of art, and that decisions about National Gallery purchases should be left to professionals. Speaking to a relatively hostile television reporter, Shirley Thomson defended the purchase in the following way: "We're interested in important works of art and great works of art.... It's part of the continual investigation of painters and intellectuals into the nature of reality" (56). Jane Martin, head of Canadian Artists' Representation asserted that "Curators are professionals and they are the ones who should do the shopping, not MP's" (58).

A second defense used the work's formal properties as its starting point and then moved to an explication of what those properties meant. Brydon Smith, the assistant director of the National Gallery, defended the purchase of the work in formalist terms: "*Voice of Fire's* soaring height, strengthened by the deep cadmium-red centre between dark blue sides, is for many visitors an exhilarating affirmation of their being wholly in the world and in a special place where art and architecture complement each other" (quoted in O'Brian 1996, 19). In a pamphlet issued by the gallery to defend the purchase, Smith continued to argue along these lines: "It is a phenomenal painting in which our sensory experience of the work is stripped of external references, and through which the emphatic qualities of purely coloured form are able to flood our consciousness with a sublime sense of awe and tranquility" (71). By excluding all realms other than the aesthetic Smith implied that one did not need knowledge to understand this work; one merely had to be receptive. This is not to say that for its defenders the work had nothing to do with contemporary culture. John Bentley Mays, writing in the Toronto *Globe and Mail*, argued that *Voice of Fire* exemplified Newman's work "at its best": "the vivid conviction about art's ability to convince, the forceful argument against the futile speediness and fretfulness of contemporary society, the summons to training for larger spiritual and intellectual life" (62).

Difficulty, it seems, had not changed much of its social function since the early years of modernism. Still eliciting visceral responses, difficulty continued to put those responses to work in familiar ways. This even went down to the uncertainty over the term itself. In the more measured critical postmortem that followed the controversy, critic John O'Brian noted: "In short, it was the monetary transaction and the 'difficulty' of the painting, rather than the exhibition of it, that provoked such strong public reaction" (1996, 7). At the end of twentieth century, then, difficulty's value (even its validity as a concept) was still contested and on the same terms that greeted the Armory Show of 1913. Difficulty, and the various responses it compels, continue to be central markers of high culture.

CHAPTER 3

Professional Romanticism: Defending Difficulty

> Every age gets the art it deserves, and every age must accept the art it gets.
> —T. S. Eliot

> Poetry belongs to the people. It does not belong to the poets, surely. That is one fact that Mr. Eliot and Mr. Pound have forgotten, among many, in their private service of song.... I should like to submit Mr. Eliot's poems to an audience of soldiers.
> —Tristram Coffin

High modernism's apologists countered the big emotional reactions to difficulty with defenses of equal size. Finding not much to *argue* against in the visceral responses to difficulty, they turned their polemics instead to specific arguments raised by modernism's detractors. As chapter 1 has shown, the big initial argument against modern difficulty was that there was so much of it. Now, difficulty's apologists did not first of all directly argue against this point. Instead, they changed its terms, addressing an implicit, nagging corollary: that since there was so much difficulty it must be deliberate. Acknowledging difficulty's prevalence, modernism's defenders nudged readers to arguments about why difficulty was *necessary*, perhaps even valuable. Articulating the reasons for difficulty's necessity was not only a way to make the question of deliberateness beside the point, it was a way to understand difficulty, sometimes by removing it completely (that is, solving it), or by making it expressive. In articulating these causes, modernism's apologists negotiated two conflicting impulses: one impulse, finding its source in professionalism, presented difficulty's necessity in terms of precision; the other, working within modernism's large romantic inheritance, presented difficulty's necessity and value in terms much less precise.[1]

Waiting for Godot in San Quentin

The state prison in San Quentin, California, may seem an unlikely place for an indication of how completely difficult modernism had conquered the cultural agenda. But what happened there on November 19, 1957, became a classic opportunity for high modern defenses of difficulty to do their work once again. That day and place saw the staging of Samuel Beckett's *Waiting for Godot*, the response to which reveals how, even at the tentative beginnings of postmodern, high modernism's understandings of difficulty still held sway, controlling how difficulty was understood and how high culture responded.

San Quentin, of course, was not the first venue for *Godot*. By the time it reached San Quentin, the play had already been staged in Paris, London, Miami, and New York. These previous stagings did not augur well; the play had garnered a prickly reputation because of its difficulty. On the major stages of the Western world the play had encountered some critical acclaim and a lot of hostile incomprehension. Peter Bull, who played Pozzo in the London production, noted that in that staging "Waves of hostility came whirling over the footlights, and the mass exodus, which was to form such a feature of the run of the piece, started quite soon after the curtain had risen" (quoted in Bair 1978, 453). After the performance, the play initiated heated conversation. American director Alan Schneider noted that the London production was "hailed in superlatives by both Harold Hobson and Kenneth Tynan," but "damned without exception by the daily critics," to become "the top conversation piece of the English season" (1993, 71). A reviewer for the *Times* described the play as a "sophisticated fantasy" that seemed "to hold last night's audience; and in the attentive silence one could almost hear the seeds of a cult growing." Journalist Marya Mannes, on the other hand, described the play as "typical of the self-delusion of which certain intellectuals are capable, embracing obscurity, pretense, ugliness, and negation as protective coloring for their own confusions" (quoted in Graver and Federman 1979, 9). Ronald Barker, writing in *Plays and Players*, skeptically noted that "people are wrong in trying to read a philosophy into this odd mass of nonsense. It should be remembered that the author is an Irishman and full of leg pulls" ([1955] 1993, 22). Going on, Barker asserted "Now that Beckett has made enough money out of pulling both legs of the audience in most European countries, he should sit down and write a real play" (23).

The play's North American premiere was at Miami's Coconut Grove Playhouse on January 3, 1956. Schneider, who directed the production, described it as a "spectacular flop." Dividing the blame equally between the Miami audience, which was "at best not too sophisticated or attuned to this type of material," and the advertising, which had billed the play as "'the laugh sensation of two continents,'" Schneider ruefully recalled that the audience "walked out in droves." As for the critical reception, Schneider noted that "the so-called reviewers not only could not make heads or tails of the play but accused us of pulling some sort of a hoax on them" (1993, 74). The play met with more critical success in New York, where its advertising called for "seventy thousand intellectuals" to attend and make the play financially succeed (quoted in Knowlson 1996, 180). Eric Bentley, writing in the *New Republic*, had much to praise in the play but he disparagingly noted reviewers who found "something of a scandal in the very existence of difficulty." Bentley went on to quote some of these reviewers, including John Chapman, who, writing in the *Daily News*, quipped: "Thinking is a simple, elementary process. *Godot* is merely a stunt." Robert Coleman of the *Daily Mirror* noted that Beckett "was once secretary to that master of obfuscation, James Joyce. Beckett appears to have absorbed some of his employer's ability to make the simple complex" (Bentley 1993, 37).

So it was not just because this was an audience of convicts that the Actor's Workshop of San Francisco apprehensively approached this performance, the first "legitimate-theatre production" since Sarah Bernhardt's performance there in 1913 ("Godot Gets Around" 1958, 73). The managing director was quoted in the San Quentin *News* as saying, "'Frankly, we were scared to death.... You had never seen us, or this type of play, and we had never seen you, or this type of audience" ("Workshop" 1957, 1). To assuage nerves on both sides, director Herbert Blau came out on stage before the show to speak to the more than one thousand inmates assembled in the North Dining Hall, reportedly telling them: "Just like jazz ... one must listen for whatever they find. It is the same with 'Godot.' For each there will be some meaning, some reaction and dressed in what we hope is good theater" (quoted in "Workshop" 1957, 1).

The performance apparently tapped into something in San Quentin. According to the *News* reporter, "the San Francisco company had its audience of captives in its collective hand. A sensitive and compelled audience closely followed the oft-times poignant, sometimes earthy, and always provocative struggles of the two wayfarers ... an almost tangible feeling of understanding and empathy could be felt" ("Workshop" 1957, 1). The reporter who is most accurately described as San Quentin's society columnist reported the following observation, under the headline "Memos of a First-Nighter:" "The trio of musclemen, biceps over-flowing, who parked all 642 lbs. on the aisle and waited for the girls and funny stuff. When this didn't appear they audibly fumed and audibly decided to wait until the house lights dimmed before escaping. They made one error. They listened and looked two minutes too long—and stayed. Left at the end. All shook" (Shrdlu 1957, 3). After the performance the managing director noted that "Responses were rapid, spontaneous" ("Workshop" 1957, 1). Speaking to a reporter from the San Francisco *Chronicle* (who, after commenting that the play had "no plot and no clear meaning," noted that the prisoners had clear theories about Godot), one prisoner identified Godot as "Society," and another commented "He's the Outside." According to an adult education teacher at the prison, this positive and perceptive response could have been predicted. Speaking of the audience, he asserted "They know what is meant by waiting.... And they knew if Godot finally came, he would only be a disappointment" (Harris 1957, 23).

That, as far as I can tell, is the basic outline of what happened at San Quentin that November. But the ways in which it would be understood were already present, to be marshaled into a defense of difficulty in Martin Esslin's *The Theatre of the Absurd* (1969), the paradigmatic apologia for absurdist theater. Esslin begins his book with the San Quentin *Godot*. In Esslin's book, the play's opening is fraught with tension and danger. As did the reporters for the San Francisco *Chronicle* and *Theatre Arts*, Esslin notes that *Godot* used an all male cast. Esslin underscores this recognition of the hazards of San Quentin with a depiction of the lone director in front of a dangerous audience: "Herbert Blau decided to prepare the San Quentin audience for what was to come. He stepped on the stage and addressed the packed, darkened North Dining Hall—a sea of flickering matches that the convicts tossed over their shoulders after lighting their cigarettes" (1). The celebrated difficulty of *Waiting for Godot* heightened the tension: "No wonder the actors and Herbert Blau, the director, were apprehensive. How were they to face one of the toughest audiences in the world with a highly obscure, intellectual play that had produced near riots among a good many highly sophisticated audiences in Western Europe?" (1). San Quentin reacted differently. Esslin reports, stretching the magnitude of the hostility accorded in other venues, that "The curtain parted. The play began. And what had bewildered the sophisticated audiences of Paris, London, and New York was immediately grasped by an audience of convicts" (1).[2]

In Esslin's book the San Quentin *Godot* goes on to provide a lesson about difficulty. Esslin asks and answers the question of the play's impact and meaning directly: "Why did a play of the supposedly esoteric avant-garde make so immediate and so deep an impact on an audience of convicts? Because it confronted them with a situation in some ways analogous to their own? Perhaps." While Esslin's "perhaps" lets us know that a more insightful answer is to follow, it makes some sense to look at the answer that Esslin discards here. Esslin puts to the side the idea that the play spoke to the convicts' own situation. That rejection is surprising, for it is a response common to all the quotations from the convicts themselves—such as the convict who said he would be around for future dramatic performances "Maybe next month, or next year—or whenever. . . . Like the man said. Nothing happens!" ("Workshop Players" 1957, 3).

But this is not the most useful answer for making absurdist theater integral to the Western literary canon—which was the purpose of Esslin's book. Setting aside this equation between the convicts and the dramatis personae, Esslin turned to what he thought was a more compelling reason for the play's impact. According to Esslin, the convicts, unsophisticated and shut off from the mainstream, came to art without any expectations, without culture. Why then did such a difficult play resonate so deeply with its audience of convicts? To his first, discarded, "perhaps" Esslin adds:

> Or perhaps because they were unsophisticated enough to come to the theatre without any preconceived notions and ready-made expectations, so they avoided the mistake that trapped so many established critics who had condemned the play for its lack of plot, development, characterization, suspense, or plain common sense. Certainly the prisoners of San Quentin could not be suspected of the sin of intellectual snobbery, for which a sizable proportion of the audiences of *Waiting for Godot* have often been reproached; of pretending to like a play they did not even begin to understand, just to appear in the know. (1969, 3)

The inmates were not "schooled" in how to respond to art. Having no pressures to respond in a particular way, the convicts responded authentically. Not coincidentally, Esslin asserts that the play was "*immediately grasped* by an audience of convicts" (1969, 1, my emphasis).

This authentic interaction with supposedly difficult art has significant implications. As Esslin understands it, difficulty is not a cultural gatekeeper, an entry into the institutions of high art; rather, the convicts' response to difficult art is a sign of their authenticity, of their escape from culture. Responding to difficulty properly is not something that convicts have to *learn*, while responding improperly is something that Esslin's elite and middle-class audiences have to *unlearn*. According to Esslin, San Quentin's *Godot* shows that there is an authentic way to respond to difficult art, one that doesn't even recognize the difficulty, and that certainly doesn't need the exegesis of literary professionals. By going to San Quentin, Esslin deftly negotiates his way through difficulty's awkward relationship with the masses and with elitism, and he uses the story to assert that "real" or "authentic" audiences can understand difficult work in a way that lesser audiences cannot.

For Esslin, what does San Quentin prove about difficulty? Citing the responses given by the reporter from the San Francisco *Chronicle*, Esslin argues that the reporter uses them as evidence that "the convicts did not find it difficult to understand the play" (1969, 2). Some works that appear to be difficult aren't *really* difficult. Esslin's argument is a way of handling both elitism and the on-again, off-again modernist search for a mass audience:

> But in the midst of my delight, I was jolted. A left-wing literary critic, whose judgment I had been led to respect, condemned Miss Stein in a sharply-worded newspaper article, implying that she spent her days reclining upon a silken couch in Paris smoking hashish, that she was a hopeless prey to hallucinations and that her tortured verbalisms were throttling the Revolution. I was disturbed. Had I duped myself into worshiping decadence?
>
> Believing in direct action, I contrived a method to gauge the degree to which Miss Stein's prose was tainted with the spirit of counterrevolution. I gathered a group of semi-literate Negro stockyard workers—"basic proletarians with the instinct for revolution" (am I quoting right?)—into a Black Belt basement and read *Melanctha* aloud to them. They understood every word. Enthralled, they slapped their thighs, howled, laughed, stomped, and interrupted me constantly in comment upon the characters.
>
> My fondness for Steinian prose never distressed me after that.
>
> —Richard Wright on Gertrude Stein, 1945

problems with difficulty are the fault of its middle-class audience. San Quentin proves the worth of the absurdist project: "The reception of *Waiting for Godot* at San Quentin, and the wide acclaim given to plays by Ionesco, Adamov, Pinter, and others, testify that these plays, which are so often superciliously dismissed as nonsense or mystification *have* something to say and *can* be understood" (3).

Defending Difficulty

Esslin begins his defense by putting the textual properties of difficulty to the side and turning to *Godot*'s audience. Aware of the charges of elitism brought against absurdist art, Esslin argues that it is "by no means of concern only to a narrow circle of intellectuals" (1969, xiii). The circle could be much wider than that, provided that *Godot* was experienced *authentically*, something verified by the play's audience at San Quentin—an audience without, apparently, preconceptions about art, one that could respond to *Godot* directly. In Esslin's logic, the reaction of the convicts, because it came from people outside of culture, could be trusted as an *authentic* reaction. Now, two problems immediately arise with this line of thinking. First, the equation between being outside of culture and being authentic does not bear much scrutiny. But Esslin's position has an additional weakness in that it too easily assumes the convicts' responses were indeed outside of culture. San Quentin's North

> Well, much has always been made about how difficult my poetry is. I never thought of this until it was first pointed out to me. It has been many times since. This has become a kind of self-fulfilling prophecy, I think. This reputation of being difficult I think discourages people from looking at my work. I found in a number of cases that people who somehow have never heard of me and who don't even read poetry and happened on it have read it with enjoyment and not found it puzzling or enigmatic. I'm thinking particularly of a handyman who occasionally worked for me who heard indirectly that I was a writer and went to the library and found some of my books. Then he began collecting them, even insisting on first editions, even though I don't think he ever [had] read anything before, not *any* book. I could see that he was really fervently involved in these poems.
>
> —John Ashbery, 1990

Dining Hall that evening was full of conventional behavior. The musclemen's expectations that were not met by the play, the matches tossed ritualistically aside, the facts that this prison published reviews and a society column and that the prisoners knew that house lights would be dimmed before the performance began—all these suggest that while San Quentin was not part of mainstream culture it did have a culture. To be more accurate, Esslin could have argued that San Quentin was a culture that was not used to the conventions of typical high art. The convicts had few preconceptions about what a play ought to do and, therefore, were less likely than the usual theater-going public to be shocked by the way the play disrupts those conventions.

For Esslin, the virtue of the audience of convicts and their authentic response is prefigured in numerous modern defenses of difficulty, including one by T. S. Eliot, who argued in 1933 that "The chief use of the 'meaning' of a poem, in the ordinary sense, may be . . . to satisfy one habit of the reader, to keep his mind diverted and quiet, while the poem does its work upon him: much as the imaginary burglar is always provided with a bit of nice meat for the house-dog." Going on, Eliot asserted that "the poet naturally prefers to write for as large and miscellaneous audience as possible, and that it is the half-educated and ill-educated, rather than the uneducated, who stand in his way: I myself should like an audience which could neither read nor write" ([1933] 1964, 151–52). As does Esslin's reading of San Quentin, Eliot's quotation reveals a central modernist uneasiness about the relationship between difficult art and the large middle-class, mainstream audience, an audience that occupies a position halfway between the authenticity of the lower classes and the professionalism of the creating writer. Casting about for an answer, Eliot and Esslin find it in the intuitive response of an audience that is not able to have the kind of response that the artist has. And this intuitive response, in contrast to the response of audiences in Paris, London, Miami, and New York, cloaks the authenticity of the convicts around the shoulders of Beckett, the actors, and Esslin himself.[3]

In making this culturally based argument, Esslin was not merely arguing for the authenticity of Beckett and the convicts, he was also putting into play several pieces of what by the middle of the century had become standard defenses of difficulty. These defenses were often different forms of a single response to the basic attack on difficulty, an attack that argued that difficulty wasn't necessary, that it was, for example, burdened with the trappings of fashion or of professionalism. These extraneous attributes revealed that difficulty was a deliberate effect; it was unnecessary, inauthentic, not inherent to great art.[4] For those suspicious of difficult modernism, deliberate difficulty was the sign of weakness. Oliver Sayler, in his 1930 *Revolt in the Arts*, noted of Stein and her followers that "It is beside the point to remind them that art which requires a key or a dictionary to be understood is futile and therefore bad art, for by deliberate intent there is little or nothing to 'understand' in their work" (1930, 106).

Modernism's defenders responded to this basic attack along recurrent lines. Particularly not wanting to ally themselves with the whims of fashion, the creators of the modern canon instead argued that difficulty was not deliberate, it was *necessary*. In his influential *A Hope for Poetry*, C. Day Lewis posited that "while some writers are of the sort to be content with a transient notoriety attained by deliberate and specious obfuscation," authentically difficult poets are undoubtedly "influenced by the poet's ancient longing to communicate." Lewis continued: "The questions then remain, must the true poet be obscure to-day? And, if so, why?" (1934, 34).[5] Answering that question was a large part of the project of Lewis's—and modernism's—struggle for canonical status.[6] Thus, when pressed in 1935 about the difficulty of her writing, Gertrude Stein responded to a reporter from the New York *Herald Tribune* that: "I cannot afford to be clear because if I was I would risk destroying my own thought. Most people destroy their thought before they create it. That is why I often repeat a word again and again—because I am fighting to hold the thought" (quoted in Mellow 1974, 420). As Mabel Dodge had asserted two decades earlier, this kind of response, arguing that difficulty had an expressivity that could *only* be reached through difficulty, "is the unanswerable argument of every sincere artist to every critic" ([1913] 172). Similarly, composer Roger Sessions in 1950 noted of his work that "I have sometimes been told that my music is 'difficult' for the listener. There are those who consider this as praise, those who consider it a reproach. For my part I cannot regard it as, in itself, either the one or the other. But so far as it is so, it is the way the music comes, the way it has to come" (Sessions 1979, 169).

This necessity, though, had a recurring uncertainty at its heart. When Eliot, focusing his attentions on the practitioner rather than the product, argues that "poets in our civilization ... must be *difficult*," the word "must" points to a fundamental ambiguity as to whether the poet is aware of the difficulty and whether he is consciously making things difficult. Eliot magnifies this uncertainty when he goes on to claim that "The poet must become more and more comprehensive, more allusive, more indirect, in order to force, to dislocate if necessary, language into his meaning" ([1921] 1975b, 65). Eliot seems to link "necessary" and "deliberate," but his use of "must" does not specify whether difficulty is *inherent* (and therefore, deliberateness is not an issue), or whether poets *ought* to be difficult (in which case deliberateness clearly is an issue). As with so many descriptions of cultural phenomena, the descriptive quickly shades into the prescriptive.

Certainly, after high modernism was established, writers could claim a deliberateness about their own difficulty, as did Vladimir Nabokov in a 1962 interview with the BBC: "Why did I write my books, after all? For the sake of the pleasure, for the sake of the difficulty. I have no social purpose, no moral message; I've no general ideas to exploit, I just like composing riddles with elegant solutions" (1973, 16).[7] But in high modernism such claims were generally more circumspect. Moderns like Eliot claimed that one deliberately worked on aesthetic solutions, but they seemed to suggest that difficulty was an accidental by-product of these solutions. As Stein's comment shows, the difficulty was not the point, but a by-product, the cost of "fighting to hold the thought."

Thus, since "deliberateness" was a quality that few would acknowledge as an aesthetic benefit, and since the apparent surge in difficulty made it hard to claim that writers and artists were unconscious of their difficulty, the "necessary" aspect of modern difficulty was crucial for its defense. For modernists like Stein and Dodge, this necessity was premised on large claims, reflecting as it did modern culture or human psychology. Claims for mimesis removed the agency of the artist: the artist was merely objective, honest. Modernists also tied difficulty's necessity to a professionalist sense of aesthetic development, in which they described difficulty as art's inevitable by-product, a value that consequently made "deliberateness" a nonissue. Using similar logic, and equally central to the formation of the high modern canon, was a more universal claim that denied that modernism presented a sudden surge in difficulty, a claim instead that difficulty was inherent to all great art or to language itself, and that difficulty was therefore *inherently* good. In these various defenses, modernism's apologists claimed that difficult art, because it was necessary, was direct, sincere, *authentic*.

Professionalism

Most typically, modernism's defenders addressed the conditions under which modern art was produced and received, defending both why modernism needed to be difficult and why that difficulty was valuable. In the first place, they presented what amounted to a sociological argument, claiming that modern literature was difficult—and necessarily so—because it was written by professionals. Writing in *High Fidelity Magazine* in 1958, the composer Milton Babbitt described what he saw as the standard relationship that had developed between the high art composer and the general public:

> I am concerned with stating an attitude towards the indisputable facts of the status and condition of the composer of what we will, for the moment, designate as "serious," "advanced," contemporary music. This composer expends an enormous amount of time and energy—and, usually, considerable money—on the creation of a commodity which has little, no, or negative commodity value. He is, in essence, a "vanity" composer. The general public is largely unaware of and uninterested in his music. The majority of performers shun it and resent it. Consequently, the music is little performed, and then primarily at poorly attended concerts before an audience consisting in the main of fellow professionals. At best, the music would appear to be for, of, and by specialists. ([1958] 1966, 235)

Writing from hindsight, Babbitt was describing (and, eventually, defending) a change in the social function of art that had solidified into the norm. High art had become professional: written for specialists, the work was "advanced," "serious."

What I mean by the term "professional" is a complex of attitudes and practices, a way of producing and consuming art that has been extensively documented by Magali Larson, Burton Bledstein, Thomas Strychacz, Louis Menand, and others. These scholars describe professionalism as a broad cultural phenomenon that encompasses large swaths of the working world, from artists and chemists to lawyers and chiropractors. A mode of organization and behavior that began in the second half of the nineteenth century, professionalism redefined and sometimes replaced "the vocational values of independence, ingenuity, and entrepreneurship" (Menand 1987, 99). Professions succeeded to a large degree because they convincingly described themselves as addressing an important problem that the general public was unable to solve; they effectively responded to a *crisis*. Consequently, the work of professionals is urgent, important. The profession argues that its activities are specialized, demanding full-time attention and education if the work of the profession is to develop and the crisis is to subside. As a sign of its complete attention to solving the crisis, professions deemphasize the individual. The professional enterprise is cooperative, and members of a profession identify themselves as part of a group, an association. With this kind of impetus and makeup, professions define themselves as objective, neutral groups, having no self-interest other than maintaining high standards.

The profession controls the definition of which objects come under its jurisdiction, which activities are professional activities—and which are *not*. This is not their only exclusion. Professions employ a specialized vocabulary that is closed to general audiences, as are the means of evaluating the activities of members of the profession. Professions thus are accountable only to themselves, for they control the methods of evaluation. The terrain of the professional consequently excludes the amateur, and the difficulty of its activities and its language both assert power over—and inspire the confidence of—those who are not part of the profession.[8] *That* is partly what makes them attractive.

In the early years of high modernism, writers of every persuasion commonly noted both that a model of art as professional activity had arisen, and that this professionalism was bound up in modernism's famous difficulty. (For many, this shift to professionalism mirrored changes in modern culture in general.)[9] Modernism's opponents noted most strenuously the impact professionalism was having on modern aesthetic expression, and it is to them that I turn first. These readers inevitably saw professionalism to be as culture driven as was fashion; indeed, for them, professionalist art *was* fashion, a dubious phenomenon, contaminated by the world, and separate from the concerns of "real" art.

Consider the following extended example. In 1923, in an article he wrote for the *English Review*, the Reverend Cyril Alington, then headmaster of Eton College, warned that modern culture had increasingly become a professionalist culture. Titling his essay "A Plea for Lucidity," and citing the "increased complexity" of contemporary life, Alington noted:

> The days of the amateur are passing. No one is nowadays thought worthy to take part in any game unless he is prepared to devote much of a lifetime to its practice, and the people love to have it so. No doubt there is much to be said for excellence in any pursuit; yet, after all, the amateur made no claim except that he loved that which he pursued, and the claim has surely some validity.... We live in days when the ordinary individual feels it increasingly impossible to resist the tyranny of the expert. (546, 548)

This professionalism, Alington believed, had even crept into art and literature, with unfortunate consequences. In fact, his central grievance against modern poetry was that "so much of it is frankly beyond our comprehension." Worried about the increasing cultural power of the aesthetic professional, Alington asked, "Are there no longer any simple and beautiful things to be said and no longer any simple and beautiful ways in which to say them?" (1923, 545, 548–49).

> Every profession is a secret society.
>
> —Composer Virgil Thomson, 1939

As Alington saw it, the problem was clear: modern poetry was dominated by young professionals who deliberately wrote difficult poems, and in so doing were overthrowing a tradition of beauty, simplicity, and love. Despite its mawkish tone, some of Alington's analysis was trenchant. Alington and others (J. C. Squire and Max Eastman, for example) did not believe that either difficulty or its professionalist source came from a pure interest in technical excellence. In step not only with their belief that modern difficulty was fashionable, but with later scholarship on professionalism, modernism's skeptics pointed out that excellent technique did not give the whole story about professionalism; rather, professionalism was enmeshed in the social, employing a complicated arsenal of attitudes, locations, and behaviors.

Modern literary professionals offered a more streamlined version of professionalism, and praised the virtues of professionalism because it supposedly had no hidden agendas; it sprang from pure motives; it was above politics and class; it was simply about producing the best possible work, work that was technically excellent and in tune with its times. As T. S. Eliot argued, in response to a *Times Literary Supplement* (*TLS*) attack on professionalism, "Surely professionalism in art is hard work on style with singleness of purpose" (1918, 61). Eliot was not idiosyncratic; there was remarkable unanimity as to what exactly was the specialized object of inquiry for writers, composers, and artists: technique. Technique usefully marked out the profession's territory, for it separated aesthetic professionals from those who were eager to assert the spiritual claims of art but were less adept at articulating the devices that might put those claims into play. Further, technique was also able to delineate difficult modernism from the art that had just preceded it and from one's contemporaries. As David Daiches noted, a writer like Eliot "employed themes which implied criticism of the emptiness and flabbiness of modern life and thought, while in technique he employed every means he could to avoid that flabbiness which he was criticizing" (1940, 115).[10] This modernist emphasis on technique also had significant long-term consequences, creating a congenial environment for the rise of formalism, an aesthetic that made art an activity that was first of all concerned with its own autonomous rules.

A central term to describe how one deployed this technical attention to style was "experimentation," a term that implied that good contemporary art *developed* some aesthetic discovery; it was not simply reciting nineteenth-century lessons. This experimentation, attacked as an empty mind game by some, was defended by modernists as being purposeful, experimentation with *consequences*. Eliot, for example, famously argued that Joyce's use of Homer in *Ulysses* "has the importance of a scientific discovery" ([1923] 1975d, 177). Eliot went on to argue that in *Ulysses* "Joyce is pursuing a method which others *must* pursue after him. They will not be imitators, any more than the scientist who uses the discoveries of an Einstein in pursuing his own, independent, further investigations (177; my italics).[11] According to Eliot, the "advance" that *Ulysses* presented was "a step toward making the modern world possible for art" (178). Opposed to this view of art, according to Eliot, was British amateurism, which he saw as the impetus "behind all of British slackness for a hundred years and more." This "dislike of the specialist," according to Eliot, was also "behind the British worship of inspiration, which in literature is merely an avoidance of comparison with foreign literatures, a dodging of standards" (1918, 60).

Eliot's argumentation, though it was quickly seen as authoritative, was also completely typical. Pound a year earlier had similarly argued that in "The Love Song of J. Alfred Prufrock" Eliot had "made an advance on Browning" (1917, 72), and he praised the poet Lionel Johnson "in part for his hardness, in part for his hatred of amateurness" ([1915] 1954, 363). Scofield Thayer, who in a few years was to publish *The Waste Land* as the triumph of modernism, asserted in 1919 that among modernist arts "there is evidence on every side that the ideas of even ten years ago no longer satisfy them, and they are making diverse—and among the better men—very earnest efforts to advance" (485). Under this paradigm, great works of art were seen as "a significant contribution to the theory and art of fiction," as W. E. Stegner described Faulkner's *Absalom, Absalom!* ([1936] 1995, 153–54).[12]

Modernist writers saw this development as occurring within a community of experts that cut across time and class. The work of earlier experts benefited other, later writers, who were not lesser imitators, but writers who were working out the implications of some aesthetic discovery. And that sense of development meant that many modern writers necessarily had a group mentality. Eliot in *The Chapbook* prescribed group associations to remedy the crisis into which literature had fallen: "Let the practitioners of any art or of several arts who have a sufficient community of interests and standards publish their conversation, their theories and their opinions in periodicals of their own. They should not be afraid of forming 'cliques,' if their cliques are professional and not personal" (1920, 9).

As Eliot's quotation suggests, such "cliques" are legitimate to those who believe that creating art is a specialized activity. Specialization, in fact, was seen to be shaping the times as a whole; there were large cultural forces at work. As F. R. Leavis would argue in his ground-breaking study of modernism,

New Bearings in English Poetry, "not only poetry, but literature and art in general, are becoming more specialized: the process is implicit in the process of modern civilization" ([1932] 1960, 213). Specialization and its resultant difficulty, therefore, had a cultural necessity—it was not merely one option among many. William Van O'Connor, participating in a 1945 *American Scholar* forum titled Obscurity in Modern Literature, wrote that "The nature of our society and literature demands an intensely specialized knowledge. The attack on specialization in criticism is neither more nor less justified than attacks on the other specialties" (359).

Professionalism's group alliances, its sense of development, and its emphasis on technique allowed professionals to claim for their art exactitude, precision. To many of their contemporaries professionals convincingly claimed that in their arguments about the canon they turned to demonstrable, textual moments; and that their emphasis on technique was, as Eliot claimed, "precise, tractable, under control" (1923a, 40). Pound early in his career announced that "Poetry is a sort of inspired mathematics, which gives us equations, not for abstract figures, triangles, spheres, and the like, but equations for the human emotions" ([1910] 1952, 14). According to Pound, "The arts, literature, poesy, are a science, just as chemistry is a science. . . . The arts give us a great percentage of the lasting and unassailable data regarding the nature of man ([1913] 1954c, 42).

Professionals made these assertions from a position of strength. As did all professional organizations, difficult modernism presented itself as the only group that could *evaluate* such arguments; witness Eliot's numerous and puzzling attempts in the early 1920s to articulate what was the proper domain of criticism and who could do it.[13] Or, consider Pound's claim:

> The touchstone of an art is its precision. This precision is of various and complicated sorts and only the specialist can determine whether certain works of art possess certain sorts of precision. I don't mean to say that any intelligent person cannot have more or less sound judgement as to whether a certain work of art is good or not. An intelligent person can usually tell whether or not a person is in good health. It is none the less true that it takes a skilful physician to make certain diagnoses or to discern the lurking disease beneath the appearance of vigour. ([1913] 1954c, 48) [14]

What were the consequences of these ways of thinking about professionalism? In the first place, they tended to flavor the tone of discussions of what art was *about*. Precision, development, a group identity—such concepts made inevitable that "seriousness" would be a hallmark of modernist art. In a review of Ezra Pound's *Instigations*, Van Wyck Brooks noted that "Ezra Pound's impossibilities are trivial enough beside the conviction that emanates from every one of his pages: of the profound seriousness, I mean, of the business of literature" ([1920] 1972, 188). Pound, in fact, was the writer most often identified with this attitude, which peppers his writing. While acknowledging that *Ulysses* was "not a book everybody is going to admire," Pound defended it as "a book that every serious writer needs to read, and that he, in our writer's profession, will be constrained to read in order to have a clear idea of the point of development of our art" ([1922] 1970, 266). To drive home his fury with the *TLS* article attacking professionalism, T. S. Eliot ended his rebuttal with the following sentence, set off from the rest of his text by a line of four asterisks: "But we must learn to take literature *seriously*" (1918, 61; italics in the original).

A second recognizable consequence of professionalism was a distancing between art and the general public. Eliot, for example, aware of the suspicion directed at aesthetic professionalism, grumbled: "any specialised activity is conceived as something isolated from life, an odious task or pastime of mandarins" (1923b, 421). But from the point of view of the literary professional, the distance between artist and public, though it did exist, had quite a different inflection, one that gave it some cultural justification. As Pound noted, "The serious artist is usually, or is often as far from the aegrum vulgus as is the serious scientist" ([1913] 1954c, 47). While Pound was willing to argue that this was a characteristic found in all serious art from all times, professionals more typically argued that much of this distance was peculiar to modernism, a result of broad cultural changes that could look quite grim. F. R. Leavis's analysis is typical:

> The important works of to-day, unlike those of the past, tend to appeal only at the highest level of response, which only a tiny minority can reach, instead of at a number of levels. On the other hand, the finer values are ceasing to be a matter of even conventional concern for any except the minority capable of the highest level. Everywhere below, a process of standardization, mass-production and levelling-down goes forward, and civilization is coming to mean a solidarity achieved by the exploitation of the most readily released responses. So that poetry in the future, if there is poetry, seems likely to matter even less to the world. ([1932] 1960, 213–14)

Thus, while modernism's promoters and skeptics might agree that the modern artist was becoming increasingly isolated, they pointed their fingers in opposing directions when assigning responsibility. Anthologist Michael Roberts, publishing through T. S. Eliot's Faber, argued that: "If it can be shown that a poet's use of language is valid for some people, we cannot dismiss his way of speaking as mere 'obscurity' and idiosyncrasy, though we may regret the necessity for such a rhetoric as we regret the necessity for scientific jargon and mathematical notation" (1936, 3–4).

The modern defense of difficult professionalism had other consequences for how elitism functioned in the first half of the century. As sociological understandings of professionalism indicate, the public can tolerate not understanding the activities and language of the profession as long as it is convinced

> The Diabolonian position is new to the London playgoer of today, but not to lovers of serious literature.
>
> —George Bernard Shaw, first recorded instance in the *Oxford English Dictionary* of the use of the word "serious" as applied to art, 1881

both of the worth of the activity and that professionals are doing things the public couldn't do on its own—valuable things that are beyond the reach of amateurs. Thus, while professions are necessarily separate from a public, they are still completely consequential to it. A tenuous relationship to uphold, this is nevertheless the relationship necessary for a culture to accept an avant-garde. Martin Esslin, for example, when he argued that absurdist theater was "by no means of concern only to a narrow circle of intellectuals," presented its value in its potential to "provide a new language, new ideas, new approaches, and a new, vitalized philosophy to transform the modes of thought and feeling of the public at large in the not too distant future" (1969, xiii).[15]

Professional difficulty's elitism, then, was not just opposed to mass culture. Modernism's turn to professionalism was not so much a retreat from the world as it was, in Louis Menand's phrase, "a reflection of worldly values" (1987, 129). Its elitism, specialization, and distance from the public were publicly recognized ways of attracting public confidence and admiration. It attempted to acquire this confidence through the assertion that it was a meritocracy, that the elitism of difficulty was professional, open to anyone with intelligence and talent. Professionalist defenses of difficulty also attempted to summon confidence by convincing general readers that literature was undergoing a crisis only professionalism could resolve, a crisis on whose resolution depended the very survival of literature as a serious enterprise. As professionals articulated things, the crisis at the beginning of the twentieth century was not the *fashion* for difficulty, as modernism's opponents argued; rather, the crisis was that there was so much sloppy writing being produced, to which difficulty was a *necessary* corrective. Van Wyck Brooks could claim of Pound that he was "within his rights when he speaks to 'the twenty-three students of Provençal and the seven people seriously interested in the technic and aesthetic of verse.'" Going on, Brooks argued that "One can not imagine an attitude more vitally important for our literature at the present time than that, not for the generality of writers, but for a few, enough to raise the self-respect of the profession" ([1920] 1972, 188).[16]

Modernism's embrace of professionalism included a predisposition for the articulable. When difficulty is defended as an important development, it is clearly tied to a context; it can be understood only in the light of a tradition or a surrounding contemporary culture that provides similarities and contrasts. And this "importance" demanded professional interpreters, who could explicate why something was important. In modernism, criticism became a necessary adjunct to artistic production. Further, the development of art, the group associations, and the specialized vocabulary all tended to privilege extended, specialized writing about the technique of art, writing that would soon evolve into the New Criticism and make other types of writings and ways of interacting with literature less culturally viable. Genteel appreciations of art were on their way out. As Eliot noted in an unguarded moment to Ezra Pound, "99% of the people who 'appreciate' what one writes are undisguisable shits and that's that" ([August 30, 1922] 1988, 567).

A further consequence of modernism's alliances with professionalism is that modernism's skeptics instantly recognized difficulty's dependence on a professionalist model, down to the smallest nuances. This produced a culture in which major arguments about professionalism could be carried out in shorthand. Writing about *The Sound and the Fury*, Harold Recht noted that "The devotees of the cult of unintelligibility are so sure of their advance that one is diffident about intruding the difficulties of the less gifted" ([1929] 1995, 34). Similarly, in an introduction to an anthology Aldous Huxley claimed that "Almost all the contents of the 'advanced' reviews are just 'Mary had a little lamb' translated into Hebrew and written in cipher" (1933, 226). As was the discourse surrounding the professionalist idea of the development of literature, language about art's seriousness was so common that those suspicious of modernism could put the term in quotation marks, as did Wilfrid Mellers in his 1947 *Studies in Contemporary Music*: "'Serious' professional musicians in this country are blithely unconcerned about popular functional music because it is so 'debased'; they forget that only if they bother their high and mighty heads about it is it ever likely to be less so" (215).

As for professionalism's group associations, they were often snidely commented on, sometimes tucked into a bit of xenophobia. Laurence Binyon, writing in response to the 1910 post-Impressionist exhibit, noted that "French art cannot get on without movements," and in a later article he would boast "We in England don't have movements if we can help it. Perhaps it is as well, in spite of the excitement we lose. It may be that we can appreciate in a truer light the actual men and their works" (quoted in Dunlop 1972, 149–51). Eunice Tietjens of *Poetry* would ask, "does not this process of specialization detract from the ultimate value of the poet's work, tend to narrow his appeal and to make him more and more the mouthpiece of a literary clique?" (1923b, 322).[17]

> The most admired writing of the twenty years' Armistice is almost impossible to read now. It dates more glaringly than the Victorians themselves. Not much of it was written by the English. It was deracinated stuff, the work of Americans living in London, or Irishmen who had settled in Paris. International, alien everywhere, it wore the stamp of no one of the kindly races of men. In every capital, international publishing houses and international galleries controlled, as often as not, by men who were at home in all countries and in none, could print or hang it for the admiration of the same drearily heterogeneous public. It was in revolt against all tradition, for it was in revolt against the ordinary man, who is compounded of tradition. And, for the same reason, it proceeded too much from the head, too little from the heart. For it was in the qualities of the heart that, when the tempest last descended upon us, the common man had excelled the intellectuals, and had earned their resentment. And so, like all those political blueprints of Utopia which ignored humanity, treating men and women as abstract units in a vast mathematical problem, the new art inevitably over-valued theory.
>
> —Lord Elton, *Notebook in Wartime*, 1941

Though they saw professionalism's ascent as an occasion for mourning or resistance rather than celebration, even those opposed to modernism recognized its grip on contemporary life. Alington himself sensed the weakness of arguing against a model of art that made art more rigorous and important (something every professionalist desires, no matter what activity is being professionalized). As a writer it is hard to gain cultural capital through the claim that art is not really as serious or rigorous as some make it out to be. The compelling arguments go the other way. In an article bravely titled "A Plea for a Revaluation of the Trite," Eunice Tietjens of *Poetry* magazine argued that "the whole tendency of the modern mind is towards specialization, towards splitting up" (1923b, 321). Clearly, both Tietjens and the magazine in which she wrote this, *Poetry*, saw themselves as battling not just a fashionable trend, but a sea-change in cultural life.[18]

Difficulty's Accuracy

One of the things that the professionalist ethos did was push to the side hoary aesthetic values like pleasure, wisdom, and beauty and replace them with ideas of development, importance, and accuracy. It is to accuracy that I now turn. Difficult modernism, the claims went, was accurate about big, important things; at times seen as faithfully re-creating the difficulty of the human mind, or, at other times, as precisely reflecting the difficulty of modern culture.

For many of modernism's proponents, difficult art was valuable because it accurately reflected the human mind, particularly the *modern* human mind.[19] At times clearly influenced by recent developments in psychology (Freud was frequently invoked in attempts to understand *Finnegans Wake*, for example), readers argued that the human mind, if portrayed accurately, was difficult. Thus, in a review of Eliot's first book of poetry, May Sinclair asserted that Eliot: "does not see anything between him and reality, and he makes straight for the reality he sees; he cuts all his corners and his curves; and this directness of method is startling and upsetting to comfortable, respectable people accustomed to going superfluously in and out of corners and carefully round curves. Unless you are prepared to follow with the same nimbleness and straightness you will never arrive with Mr. Eliot at his meaning" ([1917] 1982, 85). While the representation of human psychology was a familiar romantic concept of art, modern difficulty for the most part redirected this romantic model, giving it a professionalist slant by downplaying its expressive qualities and stressing a developmental trajectory and the *accuracy* of modern psychological representation. Thus, the difficult artist was an *exact* recorder of human psychology, a virtue Eliot reported as "a fidelity to thought and feeling" ([1921] 1975b, 62). Interior monologue was quickly seen as the most useful tool for such presentation; Edmund Wilson was typical of many when he argued that *Ulysses* is "perhaps the most faithful X-ray ever taken of the ordinary human consciousness" ([1922] 1970, 228).

In his apologia for modern poetry, Cleanth Brooks defended the psychological accuracy of difficulty in some detail. Writing about *The Waste Land*, he asserted that in the poem one finds "the effect of chaotic experience ordered into a new whole, though the realistic surface of experience is faithfully retained. The complexity of the experience is not violated by the apparent forcing upon it of a predetermined scheme." Echoing Eliot's claim about poets in modern civilization, Brooks claimed that Eliot's poem had a "fidelity to the complexity of experience. The symbols resist complete equation with a simple meaning." Brooks argued later in *Modern Poetry and the Tradition* that Yeats similarly in his poetry searched for a system "which would not violate and oversimplify experience," a strength that Brooks thought made Yeats anti-Victorian (1939, 167, 169, 175, 200).

While readers with opposing takes on difficult modernism could agree that the psychology presented in it was meant to transcribe a psychological state, not all readers saw this mimesis as a positive thing. According to Squire, for example, art ought to be more than a record. In his review of *The Waste Land*, he surmised "Conceivably, what is attempted here is a faithful transcript, after Mr. Joyce's obscurer manner, of the poet's wandering thoughts when in a state of erudite depression. A grunt would serve equally well; what is language but communication, or art but selection and arrangement?" (1923, 656). As one reviewer claimed of *Ulysses*, such writing belonged in a "madhouse," for it did not have "orderliness, sequence or interdependence" (Collins [1922] 1970, 224). It left readers not with art, but with the disconnected products of chance. Shane Leslie asserted that in Joyce's method the author "simply jots down whatever succession of thoughts might occur to his mind in certain circumstances" ([1922] 1970, 210), and *Time* magazine grumbled that Joyce's and Eliot's modernism was promoted by people who believed that it was fine if "the author writes everything that pops into his head," for to these people "Lucidity is no part of the auctorial task" ("Shantih" 1923, 12).

Be that as it may, for many readers difficult modernism was valuable precisely because it accurately portrayed the human mind (and if that meant that traditional forms of psychological representation were revealed as flawed, so be it). For some, the focus on accurate psychological representation meant that art was not first of all about communication. In a common understanding of the relationship between art and the human mind, L. A. G. Strong asserted that "poetry is not a communication but a record" (Day Lewis and Strong 1941, xv). Now, the mind that difficult modernism revealed was not necessarily the eternal, changeless human mind that linked Homer to Virgil to Dante to Shakespeare. The world had changed, many argued, and the human mind had changed along with it. Edith Sitwell was articulating a common perception when she argued that "modernist poetry is bringing a new and heightened consciousness to life" (1926, 22). More dramatically asserting that "consciousness is expanding and bursting through the molds that have held it up to now," Mabel Dodge urged "every man whose private truth is too great for his existing conditions pause before he turn away from Picasso's painting or from Gertrude Stein's writing, for their case is his case" ([1913] 174).

For modern readers, though, this brotherhood was not always transferable from person to person. Modernism was difficult not just because it mirrored the difficult human mind, but because it reflected a given *individual's* difficult mind, a specificity that exacerbated the difficulty. This stress on idiosyncrasy became a standard trope for discussing difficult art, from Hugh l'Anson Fausset, who argued that Donne's poetry showed "the intense pulse of feeling beating within the delicate nerves of a poem which was too real to be elegant and too unique to be normal" (1931, 341); to Maxwell Bodenheim's claim that Ezra Pound's poetry "carries the unmistakable stamp" of Pound's "own style and mental peculiarities" ([1922] 1972, 204); to anthologist I. M. Parsons claiming that the "difficulties and complexities" in Isaac Rosenberg's poetry stem from "his own particular and highly individual vision" (1936, xxvi–xxvii).

Even for modernism's apologists, the idiosyncrasy came with a price at times. Consider Conrad Aiken's attempt to characterize Eliot's early poetry. In his review of *Prufrock and Other Observations*, Aiken argued that Eliot's poems present "the reactions of an individual to a situation for which to a large extent his own character is responsible." Noting the "autobiographic" flavor of this work, Aiken argued that its "terms are idiosyncratic (sometimes blindly so)." This, for Aiken, was both the strength and the danger of Eliot's work: "The dangers of such work are obvious: one must be certain that one's mental character and idiom are sufficiently close to the norm to be comprehensible or significant. In this respect, Mr. Eliot is near the border-line. His temperament is peculiar, it is sometimes, as remarked heretofore, almost bafflingly peculiar, but on the whole it is the average hyper-aesthetic one with a good deal of introspective curiosity; it will puzzle many, it will delight a few" ([1917] 1982, 81). Gorham Munson similarly argued in a review of Williams's work that the difficulty of such writing came about because one item was associated with another by using subjective principles. Munson went on to argue, "since the 'association of ideas' is accidental in the first place and in the second it is personal, private, excessively subjective, therefore whether or not it produces an intended effect upon an intended reader is purely a hit-or-miss proposition" ([1928] 1980, 98).[20]

This is not to say that there was no commensurability to be found between humans. Despite these idiosyncrasies, there was yet a similar shape to diverse difficult minds. As did May Sinclair when she argued that Eliot's thought cuts all his corners and his curves," many readers implicitly argued that central to the structure of the human mind was *movement*; the difficult mind was a moving mind. After claiming that the renaissance dramatist Massinger was "lucid" but not "easy," Eliot went on to argue: "To say that an involved style is necessarily a bad style is preposterous. But such a style should follow the involutions of a mode of perceiving, registering, and digesting impressions which is also involved" ([1920] 1975c, 157). In his introduction to Marianne Moore's poems Eliot similarly described the "bewilderment" that comes from "trying to follow so alert an eye, so quick a process of association" (1935, x).[21]

Basically, modern readers saw human psychology to move in one of two different ways. Difficult writers were either rapid and urgent, or tangled and uncertain in their movements. Reviewing Woolf's *Jacob's Room* in the *Times Literary Supplement*, A. S. McDowall dismissed the rapidity of the novel's psychological representation as "This bright and endless race of things and thoughts, small acts, incongruous sensations, impressions so brief and yet pervasive that you hardly separate the mental from the external, what is it but the new vision of life as practised by So-and-so or So-and-so?" ([1922] 1975, 95). Contrasting to the pressing human mind were descriptions of the movement as uncertain, wandering. Edmund Wilson, perhaps availing himself of gendered stereotypes close at hand, argued that in the *Portrait of Mabel Dodge* Stein "seems to be groping for the instinctive movements of the mind which underlie the factitious conventional logic of ordinary intercourse, and to be trying to convey their rhythms and reflexes through a language divested of its ordinary meaning" ([1931] 1986, 61). Readers recruited these groping metaphors to help talk about the subconscious, as when critic Mark Van Doren connected Hart Crane's difficulty with "the intellectual lava that flows, sluggishly, irresistibly, somewhere down below" the surface of the brain (1930, 50).

This way of understanding difficulty, as an accurate representation of the human mind, had significant consequences. It was a fairly restricted understanding of the mind: using conceptual metaphors like UNDERSTANDING IS FOLLOWING, it was bound up in large cultural understandings of how people know, and what kinds of knowledge are valuable. It particularly subscribed to an implicit hierarchy of values found in metaphors of surface and depth: that deeper things are better things, more important, more essential. Yet this understanding of the difficult human mind was also in line with emerging models of the human mind, and so was a more usable construct than an understanding of the mind as essentially simple.

Further, though its practitioners were steeped in professionalist values, some aspects of this psychologically mimetic argument show a conflicted relationship to the emerging professionalist ethos, leaning toward romantic models of expressiveness, and describing the psychology depicted in difficult works as *authentic*. In such works culture disappears, constraints dissolve, and pure psychological expression takes over. Such a shift, if done well and accurately, was a sign of sincerity, a sign that the artist had no choice, that this form of expression was necessary. An anonymous reviewer of *The Waste Land* acknowledged that the poem's "vision is singularly complex and in all its labyrinths utterly sincere" ("Review of *The Waste Land*," [1922] 1982, 135). Herbert Read, arguing that poetic obscurity could be a positive thing, claimed that it could arise from "a fundamental obscurity in the actual thought process involved—an obscurity due to the honesty and objectivity of the poet" (1938, 99–100). Professionalist ideals do not sit comfortably next to such ideas, but in the early years of modernism default understandings of directness and authenticity could more effortlessly invoke difficulty's value than could an assertion that it was an effect deliberately taken on.

Difficulty's accuracy, though, also reached outward, to its surrounding culture. In her 1935 *This Modern Poetry*, Babette Deutsch, searching for a way to represent the actions of the modern human mind, found it by connecting the modern mind to its social context: "A method which seeks to register the motions of the mind under the pressure and the friction of modern life is peculiarly able to render back the image of that life" (231). For many readers like Deutsch, an accurate representation of modern human psychology had implications for how one represented modern culture. When Deutsch and others argued that modern times had changed what human psychology looked like, they were also implicitly making claims about modern culture, its relation to difficulty, and what made for valuable art under these conditions. As it was for human psychology, this accurate representation of modern culture would necessarily lead to difficult art. As Brooks argued in *The Well Wrought Urn*, "much modern poetry is difficult ... because of the special problems of our civilization" (1942, 76). Such claims were extremely useful in creating the high modern canon and finding a place for difficulty in it. For example, to claim that difficult writers were recording modern culture gave the difficult work a kind of necessity. Further, if such art was an accurate description, a usable solution, or a necessary thing, it also was easy to reach back to traditional aesthetic criteria and claim that it was authentic.[22]

As were so many of modern difficulty's precedents, the precedent for the relationship between writers, their culture, and difficulty was seen by many to lie in the work of John Donne. In his 1921 anthology *Metaphysical Lyrics and Poems of the Seventeenth Century*, Herbert Grierson discussed Donne's "Anniversaries" as "the fullest record in our literature of the disintegrating collision in a sensitive mind of the old tradition and the new learning" (xxvi), an argument that F. O. Matthiessen would approvingly quote in his monumental *The Achievement of T.S. Eliot*, and then note its applicability to the work of Proust, Joyce, and Eliot. Matthiessen argued that Donne attempted to create "a medium of expression that could correspond to the felt intricacy of his existence, that would suggest by sudden contrasts, by harsh dissonances as well as by harmonies, the actual sensation of life as he had himself experienced it" (1947, 11, 12). Donne was difficult, then, because his times were difficult, an assertion that in the twentieth century became commonplace in writing about Donne, but something that previous centuries, in their extensive commenting on his difficulty, had not noted.[23] It thus became an assertion that seemed peculiarly fitting to the twentieth century and could be made about difficult cultures in general, as did Selden Rodman in his *A New Anthology of Modern Poetry*: "There has been difficult poetry in every age, then. But in periods of transition and social upheaval, when ideas, attitudes and even language are uprooted or in process of reconstruction, poetry has been correspondingly complex. That it has proved, at such times, to be correspondingly rewarding, is a fact that has sometimes been left to later generations to discover" (1938, 31–32).

Difficult times create difficult art—behind different instances of this assertion lies the central modernist presupposition that aesthetic form is not a transparent vehicle, infinitely adaptable; rather, form should mirror culture. The most famous articulation of this position is found in Eliot's essay "The Metaphysical Poets," quoted earlier. Recall that Eliot, when reviewing Grierson's 1921 anthology, transferred Grierson's comments about Donne's culture to the twentieth century: "It is not a permanent necessity that poets should be interested in philosophy, or in any other subject. We can only say that it appears likely that poets in our civilization, as it exists at present, must be *difficult*. Our civilization comprehends great variety and complexity, and this variety and complexity, playing upon a refined sensibility, must produce various and complex results. The poet must become more and more comprehensive, more allusive, more indirect, in order to force, to dislocate if necessary, language into his meaning" ([1921] 1975b, 65). Perhaps because of its epigrammatic quality, Eliot's comment is by far the most frequently cited comment on difficulty in modern culture.[24] Eliot's comment had many useful resonances. First, it suggested that modernity was a time unlike any other, a time of crisis, and so it demanded this kind of complexity (note how the prescriptive tones of this and other modernist pronouncements often come out of the urgencies of a professionalist ethos).[25] But it is unclear from Eliot's statement how much of the mirroring points to the art object's form, its content, or both. That the poet should be "comprehensive" and "allusive" seems to suggest a directive for content; that the poet must "force" and "dislocate" language suggests that the mirroring of modern culture must also take place at the level of form. Eliot himself was clearer about this when he praised Joyce's *Ulysses* for creating "a way of controlling, of ordering, of giving a shape and a significance to the immense panorama of futility and anarchy which is contemporary history" ([1923] 1975d, 177). Here, form and content are interdependent in much the same way that they are in Eliot's 1923 essay on Donne, where Eliot describes "the necessity of a new form for a new content" (1923c, 332).

It is difficult to overstate how this equation shaped the modernist agenda. The poet William Carlos Williams, a modernist—but hardly one of Eliot's supporters—argued that "Literature, poetry especially, is to invent ... mechanisms of expression suitable to the keenest intelligence of the time who, struggling with emotion, finds the mechanisms formerly adequate to ensnare or vent them inadequate" (1929, 31).[26] Composer Roger Sessions, who in 1970 would use Harvard's Charles Eliot Norton lectures as an occasion for once more rising to difficulty's defense, argued in 1950 that the changes that had occurred in modern music "are the very life of music; they go to the very roots of our culture since they are only the musical equivalents—self-sufficient but deeply and, if you wish, mysteriously connected with the rest of life—of the changes that have taken place in the world as a whole" (125). This emphasis on the culturally mimetic virtues of difficulty, along with a prescription of it for art, was a central way of making difficulty seem not only necessary, but—to great artists—inevitable. As Roberts pointed out in his 1932 *New Signatures* anthology, "new knowledge and new circumstances have compelled us to think and feel in ways not expressible in the old language at all" (7). That sense of being "compelled" by culture meant that difficult artists were not sideshow hucksters, they were *authentic*. Inauthenticity resided in those who were *not* difficult. Roberts not only argued that writers were "compelled" to write in new ways, he argued that the consequences of not following this compulsion were dire: "The poet who, using an obsolete technique, attempts to express his whole conception is compelled to be partly insincere or be content with slovenly thought and sentimental feeling" (7). While in Roberts's terminology professionalist values (with "obsolete") and romantic ones (with "insincere") exist in an awkward relationship, the relationship between form, difficulty, and twentieth-century life was not negotiable.

Though many did not see *difficulty* as the central concern of modern culture, the suggestion that the artist should address the concerns of his or her culture was something relatively unproblematic for twentieth-century readers of all stripes. In her *Studies of Contemporary Poets* Mary Sturgeon even claimed it for the poet Lascelles Abercrombie, the conservative British poet for whom antimoderns most often made ambitious claims, and who, according to some apocryphal accounts, was challenged to a duel by Ezra Pound. Sturgeon noted that "Every poet in this band will be found to represent some aspect of our complex life.... But the claim for Mr. Abercrombie is that he has drawn upon them more largely: that he made a wider synthesis: that his work has a unity more comprehensive and complete. It is in virtue of this that he may be said to represent his age so fully" (1916, 11–13). In the hands of difficulty's defenders, however, the culturally mimetic argument went several steps further, not only claiming that twentieth-century art needed to address new topics, but also new *ways of addressing* topics, and that these new modes of address inevitably meant that art must be difficult. This approach to the difficulty of modern culture was probably difficulty's most striking defense because it made the project of modernism more sweeping and more ambitious. This distinctively modernist relationship between culture and form, although it was not always lauded, was easily recognized as one of modernism's central postulates. Anthologist Sharon Brown, who divided contemporary poetry into that written by "country poets" and that written by "intellectuals," noted that "The intellectuals, who get tit for tat from their country critics, have, for the most part, adopted bizarre mannerisms in an effort to represent the bewildering confusion of modern city life. At its best their style crackles with witty and pyrotechnical invention; at its worst, it is either obscure or nonsensical" (1928, 51). Yet even within such disclaimers, the shape of the argument about the cultural relevance of a distinctively modern and difficult form was clear.

As the above demurrals suggest, the more aesthetically conservative one was, the more one's comments about the changes that modern culture should make on art tended to be comments about content, not form. But this content was not understood to be merely reportage, as if a poem about an electric generator were ipso facto modern; for many conservatives a modern "content" also had an implied attitude to that content. Thus, Harriet Monroe put works like *The Waste Land* to the side because of the narrowness of their thematic response to the conditions of modern life:

> There have been poems—like Eliot's *Waste Land*—which express the terror and agony of a mind crushed and thrown aside by the ruthless rush and power of it. But there has been no presentation, apparently no realization, of the grandeur of this mass movement of the race towards comfort and ease of living beyond the wildest dreams of our forefathers, toward knowledge which brings the mysterious forces of nature to our service and presents to us every day a new miracle—knowledge which annihilates distance, unveils the invisible and the illimitable, which conquers disease and postpones death. And yet this is a subject peculiarly our own. (1927, 86–87)

Monroe resolutely believed, as modernism evolved, that to be modern involved not just a taking on of modern subjects, but also an attitude toward the twentieth century—a point she addressed in the article quoted above, when she announced the sponsorship of an annual prize for the poem that best dealt with technology. In the introduction to her anthology *The New Poetry*, she wrote: "The poets of today . . . follow the great tradition when they seek a vehicle suited to their own epoch and their own creative mood, and resolutely reject all others" (1917, vi).[27] And, as she increasingly recognized over the years that what we now know as high modernism was both at odds with her definition *and* highly successful, Monroe pessimistically noted in 1928 that the poetry written in the past year "makes us feel that the age is bigger than the poets, that there is a certain magnificence in our modern world which few of our poets seem to be aware of, which few or none command intellectually with adequate imaginative power" (1927, 86).[28]

As it did for a populist modern like Monroe, a fundamental uncertainty remained for the defenders of modern difficulty, an uncertainty that was also present in arguments about the representation of the human mind: are artists *recording* the difficulty of modern culture, or are they doing something less objective, something that is overtly *shaping* readers' perceptions of modern culture? At their least polemical, high moderns were willing to remain objective recorders. In their anthology *Verse of Our Day*, Margery Gordon and Marie King, for example, instructed the "casual reader" that, "as he reads more widely, he will find that our poets, as well as our musicians and our painters, are doing their part in recording the spirit of this modern period. What we may call the 'jazz' or cubist types in the thought, form, and theme of poetry—are they not mere excresences, temporary outbursts of the surging thought of our modern world seeking expression?" (1923, xi).[29] F. R. Leavis similarly argued that the "significance" of *The Waste Land* lay in its "rich disorganization," "seeming disjointedness," and "erudition" that together "reflect the present state of civilization" ([1932] 1960, 90).

As with Monroe's conservative modernism, for many of high modernism's apologists the value of difficulty did not lay simply in its giving an accurate record of the times. For many, there was a social function to this representation; if such readers did not go quite as far as Arthur Waugh warned they did, to "anarchy which will end in something worse even than 'red ruin and the breaking up of laws'" (1919, 39), they asserted that such writing yet went beyond mere recording (in the same way as Monroe often extended the bounds of her version of modernism). Michael Roberts pointed out that difficult modernism offered more than just formal solutions: "The poet is, in some ways, a leader; he is a person of unusual sensibility, he feels acutely emotional problems which other people feel vaguely, and it is his function not only to find the rhythms and images appropriate to the everyday experience of normal human beings, but also to find an imaginative solution of their problems, to make a new harmony out of strange and often apparently ugly materials" (1932, 10).[30]

Difficulty as Newness

Roberts's grumbling about poets who used an "obsolete technique" is a common strain of professionalist defenses of modernism. The typical articulation of this defense was a simple assertion with multiple ramifications: new works of art are *difficult* works of art. The principle was commonplace; novelist Thomas Wolfe, for instance, in a letter to his editor about Joyce's *Ulysses*, articulated a standard aesthetic judgment when he referred to "the difficulty which every new and original work creates" ([1936] 1970, 624). This comment and many others shaped the debate about modern difficulty by implicitly recognizing that, in modernism, newness was not just a chronological designation; new things have additional characteristics that make them truly new.

Now, particularly in its early years there was little disagreement that modernism presented itself as something new. In fact, the claim for its newness is probably modernism's most noticeable gesture. Newness also had a wide following; it wasn't just the high, difficult moderns who believed in newness as an important aesthetic principle. This book, though, just considers where claims for newness are attached to assertions about modernism's difficulty, and how difficulty and newness shaped each other. Such correlations are not hard to find. Bonamy Dobrée, in responding to objections about Eliot's difficulty, conceded that Eliot was difficult, but went on to argue that "every good poet is a difficult poet. Indeed, every work of art, if it is really original, if it is a new synthesis, a new exploration of life, must at first repel" (1929, 126–27).[31]

This was not a maintenance-free assertion, for the exact status of modernism's newness was under a lot of scrutiny. The scrutiny arose, again, because of the seeming deliberateness of modern difficulty. To modernism's skeptics, modernism's newness was the *wrong kind* of newness, neither the inward, self-propelled originality of the genius nor the unconscious newness of the primitive. For starters, there was too much newness. Virtually everyone, remember, saw difficult modernism as the newness of a whole generation of writers, who in addition were aware of their newness. Arthur Clutton-Brock, grumbling about the propensity for modern art and literature to organize itself into "movements," argued that much modern poetry "seems to be freed from the past altogether, expressing itself in *vers libre*. Formal verse, we are told, is dead; and it is possible now to write poetry only in *vers libres*" (1922, 633). Clutton-Brock, of course, indicated (with the phrases "we are told" and "only") his skepticism about difficult modernism's know-it-all expertise, as well as his suspicion that these phrases thinly concealed a scurrying after fashion.

Defenders of modern difficulty quickly distinguished difficult modernism from the newness of fashion and its accompanying insincerity. One of their first steps was to characterize statements like that of Clutton-Brock as being a reflex suspicion of newness, a suspicion that was on the wrong side of history. Art critic Roger Fry, in his immensely influential *Vision and Design*, noted that the "charge of insincerity and extravagance is invariably made against any new manifestation of creative art" (1921, 157). But modernism's apologists, in response, did not hold on to newness as a virtue in and of itself. First, they distanced themselves from romantic valuations of newness, which conceptualized it as personal originality and uniqueness. They recalibrated it by exploring whether this difficult newness was something more than fashion or even original self-expression, whether it had a direction that could give it value or even make it *necessary*. Modern newness, then, was not so much about personal originality as it was about aesthetic *development*; modernism was difficult because difficulty often accompanied important *developments* in art. "Development," of course, is not a neutral term, and for difficulty's defenders, "development" did not just suggest change, for that would leave one open to charges that difficulty was merely fashionable. Rather, in keeping with modernism's professionalist reflexes, "development" suggested both change and continuity along a trajectory. Comparing the "condensation of metaphor" in modernism with "the invention of a new notation ... in mathematics," Roberts argued that "the new is defined in terms of the old, it is a shorthand which must be learned by patient effort, but, once learnt, it makes possible the solution of problems which were too complicated to attack before" (1936, 20).

Newness and Revolution

As befits a professionally based justification, development had some urgency propelling it, making the changes it introduced *important*. That urgency was at times accompanied by strenuous language and large claims, language that attempted to show that the changes introduced by modern difficulty were not just those of fashion, but of something more substantial. As Edith Sitwell claimed: "There is, undoubtedly, a vast difficulty for fresh readers in the fact that modernist poetry is bringing a new and heightened consciousness to life; and this fresh perception of natural objects comes, sometimes, as a shock to people who are used to taking their impressions at second-hand—to people who want comfort and not the truth" (1926, 22).[32]

Indeed, in contexts where the claims made by the new text were strong enough, or the crisis it responded to was large enough, difficulty was seen by some as instituting changes large and important enough to be considered revolutionary. Eugene Jolas, whose magazine *transition* was condemned by one reader as an "egomaniac's dream," displaying "the acrobatic antics of ... sleazy intellectuals" (M.L., [1937] 1995, 162), made the linkage most strongly: "The final disintegration of the 'I' in the creative act is made possible by the use of a language which is a mantic instrument, and which does not hesitate to adopt a revolutionary attitude toward word and syntax, going even so far as to invent a hermetic language, if necessary" (Jolas 1932, 148).

But the revolutionary argument wasn't a big part of initial defenses of modernist difficulty. While there were many revolutionary claims for *modernism*, particularly avant-garde modernism, not many defenses clearly made difficulty central to that revolution. The reasons for this reticence are complex. Although numerous writers and artists used suggestive cognates (that difficulty was a response to a crisis, that difficulty was a break with the recent past, that difficulty required courage and audacity), the word "revolution" was a word more typically used by either modernism's most radical writers or its most virulent opponents. The major reason for revolution's lack of a broad-based appeal is its extremity as a method for change. Particularly as the heady days of high modernism modulated into the solemn years of New Criticism, most defenders of high modernism positioned themselves and difficulty not as an extreme, but as something normative, not as a radical break from tradition, but a continuation and development of it. If difficulty was universal, or at least part of a predictable development of literary history, it didn't make sense to talk about it as a radical break from what had gone on

> She is a ship that flies no flag and she is outside the law of art, but she descends on every port and leaves a memory of her visits.... The last shackle is struck from context and collocation, and each unit of the sentence stands independent and has no commerce with its fellows. The effect produced on the first reading is something like terror.
> —Publicity brochure for Gertrude Stein's *Tender Buttons*, 1914

before.[33] The professionalism of high modernism also tended to resist revolutionary understandings of difficulty. While not all did, most defenders of difficulty adopted a professionalist stance to separate aesthetic from political revolution, which for most was outside their job description. And the term "revolution" tended to be thought of in large terms; when modernism was understood as a revolution, it was understood primarily as a revolt against the past and against contemporary mass culture, not just against simplicity.

Thus, in the discussion of difficulty and newness, conservatives more readily connected art and politics and were more ready to believe that difficulty was as extreme as one could go, a total break from traditional aesthetic criteria. For such readers difficulty was at best a jejune rebellion against convention; at its worst, nothing more than lawlessness or anarchy. As a reviewer of Eliot's *Prufrock and Other Observations* claimed, Eliot "has not the wisdom of youth," his poems being merely "interesting experiments in the bizarre and violent. The subjects of the poems, the imagery, the rhythms have the willful outlandishness of the young revolutionary idea" (Review of *Prufrock* [1917] 1982a, 74). It was hard to know where the revolution might stop. Arthur Waugh argued that the current state of "poetic liberty and licence" would "hand over the sensitive art of verse to a general process of literary democratisation." The results could be catastrophic: "if the fruits of emancipation are to be recognized in the unmetrical, incoherent banalities of these literary 'Cubists,' the state of Poetry is indeed threatened with anarchy which will end in something worse even than 'red ruin and the breaking up of laws'" (1919, 14, 39).

Conservatives like Waugh tied the dangers of avant-garde aesthetic practices to bolshevism. In Squire's "The Man Who Wrote Free Verse" Adrian criticizes Reggie's poetry for not containing "the spirit of real revolt." To Adrian, Reggie had blundered by not availing himself of the many possible revolutionary devices: "You do not do it metaphorically by dissolving words as you have dissolved grammar; you do not do it literally by stating your desire to destroy society, to throw infernal machines at the comfortable, to burn libraries and pictures, to abolish education, to bombard churches and

> *Cinder Thursday*, like T. S. Eliot's *Ash Wednesday* and *The Waste Land*, though divided into sections, is in reality one continuous poem. It seeks, by means of parody, satire, mockery and passion, and even by direct statement, to point out some of the most alarming features of present-day disintegration both in literature and social life. It begins with parodies of T. S. Eliot and other modernists, explains by means of parody and direct and symbolic criticism the significance of *The Waste Land* and its influence and goes on to show how the disintegration in poetry is only the expression of disintegration in so much present-day social, national and individual life, the most alarming features of which are evidenced in what is known as Bolshevism with its relationship to Russian Communism.
>
> —Dustjacket blurb for Herbert Palmer's *Cinder Thursday* 1931

to tip the Almighty off his throne. You do not even wish you were a tiger or a motor-car" (1924, 133). Squire did not, apparently, see this list as just satiric hyperbole. Four years earlier he had asserted in an editorial: "There is something pathetic about the way in which, wherever the political Bolsheviks get into office, they print the verses and cartoons of the artistic anarchists. They don't understand them; all they know is that the bourgeois dislike them; so in Munich last Easter, and (we daresay) in Moscow now, there is an excellent opening for those who, for all anyone would be able to say to the contrary, have only to scratch out the old titles of their interlocked triangles and write underneath 'Uprising of Proletariat,' or some such thing" (1920, 387).[34] For readers like Squire, the relationship between difficulty and revolution was direct, but either alarming or trivial.

In this assertion, Squire once again was wrongheaded about the specifics, but perceptive about the general principles behind those specifics. While his assertion about bolshevism recognizes that modernism did have social implications, it is too specific about those implications. But this is not to say that Squire was foundationless. There are critics in the second half of the twentieth century, who, sympathetic to difficulty, take some aspects of modernism's understandings of difficulty and make the revolutionary argument more sophisticated and compelling. Writing from psychoanalytic, Marxist, reader-response, and reception-theory premises, critical theorists have modified standard high modern understandings of difficulty, arguing that difficulty could be an important part of social transformation. While these understandings stretch the temporal range of this book, I will spend some time on them, not only because of their importance to high culture at the end of the twentieth century, but also because they, for the most part, are completely congruent with high modern understandings of difficulty, and for the most part are working out the implications of several high modern assertions.

The belief that difficulty can lead to social change adds to modernism's own defenses the social dimension that modernism was reluctant to address, as well as having the virtue of working with difficulty's affect, with the reaction it provokes in readers. I begin with the aesthetician Victor Shklovsky, who, though one of the pioneers of formalism, is not merely a historical precedent for the asocial, new critical assertion of difficulty's universality. In his 1917 essay "Art as Technique," Shklovsky begins by noting "the general laws of perception," which, he argues, show that "as perception becomes habitual, it becomes automatic" (1965, 11). Habitualization is pernicious; it "devours works, clothes, furniture, one's wife, and the fear of war." Art, Shklovsky asserts, diametrically opposes habitualization: "Art exists that one may recover the sensation of life; it exists to make one feel things, to make the stone *stoney*. The purpose of art is to impart the sensation of things as they are perceived and not as they are known. The technique of art is to make objects 'unfamiliar,' to make forms difficult, to increase the difficulty and length of perception because the process of perception is an aesthetic end in itself and must be prolonged" (12). Despite his unabashed formalism, Shklovsky, with his address to affect and his distinction between "things as they are perceived" and things "as they are known," set the agenda for how later theorists have understood the socially disruptive consequences of difficult art.[35]

With its disruption, later theorists claim, difficulty can alert one to (or protect one from) the deadening aspects of contemporary culture. Such understandings expand Shklovsky's articulation of defamiliarization: while Shklovsky argued that art recovered "the sensation of life," he did not address its social consequences as did later theorists such as Brecht, Marcuse, Adorno, and Bürger, all of whom argue some version of the thesis that the estrangement of difficulty shocks one out of the repetitively ordinary. The writer who has developed this thesis in most detail, Theodor Adorno, argues in his *Aesthetic Theory* that central to great art is its "ability . . . to appropriate into its language of form what bourgeois society has ostracized, thereby revealing in what has been stigmatized that nature whose suppression is what is truly evil." Adorno goes on to assert that "The task of aesthetics is not to comprehend artworks as hermeneutical objects; in the contemporary situation, it is their incomprehensibility that needs to be comprehended." For Adorno, "All artworks—and art altogether—are enigmas" (1997, 93, 118, 120).

In order for art to produce alienation it must be liminally separated, if not from ordinary life, at least from how we perceive ordinary life. In *Aesthetic Theory* Adorno argues that "Insofar as a social function can be predicated for artworks, it is their functionlessness. Through their difference from a bewitched reality, they embody negatively a position in which what is would find its rightful place, its own" (Adorno 1997, 227). The very separateness of the realm of art resists commodification. For many theorists, the difficult text is inherently safe from co-optation by mass culture (or, what Adorno terms "the culture industry") since mass culture cannot understand it—it is radically different, unable to be used. Mass culture assigns a use function to everything, and difficulty makes a work useless. And it is precisely in its uselessness that art is most able to effect change, to change what people sense as the possibilities for life (or, in Adorno's grim aesthetic, to make them aware of what is deadeningly wrong about life).[36]

There are many other congruent moments in critical theory that, while not inherently a part of revolutionary difficulty, can and have been used to serve similar ends. In Jacques Lacan, for example, it is the unintelligible in a text or a dream that is important, for, as Marina van Zuylen points out, "the fragmentary encourages the beholder to relinquish the idea of psychological coherence" (1998, 44). While Lacan's is not inherently a revolutionary statement, it could easily be deployed as one, for it points to what is elided by contemporary culture, and presents difficulty in opposition to this elision. Similarly, deconstruction's assertions that a single, stable meaning in a work of art is unlocatable can be teased out for their political implications. Paul de Man, writing about Derrida's analysis of Rousseau, praises Derrida for presenting "a truly hermeneutic reading," a reading "that traces the contours of a field of significance by means of the logical points of resistance strewn throughout the text.... [W]e ignore Rousseau's chief riches by attempting to reduce him to strict coherence" (1989, 215). De Man's own theory of allegory asserts that experience itself is difficult, unknowable.[37]

Even an assertion as apparently internalized as the sense that difficult artworks close themselves to all but initiates has social implications. Consider Nietzsche's aphorism that "One not only wants to be understood when one writes, but also—quite as certainly—*not* to be understood." Nietzsche goes on to claim that "A distinguished intellect and taste, when it wants to communicate its thoughts, always selects its hearers; by selecting them, it at the same closes its barriers against 'the others.' It is there that all the more refined laws of style have their origin: they at the same time keep off, they create distance, they prevent 'access' (intelligibility, as we have said,)—while they open the ears of those who are acoustically related to them" ([1886] 1960, 348–49). As is the case with Nietzsche, these congruent theoretical positions become available to revolutionary defenses of difficulty when their ethical dimensions are stressed.[38] This ethical base is no stranger to modernism. May Sinclair, in her review of Eliot's *Prufrock and Other Observations*, disparagingly noted the probable existence of "minds so comfortable that they would rather not be disturbed by new beauty and by new magic like this" ([1917] 1982, 86). Ezra Pound, finding much to like in the poetry of Marianne Moore and Mina Loy, noted that their work "has none of the stupidity beloved of the 'lyric' enthusiast and the writer and reader who take refuge in scenery description of nature, because they are unable to cope with the human" (1918, 57).[39]

This ethic, based on an exhortation to courageous action, came with a trade-off in modernism that contemporary theory has not avoided. It seriously problematized the most common thing readers, particularly conservative readers, talked about when they talked about affect: pleasure. I will be addressing this topic in more detail in the next chapter, but for now a few remarks are in order. In a surprisingly predictable reflex, most theorists, when they assert the ethical dimension of living with difficulty, tend to oppose it to pleasure. Contemporary critical theory, especially theory that stresses the ability of difficulty to foster desirable change, is more suspicious of pleasure itself and tends to present pleasure and difficulty as opposing points on a value-laden spectrum.[40] Thus, in their *Dialectic of Enlightenment* Adorno and Horkheimer argue that pleasure's values are limited, for "pleasure hardens into boredom because, if it is to remain pleasure, it must not demand any effort and therefore moves rigorously in the worn grooves of association" (1972, 137). The consequences for art are, according to Adorno, clear: "The further artworks distance themselves from the childish desire to please, the more what they are in themselves prevails over what they present to even the most ideal viewer, whose reflexes increasingly become a matter of indifference" (1997, 92). When pleasure and ethics do make a parallel appearance, one can get a sinking sense that it is a pleasure that must be good for you. Art critic Jeremy Gilbert-Rolfe, in an article entitled "Seriousness and Difficulty in Contemporary Art and Criticism," notes that the work of art "is in a sense at the very least a kind of training ground for the very idea of difficulty, a kind of unserious zone where the serious might be properly considered as a form, and difficulty turned into a game" (1993, 142).

Contemporary theory thus has contributed in a mixed way to understanding difficulty's social function in aesthetic culture. On the one hand, writers like Adorno and Fredric Jameson have contributed to our understanding of difficulty by acknowledging that one's adopting difficulty can be deliberate, and that deliberate strategies toward difficulty can produce good art. But the social dimension of this theory, on its own terms, asks to be evaluated in terms of its efficacy. Consider the following assertions by Jameson: "it is enough to evoke the fad for rapid reading and the habitual conscious or unconscious skimming of newspaper and advertising slogans, for us to understand the deeper social reasons for the stubborn insistence of modern

> U's for the Union so Utterly Useless
> Uniting the members that make up the whole.
> Against it the Cubies wage war that is truceless:
> "Such rage for convention," they cry, "is excuseless!
> Away with cohesion, and set free the Soul!"
> —U's for the Union so Utterly Useless.
>
> —Mary Mills Lyall, *The Cubies' ABC*, 1913

poetry on the materiality and density of language.... So also in the realm of philosophy the bristling jargon of seemingly private languages is to be evaluated against the advertising copybook recommendations of 'clarity' as the essence of 'good writing'" (1971, 24). Now, the project is quite clear. In today's context, Jameson argues, clarity and simplicity are "intended to speed the reader in across a sentence in such a way that he can salute a readymade idea effortlessly in passing, without suspecting that real thought demands a descent into the materiality of language and a consent to time itself in the form of the sentence." Citing Adorno, Jameson claims that "density is itself a conduct of intransigence: the bristling mass of abstractions and cross-references is precisely intended to be read in situation, against the cheap facility of what surrounds it, as a warning to the reader of the price he has to pay for genuine thinking" (xiii). However, faith in difficulty's resistance may be too optimistic. Difficult art has been central to high culture for almost a century, and the world hasn't changed in directions congruent with this body of critical theory. Art critic Suzi Gablik notes how quickly difficulty can lose its antagonistic function: "Provocations that once seemed radical have long since lost their power to shock. Even the most difficult art has become comfortably familiar, and the unpredictable predictable.... The critic Peter Schjeldahl put it well when he wrote that the ritual anticommercialism of the late '60s and '70s has had 'roughly the impact on capitalism of a beanbag hurled against cement'" (1984, 55).

Questions of efficacy aside, writers like Adorno correctly assert the affective impact of difficulty, the idea that difficulty has consequences for behavior. But these consequences are much harder to predict than a belief in revolutionary difficulty, with its sense that reactions to difficulty are organizable and manageable, might wish. Difficulty, while it results in certain predictable effects, is not easily channeled, for it throws its reader into a state of anxiety, resulting in anger, ridicule, or boredom—aesthetic responses with very uncertain political consequences.[41]

Newness and Transitory Difficulty

Difficulty's modernist proponents more commonly extended their claims about difficult newness to the idea that difficulty was transitory, that what was difficult today would be a readable classic tomorrow.[42] Although it does complicate one's attitude, this position is not inherently skeptical about difficulty. Rather, at its most simple it argues that whatever may be the legitimate causes for modern difficulty, difficulty may disappear over time. Virtually everyone in the difficulty debate acknowledged this transitory nature of difficulty. Oliver Sayler, who characterized some forms of difficulty as "insane self-indulgence," granted that "Sometimes an esthetic revolt breaks with tradition so suddenly and violently that the public can not be expected to respond to it promptly and heartily. There has to be time to get acquainted, to make the inevitable readjustments and orientations" ([1930] 1970, 119, 120). More positively inclined to extreme forms of difficult writing, the French critic Philippe Soupault was yet only repeating conventional pieties when he argued of Joyce's *Work in Progress* that "It is only with time that the reader will be able to, if not with ease, at least with simplicity, read this great work" ([1930] 1970, 525). The process of alleviating difficulty was a slow one, as Sherwood Anderson acknowledged. Writing in the *New Republic*, Anderson noted of Stein that "She is attempting to do something for the writers of our English speech that may be better understood after a time, and she is not in a hurry" (1922, 171).

Many believed that the public needed to catch up with art, then, and modern readers claimed that for this to happen difficult art demanded not just an initial, but repeated encounters. Such repetition would make the work and its strategies familiar, gradually acclimatizing one not only to the new work, but to a whole new aesthetic language. Roger Sessions argued in 1950 that "the key to the 'understanding' of contemporary music lies in repeated hearing; one must hear it till the sounds are familiar, until one begins to notice false notes if they are played" (99). The historical precedents for this process of familiarity (precedents I have noted in chapter 1), as well as its slowness, made the removal of difficulty seem inevitable to many. L. A. G. Strong, in his tellingly titled *Common Sense about Poetry*, argued that "A great deal of modern verse is difficult: but practice makes the reading easier, and much that yields little at the first attempt becomes so clear later on that one cannot realise where the difficulty lay" (1931, 162). The difficulties not only disappear, they are unrecoverable, eventually even unthinkable. For many modern readers, the world of future aesthetic judgments was one which radically differed from the present; the future was a world that, in its assimilation of modern difficulty, would need to look to its own contemporaneous art if it were to find difficulty.

This way of thinking about future aesthetic judgments had a teleology as relentless as the professional sense of the development of art, for it believed that the judgments of the future would be infallible. On this, writers and artists of every aesthetic stripe could agree. Carl Sandburg, writing of Ezra Pound, noted that "In a world with so high a proportion of fools, it is neither disgrace nor honour when people say of a finished work, 'I can't understand it.' The last word on the merits of it will be spoken by the future" ([1916] 1972, 116). Novelist Thomas Wolfe could also confidently write to his publisher about the accuracy of later aesthetic judgments:

> A great book is not lost ... The book will make its way. That is what happened to *Ulysses*. As time went on, the circle widened. Its public increased. As people overcame their own inertia, mastered the difficulty which every new and original work creates, became familiar with its whole design, they began to understand that the book was neither an obscene book nor an obscure book, certainly it was not a work of wilful dilettante caprice. It was, on the contrary, an orderly, densely constructed creation, whose greatest fault, it seems to me, so far from being a fault of caprice, was rather of an almost Jesuitical logic which is essentially too dry and lifeless in its mechanics for a work of the imagination.

Speaking with the hindsight of the future, Wolfe continued "now, after fifteen years, *Ulysses* is no longer thought of as a book meant solely for a little group of literary adepts" ([1936] 1970, 585–86).

Granting authority to the future, as always, was a sign of one's nervousness about contemporaneous appraisals of difficult art. Arnold Bennett, writing about the ridicule accorded the 1910 post-Impressionist exhibit, noted that "it is London and not the exhibition which is making itself ridiculous," and that "in twenty years London will be signing an apology for its guffaw" (1910, 35). As French critic Louis Gillet commented: "The scandal about *Ulysses* is still remembered. And now *Ulysses* is a classic. Would one dare say that this prodigious book appeared unreadable and barbaric? It took me several years to absorb the shock and to succeed in understanding it. This recollection makes us circumspect. Let us be wary! *Finnegans Wake* is not easy reading. The labour of seventeen years cannot be absorbed in a day. Perhaps it is not for us but for the future to say the last word" ([1940] 1970, 724–25). Gillet and scores of others were not bringing in radically new evaluative criteria here; the test of time is one of the oldest tests of literature, a test that was attractive (particularly to nonprofessionals) because it required no articulation of the principles by which a work was considered great three hundred years after it was first written. This granted the test of time enormous cultural power, for it gave a sense not only of the rightness of judgments that look to the past, but also their inevitability. The present understanding of old works, understood as the culmination of what has gone on before, *always* seems the right decision. The future's judgments about the worth of earlier works of art could not have gone any other way; they do not depend on the accidents of history. Such inevitability begins to point out the consequences for modernism of the claim that new art is always difficult art. The trajectory of history, when it is seen as inevitable, merely puts difficulty in the most recent spot in line.

The apparently inevitable triumph of difficult modernism, put into play by the notion that difficulty was transitory, was also nudged along by a vagueness about difficulty's audience. After the first years of difficult modernist art, when it became possible to look back at a given work's publication as a separate, earlier moment in history, it also became possible to think of it as no longer difficult because its current audience no longer thought of it as difficult. This new audience was casually referred to; Thomas Wolfe, remember, claimed of *Ulysses* that "we no longer think of it as difficult." Who exactly was Wolfe's "we"? While Wolfe and others never explain, one can surmise. It was an audience that thought of *Ulysses*, for example, as canonical. It was an audience that was educated, that had to some degree domesticated difficulty. The gesture was easy to make. Roger Sessions, for example, referring to the difficult music of early modernism from the vantage point of 1950, would claim: "One finds immediately that what was then problematical, sometimes extremely so, has now become assimilated, and that much that is now taken for granted and considered quite harmless would have shocked the musical conservatives of a generation ago. This has happened frequently during the past hundred and fifty years, and though the present case seems more extreme, it need not in itself strike us unduly" (112). The elision of the identity of "us" points to a central problem in modernist literary history. After the first years of reviews, modernism's apologists weren't very good at acknowledging that all readers needed an initial point of entry, and that many people still needed to read *Ulysses*, or hear *Sacre du printemps*, for the first time.[43]

Further, it is awkward both to approvingly note that "we have had time" to "become accustomed" to the difficult language of a work like *Finnegans Wake* (Troy [1939] 1970, 704), and, at the same time, hold that difficulty is both necessary and valuable. That uncertainty about difficulty's value is often found within readers' claims that all new and original literature is difficult. Mark Van Doren, introducing an anthology of prize-winning poems, wrote: "Poetry which is both new and good is also difficult to read." This elision of newness and goodness required him also to have a position on the great works of literature of the past that did not, to Van Doren's readers, seem particularly difficult. Addressing this point, Van Doren continued, "In a sense all good poetry is difficult to read, but we are not aware of the fact when we are

> The cubist cul-de-sac, and, what is worse,
> The spate of senseless and amorphous verse,
> Writ by ambitious simpletons who've found
> That if you once abandon sense and sound
> And put down linkless words in disarray
> The critics really don't know what to say,
> Fearing that if they do say what they think
> Their names may, later on, be made to stink,
> Because their crassness failed to recognise
> The fire of Shelley in a Snooks's eyes—
>
> —J. C. Squire's list of his pet peeves of modern culture, 1928

considering the classics, which centuries of human experience have taught us how to read" (1930a, 10). This kind of assertion has its values, for it recognizes that difficult art has a social function, and that it is immersed in the social conditions surrounding its inception. But the assertion also reveals a fundamental nervousness about difficulty's value, a nervousness found in its offering both difficulty's skeptics and promoters something to value in difficult art. On one hand, this defense suggests that difficulty is not ultimately a very useful aesthetic quality; it is a skin that a work sheds on its way to becoming a classic. On the other hand, works that lose their difficulty in this way can seem to have fallen prey to habitualization. The results can be negative for art, as is argued by many later critics, such as the reception theorist Hans Robert Jauss. For Jauss, art is valuable in its newness and its resultant difficulty; as art loses that edge, it degenerates to the status of "culinary art," which must be read "against the grain" in order to recover its strangeness (1982, 25, 26). Perhaps, then, the unexpected inheritance of the modernist discussion of transitory difficulty is that difficulty requires vigilance.

Questioning Difficulty's Status
In addition to these defenses of difficulty, wrapped in professionalist ideas of development and precision, there were a series of defenses that more clearly arose from modernism's affinities with romanticism. Turning away from professionalist precision, these arguments asserted that difficulty's value and necessity lay in its exploitation of the imprecisions of great art. These romantically based defenses did not so much defend the qualities of difficulty or the conditions of its production as attempt to resolve that difficulty by considering such issues as whether modernism actually was difficult.

First, bracing difficult modernism against the charge of elitism, its supporters turned to meanings not based on knowledge or rationality, meanings more easily accessible. High moderns often turned to a meaning beyond language found in ambiguity, resonance, suggestion—meaning that was romantic in its antecedents and that would come to benefit from the peculiar values of New Criticism. Modulating romantic aesthetics to redefine what one meant by "understanding," many argued that the difficult work, while not rationally comprehensible, yet expressed a meaning, one that resided beyond language's ability to represent it. Marianne Moore, for example, whom Louis Untermeyer numbered among the "Cerebralists," admitted that Pound's *Cantos* "puts strain on bipedal understanding." However, Moore went on to argue, "the experienced grafting of literature upon music is here very remarkable—the resonance of color allusions, and tongues sounding one through the other as in symphonic instrumentation. Even if one understands nothing, one would enjoy the musicianship" ([1931] 1986a, 275). Often understood, as here, in terms of a work's formal properties, this meaning beyond language compensated for readers' lack of knowledge-based or propositional understanding, and it indicated a split in types and levels of reading and understanding.[44]

As was the case for understanding difficulty's necessity and its being a mirror of modern culture, this defense was most famously articulated by Eliot, who set the agenda for how a meaning beyond language might work. In his 1929 essay on Dante, Eliot asserted that "What is surprising about the poetry of Dante is that it is, in one sense, extremely easy to read. It is a test (a positive test, I do not assert that it is always valid negatively), that genuine poetry can communicate before it is understood" ([1929] 1975a, 206). Of course, these ideas did not originate with Eliot, for such ideas about aesthetic meaning had been circulating in Western culture at least since ideas of the sublime became part of the common aesthetic vocabulary. Eliot's most obvious predecessor, for example, was Coleridge, whom Eliot quoted in 1933: "Poetry gives most pleasure when only generally and not perfectly understood" ([1933] 1964, 138; Coleridge 1895, 5). Behind Coleridge, in turn, lay Aristotelian ideas of wonder, astonishment, a wonder that is precipitated by some form of subverted expectations.[45]

But the specific formulations of Eliot's phrase resonated in modern aesthetic culture. In the first place, Eliot did not reject logical understanding; his use of the word "before" suggested both a temporal trajectory of understanding and different levels of reading. Further, what Eliot called the "work" of the poem is something that he believed could be articulated (as, indeed, a professional must believe). Professional readers, under this scheme, could not be content with the passivity suggested by the above quotation. But it was not *necessary* that the "work" of a poem be articulated for a certain kind

> The so-called obscurity of modernist literature has, of course, a lot to do with the new stress on exegesis. When the overt meaning of a work can no longer be taken for granted, criticism is forced—or seems forced—to undertake the explication of the text of the work before doing anything else. But experience has shown us by now that the drift and shape of an "obscure" poem or novel can be grasped for the purposes of art without being "worked out." Part of the triumph of modernist poetry is, indeed, to have demonstrated the great extent to which verse can do without *explicit* meaning and yet not sacrifice anything essential to its effect as art. This is not to deny that we have had to get used, over more than a quarter of a century, to modernist poetry in order to see this.
>
> —Art critic Clement Greenberg, in his 1956 essay "T. S. Eliot"

of pleasure to occur, the kind of authentic pleasure that was "immediately grasped," for example, by San Quentin inmates.[46]

For the most part, those who argued for a meaning that was beyond language understood it to be meaning that went radically beyond rationality, logic, and linearity. George Williamson, writing in defense of both metaphysical and modern difficulty, argued of Donne that "his style sought to make 'apprehensible by sense' what was not 'comprehensible by reason' but might terminate in intellectual equivalents" (1931, 161). Modernism's skeptics recognized the force of this argument. Bernard De Voto, in reviewing Faulkner's *Absalom, Absalom!*, noted that the tortured sentences of Faulkner's prose "have the steady purpose of expressing the inexpressible that accounts for so much of Mr. Faulkner, but they show a style in process of disintegration." When sentences get as tortured as they are by Faulkner, De Voto grumbled, "it signifies mere bad writing and can be justified by no psychological or esthetic principle whatever" ([1936] 1995, 147).

In finding ways to move beyond the difficulties of modern texts, modernism's defenders articulated three kinds of meaning beyond language. The first was the kind of meaning acquired from the formal pleasures of pure sound, what Carl Van Vechten found in the work of Gertrude Stein. Of Stein, Van Vechten argued, "She has really turned language into music, really made its sound more important than its sense" ([1914] 1986, 34). Stuart Gilbert, who for the first generation of Joyce's readers was essential to the interpretation of *Ulysses*, looked at *Work in Progress* with an awareness that, if traditional ways of reading were inadequate for *Ulysses*, they were even more so for this next work, which was "the most curious and intricate book the world has seen." But, Gilbert argued, readers could still find pleasure, even if a lesser pleasure: if traditional forms of reading fail, "the mere sound and look of the prose, its verbal antics, are a delight in themselves" ([1930] 1970, 539).

While discussion of the pure music of language is certainly much older than modernism, in modernism it acquired an idiosyncratic function, for this music was often presented as a palliative for modernism's difficulty and as a way to inject the concept of pleasure into the difficulty discussion. In its purest form, when it was offered as the *only* pleasure a text might offer, this kind of argument was made primarily for works that were publicly acknowledged to be at the far edges of artistic innovation, works like those of Stein and the later Joyce. (To a certain degree, this view of expressibility of form alone was also held for works outside of one's own linguistic culture, as Eliot had argued for Dante.) This was not a view that impressed everyone. In the 1945 *American Scholar* forum on obscurity in modern literature, Marc Friedlaender complained: "The distillation of meaning out of literature has brought us to the obscurity that comes from the use of words as pure sound, to a poetry which, we are told, we should not try to understand, only appreciate, to an abstractionism that holds the *Divina Commedia* more beautiful if one does not understand Italian" (364). While Friedlaender here caricatures Eliot's argument, beyond the caricature lay a valid point: for most readers there had to be a tie-in to some kind of logical communication in order for there to be other kinds of meaning or significant pleasure.[47]

The tie-in to formalism implicit in these statements was a problem for modernism, for most traditional senses of the meaning beyond language turned to the sublime or to timeless emotional essences to explain what lay beyond the immediately comprehensible. Consequently, one way readers tried to articulate this extra-logical communication was through an idea explored earlier in this chapter, the idea that difficult art accurately presented human psychology, particularly the stream of consciousness—a psychology that could be experienced and recorded, but was not susceptible to rational analysis. Referring to recent psychological discoveries, Babette Deutsch argued that the contemporary writer "may discard logic altogether, and offer a poem as unreasonable as a dream" (1935, 133). As does much of modernism, this defense has more than a little romantic residue. An even more popular formulation, closely allied to the above, is further implicated in romantic aesthetics. This was the belief that the difficult work presented an emotional ensemble that was beyond the limits of rational expression. Conrad Aiken argued of *The Waste Land* that the poem was full of passages "which do not demonstrably, in any 'logical' sense, carry forward the theme, passages which unjustifiably, but happily, 'expand' beyond its purpose." Using scare quotes to acknowledge, irritably, imprecise formulations, Aiken pointed beyond such impoverishment, arguing that Eliot's poem consequently had

> Modern English poetry? No, she could not honestly say that she enjoyed it—though she had read T. S. Eliot (or was he American, too?): she preferred orthodox writers, like Francis Thompson and T. S. Eliot, because one always knew what they meant even though one could not understand what they said, and that was a great help.
>
> —D. J. Enright, *Academic Year*, 1955

"an emotional value far clearer and richer than its arbitrary and rather unworkable logical value" ([923] 1982a, 160).

Many consequences followed from the idea that difficult works had meaning beyond language. First, modernism again did not resolve the tension between its romantic and its professionalist impulses. While the music of language could clearly be tied to modernism's formalism, and so to professionalist values, other ways of talking about meaning, ways that stressed its inarticulate quality, interacted oddly with modernism's professional ethos, which showcased precision and verifiability. But, particularly in the early years of modernism, the sense of a romantically based, emotional meaning beyond language had its uses and appeal, for it was a familiar value, one readers could easily use in their interactions with art.[48]

Second, since its essence was inarticulable, the difficult text had at its core an imprecise meaning that did not reside comfortably within a professionalist ethos.[49] But imprecision had its value, for it allowed readers access to difficult texts on easier terms than if there were a specific meaning that a given difficult text had to offer. Imprecision *extended* access to difficult art through opening up possibilities rather than restricting them. Conrad Aiken's review of *The Waste Land*, in many ways typical of early attempts to understand difficult modernism, argued that the poem was part of "that symbolical order in which one may justly say that the 'meaning' is not explicitly, or exactly, worked out" ([1923] 1982a, 159). Aiken went on to argue that in his poem Eliot "catches a good deal more—thank heaven—than he pretends to," that the poem has "passages which unjustifiably, but happily, 'expand' beyond its purpose," giving the poem "an emotional value far clearer and richer than its arbitrary and rather unworkable logical value" (159, 160). Using a discovery from French symbolist poetry, Carl Van Vechten similarly argued that Stein in her writing "turned language into music," and in doing so had "suggested to the reader a thousand channels for his mind and sense to drift along, a thousand, instead of a stupid only one" ([1914] 1986, 34).

This willingness to turn one's back on precision and knowledge when it came to interacting with difficult modernism had enormous implications, for

> When I was at a dinner party at Beverly Hills in Hollywood, there were a great many of the big vedettes of the cinema. After dinner all these people were seated in front of me, and I did not know what it was all about or what they wanted, and finally one blurted out. "What we want to know is how do you get so much publicity?" So I told them, "By having such a small audience. Begin with a small audience. If that small audience really believes, they make a big noise, and a big audience does not make a noise at all."
>
> —Gertrude Stein, 1946

it highlighted a radical uncertainty about the role of knowledge in aesthetic experience. If one believed that logical understanding was not a primary part of aesthetic experience, another concern faded into the background: the concern about the knowledge that difficult art seem to assume in its viewers, auditors, and readers. (A more professionalized version of this shift, of course, would become a frequently caricatured tenet of New Criticism.) John Peale Bishop, writing about Pound's *Cantos* for *Vanity Fair*, circumvented his own lack of knowledge in the following way: "I shall have to learn at least three more languages and read seven years before I shall pretend to recognize all the references, but patchwork of erudition, of phrases in five tongues and paraphrased as it is, it still contains much that is pure poetry" ([1922] 1972, 208). Bishop's plea was typical: not dismissing the need for knowledge entirely, but putting it on hold to an indefinite future, he posited a fall-back position, a sublime moment available for first-time readers, the moment of "pure poetry." Bishop, though (and many like him), does not develop this argument. Indeed, he presents not so much an argument, as mute testimony, congenial to the late romanticism of the early twentieth century and indicated by the almost mute rebuttal of words like "yet," "still," and "pure."

The argument was frequently advanced by specifically naming the things one didn't need to know in order to appreciate the difficult work. Eliot, for example, not only claimed one didn't need Italian to read Dante; he also claimed that in reading Pound one did not need to know the Provençal, Spanish, or Italian that Pound used in his poetry. In fact, Eliot went on, "to display knowledge is not the same thing as to expect it on the part of the reader," and to expect readers to have such knowledge would be "pedantry" ([1917] 1965, 166). Knowledge could even damage the aesthetic experience. Eliot claimed that "I have always found that the less I knew about the poet and his work, before I began to read it, the better" ([1929] 1975a, 205). Eliot's position on knowledge, that at first it could be an impediment, was shared by many of difficult modernism's supporters, who, in the opening decades of the institutionalizing of modernism, believed that there had to be a way into the difficult text that did not require specialized knowledge. Bonamy Dobrée, in his 1929 *The Lamp and the Lute*, acknowledged that Eliot's allusiveness was at times "a check to full understanding," but that this difficulty was necessary, *and* that it "does not prevent our enjoying Mr. Eliot's poetry" (126).[50]

What did one gain from this rhetorical stance, other than being able to claim that the difficult text was not elitist since it did not put great demands on readers? As Bishop's support of Pound's *Cantos* suggests, removing the need for knowledge was also a way to claim for the difficult text a kind of purity, a claim that was congruent with traditional understandings of great art. Eliot claimed of Dante's writing that "if we worry too much about it at first as philosophy we are likely to prevent ourselves from receiving the poetic beauty" ([1929] 1975a, 224). Dudley Fitts, reviewing Pound's *Cantos* in 1931, posited a "thoughtless reader" who would "throw up his hands" in despair at the knowledge he needed, apparently, to understand the poem. For Fitts, this was exactly "the wrong approach, based upon a misconception not only of the nature of the Cantos, but of all pure poetry; and the reader who persists in it may as well take Mr Pound's advice and 'go back and read Tennyson.'" The problem with such readers, according to Fitts, was that they were "not reading the poem as a whole, but as a sort of historico-archaeological cypher" ([1931] 1972, 251–52). Fitts's proto–New Critical reading strategy opened up the text, lifting it to the realm of "suggestion," of possibilities. It also created a favorable environment for New Criticism, for high modernism's defenders needed to find a way to describe this "pure" reading process.

This way of understanding knowledge, in addition to making difficult texts easier to access (either because one didn't need specialized knowledge, or because it had a meaning beyond language), led some to claim that the difficult text was actually simple. As Edmund Wilson argued of *The Waste Land*, "for all its complicated correspondences and its recondite references and quotations, 'The Waste Land' is intelligible at first reading. It is not necessary to know anything about the Grail Legend or any but the most obvious of Mr Eliot's allusions to feel the force of the intense emotion which the poem is intended to convey ([1922] 1982, 143). Frequently, this defense attacked bourgeois reading habits, reading habits that unnecessarily complicated the modern text (the reception accorded *Godot* before San Quentin, for example). In this view, the uncomprehending middle-class audience was less "pure" than the audience that *could* understand the difficult work, the audience that could put to the side its "culture" and engage with the difficult work authentically.

This line of defense responded to the many reviewers and anthologists who complained that the difficult text demanded excessive knowledge.

> For those who are already engrossed in the reading of *Ulysses* as well as for those who hesitate to begin it because they fear that it is obscure, the publishers offer this simple clue to what the critical fuss is all about. *Ulysses* is no harder to "understand" than any other great classic. It is essentially a story and can be enjoyed as such. Do not let the critics confuse you. *Ulysses* is not difficult to read, and it richly rewards each reader in wisdom and pleasure. So thrilling an adventure into the soul and mind and heart of man has never before been charted. This is your opportunity to begin the exploration of one of the greatest novels of our time.
>
> —Random House advertisement for *Ulysses*, 1934

Harold Monro reported in his discussion of *The Waste Land* that "A friend came to me with the discovery that he and I could not hope to understand Mr. Eliot's poems; we had not the necessary culture: impossible for us to recognise the allusions" ([1923] 1982, 164–65). Monro's friend, of course, is a figure for the common reader—a person who in his many appearances in the difficulty debate was able to represent ignorance without that ignorance sticking to the reviewer himself. (Everyone was eager to *know* a common reader; few were eager to *be* one.) Opposed to the common reader who did not have the necessary knowledge was the specialized elite audience that did have it. Max Eastman, for example, complained that the effect of the knowledge required to understand difficult modern texts was "to narrow the circle of communication to a small group of specialists in a particular type of learning—by no means the most important type—and to communicate even to the members of this circle only a part of the content of the poem" ([1931, 70–71).

Modernism's skeptics pointed out other signs that difficult modernism improperly deployed knowledge. Many argued that the knowledge in the difficult work was not an integral part of a valid aesthetic effect; it was on display, at times being nothing more than a "pompous parade of erudition," as Louis Untermeyer described *The Waste Land* ([1923] 1982, 151). For readers like Untermeyer, as soon as the difficult work's knowledge became a display, the values of real poetry were lost. An anonymous reviewer for the *Times Literary Supplement* noted the following of Eliot's poetry: "Mr. Eliot, like Browning, likes to display out-of-the-way learning, he likes to surprise you by every trick he can think of. He has forgotten his emotions, his values, his sense of beauty, even his common sense, in that one desire to surprise, to get farther away from the obvious than any writer on record, be he Donne or Browning, or Benlowes even" ("Not Here" [1919] 1982, 98). For many conservative readers, this kind of work was neither natural, nor inevitable, nor authentic.

Such a view of the problems of difficulty implied that whatever knowledge might be required of readers and viewers of art, it should not provoke anxiety or be self-conscious. Articulating why readers were "irritated that [Marianne Moore] has not learned to write with simplicity," Marion Strobel argued that "we would rather not follow the contortions of Miss Moore's well-developed mind—she makes us so conscious of her knowledge" (1922, 210). Desmond McCarthy similarly groused of Pound and Eliot that "When either of them publishes a book, they publish at the same time that they are scholars, who have at least five languages at command, and considerable out-of-the-way erudition" ([1921] 1982, 112). Because they believed real art did not require specialized knowledge, some readers tended to think that art required *no* knowledge, that art did not and should not require a conscious (or unconscious) employment of facts (this is why they hated art that *called attention to* the use of knowledge). Strobel, grumbling about the "contortions" of Moore's mind, noted "If we find ourselves one of an audience in a side-show we prefer to see the well-muscled lady in tights stand on her head smilingly, with a certain nonchalance, rather than grit her teeth, perspire, and make us conscious of her neck muscles. Still, we would rather not see her at all" (1922, 210).

Skeptical readers described this kind of knowledge as isolated, disconnected bits of stuff; it wasn't *real*, integrated knowledge, but an idiosyncratic, haphazard collection. A standard trope for skeptics reviewing modern difficulty was to list all the sources used by the writer and to argue that what these sources resulted in was just that—a list, and a poorly organized one at that. Thus, Louis Untermeyer wrote of Pound's *Lustra*: "Poems in the imagist manner, lugubrious Cantos in a Sordello form, arrangements in the vorticist vein, epigrams from the Greek, Lalage and other ladies from the Latin, paraphrases from the German, scraps from the Spanish, idioms from the Italian, water-colors from the Chinese, echoes from Provence—one gets nothing so much as a confused jumble and smattering of erudition. The effect is less that of the man of the world than the man about literature" ([1920] 1972, 29, 128). As one reviewer noted of the learning that made up *The Waste Land*, these kinds of works were "a hodge-podge of grandeur and jargon" (J.M. [1923] 1982, 170).[51]

Such displays of knowledge made many readers not only suspect the artistry of the difficult work, it also made them conscious of their own inabilities. In shaping the reading process in this way, the too-difficult text drew readers out of the world of the text and into a situation in which they read with a key or a glossary at their elbows. David Daiches, whose support for difficulty had limits, posited in his 1935 *The Place of Meaning in Poetry* that one of the sources of modern difficulty lay in "the use of a symbolism to which the reader has not the key." Though such difficulty, Daiches noted, "*may* be dispelled by the provision of a key to the reader," to some extent the game has already been lost, for "though such a key may render the symbols intelligible it cannot invest them with the poetic value that belongs to a more immediate and universally significant set of symbols" (57). Knowledge-based difficulty, then, raised for many readers a problem for poetic value, for it made the emotional impact of the work of art less direct, less authentic.

As the high modern defense of meaning beyond language suggests, even many readers favorably disposed to difficult modernism agreed with the aesthetic principles shaping this assessment (quibbling instead with its application). In his otherwise laudatory review of *The Waste Land*, for example, Conrad Aiken argued that for a symbol to be effective, it had to be part of one's memory, something with which readers were familiar. According to Aiken, "the key to an implication should be in the implication itself, not outside of it," and it "should not be dependent on a cypher" ([1923] 1982a, 158, 159). This kind of talk implicitly argued that a difficult text that required specialized knowledge was a limited text. In what was probably the first sustained attempt to revise the modern canon, Elizabeth Atkins, in her 1936 *Edna St. Vincent Millay and Her Times*, attempted to dethrone Eliot and replace him with Millay. Decrying the "cult of intentional obscurity," Atkins argued that modernist difficulty, such as that promoted by Eliot, was premised on a limited sense of poetry's range: "The same excitement which attended the discovery that 'supralapsarianism' was the word fitting the longest line of a newspaper puzzle might, it was felt, attend the discovery that the meaning of an obscure line in a new poem depended on one's recognition of its context in Dante's *Inferno*, and the excitement of finding it might carry the phrase alive with passion into the soul" (108–9). Negative readers thought difficult art suggested that once one had the requisite knowledge, one had acquired the "key" to the cypher, and the text was "explained."[52] The difficult text narrowed aesthetic meaning, and the text no longer "suggested" meanings, radiating outward. Thus, the problem with knowledge-based difficulty was not just that it demanded an interpreting class; it was that in these poems the activity of "recognizing" allusions was both too much in the foreground and too simple an activity, resulting in a reading experience that was not rich, but impoverished. In his 1920 review of Ezra Pound, Robert Nichols argued that it was central to appreciating Pound's *Cantos* that a reader "instantly catch every literary allusion," an activity that was less than optimal, leaving readers aware "only of Mr. Pound's potential erudition, of an emotion chopped off short whenever he began, and, alas, ceased so finickly but so pertinently to render choice scraps of other poets" ([1920] 1972, 166).

In a manner similar to the strategy used by difficulty's proponents, such comments also appealed to aesthetic purity. But this time, with a turn to the idea that knowledge *is* required of the readers of difficult texts, it was difficulty's skeptics who argued that the difficult text was impure. Louis Untermeyer, for example, approvingly quoted Mary Colum's assertion that a poem like *The Waste Land* was "'of interest to critics and people professionally interested in literature; it appeals to their sophisticated consciousness, whereas great literature appeals either to our subconscious or superconscious minds—that is, to something that either transcends our experience or is profoundly buried in our experience.'" Eliot's poem, Untermeyer went on to assert, "appeals only to our acquired knowledge," for it is a work "whose intelligibility relies on other books, that points (in a poem of less than four hundred lines) to thirty-odd sources for its disjected fragments and the reading of two works of anthropology" (1924, 358). With both sides arguing for a purity that kept one immersed within the text itself, it is not surprising that New Criticism developed as the central tool for understanding modernism, and, indeed, all of literature.

Universal Difficulty

Proposing for difficult texts an intuitive meaning was a useful way to get new readers into difficult texts. However, as high modernism gathered steam and professionalist models of aesthetic discourse won the day, it became clear that claiming a meaning beyond language was not the way, ultimately, to make difficult modernism canonical. Canonization was best served by the claim lurking in many of difficulty's arguments that difficulty was essential to all great art—an assertion that is central to New Criticism, the creation of modernism as an object of study, and current critical theory. Elizabeth Drew, for example, argued that "reading poetry, if it is to mean anything at all, is not easy." Going on to assert that "It is not the things which are easy to come by which please longest and please most," Drew claimed that "Poetry is the most concentrated and complex use of language there is" (1933, 67).[53] At a time when New Criticism was establishing the range of its assertions, Donald Stauffer, in his 1946 *The Nature of Poetry*, similarly announced his "sweeping claim that *all* poetry is complex." Stauffer argued that "even the most seemingly simple poem secures its effect *as poetry* by complex means and associations. Conversely, to reduce any poem to a single mood, poetic device, or statement is to destroy it *as poetry*. A poem has not the simplicity of a machine; it has the complexity of a vital organism, of a person" (155). All art, under this view, is difficult, partly because it is self-enclosed; it has its own integrity as an aesthetic object (and not as something else).

As the texture of Stauffer's argument suggests, this universalist argument was made in ways that anticipated New Criticism, which developed a panoply of reading strategies to articulate how "the nature of poetic language invites obscurity" (O'Connor 1948, 227)—or, as I will suggest in my conclusion, to *make* all texts potentially difficult.[54] First, some argued, the kind of communication or expression that art used (emotional expression and other kinds of nonlogical meaning) resisted paraphrase, which as Stauffer argued, would "destroy it" as art. While this point has striking similarities to how I discussed meaning beyond language earlier in this chapter, I want here to stress the trajectory posited by the New Critical position on the "heresy of paraphrase." Rather than reaching to the accessibility of meaning beyond language, with which it has many similarities, the distrust of paraphrase pointed both to a professionalist concept of art as existing within its own domain, to be experienced on its own terms, and to the text's resistance. For difficulty's apologists this resistance was not inconsequential; the unparaphrasable nub at the heart of great poetry was central to it (just as in the visual arts many were arguing that those aspects that were not representational were essential to visual art). Indeed, the activity of paraphrase was seen by New Critics not just as limiting, but as damaging, even antithetical to what art was about. Paraphrase reduced art to a mere puzzle. John Crowe Ransom noted in 1947 that: "One familiar and curious consequence of paraphrasing a difficult text is the common critic's feeling that with this labor his responsibility has been fully discharged; and the general public is pretty sure to have that feeling. It is as if the poem were a truth done up in an anagram, waiting only to be deciphered" ([1947] 1984, 198).

The modernist understanding of metaphor is crucial to understanding the peculiar value attached to the unparaphrasable. As he has been several times already in this book, John Donne is a good starting point. Critics argued that Donne's metaphor, like that of difficult modernism, was not just decoration; it was necessary. In its opposition to the nineteenth century, difficult modernism stressed metaphor's necessity. Cleanth Brooks posited that a romantic sense of seeing metaphor as adornment rather than as necessity caused problems in understanding difficult modern poets. When they were understood as "ornament," Brooks wrote, the metaphors of modern poets "demean rather than adorn.... As illustration, they darken rather than illuminate" (1939, 4). For Brooks and others, metaphor—particularly its unparaphrasable character—was essential to poetry, and gave it its inherent difficulty.

Asserting difficulty as a *permanent* aesthetic value, one neither limited to modernism nor destined to disappear over time, had significant virtues. First, it turned modern difficulty into the latest moment in a long line of dif-

> In short, things that have their origin in the imagination or in the emotions very often take on a form that is ambiguous or uncertain. It is not possible to attach a single, rational meaning to such things without destroying the imaginative or emotional ambiguity or uncertainty that is inherent in them and that is why poets do not like to explain.
>
> —Wallace Stevens, 1948

ficulty, a tradition that readers already knew and had learned to read. Modern difficulty was thus not a bizarre and newly alienating form of art; it was inevitable. Second, the universalist argument not only made difficult modernism seem inevitable; when difficulty was seen as a permanent characteristic of all art, it became less interesting and explanatory to look at the unique social conditions that gave rise to difficult modernism. The modernist practice of asserting the universality of difficulty thus again attempted to pull difficulty out of its originating cultural conditions.

In this New Critical context, one in which the social aspects of art had little place, few readers recognized difficulty as a reading *practice*; for difficulty's proponents, difficulty was nothing more nor less than an inherent aspect of art. More typically, the sense that difficulty might be a reading strategy was used to attack the rising New Criticism as it spread its reading practices to nonmodernist texts. Writing to the *Saturday Review*, the Reverend Harry Taylor cajoled readers, grumbling that "frankly, isn't it about time we came down to earth. The really great poetry of the world is understandable, moving, quotable. Otherwise, by any sane standard, it would not be poetry. This modern craze to read deep meanings into drivel, and suggestions into obvious nonsense is just in line with our craziest art" (1949, 31). Difficulty, then, was not inevitable; it was a practice, one in which literary *critics* make work artificially difficult.[55]

Tilted Arc Meets Its Public

Fifty years after *Waiting for Godot*, the standard modern arguments about difficulty continue their work, as an examination of the controversy over Richard Serra's *Tilted Arc* demonstrates. Its history is instructive. From one point of view, 1985 was a great year for public art. In January of that year, the Reagan administration awarded one of the first thirteen Presidential Awards for Design Excellence to the Art in Architecture program (a branch of the General Services Administration [GSA] that was responsible for allocating one-half of 1 percent of all money spent on new government buildings to the creation of public sculpture). Pointing out that "when new works have sometimes met with puzzlement or hostility, they have usually come to be increasingly appreciated by their 'using' public," the citation commended the program for its "intelligent willingness to sustain potential risks." The award noted "Installations that may have been judged by the press, critics and others to be difficult to comprehend (or less than completely successful) are to be expected in such a courageous program and should be interpreted as an index of its continuing vitality" (Weyergraf-Serra and Buskirk 1988, 44).[56] Brave words, or more than a little ironic, given that from another angle, 1985 was a disaster, for it was the year that the controversy about Richard Serra's *Tilted Arc* boiled over.

Serra's work had been funded and approved in 1979 by the Art in Architecture program, along strictly professional guidelines. Critic Robert Storr notes that the work was selected by "an independent panel of professionals," and was finally approved after "extensive engineering studies and prolonged negotiations with the GSA's own design review panel." Nothing, it seems, could have been more bureaucratically proper. As Storr points out, though, "Given the relative blandness of much public sculpture and the intransigent if not confrontational nature of Serra's art, it was a remarkable, indeed risky undertaking for both the artist and his government patrons" (1985, 90). The confrontation began in 1981, immediately after the work, a 12-foot-high by 120-foot-long arc of two-and-a-half-inch thick rusting Cor-ten steel, was installed at Federal Plaza in New York City. The *New York Times* characterized *Tilted Arc*, which traversed the plaza, as "an awkward, bullying piece that may conceivably be the ugliest outdoor work of art in the city" (quoted in Moorman 1985, 13). Some who worked in Federal Plaza soon made their discontentment felt, writing letters to the editor and circulating a petition that collected 1,300 signatures, demanding removal of the offensive art.

There are many possible ways to understand this conflict, but a particularly useful starting point is in how Serra conceived the work's function, a conception that is loaded with the values of the difficulty debate. Before the work was installed Serra reported that "The Federal Building site didn't interest me at first." According to Serra, the difficulty arose from what was typically expected from the site: "It's a 'pedestal site' in front of a public building. There's a fountain on the plaza, normally you would expect a sculpture next to the fountain, so the ensemble would embellish the building." In short, it was not the kind of place that beckoned one of America's most austere, uncompromising sculptors. Yet Serra soon found a way to proceed, by working against the expectations generated by the site. In an interview prior to the construction of *Tilted Arc* he noted:

> I've found a way to dislocate or alter the decorative function of the plaza and actively bring people into the sculpture's context. I plan to build a piece that's 120 feet long in

a semi-circular plaza. It will cross the entire space, blocking the view from the street to the courthouse and vice versa. It will be twelve feet high and will tilt one foot toward the Federal building and the Courthouse. It will be a very slow arc that will encompass the people who walk on the plaza in its volume.... After the piece is created, the space will be understood primarily as a function of the sculpture. (Interview with Douglas Crimp, see Serra 1980, 168)

Now, this is more than just artistic hyperbole about making one's mark. Serra's position on the role of site-specific art was carefully considered, and arose from his belief that site-specific work takes a critical stance toward the context it occupies. As Serra noted: "Site-specific works invariably manifest a value judgment about the larger social and political context of which they are a part. Based on the interdependence of work and site, site-specific works address the content and context of their site critically.... It is the explicit intention of site-specific works to alter their context" (1980, 168). As he was to note at the height of the *Tilted Arc* controversy, such an interaction, requiring a change in people's perceptual activity, "may startle some people" (Weyergraf-Serra and Buskirk 1988, 65).

In 1984 a new regional commissioner for the GSA, William Diamond, was appointed, and he set to work reigniting the initial controversy, which had cooled considerably after the initial furor. Diamond first attempted to have *Tilted Arc* relocated, a move that Serra, insisting on the work's site specificity, strenuously resisted. Upon hearing of the proposed move, Serra wrote to the Art in Architecture program, arguing that *Tilted Arc* "is a site-specific work and as such not to be relocated. To remove the work is to destroy the work" (Weyergraf-Serra and Buskirk 1988, 40). As Serra testified, "I don't make portable objects; I don't make works that can be relocated or site-adjusted" (Weyergraf-Serra and Buskirk 1988, 64). Diamond also placed a petition in the two buildings that adjoined the site, a petition whose signatories claimed to "find no artistic merit in the Serra artwork" (quoted in Senie 1989, 298). Aided by Judge Edward D. Re, chief justice of the U.S. Court of International Trade, who worked in one of the adjoining buildings, the controversy was soon back in the news and culminated in three days of hearings in March 1985—hearings presided over by Diamond and attended by many art world celebrities, including art critic Rosalind Krauss, art dealer Leo Castelli, Museum of Modern Art director William Rubin, artists Donald Judd and Frank Stella, and composer Philip Glass. Given the public nature of the debate and the time that had elapsed since protests were first launched, it was natural for art critic Patricia Phillips to quip that the hearing was a time "during which positions and sentiments were publicly confirmed" (1985, 101). Testimony at the hearings was heated, revealing how many of the sentiments about difficulty that were operative near the beginning of the twentieth century were still in good health near the century's end.

While a few of Serra's opponents argued for more time to understand the work, most of those speaking against *Tilted Arc* had two basic arguments against it. The first was that the work was shocking, twisted, ugly. His eye on the cameras, congressional representative Ted Weiss noted that the work's "appearance of a rusted metal wall" added to its "shock effect." Going on, Weiss claimed that "many who first viewed *Tilted Arc* regarded it as an abandoned piece of construction material" (Weyergraf-Serra and Buskirk 1988, 113). Other public figures lined up. Paul Goldstein, representing Manhattan County Board 1, called the plaza a "potentially wonderful area" that had been "turned into a virtual no-man's-land" by the sculpture, which "contributed to the public's rejection of this space." Indeed, Goldstein went on, "Many people are even bewildered when they are told that this large metal structure is not a piece of leftover construction material, but is, in fact, a piece of art" (126–27). Norman Steinlauf, a worker at Federal Plaza, told the hearings that *Tilted Arc* "represent[s] an irritant and an impediment" (110). One speaker, referring to *Tilted Arc* as a "so-called sculpture," ended his testimony with what ought to be done with Serra's supporters: "you can bring up buses, take them over to Bellevue Hospital and sign them into a mental ward. That is where they belong" (118–19). Another speaker attacked the art establishment that approved the installation of the sculpture: "These artists are part of a larger, but still small but tightly organized and very controlled clique of galleries, curators and critics. They all write about each other, recommend and promote each other and, as in the case of the Serra sculpture, they sit on each other's boards and advise and give grants and monies to each other." The speaker went on to grumble that such groups "intimidate" the public with "a smoke screen of intellectual mumbo-jumbo about art," whose purpose is "to make you feel you know nothing, should have no opinion, and just generally get rid of you" (119–20).

It is in support of testimony like this that the second major objection to the piece was raised, that *Tilted Arc* worked against the wishes of the public. One speaker argued that "those who support it do not work at 26 Federal Plaza"; another, that the work was "hostile both to its environment and hostile to the public" (Weyergraf-Serra and Buskirk 1988, 118, 123). Congressman Weiss, in a flourish of democratic piety, ended his testimony with the argument that "The rights of a large number of people who live and work here have been overlooked and ignored. I would like to see their rights restored" (115).

Statements in support of Serra's work can be seen within the context of Serra's later legal challenges to the removal of the work, which argued that, on the basis of the work's site-specificity, to move it was to destroy it, and therefore to violate Serra's right to free speech and the government's moral rights not to destroy the art it had bought. Yet, while these other arguments

> From the time it was built it was hard to see
> just what it was supposed to be.
> A windbreaker was the general guess
> or a tilted wonder more or less.
> We soon found it was none of the above
> but a great work of art we would grow to love.
> Unfortunately it just didn't work out that way
> but has dampened our spirits every day.
> It has turned into a hulk of rusty steel
> and clearly, at least to us, doesn't have any appeal.
> It might have artistic value but just not here,
> so put it in some other place where it should appear
> and for those of us at the plaza I would like to say,
> please do us a favor and take it away.
>
> —Hank Perveslin, employee, U.S. Department of Education, at the GSA hearing, 1985

show that the *Tilted Arc* controversy was not just about difficulty, without difficulty, none of this would have happened, and the other arguments wouldn't have the timbre they acquired. (It is difficult to imagine a massive public protest against a manifestly banal work of art.)

One defense of the work was that of professionalism, with art historian Benjamin Buchloh and others suggesting that Diamond and his supporters were incompetent to judge the art of professionals. As did Congressman Weiss, Buchloh insisted that he was on the side of democracy, arguing that "the successful operation of the institutions of democratic bourgeois society depends on the competence and specialization of its members in all fields." Using the analogy of doctors and judges, Buchloh warned that "When these professional standards are abandoned on a large scale throughout society, we would speak of chaos and anarchy" (Weyergraf-Serra and Buskirk 1988, 90, 91). Sculptor Claes Oldenburg also defended the "expertise" of the artist, warning that the removal of *Tilted Arc* would "symbolize the giving-in to escapist motives and notions of inoffensive 'beauty'" (78, 79). Testifying at the hearing, Marion Javits, reading a statement from former New York Senator Jacob K. Javits, argued that the removal of the sculpture would be "discreditable ... to the development of serious artists" (98). Writing some years after the hearings, Serra quoted a 1903 ruling by Justice Oliver Wendell Holmes that "it would be a dangerous undertaking for persons trained only in the law to constitute themselves final judges of the worth of

> Sculpture which may be provocative to our eyes can be seen more clearly by those who come after us. I recognize the difficulty of your position, but I hope that in the interest of American art for future generations that you will let this piece stand and permit time and history to judge it.
>
> —Joan Mondale, wife of former Vice President Walter Mondale, at the GSA hearing, 1985

pictorial illustrations, outside the narrowest and most obvious limits. At the one extreme some works ... would be sure to miss appreciation. Their novelty would make them repulsive until the public had learned the language in which their author spoke" (quoted in Serra 1989, 43).

Many at the hearing argued that the work needed more time for its public to get used to it. Museum of Modern Art director William Rubin, for example, noted that "truly challenging works of art require a period of time before their artistic language can be understood by a broader public" (Weyergraf-Serra and Buskirk 1988, 101). Lurking in much of this testimony, however, was a more explosive issue: the work's uncomfortableness, a discomfort that was seen by both the work's defenders and its critics as central to it. As noted earlier, Serra meant his work to "dislocate or alter the decorative function of the plaza," and surmised that site-specific works like *Tilted Arc* "address the content and context of their site critically." The language of more than a few at the hearings testified to the anxiety raised by this critical function. Echoing another witness, who had claimed that "good new art ... lives at the edge of human experience" (92–93), Victor Ganz, chairman of the Battery Park City fine arts committee, pleaded that "Everybody knows and almost everybody forgets that the art that discomforts us the most eventually becomes our proudest possession. Please, let us remember and let us collaborate in avoiding this backward step. Let us have the courage to be elitist enough to be truly democratic" ("Tilted Arc Hearing" 1985, 99). Roberta Smith noted that *Tilted Arc* "is a confrontational, aggressive piece in a confrontational, aggressive town, in a part of the city where confrontations in court are particularly the order of the day." Going on, Smith noted that *Tilted Arc* "is not wide entertainment and it is not an escape from reality, but it does ask you to examine its own reality, its scale, its material, its tilted sweep, and so the other things around it' (Weyergraf-Serra and Buskirk 1988, 103). Critic Robert Storr noted that *Tilted Arc* "was meant to actively subvert" its social context, governed by "the tyranny of architects and the bland conventions of most of public art" (92).

Several art critics argued that *Tilted Arc*'s revolution took an aesthetically powerful, but socially unfortunate form. As Patricia Phillips summarized in *Artforum*, *Tilted Arc* was as dehumanizing as the totalitarian environment it attacked. According to Phillips, Serra had created a "behavioral autocracy": "Everyone who walks through the plaza has been condemned to participate in the artist's investigation of the expectation of passage in an open public space." That authoritarianism resulted in "the failure of Serra's work as criticism," for it was "as awkward and sadistic as the environment he attacks" (1985, 101). Writing several years after the destruction of *Tilted Arc*, Gregg Horowitz agreed, noting that while "Serra did not cause the deadness and unusability of Federal Plaza, . . . he did make it manifest" (1996, 13).

This revolutionary aspect of the work made it inevitable that those who did not like it were condemned as reactionary by those who did. Thus, Benjamin Buchloh generously allowed that "everybody should have the right to detest contemporary art—especially art like that of Richard Serra that addresses the condition of alienation." However, Buchloh distrusted the politics of turning such personal "prejudice" "into public judgment or political action" (Weyergraf-Serra and Buskirk 1988, 90). At the hearing Douglas Crimp quoted *Tilted Arc*'s nemesis Judge Re, who had written the previous year to the GSA, "Finally, but by no means of minor importance is the loss of efficient security surveillance. The placement of this wall across the plaza obscures the view of security personnel who have no way of knowing what is taking place on the other side of the wall." To this, Crimp responded "Well, I would submit that it is we—the public—who are on the other side of the wall and it is we who Judge Re so fears and despises that he wants that wall torn down in order that we may be properly subjected to surveillance" (29, 74).

As Harriet Senie noted several years later, this response to *Tilted Arc* was an inherent reaction to difficult art. Senie cites the famous testimony of Vicki O'Dougherty, a physical security specialist for the Federal Protection and Safety Division of the GSA. O'Dougherty had testified that the sculpture's shape resulted in "a blast wall effect," which made it "comparable to devices which are used to vent explosive forces." *Tilted Arc*, she claimed "could vent an explosion, both upwards and in an angle toward both buildings" (Weyergraf-Serra and Buskirk 1988, 116). For Senie, this testimony, while representing the extreme of reactions to *Tilted Arc*, "did underline a recurring theme of a perceived threat of physical violence associated with the sculpture" (1989, 299). Senie noted that these perceived threats (another participant feared the sculpture could hide rapists) were part of a larger reaction to art and difficulty: "Although these and comments like them are initially amusing, they reveal that serious issues are at stake for those who utter them. Feelings of helplessness frequently result in expressions of hostility. Over and over again, we see the public rendered helpless and hostile by art they don't or can't understand" (299).

The furor created an environment of great journalistic interest. The press wanted easy stories; *People* magazine headlined its story with "A Rusty Eyesore or a Work of Art: Sculptor Richard Serra Defends His Controversial 'Tilted Arc'" (April 1, 1985, 140). More centrally, the press portrayed *Tilted Arc* as a story of the people rising against effete artists and bureaucratic bungling—never mind that 120 of the 180 people testifying argued to keep the sculpture, or that about 85 percent of the letters to the GSA about *Tilted Arc* were in its defense (Senie 1989, 299). Diamond also apparently wanted an unambiguous story. As early as the end of the hearing's first day he declared in a television interview his wish to have the sculpture removed. So, it is not surprising that after two more days of testimony Diamond's panel recommended that *Tilted Arc* be moved to a new location, a recommendation that a later National Endowment for the Arts panel decided would destroy the work's integrity. Eventually though, on March 15, 1989, after several further legal battles, *Tilted Arc* was—depending on whom you quote— either put in storage or destroyed. Diamond was quoted in the *New York Post* two days later as saying "This is a day for the people to rejoice because now the plaza returns rightfully to the people" (quoted in Serra 1989, 35). A few months later, posters appeared announcing that July 6, 1989, would see a "special rededication of Federal Plaza." Diamond was present and announced "It will be a real pleasure to celebrate this anniversary with the opening of this concert series and the return of Federal Plaza to the local workers and people of this community" (quoted in Senie 1989, 301).

As it did in *Tilted Arc,* sanctimony like Diamond's has always played a part in the realpolitik of public art. But it should not be allowed to hide difficulty's tremendous affective consequences, which put into play a tangled mass of things such as anxiety, anger, morality, professionalism, celebrations of democratic principles, and even state security. The success of difficulty as an aesthetic force depends on harnessing those consequences, and, as was the case in the first half of the twentieth century, the consequences in the 1980s were very hard to manage.

CHAPTER 4

Difficulty, Vigor, and Pleasure

> But no person capable of sympathy and the love of beauty need be frightened away from poetry by the abracadabra of critics. For poetry is not, after all, an intricate puzzle game for sophisticated intellects. It is, like music, like sculpture, a natural, joyous, life-sharing art, concerned with feelings that we all share and appealing to sympathies engendered and fostered by the imagination.
> —Marguerite Wilkinson

> This tradition took its rise in the period of the great Romantics. It involved a prejudice against recognising as poetry anything that was not in the most obvious sense of Milton's formula, "simple, sensuous and passionate." Poetry, it was assumed, must be the direct expression of simple emotions. The "poetical" emotions were of a limited class: the tender, the exalted, the noble, the poignant—in general, the sympathetic.... Wit, play of intellect, stress of cerebral muscle had no place; they could only hinder the correct response, which was to be "moved."
> —F. R. Leavis

In their large arguments, presented in the previous chapter, modernism's defenders did not argue directly about difficulty's affect, often sliding by the visceral anxiety that accompanied difficulty. But difficult modernism, if it was to convince a larger readership, required not just large cultural arguments; it also needed to present an affect of similar weight to those visceral reactions. In particular, difficult modernism needed to deal with pleasure, a central affect of art, and one that conservative readers argued difficult modernism had destroyed. Pleasure was a nub of irritation in modernism, for high moderns had to work against the common assertion that resulted from anxious reactions to difficulty, the assertion that the pleasures of difficult modernism were at best trivial, akin to those of solving a crossword puzzle.

Unlock the cypher and you've solved the poem. High moderns approached pleasure in two ways, both of which worked with the inevitable anxiety surrounding difficulty. One approach was to attack then-dominant ideas of pleasure as being passive and irrelevant. Indeed, modernism's apologists often seemed opposed to pleasure—as Richard Poirier argues, "Modernism happened when reading got to be grim" ([1978] 1992, 105). But high moderns also used what was eventually to become a much more successful tool for making difficult modernism central to art in the twentieth century. Unable (or unwilling) to shake off many of the traditional aspects of pleasure, they redefined it and claimed that difficult texts were important providers of this pleasure. In the face of difficulty's anxiety, they claimed that the difficulties of the modern text were not weak and passive pleasures; they were direct and virile, heroic and muscular. This bracing quality of difficulty was essential to the high modernist sense of pleasure, which had a vigorous ethical claim to it, a vigor redolent of Victorian values.

In a 1923 comparative review in *Poetry*, editor Harriet Monroe set T. S. Eliot's *The Waste Land* next to Lew Sarett's *The Box of God*. Eliot's poem was already one that people had noticed; *Time* magazine in the same month ran a short article that cheerily harpooned the cultural heft of it and *Ulysses* ("Shantih" 1923), and it had by this time also won the *Dial* prize for the best poem published the past year. In commenting on the prize, *Dial* noted in 1922 that Eliot was "an exceedingly active influence on contemporary letters" (Announcement of *Dial* Prize [1922] 1982, 136). The *New York Times Book Review* concurred; noting the awarding of the *Dial* prize, the anonymous reviewer wrote that "Mr. Eliot's work is marked by an intense cerebral quality and a compact music that has practically established a movement among the younger men" (1922, 136). This is not to say that the poem sailed into triumph unopposed. While it was hailed by Edmund Wilson as a poem that speaks "for the starvation of a whole civilisation," it had scandalized many other reviewers, one of whom called it "a mad medley ... a smoke-screen of anthropological and literary erudition," and went on to argue that the poem "just is, to all but anthropologists and *literati*, so much waste paper" ([1922] 1982, 144; Powell [1923] 1982, 194, 195).

Sarett's title poem had also won a prize, the Helen Haire Levinson Prize, which was awarded to the year's best American contribution to *Poetry* magazine. It was not a surprise, then, that Sarett's book occasioned a review in *Poetry*. But this was not mere boosterism; Sarett was recognized as a serious poet in other venues as well. The author of several books of poetry, Sarett had won respectful reviews in magazines other than *Poetry*. His poem "Maple Sugar Chant," which appeared in his *Box of God*, was praised by David Morton in the *Bookman* as "simple and direct utterance, exalted beyond self-consciousness by a fine and stirring passion"; in a similar vein, the anonymous reviewer for the *New York Times Book Review* called the expression of nature in the book's title poem to be "profoundly sincere, and the expression of it is genuine and sincere" (1923, 765; "Pushcarts," 1922). As late as 1930 Bruce Weirick of the University of Illinois pronounced Sarett's *Box of God* a poem that "would indeed adorn any decade able to produce it," and went on to claim that "In this poem Mr. Sarett definitely announces his arrival among America's permanent poets" (1930, 203). Sarett also was published in *Broom*, an expatriate magazine located in Rome and clearly connected to art of this century, publishing art by Picasso, Man Ray, and Matisse, and writing by Wallace Stevens, Amy Lowell, Conrad Aiken, and Sherwood Anderson, to name just a few. Sarett would become part of *Broom*'s editorial board, in which position he rubbed shoulders with Alfred Kreymborg and Harold Loeb, the model for Jake Barnes's nemesis in *The Sun Also Rises*.

Monroe thus reviewed together two texts that had claims for, and which she believed deserved, cultural prominence. She called both poems "important," and ended her review with the claim that both poems succeeded at what they attempted: "they do excellent-well what they set out to do, and they suggest more than they say—they invite to thought and dreams" (1923, 325, 330). That is not to say Monroe saw the poems as equally valuable and springing from a single vision of the world. Calling Eliot's poem "kaleidoscopic, profuse, a rattle and rain of colors that fall somehow into place," she diagnosed it as a symptom of modern times. According to Monroe, *The Waste Land* "gives us the malaise of our time, its agony, its conviction of futility, its wild dance on an ash-heap before a clouded and distorted mirror." Turning to textual evidence to illustrate the poem's theme, Monroe found the poem's central assertion in Eliot's phrase "I will show you fear in a handful of dust." Monroe argued that the poem "shows us confusion and dismay and disintegration, the world crumbling to pieces before our eyes and patching itself with desperate gayety into new and strangely irregular forms." But, Monroe pointed out, *The Waste Land* was a selective portrayal, congenial primarily to one specific group. Within this poem, Monroe asserted, Eliot portrayed the cultural life of "what many an indoor thinker thinks about life today, what whole groups of impassioned intellectuals are saying to each other as the great ball spins" (326).

Monroe's coolness ended when she turned to Sarett's poem—not surprising, since she had awarded it the Helen Haire Levinson Prize. In contrast to the impassioned intellectuals represented by Eliot's poem, Sarett was a man for whom "the miasma which afflicts Mr. Eliot is as remote a speculative conceit, as futile a fritter of mental confectionery, as Lyly's euphemism [*sic*] must have been to Elizabethan sailors" (1923, 327). Monroe enthusiastically quoted from Sarett's poem the following lines, which are narrated through the voice of a "long-dead Indian guide":

> Somebody's dere.... He's walk-um in dose cloud....
> You see-um? Look! He's mak'-um for hees woman
> De w'ile she sleep, dose t'ing she want-um most—
> Blue dress for dancing. You see, my frien'? ... ain't?
> He's t'rowing on de blanket of dose sky
> Dose plenty-plenty handfuls of white stars;
> He's sewing on dose plenty teet' of elk,
> Dose shiny lookin-glass and plenty beads.
> Somebody's dere ... somet'ing he's in dere ...
>
> Sh-sh-sh-sh! Somet'ing's dere!.... You hear-um? ain't?
> Somebody—somebody's dere, calling ... calling ...
> I go ... I go ... me! ... me ... I go....

Seventy-five years after Sarett wrote them, readers may have some difficulty understanding what Monroe admired about these lines, which to my ears, at least, manage to come across as both well meaning and bizarre. Be that as it may, there were good reasons why Sarett's poem should not be dismissed. Sarett deserved serious attention not only because of his recognized stature as a poet, but also because of the premises of Monroe's argument, premises consistent with her argument about *The Waste Land*, premises shared by many readers of her time. Sarett's poem, too, was a manifestation of its age; Monroe presented Sarett as the ideal American poet, living an optimistic life of action, of which his poetry was only one facet. According to Monroe, Sarett "last summer, while taking his vacation as a forest ranger of the government, chased a pair of bandits through Glacier Park for forty-eight hours alone, and single-handed brought them back to camp for trial" (168–69). Sarett was someone who knew the world; according to Monroe "[h]e could talk with Thomas A. Edison, or perhaps with a sequoia or a skyscraper" (329).

Eliot, Monroe thought, could not meet this ideal, for Eliot was out of touch with the modern world. By contrast, the kind of people represented by Sarett's poem had an important social function, for they were "creating that modern world which the half-aware and over-informed poets of London and Montmartre so darkly doom" (Monroe 1923, 327). Monroe claimed that Eliot's world differed vastly from Sarett's: "Mr. Eliot lives with specialists—poets of idle hands and legs and supersensitized brains; varied by a bank clerk routine with second-rate minds. One can not imagine him consorting with heroes or highwaymen, or getting on intimate terms with Thomas A. Edison if he were granted a confidential hour" (328). Monroe's central point was that Eliot was a pessimist, removed from the constructive energies of his time; Sarett, by contrast, was an optimist. While both poets wrote acceptable forms of pessimistic and optimistic poetry, Monroe clearly preferred Sarett's optimism. From Eliot and his pessimism, Monroe claimed, it was "hopeless to expect an all-round great poem of our time" (328).

Pleasure

But outside the pages of *Poetry* the comparison did not stop in Glacier Park, with Sarett triumphantly squatting by a campfire. Within seven years after the publication of *The Waste Land*, Eliot was a decidedly more major figure than Sarett. Bonamy Dobrée enthused "I would be prepared to lay odds that the year 1922, which saw *The Waste Land*, will prove to be as important a year in the history of the development of English poetry as the year 1798, in which Wordsworth and Coleridge produced their transforming volume, *Lyrical Ballads*" (1929, 130).[1] However, despite its portrayal as a zero sum game, this is not simply a story of two worlds colliding, with writers on opposing sides having no values in common. Although they developed their arguments with different emphases and nuances, readers on either side of the difficulty debate shared some starting principles. Both, for example, made vigor a sign of aesthetic and moral value. Thus, as did Monroe for Sarett, Dobrée claimed for Eliot the macho high ground. Eliot's difficulty was important because it was real art, which according to many readers and to Dobrée had some inescapable characteristics: "Art is not a gentle soporific, an escape, an ornament: it is a terrifying thing that must be grappled with, overcome, absorbed" (127). As a difficult writer, Eliot, too, lived strenuously, dangerously, authentically—only, Sarett's *life* of action was transmogrified into Eliot's *mind* of action. While according to high modernism's proponents Eliot was a more important writer than Sarett because he was "vigorous" and "serious" in a way that Sarett wasn't, Dobrée's aesthetic yet shares fundamental principles with Monroe's.

Thus, for readers of all allegiances, art at the beginning of the twentieth century was made by manly men. As did Monroe's version, high modernism's vigor had recognizable contours. In the introduction to his anthology *Prize Poems 1913–1929*, Mark Van Doren, after claiming that all good, new poetry was difficult, asserted that "Good poetry requires a discipline in the reader. . . . It cannot be read by a mind asleep" (1930a, 10). Claims for difficulty's virility ranged from Marianne Moore archly suggesting that Eliot might want "to publish a fangless edition of 'Prufrock and Other Observations' for the gentle reader who likes his literature, like breakfast coffee or grapefruit, sweetened" ([1918] 1986c, 35), to F. R. Leavis's more strenuous assertion that Yeats's new verse, which "belongs to the actual, waking world, and is in the idiom and movement of modern speech," was "spare, hard and sinewy and in tone sardonic," or that the rhythms of Ronald Bottrall, although "difficult at first," had great value, for "they are subtle, varied and sure: he uses the body and sinew of the language" ([1932] 1960, 42, 209). Indeed, readers claimed difficulty's virility so loudly that their assertions look less like the marshaling of argument than like exhibitions of machismo.

But despite their shared affection for machismo, Eliot's modernism *did* eventually win the day and Sarett's did not. How did this happen? The change in high culture, although not inevitable, was made more likely because pleasure, as it was articulated in Sarett's modernism, was vulnerable. Initially, this might not seem to be the case; at the turn of the century pleasure seemed a robust aesthetic. For most readers pleasure was central; to them it was inconceivable that a great work of art would not have pleasure as its central effect. Although Eliot himself never connected pleasure to difficulty, and most often associated pleasure with meaning beyond language, he would on occasion make the expected noises about pleasure, arguing that "there is no doubt that a poet wishes to give pleasure, to entertain or divert people; and he should normally be glad to be able to feel that the entertainment or diversion is enjoyed by as large and various a number of people as possible" ([1933] 1964, 31–32).

So, pleasure had shared adherents. But they rarely subjected it to scrutiny; while pleasure showed up in differing discussions of modernism, people rarely defined it. Pleasure had the grand but ghostly presence that Mark Van Doren invoked when he claimed that difficult poetry "gives one of the amplest and acutest of all pleasures, the pleasure that there is in poetry itself" (1930a, 14). As it is yet today, "pleasure" was a wobbly term; its wobble was inevitable partly because pleasure was acknowledged to be subjective, and it was described not so much as art's property as its *affect*. Yet although pleasure had only a vaguely agreed upon definition, it had predictable inflections. These various inflections of pleasure tended to make it more smoothly used as a counter to difficulty than as a promoter of it. Pleasure had qualities that allowed traditionalists to write about it with less anxiety than would radicals, qualities that would make unproblematic for them assertions such as that pleasurable works are simple, and (as my next chapter will show) that simplicity is the most effective tool for giving rise to beauty and pleasure. Generally, the more that readers distrusted difficult writing, the more they buttressed their arguments with these points.

The more conservative one's tastes, then, the more emphatic the insistence upon pleasure. Difficult modernism was consequently a problem, since for many readers it seemed to block reading pleasure, creating anxiety and irritation instead. Untermeyer's fellow anthologist Marguerite Wilkinson argued against difficult modernism's assault on pleasure by its practitioners and critics, asserting that "no person capable of sympathy and the love of beauty need be frightened away from poetry by the abracadabra of critics. For poetry is not, after all, an intricate puzzle game for sophisticated intellects. It is, like music, like sculpture, a natural, joyous, life-sharing art, concerned with feelings that we all share and appealing to sympathies engendered and fostered by the imagination" (1919, 9).

Difficulty, Vigor, and Pleasure   151

> The reader does know because he enjoys it. If you enjoy you understand if you understand you enjoy. What you mean by understanding is being able to turn it into other words but that is not necessary. To like a football game is to understand it in the football way.
>
> —Gertrude Stein, in response to a 1934 interviewer's question about the meaning of her phrase "Pigeons on the grass alas"

Most strikingly, the pleasure derived from a text was distinguished by what was missing in the experience of reading that text, by a *lack*. Not only were pleasurable texts not rhetorical (or "deliberate"), they also had no extraneous "stuff" in them; they were direct and not tangled. For many readers, aesthetic pleasure was more about what was *not* present than by what *was*. The first, immediately noticeable aspect of the lack that gave rise to pleasure was found in the act of reading itself, in which the outside world should fade away. There was a general consensus about this; even readers most sympathetic to difficult writing agreed that the pleasurable text was best pursued in a physical location removed from the world. In a positive 1940 review of Joyce's recent writing (practically titled "How to Read *Finnegans Wake*"), Walter Rybert argued that reading *Finnegans Wake* properly required the following conditions: "Be 'given time to read' is one, or 'take it easy.' It can't be done while hanging on a strap or sitting in a railway station. You've got to be where you won't be ashamed to laugh out loud, murmur 'ah!' or satisfy the desire to read something of what you've just discovered to an appreciative listener, preferably feminine. An easy chair, nothing else to do, are essentials" ([1940] 1970, 731–32).[2] Distractions and social restraints on behavior had to go, leaving just the text, physical comfort, and a properly receptive audience at one's command.

Many readers transferred that sense of pleasure's minimalist requirements to the text itself, in which a reader's pleasure was hampered by anything "extra" left lying around. And this is where ambivalent readers thought many difficult texts ran into trouble. David Daiches, in his *Poetry and the Modern World*, found much to admire in *The Waste Land*. But yet, Daiches argued, a central problem remained, for the poem's myth-based structure was "too complex for any reader to be able to read the poem fully at any given time." Daiches went on: "our enjoyment is frequently spoiled by our tripping over cultural lumber that has been deliberately left lying about by the poet" (1940, 124). John Middleton Murry complained of *Ulysses* that "the curse of nimiety, of too-muchness, hangs over it as a whole" ([1922] 1970, 197), and Lewis

Bettany, writing in the London *Daily News* about Woolf's *Jacob's Room*, noted that the novel "is so full of parentheses and suppressions, so tedious in its rediscoveries of the obvious, and so marred by its occasional lapses into indelicacy, that I found great difficulty in discovering what it was all about" ([1922] 1975, 98). The pleasure-crushing excesses of difficult writing provoked some astonishing responses. In a startling reading of Stein, Wyndham Lewis wrote: "Gertrude Stein's prose-song is a cold, black suet-pudding. We can represent it as a cold suet-roll of fabulously reptilian length. Cut it at any point, it is the same thing: the same heavy, sticky opaque mass all through, and all along. It is weighted, projected, with a sibylline urge. It is mournful and monstrous, composed of dead and inanimate material. It is all fat, without nerve. Or the evident vitality that informs it is vegetable rather than animal. Its life is a low-grade, if tenacious, one, of the sausage, by-the-yard, variety" ([1927] 1970, 55).

To use a less glutinous image, the difficult text, then, left extra "lumber" lying around. Readers described this excess as being of two kinds. First, there was difficulty of excessive structure, of technique. An unidentified reviewer of William Faulkner's *Absalom, Absalom!* argued that Faulkner's technique of using "negatives of words—such as 'not-husband,' 'not-people,' 'not-language,' 'un-amaze' . . . recalls the acrobatic antics of the sleazy intellectuals who used to write for *transition*, that egomaniac's dream, some years ago." While such writing would "gain the adulation of weakish ladies and gentlemen who adore anything they can't understand," its technique was not an inherent problem. The reviewer went on to argue that while Faulkner's technical innovations could have some merit "if they simplified the reading, if they rendered the story more lucid, if they clarified the text, or heightened the emotional content"—that simplification does not happen here. Instead, the innovations "make reading difficult, they becloud the outlines of the story, they encase the details in a fog, and they add nothing to the understanding of the thought processes" (M.L., [1937] 1995, 62).

But the extra material that littered the difficult text and tripped up pleasure was not just the work's technical features; it was also at times the amount of *knowledge* required to understand it. Early in his lifelong grappling with T. S. Eliot, Louis Untermeyer wrote of the "amazing virtuosity" with which Eliot "balances and tosses fragments of philosophy, history, science, tea-table gossip, fetishes of literature." For Untermeyer, this extra material diminished the writing, a diminishment that was signaled by the makeup of the audience that liked it. According to Untermeyer, in response to Eliot's juggling "only the intellectuals applaud. Simplicity is more foreign to Eliot than the mountains of the moon. His recondite euphuisms twist their length through tortuous lines" (1924, 352). Such demands on readers' knowledge stymie aesthetic pleasure.

> He who does not take a thorough pleasure in a simple chord progression, well constructed, beautiful in its arrangement, does not love music; he who does not prefer the first "Prelude" in the *Well-Tempered Clavier* played without nuances, as the composer wrote it for the instrument, to the same prelude embellished with a passionate melody, does not love music; he who does not prefer a folk tune of a lovely character, or a Gregorian chant without any accompaniment to a series of dissonant and pretentious chords does not love music.
>
> —Camille Saint-Saëns, 1913

As a result of understanding the difficult text to be excessive in the ways outlined above, a dubious hierarchy was set in place. The unmediated *experience* of the text was more important or primary than the *knowledge* that one used in the reading process. Thus, anthologist Marguerite Wilkinson argued "poetry should not be analyzed until it has been enjoyed. Like religion, it should come to people first of all as an experience" (1923, 3). In his career-long attempt to establish a canon of homegrown, populist authors over internationalist expatriates, Untermeyer claimed that domestic authors had set in motion a renaissance of reading practices, that readers of what Untermeyer called the "new" poetry (by which he meant the work of such writers as Frost, Sandburg, Lindsay, and the Imagists) "discovered that for the enjoyment of poetry it was no longer necessary to have at their elbows a dictionary of rare words and classical references; they were not required to be acquainted with Latin legendry and the minor love-affairs of the lesser Greek divinities." As it was for Monroe's Sarett, for these readers "Life was their glossary, not literature. The new work spoke to them of what they rarely had heard expressed; it was not only closer to their soil but nearer to their souls" (Untermeyer 1930, 16).[3]

This experience of pleasure, in tune with the concepts of lack that surrounded discussions of pleasure, was often described as a passive activity. In aesthetic discussions, readers first signaled this passivity in the typical syntax of their descriptions of the reading process. In discussions of pleasure, particularly conservative discussions, the artwork typically is the agent, while the reader is the object of that action. As often, readers used the passive voice to describe the experience of pleasure, as when Marguerite Wilkinson claimed that "poetry should not be analyzed until it has been enjoyed" (1923, 3). This grammatical construction set one in line for a quiescent reading activity, one in which the work of art, acting upon the reader, was the agent. The reader was not the hero; the reader was almost invisible. This belief was supported

> Works of great originality, the result of long labor on the part of superior mind, are not grasped in a moment by hasty, lesser folk. This is not ground for despair.
>
> —"The Editors," *transition*, vol. 1, 1927

by the commonsense conviction that whatever the experience of art was, it was initiated by the artwork, whose agenda controlled the experience. Not surprisingly, this belief was relatively widespread, not limited to a conservative agenda. At the height of his career as the grand man of modernism, Eliot would write of what happens when "we are moved by a poem" (1942, 456). At the more conservative end of the spectrum, William Payne, reviewing Robert Frost's first book of poetry, claimed of its contents that "In their simple phrasing and patent sincerity, his songs give us the sort of pleasure that we have in those of the 'Shropshire Lad' of Mr. Housman" ([1913] 1977, 5). Payne, of course, attached his passive reading experience to a very different sort of text than Eliot would, but the two share a starting premise: the text initiates the aesthetic experience, which can occur only if the reader submits to the text.

As the grammar suggests, many readers understood this kind of pleasure as something that came unbidden. Harold Monro, in his introduction to the 1920 *An Anthology of Recent Poetry*, noted that the "first object of poetry is to give pleasure," and then made the following claim: "Pleasure is various, but it cannot exist where the emotions or the imagination have not been powerfully stirred. Whether it be called sensual or intellectual, pleasure cannot be willed" (1920a, v). In this unbidden experience of pleasure, giving some sense of presence to the reader's experience of the artwork was tricky, particularly if you valued difficult writing. In the introduction to his anthology of modern poetry, Hermann Peschmann argued that poetry "asks the reader to meet it half-way; to make some effort to enter into the imaginative or emotional experience of the poet: to seek to apprehend the essence of the poetic experience rather than to comprehend its every detail. But the materials for a full appreciation and enjoyment must at least be latent in the poem if the reader will but surrender himself to it" (1950, xlii). In his *Sense and Poetry* John Sparrow argued that Yeats's "The Cap and Bells" "only seems obscure if we try to interpret what we should be content to enjoy" (1934, 87). As befits his generally conservative stance, Sparrow put the work of interpretation and pleasure at odds: contentment, not exertion, leads to pleasure. This quiescence sits uneasily next to assertions of vigor, both in Monroe's version of modernism and that of the high modernists. That unease would have large consequences for the formation of the modern canon. The opposition between "interpretation" and "contentment" also points to something important about reading practices and the relationship of difficulty to interpretation: interpretation tries to do *more* than what contentment does. Sparrow, a few pages later, repeated the hierarchy: "Modern literature, we have seen, is most often called obscure because its readers seek to understand what they should be content to feel. They think that the writer is trying to tell them something, when in fact he is only anxious that they should enjoy listening to him" (1934, 90). The more the work required interpretation, the less pleasurable it was.

Difficulty's adherents, particularly when they worked with ideas of the sublime and of meaning beyond language, suggested a reading process that also had many affinities with default notions of aesthetic pleasure. Many readers asserted that understanding difficulty was like receiving grace: you just had to be receptive. One had to be passive in order to experience this kind of meaning and to receive pleasure from it. This kind of advice for understanding modernism was everywhere: Mabel Dodge (1913, 174) suggested "letting one's reason sleep for an instant" while looking at Picasso; a writer for *The Week-End Review* advised reading Auden's *Ode to my Pupils* "as passively as possible ... without letting intellect interfere" (G. R. Mitchison, quoted in Sparrow 1934, 152); and a reviewer of *Finnegans Wake* argued that "To understand it one has, in truth, only to allow himself to be carried and to descend the course" (Pelorson, [1939] 1970, 682).[4] This kind of imprecision not only allowed easy access to difficult texts, for some readers it was the primary way in which one could receive pleasure from them. Echoing Coleridge's phrase that "Poetry gives most pleasure when only generally and not perfectly understood," Leonard Woolf, husband of Virginia and owner of the Hogarth Press, posited the pleasure of reading Eliot (whom he granted was "difficult to understand") in the following way: "But if anyone will read the opening of 'The Waste Land,' and the whole of 'Gerontion,' without fussing very much about whether or not he is understanding exactly what the author means, he will suddenly be amazed and delighted by the mere beauty of the poetry" ([1925] 1982, 214).

Full Pleasure

But such a reading practice tells only part of the story of high modernism's ascendancy and does not explain how great swaths of other texts dropped out of sight. *That* narrative requires more excavation, a sorting through of more nuances of the argument about pleasure and vigor. One of the nuances was that readers posited different levels of pleasure, ranging from the trivial to the sublime. These different levels are elucidated in discussions about the knowledge required in the reading of difficult texts, and the widespread sense that the difficult text's required knowledge was implicated in the text's pleasure, either by being necessary in order for a reader to experience full pleasure, or by removing the possibility of it. Clive Bell defended Virginia Woolf's writing by aristocratically noting that Woolf's "style is sometimes accused, injuriously, of being 'cultivated and intellectual', especially by people who themselves are not particularly well off for either culture or intellect." The cultivation that produced Woolf's writing resulted in a text that, in order to enjoy it "thoroughly," "a reader must himself have been well educated" ([1924] 1982, 145). Readers frequently made these kinds of qualifications. Dudley Fitts argued that "technical information" would "add a certain richness to the enjoyment" of Pound's *Cantos* and Stravinsky's *Sacre du printemps* ([1931] 1972, 252); and F. W. Dupee claimed that in his reading of difficult poetry there was always "a margin of obscurity which had to be overcome by study before my enjoyment was at all complete" (1945, 355). These texts therefore provided "full" pleasure only to certain readers, or after certain kinds of reading.

This distinction between "pleasure" and "full pleasure" implicitly argued that there was a full aesthetic pleasure, typically based upon an idea of art as emotional or self-expression, that didn't *need* knowledge. Anti-difficulty readers exalted this pleasure as being central to art and condemned difficult, knowledge-based pleasure as trivial, for it made knowledge rather than experience central, books rather than life. For them, the difficult text did not allow for *full* pleasure. For such readers, whatever pleasures might hypothetically accrue from the excesses of the difficult text were diminished ones, the formal pleasures of a technical game: clever, intellectual, with little substance. Marguerite Wilkinson, recall, claimed that "poetry is not, after all, an intricate puzzle game for sophisticated intellects" (1919, 9). Henry Parkes, discussing Pound's *Cantos* in the course of a review of the *Objectivist Anthology*, began by acknowledging that "Few qualified students of contemporary literature would deny that for the last twenty years Pound has been the most serious and accomplished man of letters in the English-speaking world" ([1932] 1972, 240). Parkes, though, saw that Pound's early adherence to Imagism created problems for a long poem like the *Cantos*, because his Imagist principles resulted in the poem becoming a disconnected series of images in which the poet "cannot find among these objects any inherent unity; his poem becomes a kind of catalogue" (241). For Parkes, Pound's Imagism resulted in a lack of personal expression which caused the poetry to "lack vitality": "Any other conception of poetry causes it to degenerate into a mere intellectual amusement, more difficult but scarcely more valuable than designing a tapestry or a vase" (242).

> It is a matter of general agreement that professional musicians who cultivate so-called serious music are high-brow and long-haired individuals, and this is being held against them. The reason usually brought forward in support of such criticism is that the music written and performed by those individuals cannot be enjoyed by the common man because of its complexity and lack of emotional appeal.
>
> —Ernst Krenek, "The Ivory Tower," 1966

While, as the previous chapter showed, some readers sympathetic to difficult writing used the argument about personal and emotional expression to further the cause of difficulty, typically the reliance on emotional expression as the chief agent of *pleasure* was more noisily asserted by those who distrusted difficult writing. For these readers, emotional expression was always simple and direct. They believed that the difficult text, lacking this emotional or self expression, offered the trivial pleasure of a game—a nonhumanistic pleasure, technical, cold, and deliberate. Cynics labeled the writers who made such texts as being from the "crossword puzzle" or "puzzle-picture" school, in these phrases pulling together ideas of trivial pleasure, professionalism, and fashion. Louis Untermeyer, for example, argued in his *American Poetry Since 1900* that *The Waste Land* "is a poetry not actuated by life but by literature," a poem that "appeals only to our acquired knowledge." What the reader finds in Eliot's poem "is not so much a creative thing as a piece of literary carpentry, scholarly joiner's work; the flotsam and jetsam of desiccated culture stuck together in the puzzle-picture manner of Pound's 'Sordelloform' cantos" (Untermeyer 1924, 358). In his review of *The Waste Land* Untermeyer argued that "the pleasure which many admirers derive from 'The Waste Land' is the same sort of gratification attained through having solved a puzzle, a form of self-congratulation" ([1923] 1982, 152–53). Real pleasure, then, was something different from *The Waste Land's* puzzle pleasure. As David Daiches wrote, in reference to Gertrude Stein's work: "But an art which is all form and no content, as it were, can never be among the greatest of human activities, and certainly beside poetry proper it sounds empty and feeble. Such an art can never quicken the pulse or heighten the emotions" (1935, 60). The game-like pleasures of the difficult work were often seen to reduce art's expressive/cultural abilities; they were pleasures that could not reach common readers because their impetus came from professional interests.[5]

In a passage of *The Literary Mind* in which he argued against poets Robert Graves and Laura Riding, Max Eastman claimed that the knowledge required

> B is for Beauty as Brancusi views it.
> (The Cubies all vow he and Braque take the Bun.)
> First you seize all that's plain to the eye, then you lose it;
> Next you search for the Soul and proceed to abuse it.
> (They tell me it's easy and no end of fun.)
> —B is for Beauty as Brancusi views it.
>
> —Mary Mills Lyall, *The Cubies' ABC*, 1913

to read many modern texts was unfortunate, for "Its actual effect is to narrow the circle of communication to a small group of specialists in a particular type of learning." Eastman continued: "Most of the 'cognoscenti,' as I know them, will be so tickled by the poet's assuming they know everything he is alluding to, that they will get along better than others without the more specific pleasure of finding out what he is alluding to. Even those who do find out will have enjoyed a cerebral exercise rather than the emotional and intellectual experience of the poem" (1931, 70–71). Oliver Gogarty, maintaining the cynical skepticism toward intellectual life for which he was pilloried in Joyce's *Ulysses*, cast a jaundiced eye over the Atlantic to ask: "How does it happen that America should have become the chief infirmary for Joyceans? The answer is because America is the country *par excellence* of the detective story, the crossword puzzle, and the smoke signal. All these are supplied by *Ulysses*. Here, too, where mental homes are numerous, are to be found that unique class who think that the unravelling of an enigma or a puzzle is the height of poetry" ([1950] 1970, 765). One of the things this accusation of crossword puzzles did was make the difficult text, paradoxically, easy. The text was completely explainable through a mechanical procedure of finding a cypher, of filling in the blanks. The difficult crossword puzzle text had none of the resonance of the great work of art.

Further, for high modernism's skeptics, difficult, "game-like" art teetered on the brink of being a hoax, and "clever" became the operative term. Describing the difficult, "radical" poets of her time as being "undeniably alarmingly clever," Marguerite Wilkinson singled out the opening metaphor of Eliot's "Love Song of J. Alfred Prufrock" as deserving particular abuse:

> The comparison would never come into the mind of a stupid man, of an unsophisticated man. It is clever, also, to speak of the "damp souls of housemaids." It is clever to say that the laughter of a certain Mr. Apollinax "was submarine and profound." It is such cleverness that one finds in Mr. Eliot's work. It is for such things, as much as for anything else, that his admirers praise him. His sketches of personality are dry and

> One of the incidental, but characteristic, features of the post-war artistic cults was that they took the line of least resistance, made the practice of art so phenomenally easy. To draw and paint like Rubens meant arduously acquiring a high degree of professional skill; to exhibit a formless mass of crude pigment, or a couple of faintly-tinted triangles, or to suspend a herring and a pair of stays from an easel, whatever its other merits, at least absolves the performer from a great deal of preliminary labour. *Vers libre* dispensed the poet from mastering those exacting accomplishments, rhyme and rhythm, and the principle of free association from learning structure and intelligibility. The Dadaist who exhibited a blot of ink as a portrait of the Virgin Mary had needed little training at art school.
>
> —Lord Elton, *Notebook in Wartime*, 1941

hard. His comment on the complex lives of worldlings is all entertaining. But a poet must be more than clever and entertaining to merit the attention of many readers. A brittle aestheticism is not enough. (1929, 182–83)

Eunice Tietjens, associate editor of *Poetry*, approvingly quoted Sara Teasdale, who put all the associations together: "The poet must put far from him the amazing word, the learned allusion, the facile invention, the clever twist of thought, for all these things will blur his poem and distract his reader. He must not overcrowd his lines with figures of speech, because, piling these one upon another, he defeats his own purpose." Clever technique stood in the way of both the readers' abilities and the emotional resonance of great poetry. According to Tietjens, "The mind of the reader can not hold many impressions at one time. The poet should try to give his poem the quiet swiftness of flame, so that the reader shall feel and not think while he is reading. But the thinking will come afterwards" (1923a, 151–52).[6]

When they saw the pleasures of a difficult text as trivial, many readers predictably announced they were unable or unwilling to do the necessary work to achieve such pleasures. Reviewing Frost's first book of poems, *A Boy's Will*, a writer for *The Nation* commented favorably on the annotations that Frost had put beneath the title of each poem, thus creating a central persona and something of a narrative for the book. The reviewer went on: "I object personally to researches into obscure poetic meanings, not merely from the healthy human disinclination to overwork, but from a sense that the faculties which the assessing of probabilities and the summing up of evidence call into play are destructive of the moods in which poetry is absorbed and enjoyed" (Firkins [1915] 1977, 8). That "human disinclination to overwork" may be disingenuous, but more than a few reviewers announced a similar refusal. This is seen most clearly in the response to James Joyce, whose writing increasingly showed a negative correlation between work and pleasure. Donald Adams, reviewing *Finnegans Wake* in the *New York Times*, gave what for many readers was (and remains) a fearsomely recognizable trajectory to Joyce's career:

> In his early work, in *Dubliners* and *A Portrait of the Artist as a Young Man*, Joyce made no extraordinary demands upon his readers; in *Ulysses* they are heavy; in *Finnegans Wake* they pass beyond all reasonable bounds. It was natural that his contemporaries should make the effort to determine what Joyce was about; one wonders how many, in the years to come, other than literary historians and writers absorbed in the technique of their craft, will find that necessary effort sufficiently rewarding. In the case of *Ulysses* there is little doubt that readers of sufficient tenacity and knowledge will be numerous, for in spite of its frequent obscurity and its occasional dullness there is an abundance of life between its covers, revealed in a manner not paralleled in any other writer. But *Finnegans Wake* seems destined to be one of the dipped-into but unread curiosities. ([1941] 1970, 754)

Richard Aldington, who in 1923 had been upbraided by Eliot for having a naively simplistic (albeit positive) reading of *Ulysses*, came to a very different estimation of *Finnegans Wake*, and let fly in the mainstream *Atlantic Monthly*: "Common honesty compels this reviewer to state that he is unable to explain either the subject or the meaning (if any) of Mr. Joyce's book; and that, having spent several hours a day for more than a fortnight in wretched toil over these 628 pages, he has no intention of wasting one more minute of precious life over Mr. Joyce's futile inventions, tedious ingenuities, and verbal freaks." Aldington went on, "The problem of what Mr. Joyce has to say in *Finnegans Wake* may be left to those who have time and energy to waste" ([1939] 1970, 690).

But readers sympathetic to high modernism did not accept the terms and structure of this argument about the diminished pleasures of the difficult text. Thus, while Marguerite Wilkinson tidily separated the pleasure designed for "sophisticated intellects" from the "natural, joyous, life-sharing art, concerned with feelings that we all share" (1919, 9), proponents of difficult art did not comfortably settle into the slot she assigned them. Bonamy Dobrée, for example, noted the difficulty arising from the specialization of Eliot's poetry, but went on to argue that "this does not prevent our enjoying Mr. Eliot's poetry" ([1929] 1986, 126). Tying the pleasure of difficult modernism to one of its classic defenses, many tried to subvert what others saw as the necessary conditions for pleasure. They argued that full pleasures were possible without "understanding" a text; indeed, a properly quiescent reading practice demanded that understanding be put to the side. In his review of

Finnegans Wake, Walter Rybert argued that "it's not a matter of reading it 'as one would a foreign language, translating each word,' etc. etc. This is *one* thing that must not be done. If you have a scholar's yen for that sort of job, put it off until you have gotten what the book was jolly well made for—esthetic pleasure. You don't need Mr. Joyce's erudition any more than you need Herr van Beethoven's musical education in order to enjoy his Fifth Symphony" ([1940] 1970, 32). Relatively early in modernism, Floyd Dell noted that although the poems in Pound's *Provença* "have often an unconventional form, bizarre phraseology, catalectic or involved sentence structure and recondite meanings," the book yet gave the "sense that effects which are beyond one's immediate power of comprehension have been exquisitely designed and exactly carried out." That relationship to comprehension, for Dell, was universal; it was "at the base of the pleasure afforded by all art of a high order" ([1911] 1972, 70, 71). Ernst Curtius, in discussing Eliot, claimed that "A line of verse that causes us to vibrate musically, that excites us with its rhythm and haunts us with its melody—must be a good line, even if its meaning is still hidden from us" ([1927] 1973, 356).

Virility

When high modernism's defenders insisted on its pleasures, they revealed that there were ways for difficult texts, by utilizing a sense of the sublime, to tap into traditionally romantic understandings of pleasure. But the relationship was fraught with inconsistencies and overshadowed by a more aggressive strategy. While all involved in high culture might affirm, if pressed, the general goodness of pleasure, things got more heated when it came down to specific formulations of what pleasure meant. High moderns set themselves against a form of pleasure that was heavily inflected by default values peculiar to the beginning of the twentieth century. According to high modern writers, the pleasures of traditional contemporary writing (which used versions of the same values of resonance and suggestion as the high moderns occasionally did) were suspect. Quick to denounce the pleasures of traditional contemporary writing, high modern writers used a version of the usual route for attacking pleasure and presented an ethical critique of traditional pleasure's limitations. Trivializing the pleasures of traditional contemporary writing, the supporters of difficult modernism attacked an attitude it saw lurking in conservative accounts. Recall, from earlier in this chapter, that John Sparrow, in writing about Yeats, noted that one of his poems "only seems obscure if we try to interpret what we should be content to enjoy" (1934, 87). Sparrow's use of "content" gives him away, for contentment was not something difficult moderns valorized; it was something they were eager to castigate. Using the same argumentative strategies as their opponents did for the idea of difficulty as a game, high modern readers caricatured conservative ideas of pleasure,

> "I don't see the point. More people would enjoy it if it was more straightforward."
> "Difficulty generates meaning. It makes the reader work harder."
> "But reading is the opposite of work," said Vic. "It's what you do when you come home from work, to relax."
> "In this place [Rummidge University]," said Robyn, "reading is work. Reading is production. And what we produce is meaning."
>
> —Robyn Penrose, English professor, in conversation with a businessman about the difficulty of *Wuthering Heights*. David Lodge, *Nice Work*, 1988

portraying its tropes of lack as a weak-kneed diminishment of art's scope and ambition. Difficulty, on the other hand, presented the pleasures of its own texts as heroic, virile.

What, according to modernism's apologists, did conservative pleasure and its art look like? While there was some sniping at the purveyors of pleasure, such as "the comparatively timid Georgians" (Murphy 1938, xv), for the most part high moderns directed their concern at a readership that, they argued, desired not so much art as a tranquilizer. (This tendency to discuss conservative aesthetics in terms of reading rather than writing practices gave more sweep to difficulty's assertions, for it also implicitly accounted for high modernism's own initial lack of acceptance by the general reading public.) David Daiches acerbically noted that Eliot's writing "has to be read much more carefully than that of the Georgians," whose writing encouraged its readers to be "carried along on a murmuring stream with our eyes and ears half shut" (1940, 111). As such quotations suggest, high moderns did not just disagree with traditional aesthetic principles and their social actualization; they were morally averse to them. Casting a jaundiced eye over the common reader, Cleanth Brooks, in discussing Yeats's writing, asserted that "the average reader will balk, not so much at the images as at the amount of intellectual exercise demanded of him" (1939, 63–64). In her 1932 *Fiction and the Reading Public*, Q. D. Leavis located the source of such intellectual laziness in contemporary culture: "The training of the reader who spends his leisure in cinemas, looking through magazines and newspapers, listening to jazz music, does not merely fail him, it prevents him from normal development ... partly by providing him with a set of habits inimical to mental effort" ([1932] 1965, 224). This attitude to the common reader was widespread. For example, Riding and Graves condemned the "lazy reading habits" of modern readers (1927, 10); Hugh Ross Williamson (1933, 12) and, seventeen years later, Roger Sessions (1950, 126), described the contemporary audience's desire for easy art to be similar to the wish for a "drug"; and Edith Sitwell grumbled that difficult poetry came "as a shock to people who are used to taking their impressions at second-hand—to people who want comfort and not the truth" (1926, 22). Thus, when readers argued that a given text required too much work, they were setting themselves up to be criticized by high moderns as being indolent and feeble. Pleasures such as these readers desired were at best, beside the point, at worst, corrupt and lazy.

According to many high moderns, such were the reading practices that accompanied the pleasures of conservative art. Eager to dismiss them, modernism's apologists asserted that whatever the antithesis of this traditional pleasure might be, it was not a lack, a diminution. In their search, though, high moderns did not *replace* pleasure with difficulty, for they understood difficulty as a *property* of texts and not an *affect*. What did they see as the kind of reading necessary for, and effect produced by, difficult art? High moderns didn't deny reading's strenuousness; they often acknowledged, rightly, that difficulty did require hard work, that the effort of reading high modernism was an effort that encountered resistance. Such an understanding made reading into a struggle, for modernism's texts were not, first of all, cooperative. Difficult art, in the high modern aesthetic, was serious and important; the effect it created and the reading it required were vigorous.[7]

This aesthetic dominated high modern articulations of pleasure and the reading process, and was central to its canonization. But it was not an aesthetic without awkwardness, for it necessitated casting to the side large chunks of romanticist defenses of difficulty, which argued that one needed to passively accept the difficult text, and that such a relaxed reading practice allowed one access to the difficult work's meaning beyond language. Difficulty's defenders instead called for vigilance, energy, machismo. Bernard Bosanquet argued that difficult works demanded "profound effort and concentration to apprehend them" ([1915] 1963, 48); Elizabeth Drew similarly claimed that reading Hopkins required "real toughness of intellectual effort" (1933, 85). Ezra Pound, implicated more than most in high modernism's virility, noted that "Intense emotion causes pattern to arise in the mind—if the mind is strong enough" ([1915] 1973, 374). Instead of passively drifting along, readers and writers of difficult work needed energy. If there is something analogous to pleasure in the difficult text, then, it is the pleasure of vigorous exercise, with bracing whiffs of danger and moral rectitude.

Richard Aldington, castigating "the pleasant little rhymes now current," contrasted them to the work of Eliot, which he saw as "a healthy reaction against the merely pretty and agreeable, against shallowness and against that affectation of simplicity which verged on dotage." Aldington went on to congratulate Eliot for, in contrast, bringing "new vigour to the intellectual tradition of English poetry" (1924, 190–91). For high moderns, vigor's inherent value allowed few nuances. Mark Van Doren, in his introduction to the anthology *Prize Poems 1913–1929*, made the following claims:

> Poetry had been soft, both in its sound and in its sentiment. Now it became hard, with edges and structure, and with a bold, protruding skeleton of idea. The poet was no longer content to lull his listener; he would shock him, wake him up, jolt him into attention; he would force him to use his mind as he read. Hence a diction which met with opposition because it was not "poetic diction"—the sort of language that had become customary in verse. Hence a complicated syntax, surprising combinations of words, and positively embarrassing riches of concrete, homely, sometimes "ugly" words alternating, it might be, with abstractions, technical terms, and far-fetched phrases. Hence a preoccupation on the part of some poets with the mysteries of the subconscious. (1930a, 12–13)

The crisp causality of Van Doren's repeated "hence," while it may or may not precisely articulate how these texts came into being, does accurately describe how modern readers of all persuasions understood the changes introduced by modern difficulty. Under the old dispensation, the standard metaphors depicted the text as a limpid, bottomless, clear, direct thing, easily plumbed. In contrast, modernist tropes presented the difficult text as a spiky, hard thing that attacked readers. The text under this conceptualization became not a clear vessel waiting to be penetrated, but an active thing that acted upon its readers (in modernist aesthetics, the sexual connotations for many of these metaphors, whether conscious or not, were certainly used freely).

So strong was the linkage between difficulty and virility that both difficulty's supporters *and* its detractors connected difficulty to the virile posture of high modernism.[8] In "The Man Who Wrote Free Verse," remember, Adrian castigates Reggie for not "really expressing the spirit of real revolt," by, among other things, not even wishing he were "a tiger or a motor-car" (Squire 1924, 133). When in his anthology of modern British poetry Untermeyer turned his attention to the three Sitwells, he noted that, "mocking the softness of 'Georgianism,' these writers send up showers of indignant though sometimes esoteric brilliance wherever their work appears" (1925, 18). Marion Strobel, reviewing Williams's *Spring and All* for *Poetry* magazine, argued that Williams "hasn't the guts to be simple," and that instead he showered the public with fake machismo, "a barrage of words to show that he—by Jove—is no lily-livered ninny singing of love" ([1923] 1980, 75).

Claims for machismo and virility weren't the sole property of difficulty, of course.[9] For example, while Hemingway was occasionally seen as difficult, when writers characterized his writing as muscular they often did so without reference to the difficulty of recognizing his writing as *art*, as when one reviewer described his writing as having a "lean, pleasing, tough resilience,"

> P's for Picasso, Picabia and Party
>   (Who deal in abstractions, distractions and such.)
> When, with vision chaotic and expletives hearty,
> You beg of a Cubist their sense to impart, he
>   Profoundly makes answer: "In little is much."
> —P's for Picasso, Picabia and Party.
>
> —Mary Mills Lyall, *The Cubies' ABC*, 1913

with language that was "fibrous and athletic" ("Preludes to a Mood" [1925] 1977, 7). Further, startling virile claims were often made for the *newness* of modernism, again without necessarily referring to difficulty, as in this 1910 manifesto of the futurist painters:

> The cry of rebellion which we utter associates our ideals with those of the Futurist poets. These ideals were not invented by some aesthetic clique. They are the expression of a violent desire which boils in the veins of every creative artist today.
>
> We will fight with all our might the fanatical, senseless and snobbish religion of the past, a religion encouraged by the vicious existence of museums. We rebel against the spineless worshipping of old canvases, old statues and old bric-a-brac, against everything which is filthy and worm-ridded and corroded by time. (Boccioni et al. [1910] 1973, 24)

So, claims for virility flew fast and furious in the first decades of the twentieth century. But difficulty was virile in idiosyncratic ways. First, difficulty was often implicated in these other claims for virility; many of the "new" works that were seen as macho were also seen as difficult. Second, difficulty's virility had a larger range than that claimed for a writer like Sarett. Claims for the virility of nondifficult art were circumscribed, with its proponents usually asserting that this virile art received its vigor from its authentic relation to life in the twentieth century. Difficulty's virility was not related primarily to biographical details of the artist's life, as in the case of Sarett. Difficulty's machismo was larger, embracing style as well as content, and encompassing readers as well as writers. Difficulty's machismo was prompted by content, by style, and by the visceral experience that many had of it.

The fact that they overwhelmingly portrayed difficulty as the occasion of a physical struggle says much about how modernism's apologists allied difficulty with moral values. According to most involved in the difficulty debate, difficult works required not just effort, but an effort with struggle, an effort that encountered resistance. This, of course, makes sense with difficult modernism, whose texts are premised on a resistance that must be engaged. John Middleton Murry, reviewing Yeats in 1919, reached back in history to find the following analogue. Noting that "even in Blake's most recondite work there is always the moment when the clouds are parted and we recognise the austere and awful countenances of gods," Murry claimed that "the sheer creative will of the poet" had overcome in struggle: "Like Jacob, he wrestled until the going down of the sun with his angel and would not let him go" ([1919] 1977, 217). In his arguing for the centrality of difficult poetry to the modern tradition, Cleanth Brooks similarly looked to the past, arguing that the unity of a metaphysical poet "is a perilous one, wrested by his own effort from a world of incongruities" (1939, 45). Critics compulsively pressed these metaphors into service, even in unlikely circumstances. Winifred Bryher, defending Marianne Moore in the ambivalent surroundings of a *Poetry* symposium on her work, noted that Moore did not have a "passive" temperament. Instead, Bryher argued, "the spirit is robust, that of a man with facts and countries to discover and not that of a woman sewing at tapestries" (1922, 209).

Such exercise, according to the logic of its defenders, inevitably resulted in healthy art. Geoffrey Grigson, reviewing Pound's *Cantos* in 1933, described it as "athletic writing, of a kind which has only been made possible by long severe training and dieting" ([1933] 1972, 262). More than a few writers used the term "vigor" to discuss this aspect of difficult writing, from Riding and Graves's assertion that "poetry obviously demands a more vigorous imaginative effort than the plain reader has been willing to apply to it" (1972, 10), to Aldington's assertion that "Mr. Eliot is to be honoured as a poet who has brought new vigour to the intellectual tradition of English poetry" (1924, 191).

Critics pictured difficult modernism as the triumph of good health that only right living can bring; inexorably seeping into descriptions of difficulty's vigor was an implied ethics based on courage. For high modernism's proponents the vigor of difficulty was not the kinetic frenzy of madness, but the strenuousness of good health. As David Daiches claimed of Eliot, "In subject matter he employed themes which implied criticism of the emptiness and flabbiness of modern life and thought, while in technique he employed every means he could to avoid that flabbiness which he was criticizing" (1940, 115).

The equation between health and morality is an ancient (albeit logically untenable) one. It was also close at hand, in the late nineteenth-century sense of the moral life as a strenuous life. In fact, the values surrounding difficult art had overtones of a moral call to action that sounds more at home in late Victorian culture than in high modernism.[10] Marianne Moore noted that her value of "precision" was "a matter of diction, of diction that is virile because galvanized against inertia" ([1944] 1986b, 397). Calling Blake's use of metaphor "vigorous," Cleanth Brooks argued that Blake marked "the return to the daring of Elizabethan metaphor, to the use of serious irony, to a bold willingness to risk obscurity, and even something very close to metaphysical wit"

(1939, 234–35). While she had some problems with the coarseness of *Ulysses*, Virginia Woolf noted of Joyce: "Mr. Joyce is spiritual; he is concerned at all costs to reveal the flickering of that innermost flame which flashes its messages through the brain, and in order to preserve it he disregards with complete courage whatever seems to him adventitious, whether it be probability, or coherence, or any other of these signposts which for generations have served to support the imagination of a reader when called upon to imagine what he can neither touch nor see" (1925, 190–91).

Using a romantic aesthetic that lay close at hand, high moderns claimed for this courage the romantic values of directness, authenticity, and sincerity. Indeed, readers instantly employed and understood the macho claims as ethical claims because these romantic values were still the default ones. Writing in 1927, William Carlos Williams asserted that "the difficulty of modern styles is made by the fragmentary stupidity of modern life, its lacunae of sense, loups, perversions of instinct, blankets, amputations, fulsomeness of instruction and multiplication of inanity." Going on, Williams argued that "to avoid this, accuracy is driven to a hard road.... The only human value of anything, writing included, is intense vision of the facts" ([1927] 1969, 71). Four years earlier, in his manifesto *Spring and All*, Williams had commented on the work of Marianne Moore, noting that "the incomprehensibility of her poems is witness to at what cost (she cleaves herself away) as it is also to the distance which the most are from a comprehension of the purpose of composition." The ethical generalization he was able to draw from this was clear: "The better work men do is always done under stress and at great personal cost" ([1923] 1986b, 188). The sentiment was commonplace. George Williamson, in his contribution to the critical anthology *A Garland for John Donne*, tied the integrity of Donne to that of contemporary difficult writers, at one point noting of the poet Herbert Read that "In Read there is the hard integrity of thought which marks Donne, and there is no intention to be satisfied with any such dream-world as solaced the poets of the nineteenth century" (1931, 172).

This ethical machismo did not, however, base its identity solely in romanticism; there were aspects specific to *modern* difficulty that invited moral strenuousness. Most generally, other aspects of modern culture, such as its professionalism, pressed to make difficulty more, rather than less, important. To claim morality for difficult work was congruent with other attempts to enlarge difficulty's importance. Further, high moderns were not immune to the attractions of having an ethical basis for what they spent most of their time on. In that, difficult modernism did not differ from earlier aesthetic periods or from other human activities. More concretely, it should be remembered that conservative moderns had launched a multipronged attack on the morality of difficulty, claiming that it was elitist, that it was a hoax,

> Unintelligibility is one of the inevitable results of a developing individualism; and individualism, frequently intensified by the adjective "rugged," has been regarded as one of the prime virtues of our age—the chief embodiment of courage, strength, initiative, heroism, leadership, and self-respect—the necessary attributes of the indefatigable pioneer.
>
> —Edward Rothschild, *The Meaning of Unintelligibility in Modern Art*, 1934

that it was created by charlatans, and that it was unnatural. Few, finding themselves in that position, were tempted to counter that moral barrage by stepping down their own claims, by claiming that their difficulty, and its strenuousness, was too unassuming to have moral claims made for it. In the face of such attacks it made more sense to claim that difficulty had morality on its side; indeed, that it was *more* moral than the work of its opponents.

As for the machismo of this ethical stance, it can be partly accounted for by the larger cultural situation in which modern writers found themselves. In his *Modernist Quartet* (1994), Frank Lentricchia convincingly describes modern American poets' anxiety about the public perception of them as an effete cultural elite separate from the rest of society, which was vigorous, active, and healthy. Particularly in his chapters on Stevens and Frost, Lentricchia argues that these poets' public stances can be understood as a reaction to this perception. The vigor of difficult art is also part of that response to that cultural perception, both as an attempted denial and as an implicit acceptance of its terms.[11] This larger cultural situation also saw the rise of professionalism, which similarly distrusted pleasure as a basis for significant human activity and emphasized vigor. Professional activity, seen as a serious response to a crisis, was frequently described with macho language that emphasized risk, importance, and virility. Professionals saw themselves as special people, intelligent and brave pioneers, virile, proud, and unflinching, who realized that art, like all professional activity, was inevitably difficult.[12]

Thus, modernism's moral strenuousness can be found both in its near historical antecedents and in specific aspects of the modern cultural situation. But also, linguistic and physical aspects of the difficult experience helped to link difficulty, vigor, and morality even more strongly. The metaphoric language in which modernism's strenuousness and morality came packaged helped facilitate such connections. This language is telling, both in how it described the structure of difficult texts and how it exuded an attitude to that structure. First, notice the structure. The conceptual metaphors surrounding difficulty considerably overlap the standard metaphors and language of strength, force, and power, and they create a sense of what the experience of difficult modernism felt like. May Sinclair, writing in the friendly confines of the *Little Review*, described Eliot's writing in the following way: "He does not see anything between him and reality, and he makes straight for the reality he sees; he cuts all his corners and his curves; and this directness of method is startling and upsetting to comfortable, respectable people accustomed to going superfluously in and out of corners and carefully round curves." Eliot's readers, Sinclair asserted, needed to have the right stuff: "Unless you are prepared to follow with the same nimbleness and straightness you will never arrive with Mr. Eliot at his meaning." In these phrases, Sinclair employed the standard conceptual metaphor UNDERSTANDING IS FOLLOWING, adding, by availing herself of the understanding that difficult texts were excessive in some way, the idea of speed. One needs physical/intellectual stamina to read difficult Eliot. With writing like Eliot's, Sinclair asserted, one either followed along or contented oneself with a diminished response, such as the following: "Therefore the only comfortable thing is to sit down and pretend, either that Mr. Eliot is a 'Helot' too drunk to have any meaning, or that his 'Boston Evening Transcript' which you do understand is greater than his 'Love Song of Prufrock' which you do not understand. In both instances you have successfully obscured the issue" ([1917] 1982, 85).[13]

Eliot himself found the historical precedents for this way of thinking about the reading process in the metaphysical poets. In his famous review, Eliot noted that in metaphysical writing one found "instead of the mere explication of the content of a comparison, a development by rapid association of thought which requires considerable agility on the part of the reader" ([1921] 1975b, 60). One year earlier, using the same conceptual strategies, Marion Strobel noted of Eliot that his poetry was "a perilous leaping from crag to crag" in which Eliot "with a 'Whoop-la'—for he is in beautiful condition . . . swings from romance to realism, to religion, to history, to philosophy, to science, while you and I climb pantingly, wearily, after him" ([1920] 1982, 119).[14] In the writing of modernism's more dramatic proponents, this swiftness was violent. Noting that many readers had found Stein's word portraits to be "particularly incoherent," Mabel Dodge dismissed such responses with the observation that "Many roads are being broken—what a wonderful word—'broken'! And out of the shattering and petrifaction of today—up from the cleavage and the disintegration—we will see order emerging tomorrow. Is it so difficult to remember that life at birth is always painful and rarely lovely?" (1913, 174).

Difficulty has further conceptual alliances with vigor in its metaphors of entanglement and compression. These metaphors were difficult to manage and under some contention. Although to contort, to tangle, or to twist language were all ways of articulating the forcefulness of difficulty, such

> Popular music speaks to the unsophisticated, to people who love the beauty of music but are not inclined to strengthen their minds. But what they like is not triviality or vulgarity or unoriginality, but a more comprehensible way of presentation. People who have not acquired the ability of drawing all the consequences of a problem at once must be treated with respect to their mental capacities; rapid solutions, leaps from assumptions to conclusions would endanger popularity.
> —Arnold Schoenberg, 1950

language was particularly useful for claiming the *unnaturalness* of difficulty, by allying one's language with conceptual metaphors that think of health and normalcy as straight and illness and perversion as crooked. Thus, Marion Strobel asserted that "we would rather not follow the contortions of Miss Moore's well-developed mind—she makes us so conscious of her knowledge" (1922, 210), and a reviewer of *Absalom, Absalom!* grumbled that "Faulkner, macabre and sadistic, delights in rendering his plots so that the reader will not easily untangle them" ([1937] 1995, 161). Steering away from this association with ill health and unnaturalness, difficult modernism's proponents turned less often to images of twisting than they turned to metaphors of directness or of compression, as when May Sinclair noted Eliot's "directness of method," in which "he makes straight for the reality he sees; he cuts all his corners and his curves" ([1917] 1982, 85). Marianne Moore, in a 1934 review of William Carlos Williams, noted that "Struggle, like the compression which propels the steam-engine, is a main force in William Carlos Williams" ([1934] 1986d, 325).

While conceptual metaphors encouraged assertions of difficulty's vigor and morality, these metaphors were abetted by the visceral experience of difficulty. The language that I have quoted in this chapter is loaded with values stemming from difficulty's viscerality, with words such as "courage," "terror," "repel," "terrifying," "strong," "bold," and "cost." These words recall the anxiety of the difficult experience described in chapter 2, but modernism's apologists, instead of morally condemning the instigator of this experience, lauded the moral courage of those who were able to endure it (except for when they claimed that the difficult text was actually simple, high moderns didn't disavow difficulty's large anxiety). The proponents of difficulty modulated the anxiety surrounding difficulty into a sense of macho pleasure. This reversal in valuation required some maneuvering, for it is easy to account for difficulty's negative value-laden words. The violation of entrenched things does

> With Donne, whose muse on dromedary trots,
> Wreathe iron pokers into true-love knots;
> Rhyme's sturdy cripple, fancy's maze and clue,
> Wit's forge and fire-blast, meaning's press and screw.
>
> —Samuel Taylor Coleridge

attract moral responses, but negatively: survival dictates that people need to be able to figure things out, and being unable to do so triggers anxiety. In a reworking of romantic ideas of the sublime, difficulty's apologists presented the difficult artist or the successful reader as someone who had managed to deal with the unknown, either by solving it or by riding it out. Marion Strobel argued that "Lovers of exercise will find their minds flexed, if not inert, after following the allusions and ellipses of 'Gerontion'" ([1920] 1982, 119). Addressing this kind of writing, L. A. G. Strong noted:

> A common source of obscurity is the speed with which a great poet's imagination leaps from point to point. The logical connections are left out. In a flash, the kindled mind apprehends a series of conclusions, and has sped across them to a new peak while the pedestrian reader is boggling at the preliminaries to the first leap. For this sort of difficulty there is no cure except study and the development of our own intuition. Fine poetry is not to be mastered cheaply. The man who reads it in bed, last thing at night, seeking an amiable soporific, will succeed only too well in his object. (1931, 156)

Difficult modernism's machismo and the moral values attached to it, then, were inescapable, given modernism's cultural situation as well as the conceptual structures that articulated that situation, and the visceral reactions difficulty provoked. The machismo made the morality inevitable, and it made someone as mannered as, say, Paul Rosenfeld part of a larger intellectual enterprise. Writing of William Carlos Williams, Rosenfeld noted that Williams's "words shock with the unexpectedness of their thrusts," and that they "bear unflinchingly the pain of violent cauterizations": "The poems of William Carlos Williams are good biting stuff. Lyric substance has gotten a novel acidulousness of him. Scent bitter like the nasturtium's, and like the nasturtium's freshingly pungent, mounts off his small spikey forms. The sharp things make gay dangerous guerilla upon the alkalis coating his brain. Corrosive fluid destroys the properties characteristic of ubiquitous Huyler's; leaves crystal of valuable salt. Poems start with sudden brandished cutlery. Poems writhe with the movements of bodies vainly twisting to loose themselves from fixed scorching points" ([1924] 1980, 76–77). To a large degree, high modernism succeeded in gaining the moral high ground and canonical status because language like this, although exaggerated and stylized, was understandable.

While modernism's apologists effectively redirected anxiety into morality and vigor, it would be overly dramatic to assert that they consciously cast about for a specific modulation of the sublime that would give their texts more authority. The written record gives no indication of such deliberateness. Difficult moderns did not deliberately add ethics to the experience of difficulty *in order to* give their project more cultural weight; a more accurate description would be that they were nudged along by various factors, some cultural, but particularly by the bodily experience of difficulty and the conceptual metaphors that structured aesthetic descriptions of this experience. However, the consequences for modernism of the peculiar alliances among difficulty, ethics, strenuousness, and pleasure are hard to exaggerate. In the first place, high modernism domesticated difficulty without *appearing* to have done so. Their difficulty wasn't just terror; high moderns gave its anxiety the focus and predictability of morality, of an ethical trajectory. By giving difficulty an ethic, high moderns made the anxiety manageable; by making this ethic virile, they avoided tying the pleasures of difficulty to habitualization. That management was important, for the wildness of difficulty was not only a part of many reading experiences; it was also a potentially valuable affect.

Thus, the morality of modernism's machismo was the flip side of the morality directed against modernism in the form of laughter and anger. High moderns acknowledged difficulty's anxiety, but claimed they were able to handle it, and that doing so was a sign of their virtue. This assertion was not mere grandstanding on their part, but neither was it unproblematic. Dealing with the same texts as their skeptics, and articulating difficulty as a textual *property* rather than the result of an interaction between text and reader, difficulty's proponents presented their experiences with difficulty as being the same as those of, say, the common reader. But high moderns asserted that their *reactions* differed. That being the case, they presented a simple explanation: difficulty's proponents were simply braver, more energetic, less lazy than those who panicked in the face of difficult art.

Now, while it is easy to see how high moderns arrived at this position, such logic works only if one considers difficulty to be a property that everyone experiences similarly. But in giving difficulty an ethical value there was some slippage: while being different degrees of the same experience, the anxiety that leads to pleasure and the anxiety that leads to terror and anger arise from differing intensities of anxiety. Recall that research on emotion in art reveals that as the difficulty/complexity of a situation increases, people's arousal/pleasure increases—until a moment of maximal arousal, at which point there is a sudden shift to panic, and pleasure drops off sharply. Where that moment of panic occurs is highly individualized and depends, among other things, on one's own habitualization with art and with the specific forms of difficulty being presented. For those who found difficulty exhilarating, the boundary into real terror hadn't been crossed. The boundary, when crossed, led to a radically different experience, one in which exhilaration collapsed into panic and mild anxiety suddenly modulated into anger. Thus, it is not inevitably the case that difficulty's proponents experienced the same degree of anxiety as its skeptics did, and it is particularly suspect to blame anxious reactions on the morality of a large class, such as the common reader, without considering all the factors that might separate the common reader from the professional.

Further, as exhilarating as their ethical rigor might be, high moderns moved too briskly away from mainstream notions of pleasure. Looking askance at forms of pleasure that didn't have its vigorous ethic attached to it, difficult modernism presented the hard and serious work required for reading *Ulysses* as the only worthwhile pleasure. Thus, even though difficult modernism shed light on an important aspect of art when they described difficulty's anxiety, and why that anxiety might be important, it was less adept at imagining the validity of other forms of pleasure. As with its attitude to the formation of modernism in general, difficult modernism didn't tolerate multiplicity. Only purity was possible. By *opposing* itself to how traditional ideas of pleasure seemed to interact with difficulty, difficult modernism may have cut itself off from too much. Its blind spot obscured pleasures that do not arise from hard work, but that arise from such activities as being really adept at something and doing it well. When they asserted their vigorous morality, difficulty's apologists also couldn't deal with the pleasure of physical abandonment and sensual indulgence.

Other problems obtrude as well. In focusing on its peculiar form of pleasure, difficult modernism's attempt to elide any split between pleasure and ethics seems only partially successful. Is it really pleasure if you always have one eye on the ethic meter? Pleasure, when it is *inextricable* from an ethic, doesn't seem much like pleasure anymore. Granted, there may not be such a thing as *pure* pleasure; it may be that pleasure is always mediated, so there is a pleasure of ethics, a pleasure of reading, a pleasure of any number of human experiences. But this opens pleasure up to multiplicities of experiences, not singleness. Further, difficult modernism only partly overcame resistances to its redefinition of pleasure, for traditional forms of pleasure still look like the default notions, unmarked, while high modernist forms look marked. Perhaps because high moderns reworked and limited the concept too much for it to be really workable, the high modern version of pleasure isn't the first thing that one thinks of when using the term.

Pleasure and the difficulties of the professional artist remain uneasy bedfellows, an uneasy opposition that still shapes contemporary culture. For example, Kenneth Silver writing in 1998 in *Art in America*, explored modernist artists working on the Côte d'Azur. Noting that it has taken long for this work "to come into its own as a subject of esthetic inquiry," Silver says the "obvious" explanation "is the 'problem of pleasure'": "Although many of the greatest artists of the first half of our century created extraordinary work on the Riviera, our associations with the place work at cross-purposes with this realization. Notions of pleasure, frivolity and sensual fulfillment do not sit comfortably with received ideas of serious endeavor, let alone with a currently popular effort to rewrite modernism's history as one dominated by absence, rupture and darkness" (1998, 85–86).

High modernism's strenuous, ethical metaphors have two further important characteristics. The first is that many of them are gendered male, even to the point of seeing Marianne Moore as a man. What is more striking, everyone involved in proselytizing for difficult modernism accepted this inflection. The gender of modernism, has, of course, been discussed often, and this book was not written primarily to advance that discussion. This does not mean that gender has little interaction with the difficulty debate: it clearly impinges upon individual discussions of difficulty (for example, readers' tendency to see Gertrude Stein's work in terms of her personality). And it is striking that gender-nuanced references are so frequent and so wrapped up in difficulty (and, consequently, the central aesthetic principles governing the construction of the modern canon). However, gender does not interact with difficulty in a sufficiently predictable way to *organize* my discussion around that interaction; while gender enters the difficulty debate, it doesn't explain its outlines. For example, difficulty's promoters often directed at nondifficult writing stereotypes frequently aimed against women: simplicity, weakness, lightness, and triviality. However, the gendered language could also move in the other direction, for modernism's skeptics at times tied women to the sense of difficulty as fashion. To further complicate things, correlations between gendered language and individual women were not inevitable—Marianne Moore escaped this conjunction, for example. The slippage of gender reference is important: in the difficulty debate the feminine-inflected language of disparagement was directed at both genders. Difficulty's virility was thus a complicated instrument: the gendering of difficulty was useful not just in making T. S. Eliot a central modernist and excluding Edna St. Vincent Millay, but also to the inclusion of Virginia Woolf and Gertrude Stein and to the demotion of Robert Frost.

Second, the vigorous talk around difficult texts helped make difficulty more ambitious and important; tying morality, difficulty, and virility gave difficulty more cultural weight. This moral strain had important cultural consequences, for it affected what both formalism and New Criticism look like. While in New Criticism the images of a particular work may have nothing to do with morality, the proper deployment of them has everything to do with it. In this process the trick for difficult moderns was to assert both that they were professionals (which was primarily an assertion of technical, not bardic, expertise) and that the difficulties of the modern text were not just a game. It seems in particular that they were nervous about the "game" aspects of difficulty, for the characteristics of machismo are all extra-formal things, moving difficulty out of the trivialities of the Sunday crossword puzzle. High moderns consequently employed many romanticized, ethical metaphors, and they needed them. Modernism's vigorous morality, based on difficulty, then, shaped both formalism and New Criticism, and it continues to govern both current literary criticism and attempts to expand the canon. The ethical pleasures of difficulty still hold us in thrall.

John Caputo Goes to the Wall

The extent to which high culture continues to work with modernist protocols of difficulty can be startling. While it shows up in such explosive events as the dismantling of *Tilted Arc*, it governs smaller activities as well, such as everyday academic discourse, even swatches of postmodernism apparently most at odds with high modernism's various agendas. Consider John Caputo's 1987 *Radical Hermeneutics: Repetition, Deconstruction, and the Hermeneutic Project*. In the introduction, Caputo announces the project his book attempts to undertake, a project that refutes metaphysics, for metaphysics "makes light of the difficulty in existence." Caputo contrasts metaphysics with hermeneutics, which he defines "as an attempt to stick with the original difficulty of life, and not to betray it with metaphysics" (1). This large claim for the "difficulty of life in general" wanders toward some more specific claims. Caputo's language gets muscular, as he asserts that "Hermeneutics thus is for the hardy" (3). Hermeneutics is "a radical thinking which is suspicious of the easy way out, which is especially suspicious that philosophy, which is metaphysics, is always doing just that" (3). Caputo argues that good thinking stretches to "the forbidding regions of *différance*, where things really get difficult" (5). Tying his work to the project of deconstruction, he insists that "Derrida—along with a few other Parisian philosophers—is exceedingly good at throwing difficulties in the path of metaphysics, at blocking off the superhighway that metaphysics seeks to build across the flux, at disturbing the consolations of philosophy" (4). An extension that reaches to postmodernism's literary activities is thus not surprising:

> [D]econstruction is an "undoing," a kind of *Ab-bauen*, which does not raze but releases and which is ready for what is difficult, indeed ready for the worst....

With deconstruction, hermeneutics loses its innocence and in so doing becomes even more faithful to the appointed way, which, as the young Heidegger said, means to remain faithful to the difficulty in life. *Différance* is very good at making things difficult. It puts in the place of the solemnities of Heideggerian hermeneutics a nontheological, nonrabbinic, more freewheeling, impious, poetic kind of reading; and in the place of Heidegger's Greco-Germanic poets it puts Artaud and Bataille, James Joyce and Mallarmé. (5)

Now, the rhetoric here is familiar, an introduction to a scholarly text, some academic throat-clearing that in its drama perhaps overstates the importance of what follows. But despite their aggressive insistence on separation from much of cultural history, Caputo's ideas are as conventional as his rhetorical stance. These are brave words that enact their bravery and independence, but they are totally culture-bound.

Though he would bristle at the comparison, Caputo is cheek by jowl with central high modern thinkers, such as Cleanth Brooks, who also argued that the difficulty of *The Waste Land* was a result of Eliot's "fidelity to the complexity of experience," and that Yeats searched for a system "which would not violate and oversimplify experience" (1939, 169, 175). He is equally related to Eliot's claims in "The Metaphysical Poets." Now certainly, Eliot and Caputo would see each other as ideological opposites, for Eliot presents the very metaphysical desire that Caputo loathes. But for understanding Western twentieth-century cultural activity, it is the similarity and relation between Caputo and Eliot that is more important than their differences. Eliot and Caputo are part of a single cultural history. So one should put to the side for the moment the proof for Eliot's and Caputo's claims that the world is "actually" difficult, and whether it is best represented by a metaphysical or antimetaphysical interpretive frame. Instead, note that both claim difficulty as a *necessary* value. For both, difficulty is calmly announced as necessary for honest cultural work, and it is necessary because the world really is difficult. For both, that claim is breathtakingly abrupt. While Caputo thinks it necessary to argue at length that one *ought* to return to the real difficulty of life (itself a curious imperative), he doesn't seem to think an argument is necessary to prove his point that life *is* difficult, or why it would be desirable to make difficulty into an aesthetic experience.

Further, while it is startling that they both represent the difficulty of life as a fact, more startling is that Caputo and high moderns find it both exhilarating and ethically proper. Caputo titles his preface "Restoring Life to its Original Difficulty," and moral suasion saturates his writing, from his claim that he will not "betray" life's difficulty, to his assertion that his work is "for the hardy," that it enters "forbidding" regions, that it is "faithful to the appointed way" and doesn't seek "consolations." This ethical view of difficulty also clings to the modernist belief that this display of vigor is a way of asserting personal authenticity. Caputo adopts the incoherent stance (for a postmodernist) of insisting on the individualist authenticity of his argument. And it is surprisingly universalist—Caputo's muscular language of difficulty is never presented as culturally determined. While Eliot defended difficulty by gesturing outside of the text, to early twentieth-century culture, claiming that difficulty for modern writers is uniquely necessary; Caputo steps outside of culture and gestures to life in general. As long as those gestures and their machismo seem unexceptional, modernism's difficulties, for better and for worse, are ours.

CHAPTER 5

Simplicity and the Modern Canon

> Mr Frost seems the nearest equivalent to an English poet, specializing in New England torpor; his verse, it is regretfully said, is uninteresting, and what is uninteresting is unreadable, and what is unreadable is not read. There, that is done.
> —T. S. Eliot, 1922

> What troubles me most about the defense of obscurity in Modernist and later poetry is the intolerance for other things it breeds. I am content to study Rosicrucianism to make sense of Yeats but I cannot abide denunciations of Frost for selling out by writing poems that do not require such research.
> — Joseph Aimone, 1995

Weighty values accompanied modern difficulty's assertions of its centrality; as the previous chapter argued, high modernism claimed for its difficulty the virile high ground, arguing that writers such as those given pride of place in Untermeyer's and Wilkinson's anthologies were working with a lesser idea of the possibilities of art. This chapter turns to modernism's skeptics' own version of what created great art. Early in the twentieth century, these readers' version of simplicity was the default way of understanding literature for the majority of "literate" readers, a simplicity that was not just based on comprehension but was encrusted with peripheral, socially inflected values. For these readers, simplicity was central to great art—simplicity and the terms that it shaped and carried with it, such as directness, purity, and sincerity.

But during the years when the high modern canon was formed, simplicity became an increasingly weak principle around which to marshal arguments about the canon. Difficulty was its undoing. Simplicity was not an effective counter to the ways in which difficulty was valorized, and it eventually became incomprehensible as a way of understanding significant aesthetic experience. In the triumph of high modernism, difficulty replaced simplicity, but in so doing, it also took on the *kind of work* that simplicity did; difficulty became the "default" aesthetic, the principle of aesthetic value that most readers turned to automatically, a principle that was encumbered with powerful and often unannounced values. This turn away from simplicity and toward difficulty made possible and inevitable the shape of the high modern canon as it existed by, say, 1960.

Simplicity began to disappear in the first decades of the twentieth century, the signs of its inevitable demise recorded in the pages of anthologies and literary and mass market magazines. I begin with a typical moment, by returning to Cyril Alington's 1923 article in the *English Review*. Alington warned that modern culture had increasingly become a culture of difficulty. Citing the "increased complexity" of contemporary life, Alington noted that "We live in days when the ordinary individual feels it increasingly impossible to resist the tyranny of the expert" (548). This professionalism and its difficulty, Alington believed, had even crept into contemporary art and literature, with unfortunate consequences; in his essay he grumbled that so much contemporary literature was "frankly beyond our comprehension." Finding himself shut out from contemporary literature, Alington grumbled that "Youth at the present day expresses itself in literary and artistic forms that are so extremely hard to understand" (545). Alington, worried about the increasing cultural power of aesthetic difficulty, commented that it threatened simplicity, which to him was "the essence of greatness" (549). He asked, "Are there no longer any simple and beautiful things to be said and no longer any simple and beautiful ways in which to say them?" Now, Alington's article is not an intellectually compelling piece of rhetoric—indeed, his *Times* obituary noted that Alington was "not a very profound scholar" (Roberts 1979, 13). But Alington's argument is important, for its strategies were the typical ones employed against difficult writing, strategies that fought an ineffectual rearguard action for the virtues of simplicity.

As its presence in the writing of "not a very profound scholar" like Alington might indicate, the virtues of simplicity had a lot of cultural weight. That weight is strikingly signaled by the enduring popularity of Francis Turner Palgrave's *Golden Treasury of Poems and Songs*. Initially published in 1861, and selling over 300,000 copies in that decade, the anthology was still very much in print in the second decade of the twentieth century, and had enough cultural weight for Pound in 1916 to petition Macmillan, then publisher of *The Golden Treasury*, for "something to replace that doddard Palgrave" (quoted in Stock [1970] 1974, 266). Palgrave's preface is a repository of the default understandings of simplicity that were operative at the turn of the century. Palgrave dedicated all editions of the anthology to Alfred Lord Tennyson and prayed that the book may be found by many a lifelong fountain of innocent and exalted pleasure; a source of animation to friends when they meet; and able to sweeten solitude itself with best society,—with the companionship of the wise and the good, with the beauty which the eye cannot see, and the music only heard in silence. If this Collection proves a storehouse of delight to Labour and to Poverty,—if it teaches those indifferent to the Poets to love them, and those who love them to love them more, the aim and the desire entertained in framing it will be fully accomplished. (Palgrave 1861, iii–v)

Poetry meant *lyric* poetry, the art's highest form, and Palgrave defined the lyric in terms of unity and exclusion, arguing that "each poem shall turn on some single thought, feeling, or situation." He wrote that in his selection process he had made it a principle "that passion, colour, and originality cannot atone for serious imperfections in clearness, unity, or truth" (v, vi). Vague blessings and improvements would ensue from this kind of writing; sounding a bit like Matthew Arnold with a head cold, Palgrave asserted that "Like the fabled fountain of the Azores, but with a more various power, the magic of this Art can confer on each period of life its appropriate blessing: on early years Experience, on maturity Calm, on age Youthfulness. Poetry gives treasures 'more golden than gold,' leading us in higher and healthier ways than those of the world, and interpreting to us the lessons of Nature. But she speaks best for herself" (viii–ix).[1]

As Palgrave's and Alington's arguments suggest, simplicity, as it was understood early in this century, was not just concerned with readers' comprehension, which would be facilitated or hindered by certain kinds of diction or sentence structure. As did difficulty, simplicity brought with it ideas about life and the function of art: beliefs about optimism, about democracy, about art as emotional expression, about a vaguely spiritual quietism, and about removal from the world. Of course, different people believed differing combinations of these peripheral ideas. Simplicity's proponents at Chicago's *Poetry* magazine, for example, tended to think of simplicity as a sign of democracy and of the *new*; British proponents of simplicity tended to tie it to universal values, to tradition, and to antiprofessionalism. As was the case for difficulty, one's attractions to simplicity depended on the appeal of ambient ideas that often accompanied but weren't inherent to it.

Simplicity, then, was a complex of ideas, and it is to crucial aspects of this complex—its inevitable ties to emotional expression, sincerity, familiarity, and the common reader—that I now turn. First, people who believed in simplicity believed in it a lot; it was nonnegotiable. Charles Wharton Stork, in the introduction to his *Second Contemporary Verse Anthology*, intoned: "Let all decorative qualities be conditioned upon sincerity and simplicity" (1923, xxi); Harriet Monroe, in the introduction to her 1917 anthology *The New Poetry*, argued that the simple "new poetry" of America "has set before itself an ideal of absolute simplicity and sincerity" (vi); and Louis Untermeyer in his 1924 edition of *American Poetry Since 1900* claimed the "great" writers "are essentially simple and direct" (350). Eunice Tietjens, writing in 1923 in *Poetry*, found that modern poetry was in crisis, and that what was most needed was "a way of going back of, and under, the specialization of our day, to the great underlying simplicities, to the major themes" (1923b, 325). Tietjens found the "great simplicities" to reside in art that presented itself as emotional expression. Arguing on another occasion that the "first essential" of a lyric was that "it shall deal with a fundamental, a universal emotion of the human heart," Tietjens asserted that the lyric poet "must be able to see through the swathings of thought the eternal core of emotion" (1923a, 150–51).

In stressing emotion, Tietjens and others were putting into play a standard dichotomy—that between emotion and thought—and allying the second half of that dichotomy with difficulty. Approvingly quoting Sara Teasdale, Tietjens noted that "The poet must put far from him the amazing word, the learned allusion, the facile invention, the clever twist of thought, for all these things will blur his poem and distract his reader." Tietjens quoted Teasdale further: "The poet should try to give his poem the quiet swiftness of flame, so that the reader shall feel and not think while he is reading. But the thinking will come afterwards" (1923a, 151–52).[2] Louis Untermeyer, in a 1919 reading of Robert Frost, claimed that "The living poem is something that is felt first and thought out afterwards" (1919b, 39). Writing twenty years later, Untermeyer remained steadfast in his belief that "many of the best poems are so straightforward, so really simple, that they need nothing more than attention and sympathetic reading" (1938, 9).

Emotional expression was also generally understood to be eternally true, not subject to the vicissitudes of culture. Not surprisingly, as a corollary to this idea of emotional expression came a belief that great, simple art was not self-conscious or deliberate; it was sincere, and, in perhaps the most common term, *direct*. John Cooper Powys, reviewing Edgar Lee Masters in 1929 (well *after* high modern excitement at the realism of his work had faded into disgruntled disappointment at Masters's simplicity and facility of composition), set Masters's simple directness as a clear rebuke to the current fashion for difficulty: "Mr. Masters touches a chord of emotional intensity such as, just because we have acquired a certain clever shame at feeling directly and simply, has become rare among us" (655). Reading from the same script, a reviewer of Lew Sarett praised the poet's "Maple Sugar Chant" for its "simple and direct utterance" (Morton 1923, 765). Works that lacked this directness had some predictable qualities. An anonymous reviewer of Wallace Stevens's 1931 edition of *Harmonium* found the following things to worry about in Stevens's poetry: "Mr. Stevens renders the mood of thought rather than thoughts about mood. He escapes into intellect, and his obscurities are due to excess of light—match-flames invisible in the dazzle of sunshine. He thinks more than he feels, and so life remains for the most part a comedy. The hard surfaces of his thought take no soilure from emotion." After setting out these failures, the reviewer worried that Stevens might never "attain the heights of a simple, direct unself-conscious art" (Review of *Harmonium* 1931, 207).

Simplicity towed further characteristics in its wake. For example, conservative readers overwhelmingly thought of simple art as familiar art. Harold Monro claimed that contemporary poetry (i.e., the poetry he published) was "readable and entertaining" because it "deals with familiar subjects in a familiar manner; that, in doing so, it uses *ordinary* words literally and as often as possible" (1920a, ix–x; italics in the original). Untermeyer turned to Walt Whitman for exactly these values. Whitman, Untermeyer claimed, "with his emphasis on the beauty that lurks in familiar things and his insistence on the 'divine average,' was the greatest of the moderns who showed the grandeur of simplicity, the rich poetry of everyday" (1919a, vii).[3] For many of simplicity's advocates, if familiarity was not exactly the same as universality, it was a close relative. Thus, Charles Wharton Stork asserted the motivating principle of his anthology in the following way: "CONTEMPORARY VERSE wants poems with the appeal, not of novelty, but of universality; poems that affirm, not the superiority of the few, but the kinship of the many." For Stork and others, such universality allowed for a trouble free relationship with the common reader. As Stork went on to claim, "This does not mean an attempt to write down to a vulgar level, it means that a given poet finds his deepest vitality to be in tune with his fellows" (1923, xx). Bonaro Wilkinson, in his *The Poetic Way of Release*, noted that "It appears that most of those whom we may call 'modernistic poets' have fairly lost sight of the fact that truly significant poetry is more intelligible than experience itself, not less intelligible. The great poet must have the ability to clarify by selection and emphasis that which is in reality often blurred by unrelated and uninterpreted details. And he must be above the desire merely to amuse himself, at the expense of the reading public, by the fabrication of clever obscurities" (1931, 212–13).

High modernism's apologists made this complex of values a favorite target, and often had elements of the complex stand in for simplicity. Taking a page out of their attackers' book on difficulty, difficulty's apologists saw simplicity as immersed in culturally conditioned values, and therefore impure. As their opponents did for difficulty, high modern readers tended to see these relationships between simplicity and its cognate values as an unthinking alliance, and a sign of weakness, not toughness. But simplicity, although immersed in culturally conditioned values, missed the one value that was essential for a modern writer: it had nothing to do with newness, with the current conditions of modern life. Simplicity instead was enmired in naivete and nostalgia. Modern life is complex, the belief went, and a writer like Willa Cather, for example, could not very easily be complex by nostalgically turning to the past. High modern readers also tended to identify simplicity with regionalism, with gender, an identification compounded by the high modern predisposition to see regional and female writers as unambitious. As Alfred Kazin remarked in 1942, Cather had "carved out a subtle and interesting world of her own, if the world became increasingly elegiac and soft, it was riches in a little room" (257)."

This gives some sense of why high modernism jettisoned simplicity as a criterion of aesthetic evaluation. Modernism was opposed to the cultural inflections it saw accompanying simplicity, particularly to what F. R. Leavis caricatured as the inheritance of romanticism, a tradition that had "a prejudice against recognising as poetry anything that was not in the most obvious sense of Milton's formula, 'simple, sensuous and passionate.'" (Perhaps Leavis had in mind someone like J. C. Smith, who in the preface to his 1925 anthology *A Book of Modern Verse* quoted Milton's phrase as containing the "marks that have distinguished the best poetry in all ages" [Smith 1925, iv].) Going on, Leavis characterized this aesthetic as asserting that poetry "must be the direct expression of simple emotions. The 'poetical' emotions were of a limited class: the tender, the exalted, the noble, the poignant—in general, the sympathetic.... Wit, play of intellect, stress of cerebral muscle had no place; they could only hinder the correct response, which was to be 'moved'" (1931, 346).

But while such statements suggest why high moderns disliked simplicity, they do not indicate how they *won* the argument. A big part of the answer to that is found in simplicity's inherent weakness as *argument*, a weakness that can begin to be seen in how simplicity's advocates argued against difficulty. As earlier chapters indicated, simplicity's champions thought that everything about difficult art was excessive. The difficult text demanded too much knowledge from its readers; it drew too much attention to its technical virtuosity; it announced too clearly the coterie from which it came; it was too invested in fashion. As well, the intentions of the difficult author were too clear: the difficult text *intended* to obstruct comprehension. All of these complaints signaled that, in the difficult text, what should be unarticulated becomes foregrounded: the struggle for comprehension becomes highlighted, as do the social conditions under which this art has been created. As such things become foregrounded, they become forms of entanglement, ways of removing the artwork's directness. Whatever consequent pleasures the difficult text might bring are those of a technical game: clever, intellectual pleasures, far removed from the lucid pleasures of the great work of art. Unlike great, simple art, which was direct, difficulty, with its excesses, entanglements, and barriers, was not direct enough. As a writer for the *TLS* claimed in 1918, readers of difficult writing were "aware of the difficulty, not of the

> Simplicity in our time is arrived at by an ambages. There is, at this moment, no such thing as a simple poem if what is meant by that is a point-to-point straight line relation of images. If I said that this was so because on the level where the world is mental occurrence a point-to-point relation is no longer genuine I shd be accused of mysticism. Yet it is so.
>
> —"Preface and Statement," Ern Malley, pseudonym for authors of literary hoax, published in *Angry Penguins*, Australia, 1944

art" ("Professionalism" 1918, 49). Lew Sarett, writing a few years after Harriet Monroe had celebrated his *Box of God* in *Poetry*, grumbled about the tendency for modern poets to write "cerebral" poetry that was marked by a "cold brilliance." Modern difficult writers, Sarett charged, create work that "is certain to lack power, depth, and sincerity" (quoted in Ellsworth 1928, 157).

Simple writing was the inverse, and its weakness, as an aesthetic that could be argued about, lay in the terms of that inversion. According to simplicity's proponents, the central virtues of simplicity opposed the deficiencies of difficulty, for simplicity was minimal, "pure," "direct." Marguerite Wilkinson consistently argued for the virtues of simplicity over difficulty, asserting that the purity of a simple text let readers directly into the heart of the poet. Writing in the introduction to her anthology *Contemporary Poetry*, Wilkinson noted that "poetry is sometimes hidden from the wise that it may be revealed to babes," and that "the simple and sincere approach to poetry is of great assistance," an approach in which "the reader should simply receive and share the poem" (1923, 6, 8). The word "simply" is telling, for it is essential to what Wilkinson believed about art. In the introductions to the various poets in her anthology, Wilkinson writes that Sara Teasdale's "The Coin" "is simply a wise little maxim admirably made into verse" (173); that George Sterling's "The Last Days" "simply tells how one person feels about the coming of the autumn" (65); that E. A. Robinson's "Neighbors" "is simply the story of the woman who can never afford to dress well" (67); that Carl Sandburg's "Fog" "is simply a small, masterly metaphor" (121); that a poem by Vachel Lindsay "simply tells a tale that touches our hearts" (143). The repeated "simply" reveals not only that Wilkinson's gesture is her default aesthetic position, one that needs no justification, but also that it does important work: simply put, the term "simply" limits the reach of interpretation, closes off inquiry.

Indeed, in her discussion of the poems in her anthologies, Wilkinson repeatedly argued how the simple poem "needs no explanation," a comment which she directed to at least five different poets (1923, 37, 54, 109, 173, 201).[4] According to Wilkinson, "poetry should not be analyzed until it has been enjoyed. Like religion, it should come to people first of all as an experience" (3). Writing of John Drinkwater's poetry, she argued that "like all good poems, these lyrics should be enjoyed first of all and analyzed afterwards. We have no right to take poems seriously until we have taken them happily" (342). In this position, Wilkinson was typical of many anthologists; her aesthetic lines up unproblematically, for example, with Untermeyer's claim quoted earlier, that great poetry "is felt first and thought out afterwards" (1919, b39).

Simplicity's proponents, then, thought laborious argument could never demonstrate the greatness of art; aesthetic greatness was self-evident, mute. This attitude against argumentation was congruent with the content of simplicity and its various extensions and peripherals, for they all moved in the same direction; they all posited that great, simple art was defined by what it excluded from consideration.[5] This lack shapes all the central propositions of the simplicity argument: for example, that great literature is pure, that it is inspired, and, as the previous chapter has argued, that it provides pleasure. Each of these propositions rests not on what the text does do, but on what it doesn't do, what it has removed from consideration. Thus, in her home-grown anthology *The New Poetry*, Harriet Monroe championed poetry that, in contrast to more difficult writing, was "less vague, less verbose, less eloquent.... It has set before itself an ideal of absolute simplicity and sincerity" (1917, vi). The almost de rigeur modifiers that accompany "simplicity" in such statements are telling. Simplicity is "absolute" (Monroe, above); the great writers are "essentially" simple (Untermeyer 1924, 350); the simple lyric is "the pure essence of song" (Tietjens 1923b, 322); "simplicity is of the essence of greatness" (Alington 1923, 549). The making of great art is a process of distillation, of removing the extraneous. Instead of being entangled, the simple text is "direct."

The central consequence of this lack was that critics who championed simplicity, as Craig Abbott has pointed out for Wilkinson, not only needed "no critical apparatus" when they discussed simple literature, they *couldn't* provide one (1990, 217). Neither could they supply a critical apparatus for simplicity's cognates and effects. The central aesthetic effects of simplicity (purity, pleasure, authenticity, sincerity, directness) could not be supported with evidence; at best, they could be advocated only with a silent gesture to the texts themselves. One could not point to specific moments in a text and discuss at any length why, at this point, the text was particularly simple, or inspired, or pleasurable. Readers could only quote the text, note its affect (that they, for example, experienced pleasure in the presence of these lines), and register what was *not* present at these moments. In short, the simple claims for what made great literature were inherently unverifiable. And, in a culture that was increasingly defining itself as a professionalist culture, that unverifiability came with a cost, for simplicity could not justify itself as an impetus for academic study; it couldn't do close reading. Given that arguments for simplicity inherently had no evidence to present (other than a silent gesture to the texts themselves), simplicity was doomed as an argument, and a form of art, that could be central to a canon based on interpretation and evidentiary arguments.

Consider, for example, William Morton Payne's ([1913] 1977) review of *A Boy's Will* for *Dial* in 1913.[6] Payne begins his review with the comment that "A dream world of elusive shapes and tremulous imaginings is half revealed to our vision by the subdued lyrics which Mr. Robert Frost entitles 'A Boy's Will.'" Words like "elusive," "tremulous," "half revealed," and "subdued" announce the presence of a simplicity aesthetic, and such words continue over the course of the review. Payne goes on: "It is a world in which passion has been stilled and the soul grown quiet—a world not explored with curious interest, but apprehended by the passive recipient. The sun does not shine, but the pale grey of twilight enfolds nature with a more gracious charm. The song called 'Flower-Gathering' offers an exquisite example of the wistful and appealing quality of the author's strain." Now, the poem that Payne cites does in its imagery illustrate his point quite well. Its first lines, which Payne quotes, read:

> I left you in the morning,
> And in the morning glow,
> You walked away beside me
> To make me sad to go.
> Do you know me in the gloaming,
> Gaunt and dusty grey with roaming?

The rhyme, the easily available narrative situation, the fussy diction, the question that gets no response—all these make the poem a plausible instantiation of the critic's generalization. But the poem does not, under Payne's aesthetic, need to be analyzed or interpreted—what academics today, in a telling phrase, call *read*. There is no sense that there are things going on in this poem with which a reader might require help, no need to tells us what the poem *means*. Payne provides no analysis of how the quotation achieves its apparent effects; the quoted lines are just an example of a stunning quality of the poet, presented without analysis or comment and encouraging no consequent elucidation. Quoting the poem in its entirety, Payne follows it not with analysis, but with what, by today's standards, looks like a non sequitur:

The desire of the solitary soul for companionship has rarely found such beautiful expression as it receives in this quotation:

> We make ourselves a place apart
>   behind light words that tease and flout,
> But oh, the agitated heart
>   Till someone find us really out.

Payne has simply moved on, in order to display another unarguable aspect of Frost's excellence. The review has no logical development: the first part of Payne's review could switch places with the second and leave the review basically unchanged. The rhetorical trope of the grand gesture toward the poem, followed by a swatch of poetry, is repeated, just as it is repeated in the conclusion to his review. Payne introduces his last example with the phrase "'Reluctance' is the poem that closes the collection—a lyric of lassitude with just a faint flicker of the spent fire of life." He then quotes four six-line stanzas, and ends the review with: "If Mr. Frost's verses show the cast of melancholy, there is at least nothing morbid about it. In their simple phrasing and patent sincerity, his songs give us the sort of pleasure that we have in those of the 'Shropshire Lad' of Mr. Housman" (4, 5). Now, this is not the sort of writing that could hold up under New Critical scrutiny. But one should remember what this review sets out to do. It is not that Payne is a poor reader under his terms, and that he should have given more analysis. His aesthetic is simply uninterested in and unsuited to argumentation.

Difficulty's aesthetic, on the other hand, proffered a different interaction, both from its proponents and from within the art itself. This interpretive impetus was apparent early on, across the reading community. Early reviewers of *The Waste Land* or *Ulysses* overwhelmingly concerned themselves with what these texts *meant*, and they realized it wouldn't do to begin a review of either of these works with the phrase that this was "simply" a work that "needs no explanation." J. C. Squire began his review of *The Waste Land* with the following telling phrase: "I read Mr. Eliot's poem several times when it first appeared; I have now read it several times more; I am still unable to make head or tail of it" (1923, 655). Rather than assume, in a moment of panic, that because these texts did not fit high culture's default aesthetic they must necessarily be flawed, high moderns convincingly claimed that they turned to the text, to demonstrable, textual moments; and that their emphasis on technique was, as Eliot claimed, "precise, tractable, under control" (1923a, 40). Now, much of this may have been smoke and mirrors; Eliot's criticism, for example, shows very little close reading. But it was making the right kind of noises, and in New Criticism high modernism eventually produced an argumentative apparatus that was capable of such looking. As a result, early difficult readings of high modernism, although they can seem crude and lacking in detail, are clearly part of the same genre as contemporary literary criticism. There is not a difference of kind between Pritchard's 1984 *Frost: A Literary Life Reconsidered* and Riding and Graves's 1927 *A Survey of Modernist Poetry* (perhaps the first example of modern close reading). And, the texts of high modernism were also considered to *reward* evidentiary argumentation; they could sustain a look conducted on these terms. Just as a simple aesthetic seemed completely askew to the aims of difficult modernism, so too simple texts seemed unable to produce rewarding readings under high modern reading practices.

This is not to say that the difficulty aesthetic proceeded, at each of its stages, on the basis of sound evidence. Modern difficulty, like every aesthetic system, has an element of arbitrariness about it, a founding moment that needs to be accepted a priori, a moment where the goodness of difficulty simply has to be accepted as a given in order for the aesthetic to proceed. Unlike simplicity, however, difficulty was, after that foundational moment, seemingly able to proceed forward on the basis of evidence. Simplicity, and its cognates "sincerity" and "authenticity," were vulnerable at this point, for they did not produce the *kind* of argument that difficulty was. This disjunction has had consequences. "Simple" literary criticism—unlike that of Eliot, for example—no longer fits into the category of what we think of as "literary criticism." It is not that Wilkinson and Monroe are wrong in saying that one should "simply receive" art, for how could one evaluate such arguments? Their wrongness or rightness is not the central issue; much more unsettling is that they are not *understandable*; they seem to be making a category mistake. Simplicity has been so completely eradicated that, even if one understands the pressures that excised it from aesthetic discussion, twentieth-century aesthetic writing that works within early twentieth-century understandings of simplicity seems more alien than wrong. And that is a much bigger victory for difficulty. It is impossible anymore to write literary criticism as William Morton Payne did in 1913. By today's understandings of what it means to read a poem, simple readings of literature are incomprehensible. And, because simplicity-based arguments are unrecognizable as literary criticism, some of the presuppositions of high modernist criticism against simplicity (such as difficulty) seem so natural as to be beyond discussion.[7]

Robert Frost and Willa Cather

The reception histories of numerous twentieth-century writers, from A. E. Housman to Carl Sandburg, from John Steinbeck to Edna St. Vincent Millay, indicate how completely simplicity has been eliminated. Focusing my attention on the work of Robert Frost and Willa Cather, I begin with a curious but typical moment, William Pritchard's 1984 biography of Robert Frost. In it, Pritchard observes that many of the early laudatory reviews of Frost praised the poet's simplicity. That simplicity makes Pritchard uneasy. While he doesn't mind the initial praise of Frost, Pritchard is nervous about the reasons for this praise—for simplicity is not a useful virtue to claim for Frost if one is bent on establishing him as a central modernist. Citing the concluding lines of Frost's "Storm Fear," Pritchard notes that these are the kinds of lines "that readers of *A Boy's Will*, including Pound, might naturally have thought of as simple: there are only two words of more than two syllables in the whole of it, while the feeling of helplessness and fear is an easily available one.... But almost immediately one is struck by how the disposition of words and line lengths and rhymes is not simple at all, is certainly more complicated than what passed for 'technique' in most of the writers from the 1927 *Oxford Book of American Verse*." Indeed, Pritchard argues, there are effects in these lines "for which 'simplicity' will hardly do as a name," and that there is "nothing the least bit 'simple'" about the poem (1984, 19, 20).

The values enfolded within Pritchard's comments are telling. Pritchard not only believes that Frost's first readers liked his poetry for a quality that it did not, in fact, have (its simplicity); he also believes that the term "simplicity" itself is a problem. As the polemical tone and scare quotes suggest, "simplicity" is a contested term, one that Pritchard believes has more negative values than positive, values that are generally accepted by today's readers and that, according to Pritchard, do not need to be articulated. Now, Pritchard may be right about Frost; Frost may in fact (by today's reading protocols) not be simple. But how did it happen that asserting a lack of simplicity became a necessary move for establishing Frost's value—not only for Pritchard but for virtually all of Frost's critics, for critics of Willa Cather—indeed, for critics of all the simple moderns?

The history of Cather and Frost shows that for the most part high culture does not think of difficulty as an incidental quality of great art, a quality that a great work may or may not have. Difficulty's virtues are not on the order of, say, iambic pentameter, or counterpoint, or sfumato. Rather, difficulty is an essential quality of what literary critics consider great art. It is not a coincidence that none of the simple moderns have triumphed, particularly as long as they have continued to be thought of as simple. Without difficulty, and without the particular form of difficulty taken on by high modernism, canonization doesn't happen. Further, in the reception history of Frost and Cather (and, I would wager, many others), the turn to difficulty has a peculiar temporal shape, driven by the modernist debate on difficulty. Both writers were (1) early lionized for their simplicity and realism, (2) then rejected as "unmodern" because of their simplicity, and (3) then recanonized—but only partially—by critics claiming for them not simplicity, but an essential difficulty. It is intellectually more exciting, and canonically it is a better strategy, to make Frost difficult than it is to make him simple. This is not to say that the recovery has been complete: Frost's and Cather's return to the center of the canon, since it depends on a form of difficulty structurally different from that of the canonical high moderns, could only be partial.[8]

In the early stages of their careers, Frost and Cather were initially well received by a diverse audience, including high modernists. Moreover, their simplicity was considered an integral part of their realism, and for all readers it was a positive aesthetic criterion. Writing with a little condescension showing through, Ezra Pound described Frost's *A Boy's Will* as "simple . . . without sham and without affectation." Pound thought the work "a little raw, and [having] in it a number of infelicities; underneath them it has the tang of the New Hampshire woods, and it has just this utter sincerity. It is not post-Miltonic or post-Swinburnian or post-Kiplonian. This man has the good sense to speak naturally and to paint the thing, the thing as he sees it" ([1913] 1977, 1–2). Pound argued that Frost's work "comes direct from his own life," a formula that he was to repeat the next year in his review of *North of Boston*, in which he depicted Frost as "an honest writer, writing from himself, from his own knowledge and emotion; not simply picking up the manner which magazines are accepting at the moment, and applying it to topics in vogue. He is quite consciously and effortlessly putting New England rural life into verse" ([1914] 1954c, 16). F. S. Flint, who in the years preceding this had been working alongside Pound in founding Imagism, noted of *A Boy's Will* that "simplicity" was "the great charm of his book; and it is a simplicity that proceeds from a candid heart"; that each poem was "the complete expression of one mood, one emotion, one idea" ([1913] 1977, 3). Flint argued that "behind" all of the poems was "the heart and life of a man, and the more you ponder his poems, the more convinced you become that the heart is pure and the life lived not in vain" (4). Amy Lowell noted that Frost "tells you what he has seen exactly as he has seen it," and that he does so with words that "are simple, straightforward, direct, manly, and there is an elemental quality in all he does which would surely be lost if he chose to pursue niceties of phrase" ([1915] 1977, 20).

In this, these high modern readers did not make very different noises from those made by more conservative readers, such as this anonymous writer in *The Academy*, who found the writing in *A Boy's Will* to be "so simple, lucid, and experimental that, reading a poem, one can see clearly with the poet's own swift eye, and follow the trail of his glancing thought. One feels that this man has *seen* and *felt*; seen with a revelatory, a creative vision; felt personally and intensely; and he simply writes down, without confusion or affectation, the results thereof" ("Procession" [1913,] 1977, 5). George Browne claimed that Frost's poetry was popular with common readers because it "is written in a language they can understand and enjoy, because it is the language they speak, vibrant with the feeling and force and form of the familiar spoken

> At least I am sure I can count on you to give me credit for knowing what I am about. You are not going to make the mistake that Pound makes of assuming that my simplicity is that of the untutored child. I am not undesigning.
>
> —Robert Frost, letter to Thomas Mosher, July 10, 1913

sentence" ([1916] 1977, 36). Frost's most influential conservative proponent, Louis Untermeyer, repeatedly praised Frost in his anthologies, noting in a review of *New Hampshire* that Frost had an "absolute freedom from contemporary fashions, technical trickery, or the latest erudite slang," and that "in the very simplicity of these lines we have the unaffected originality of Frost" ([1924] 1977, 65).

Cather's work initially received the same reaction. Eva Mahoney, writing in the *Omaha World-Herald*, noted in 1921 that anyone writing about Cather "must approach his subject with simplicity and sincerity. If he does not he will sin ... against the canons of art" (quited in Carlin 1992, 3). In her 1927 book *Fire under the Andes*, in which she described Frost as "one of the few authentic poets of his age" (300), Elizabeth Sergeant argued of Cather that "her life, her work, and her personality have a simple unity and consistency" (261). Looking over the scope of Cather's writing, Sergeant returned with favor to the early works, which, she thought, "comprehend youth and simplicity so largely and profoundly" and thus were more successful than her late work, "where the ugliness, the complexity of middle or old age pierce through." The problem with the later work, Sergeant argued, was that "this 'modern life' from which Willa Cather had tried to protect her writing had 'got in at' her after all. She does not want to probe its depths, and its surfaces wound her." For Sergeant, Cather "feels the large, bold essentials and simplicities to be thus obscured" in an urban setting (279, 282). Carl Van Doren noted that Cather wrote "beautifully and delicately," with an "utterly artless handling" of character, and that she produced writing which was "clear and fresh and simple" (1940, 283, 289). Thus described, Cather's writing eventually came to be seen as a sign of defiance against high modernism's tyranny. As early as 1927, Herschell Brickell noted in an advertising supplement in the *North American Review* that "Miss Cather has given the younger generation who think the overtones of life can only be caught in murky, obscure, amorphous prose a lesson, if they will heed it." Alfred Kazin in his *On Native Grounds* similarly celebrated Cather for bringing to her work "none of the formal declarations and laborious experiments that Hemingway and Dos Passos brought to theirs" (1942, 248).

But simplicity could not canonize an author on high modern terms; indeed, with high modern terms rapidly becoming the only terms in play, simplicity quickly became a handicap. High moderns discarded simplicity as much for itself as for the ideas that accompanied it. High modern teeth were set on edge because of the company that simplicity kept, as when a reviewer for the *Christian Century* in 1929 praised Frost's work for having "a narrowly world-accepting philosophy, a calmly but pungently life-affirming mood, a grey elfin mysticism" (Root [1929] 1977, 74). Further, the kind of realism that came along with simplicity (frequently accompanied with such terms as "authenticity" and "sincerity") increasingly became an inadequate criterion for entry to the center of the modern canon, and these writers' accompanying simplicity was even more of a problem, for high modernism soon jettisoned the idea that simplicity was one of the characteristics of realism. Reality, they believed, was more complicated than that. Simplicity was simplistic.

As high modernism gathered steam, Cather's and Frost's early acceptance became qualified, and more dismissive statements were made about them, particularly because of their surface simplicity and the qualities that apparently came with it. R. P. Blackmur, writing of Frost, distinguished between the bard (someone who "is at heart an easygoing versifier of all that comes to hand") and the real poet, to Frost's discredit. Blackmur claimed that Frost, "when ... he attempts to make poems of his social reactions without first having submitted them to the full travail of the poetic imagination," has become a bard, someone who looks for "escape" (1936, 818). Writing in the *Yale Review* in 1928, Frederick Pierce damned Frost's work as "charming," in that, "From the roar and bustle of Wall Street and the overelaborate intellectual life or our educational system, it calls us back to childhood's dreams among the green fields." But this was also Frost's limitation, according to Pierce: "Our admiration is for the sincerity and delicate insight with which the theme is handled. Our disappointment is because of the smallness, limitation, almost barrenness, of the theme itself. It may be true that a perfectly carved cameo is a greater work of art than a clumsily constructed pyramid; but it is equally true that the greatest poems lead us out into the vast complexity of life and do not keep us indefinitely in a little walled-in nook, however beautiful" ([1928] 1977, 70). As this kind of thinking became more dominant, Frost's apparent simplicity at times became a caustic sound bite. Apparently Dylan Thomas, after being chastised for his obscurity, acerbically replied: "Read Frost" (quoted in Meyers 1996, 297).

Cather's reputation suffered similar attacks. Even some of her supporters, nervous perhaps at the apparent lack of ambition in simple writing, helped set the agenda for her dismissal. Rebecca West compared, to Cather's discredit, the limited goals of Cather to the "courage" of a writer like D. H.

> The facts of nature and of life are more apt to be complex than simple. Simplistic theories are generally one-sided and partial.
>
> —J. F. Clarke, first recorded instance in the *Oxford English Dictionary* of the use of the word "simplistic," 1881

Lawrence: "Does not such transcendental courage, does not such ambition to extend consciousness beyond its present limits and elevate man above himself, entitle his art to be ranked as more important than that of Miss Cather?" (1928, 243). Lionel Trilling, turning his attention to Willa Cather, grumbled that "the 'spirituality' of Miss Cather's latest books consists chiefly of an irritated exclusion of those elements of modern life with which she will not cope" (1936, 54). David Daiches argued that Cather "was not interested in any kind of radical experimentation with the technique of the novel, and some interest of that kind was necessary to achieve the delicate texture of such a novel as *To the Lighthouse*" (1951, 139). Even Alfred Kazin, although supportive of Cather, ended his famous 1942 essay on her work with the following qualified appraisal: "There was no need to apologize for her or to "place" her; she had made a place for herself, carved out a subtle and interesting world of her own. If the world became increasingly elegiac and soft, it was riches in a little room" (1942, 257).

That, of course, is not where things have stayed; one cannot today exclude Frost and Cather from a modern canon and remain unchallenged. But Frost and Cather were resuscitated on high modern terms, for when critics began to recuperate Frost and Cather, they did so by claiming for them a kind of difficulty, by claiming that simple, univocal readings of these writers were not a naive start in the right direction, but were fundamentally inadequate. Critics argued that below the surface of these writers' texts lay interesting difficulties, that their simplicity was deceptive, that it was, in fact, a form of difficulty.

For Frost, the recuperation started much earlier than Pritchard's biography. As early as 1939, Cleanth Brooks was arguing that Frost "is popularly supposed to be homely, salty, direct, whereas poets like Ransom and Tate are reputed to be tortured intellectual obscurantists." The difference, Brooks argued, was illusory; Frost shared an essential difficulty with these poets, and with all great writers (1939, 110). Brooks's assertion was paralleled in two later, famous moments. In his late 1940s essay "The Other Frost," Randall Jarrell similarly argued against the common perception of Frost as "the one living poet who has written good poems that ordinary readers like without

> The boys have roared and fought; they have left out the commas and added the hyphens; they have galloped to Paris or Moscow; they have dived into degeneracy or phony holiness; but quiet and alone, Willa Cather has greatly pictured the great life.
>
> —Sinclair Lewis in *Newsweek*, 1938

any trouble and understand without any trouble; the conservative editorialist and self-made apothegm-joiner, full of dry wisdom and free, complacent, Yankee enterprise; the Farmer-Poet—this is an imposing private role perfected for public use, a sort of Olympian Will Rogers out of *Tanglewood Tales*; and, last or first of all, Frost is the standing, speaking reproach to any other good modern poet: 'If Frost can write poetry that's just as easy as Longfellow you can too—you do too'" (reprint 1953, 26). This view of Frost, Jarrell argued, "has helped get him neglected or depreciated by intellectuals." Jarrell went on to press the virtues of the "other" Frost, the Frost who at his best writes poems that, "so far from being obvious, optimistic, orthodox, many ... are extraordinarily subtle and strange" (27).[9] Several years later, on the occasion of Frost's eighty-fifth birthday, Lionel Trilling (in remarks that we will return to later in this chapter) made essentially the same kind of point. That, essentially, has been the turn that almost all critics make in asserting Frost's canonical status: that careful reading will uncover not a surface simplicity but an essential difficulty. The logical awkwardness that critics then have to negotiate their way around is the commerce that these poems also have with simple readings. Many try to find a way to honor the simple, but even in doing so the default trajectory is to argue that the difficulty is what is *essential* about Frost. Critics typically find a way to assert, as Kathryn Van Spanckeren (2002) and Jeffrey Meyers (1996) (and, forty years before him, Robert Spiller [1955, 183]) point out in a tellingly popular phrase, that Frost's poems have a "deceptive simplicity."

Cather was similarly resuscitated. In 1943 Maxwell Geismar argued that Cather possessed "one of the most complex, if not difficult and contradictory minds in our letters," and he cited Cather's "persistent concern with the 'darker' instincts: that is, with those temptations and acerbations of the flesh which have rested beneath the cultivated surface of her art, and have actually been responsible for the tension of her work" (1943, 155–56, 195). Concurring, Edward and Lillian Bloom argued that Cather's work exhibited a "deceptive simplicity" (1949–50, 72), a formulation repeated by Lois Feger in 1970 when she described *My Ántonia* as "deceptively simple" (774), John Murphy, who in 1984 described Cather as "a writer of apparent simplicity, actual complexity" (2), and Jo Ann Middleton in her 1990 *Willa Cather's Modernism*, who noted that Cather's work was "deceptively simple to read" (21). In a teleological summation of Cather criticism, Sharon O'Brien notes, "Earlier readers both praised and dismissed Cather for her simplicity and conservatism, but in the last decade critics have begun to discover the complexity beneath the apparent surface of simplicity and the resonance of her seemingly transparent, luminous prose" (1984, 598).

These rereadings of Frost and Cather do not just stretch out early readings, continuing their implications. Most canonizing critics, such as these I have just quoted, argue that the initial simple readings of Frost and Cather are not authentic readings, they are fundamentally incomplete. Something has gone wrong; that is why the work has to be described as having an "*actual complexity*" or being "*deceptively* simple." In this model of the deceptively simple, simplicity takes on the function that the techniques of difficulty do for those, like Alington, opposed to difficult modernism. Simplicity is the entanglement, the barrier to a "real" understanding. John Ciardi, arguing against critics who had dismissed Frost from serious consideration, posited that, "misled by the surface simplicity of Mr. Frost's poems, they have dismissed them as being simple—all the way down" (1962, 16). D. H. Stewart, writing in the *Queen's Quarterly* in 1966, noted a similar deception in Cather, claiming that Cather's *Death Comes for the Archbishop* "is one of the most elaborately contrived novels ever fashioned by an American, rivaling in artistic allusiveness Eliot's *Wasteland* [sic], and in technical complexity Faulkner's *Absalom, Absalom!* So adroit had she become in the practice of her much publicized '*démeublé* form' that she could use it as a mere facade. Behind its plain face she built, as it were, a complicated cathedral into which busy critics of her time and ours seldom glance" (244).

This redeployment of simplicity as a barrier to what is "really" going on in a text is a method of canonization idiosyncratic to the twentieth century and steeped in its conceptualizing of difficulty. As a canonizing gesture, it differs from traditional notions of inexhaustibility, of works that grow ever richer as one continues to look at them. Inexhaustibility is not premised on a disjunction between surface and depth, and so it does not discount first-level simplicity. (Think of the inexhaustible text as an onion, with inner layers just working out the implications of the outer.) Inexhaustibility does not denigrate the kind of reading one may have engaged in before one recognizes (and to some degree solves) the complexity; it is not premised on an interpretive crisis the way that difficulty is. Such a disjunction, however, governs the appropriation of Frost and Cather. So, while according to premodernist principles of canonization it could conceivably be argued that Frost is inexhaustible, for him to be central to the modern canon his first-level simplicity must be deceptive, a barrier, difficult. (Difficulty always urges readers

196   The Difficulties of Modernism

> Housman's poetry, like his life, is deceptively simple: this volume shows some of the complex currents below the surface
> —Publisher's blurb for *A. E. Housman: A Reassessment*, 1999

forward, suggesting that they discard what they have done so far, that they haven't done enough, and that they haven't done the important work.) It was not enough to make Frost inexhaustibly rich; his texts needed the duplicity of difficulty.[10] As a result, in canonizing the simple moderns, critics typically deny legitimacy to the simple level and claim that only the underlying difficulty is "real."

That first layer produces the crisis in the reputations of Cather and Frost. One is left with what critic Allon White, borrowing a phrase from Althusser, calls "symptomatic reading." The consequences are great: "Symptomatic reading has become an intellectual reflex of our age. By refusing to take an utterance at its word it treats it as the symptom of a hidden 'problematic' or 'sub-text'. Its initial gesture is one of suspicion or refusal, and above all it refuses to treat a work of literature or a conscious utterance as complete. There is always something further which has been disavowed, repressed, or avoided. Nothing can be taken at face value." White goes on to argue that one of the problems of such reading is that it does not account for reading pleasure, and it treats the phenomenal text as the equivalent of a "sore throat" (1981, 6).

This dismissal of surface creates a disjunction between these texts' surface and their depth, and it avails itself of standard Western conceptual hierarchies in which surface is inconsequential, and real value is to be found in depth. Thus, as noted previously, John Ciardi complained that critics of Frost had been "misled by the surface simplicity," and had consequently read the poems as being simple "all the way down"; D. H. Stewart distinguished between the "mere facade" of Cather's writing, a facade that had a "complicated cathedral" "behind its plain face." As chapter 2 discussed, such metaphors of layering, surface, and depth are central to talk about difficulty. Twentieth-century aesthetics was nervous about the value of the outer layer of a work of art, with most people seeing it as the least important, something to be done with quickly, before one moved on to what was central to the work.[11]

This shared agreement was stable in modern argumentation, despite the fierce disagreements about difficulty's value. All agreed that below the surface lay what was "real" and essential, such as emotion, the truth of the heart, or depth of thought. Donald Stauffer, writing of the poetry of A. E. Housman,

> "I really do feel," Gwyn was saying, angling his head to accommodate the photographer who crouched at his feet, "That the novelist has to find a new simplicity."
> "How, Gwyn, how?"
> "By *evolving* into simplicity. By deciding on the new direction and heading for it."
> "To where, Gwyn, where?"
> "How about if we loop the *Post* guy," called the publicity boy, "and he can just *watch* you do the radio spot?"
> "To fresh fields. Okay: the guy from *EF* can listen to me do the TV spot—from the audio booth. And pastures new."
>
> •
>
> Gwyn liked being taken seriously and wanted—and expected—much more of it. He felt strongly attracted to the idea that his work was *deceptively* simple. But he wished they'd make their questions easier.
>
> —Martin Amis, *The Information*, 1996

asserted that a poem, for a "reader of sensitivity and experience, . . . will not have a single simple key; the literal meaning . . . is usually the least satisfactory; and the further a reader progresses toward meanings difficult to formulate, the closer he seems to be to the heart of the poem" (1946, 157). This is the same fundamental value that is seen in F. L. Lucas' review of *The Waste Land*, in which Lucas argued that poetry like Eliot's "replaces depth by muddiness" ([1923] 1982, 195). (In arguing this Lucas also implied, as did many conservatives, that the layers of meaning in a poem had to be something that could be seen through.) And so, a writer like Edith Sitwell, herself lambasted by Squire as part of the first generation of modern obscurantists, argued that the *second*, younger generation of modernist poets (such as Auden and Zukofsky), "present surface difficulties," but not to the advantage of their art: "This surface difficulty gives the average person the impression that the poems conceal great depths. But this is rarely so" (1934, 231).

But even though the surface might not be ultimately important, if the surface was difficult, conservative readers found it hard to value the poem, because the difficulty presented a barrier to the depth. Arguing that difficulty had a "tenuous legitimacy" in fiction, George O'Donnell asserted that it was "dangerous because it may perform the decidedly illegitimate function of standing between the reader and his final understanding of the characters and of the story, instead of helping him toward that understanding"

([1936] 1995, 143). Similarly, novelist Sinclair Lewis panned the writing of Marguerite Young, finding Young guilty of "surrounding her real garden of beauty with a fence of fog through which no reader can peer" (1945, 51).

Given that its difficulty was invariably a difficulty of surface, high modernism also had to find a way to make this aspect of the work aesthetically valuable. It was a tricky business, even from within high modernism, for the general distrust of surface reveals itself in some of the nervousness about the value of difficulty, and also shows in comments about transitory difficulty, about difficulty as being essential to all great art. Now, seemingly in the face of this distrust of surface, high modernism privileged *surface* difficulty and did it so successfully that it is a privileging that has not left us. Most notably, there was an interest in the texture of difficulty itself; many valued surface difficulty because of its engagement with such issues as the nature of knowledge, pleasure, literature, and comprehension itself. These issues were engaged so productively because they were at the surface, the *first* things the reader noticed about these texts. Surface difficulty resulted in a reading experience in which the text's difficulty had to be engaged with *immediately*; it presented an interpretive crisis whose anxiety demanded interpretation. Readers like Conrad Aiken valued this immediacy because of its apparent mimesis, reproducing the texture of contemporary experience; to others it had additional values because of how it limited and directed its readership and because of its apparent fearlessness.

This valuable surface difficulty was not paralleled by a congruent difficulty of depth. High modern critics did not show that the difficult work, at its heart, was difficult as well. The trajectory was different. For modernism's apologists, difficult works had a thematic consistency in which the depth explained the surface. In their early formalist anthology, *Reading Poems: An Introduction to Critical Study*, Wright Thomas and Stuart Gerry Brown asserted that "The mastery of the reading of *The Waste Land* means moving from an initial experience of the terrifying futility of modern living to ever richer perception and experience as the many levels of meaning are comprehended" (1941, 719). The depth justifies the surface, and the critic who explicates this relationship is the successful professional who defuses the crisis that the difficult surface had initiated.

Simple texts didn't work this way. Unlike with most canonized high modern authors, the first level of Frost and Cather is the simple level, from which difficulties must be extracted in order for the activity of interpretation to be plausible (the impulse of high modernism is exactly the reverse). There is a different interpretive trajectory. With the canonical high moderns it is from a surface difficulty to an underlying unity, even simplicity; with the simple moderns the trajectory is reversed, from an initial simplicity to an underlying difficulty.[12] As a consequence, with writers like Frost and Cather the only way to create difficulty and an ensuing interpretive crisis (one that can be resolved only by literary professionals) is by positing a radical disjunction between surface and depth. As a canonizing gesture, that push to interpretive difficulty (and the consequent idea of deceptive simplicity) was inevitable, since these writers' apparent surface simplicity also seemed patently bankrupt: there was nothing to say about it, and critics were attracted to texts that gave them something to write about, something that *needed* their professional expertise. Consequently, critics needed to talk about deceptive simplicity; the task of criticism became making difficult that which initially seemed obvious, to create a *crisis*. But the plausibility of an underlying difficulty of these writers was not enough; the simple moderns' lack of surface difficulty continues to create a barrier for their full admission to the canon.

Dissenters

Two distinct groups have dissented from these canonizing moves. First, many critics have not been convinced either of these writers' centrality or their deceptive simplicity. As Sharon O'Brien notes, Cather's position in the American literary canon is tenuous: "she has been considered an important writer and yet somehow not a 'major' one, somehow not an equal colleague of Hawthorne, James, or Faulkner, and perhaps not even in the same realm as Fitzgerald, Hemingway, or Dreiser" (1988, 110). In 1994, Frank Lentricchia could unproblematically state that Frost "is the least respected of the moderns" (76). The lack of complete success can to a large degree be explained by the fact that literary critics have for the most part accepted the way high modernism framed the debate on difficulty and the privileging of surface difficulty. Within this framework, Frost and Cather's difficulty isn't difficulty's most exciting or ambitious form, and so the place they are given in the canon is not front row center, but an aisle seat somewhere in the balcony.

But at the heart of critical uneasiness lies the suspicion that these two writers are, in a central way, simple, and that "deceptive simplicity" just doesn't account for the effects of their texts. For many academic writers, the surface simplicity of these writers is central to the claims that these texts make, and it seems counterintuitive to dismiss the simple aspects of these texts by characterizing them as a ruse. The amount of work that needs to be done to make their writing essentially difficult ends up producing a schizophrenic text, a text which seems to offer at its core a meaning that is at odds, both in terms of its content and the *type* of statements that it makes, with its language, sentence structure, and narrative situations. This unwillingness to dispose of Frost's and Cather's simplicity should not be understood as an implicit endorsement of these writers, for the allegiances to simplicity in these writers is, for most critics, their least attractive feature. It is unattractive not only because there is not much to say about it, but also because of the predominant belief that all language really is difficult, and that texts that we think of as simple are not really using language for its natural potential. In fact, they are being dishonest.

Moreover, in their public presentation of themselves and in their own critical pronouncements, Frost and Cather seem inextricably more connected to the simple side of things than to the difficult. Willa Cather, writing as a young reporter in the *Nebraska State Journal*, made more than a few comments that sound like Marguerite Wilkinson. In November 1893, for example, Cather noted that "One can only say of perfection that it is perfect; we have no adjectives which can go any higher" (1966, 262). Warming to her topic, Cather went on: "Men cannot say where art gets its beauty, where power gets its strength. The greatest perfection a work of art can ever attain is when it ceases to be a work of art and becomes a living fact. Art and science may make a creation perfect in symmetry and form, but it is only the genius which forever evades analysis that can breathe into it a living soul and make it great" (263). Taking on the mantle that J. C. Squire would wear with such panache, Cather three years later would grumble "realism has been pushed to its last limit until we are sick of the barnyard and the gutter, and as for the weird and fantastic—heavens, is there one more nerve left in us that has not been jangled and jarred by these craftsmen of the impossible? *Vive la bizarrerie!* is the literary watchword; we have studies in color, studies in environment, studies in heredity, studies in sex, studies in anything but common sense. Anything that is odd, unheard of, unnatural 'goes.' We translate from other languages not what is good, but what is bizarre." Advocating a return to "some quiet place in the country" where one could go to "drink spring water and go to bed with the robins," Cather asserted that "satiated we have come back to nature acknowledging that she is best, amid the wrecks of an old life we are beginning anew" ([1896] 1966, 342).

Granted, this is Cather when she was young, and not afraid to toss out such pronouncements as "art ought to simplify" ([1913] 1966, 447). But in 1936, nearing the end of her career and sensing that she was out of step with the high moderns, Cather published her collection *Not under Forty*, explaining that the title "means that the book will have little interest for people under forty years of age. The world broke in two in 1922 or thereabouts, and the persons and prejudices recalled in these sketches slid back into yesterday's seven thousand years" (v). Thus separating herself from the generation that identified with the great works of 1922, *The Waste Land* and *Ulysses*, Cather undertook in her *The Novel Démeublé* to defend her art.[13] Attacking the cheapness of much realism as writing "manufactured to entertain great multitudes of people," Cather claimed that such art "must be considered exactly like a cheap soap or a cheap perfume, or cheap furniture" (1936, 44). Instead, one should proceed by "suggestion." Citing the greatness of Tolstoy, Cather noted that the details in his writing, "the clothes, the dishes, the haunting interiors of those old Moscow houses, are always so much a part of the emotions of the people that they are perfectly synthesized; they seem to exist, not so much in the author's mind, as in the emotional penumbra of the characters themselves" (48). Within this kind of thinking, Cather's conclusion seems natural: "The higher processes of art are all processes of simplification. The novelist must learn to write, and then he must unlearn it; just as the modern painter learns to draw, and then learns when to utterly disregard his accomplishment, when to subordinate it to a higher and truer effect" (48–49). While it must be acknowledged that Cather here is denouncing the descriptive and contextual excesses of some forms of realism (what she calls "tasteless amplitude") and is propounding instead what she sees as an authentic realism rather than simplicity first of all, it is undeniable how close her language is to the classic defenses of simplicity.[14] In her analysis of *The Scarlet Letter*, for example, she praises the novel for its "consistent mood, [in which] one can scarcely ever see the actual surroundings of the people; one feels them, rather, in the dusk" (1936, 50). She follows this with her most quoted aesthetic statement: "Whatever is felt upon the page without being specifically named there—that, one might say, is created. It is the inexplicable presence of the thing not named, of the overtone divined by the ear but not heard by it, the verbal mood, the emotional aura of the fact or the thing or the deed, that gives high quality to the novel or the drama, as well as to poetry itself" (50). Lionel Trilling, as part of the Marxist generation of critics who were among the first to de-accession Cather's work, argued that this suggestivity by absence had made her work "irrelevant and tangential—for any time" (1936, 54). Whatever one might think of Trilling's value judgment, Trilling was right to sense that the amalgam of values that one finds in Cather's critical writing allies her much more closely with Marguerite Wilkinson, Cyril Alington, and Louis Untermeyer than with Gertrude Stein, Ezra Pound, and T. S. Eliot.

But it is curious that in the history of Cather criticism critics have widely quoted her articulation of "the thing not named" in order to defend her actual difficulty. Edward and Lillian Bloom, for example, note that her work has "a deceptive simplicity since it emerges not from naiveté but from her deliberate and conscious theory of art." Quoting Cather's "the higher processes of art are all processes of simplification," the Blooms go on to assert that "Willa Cather derives her simplicity from the effort to subordinate all details and subsidiary meanings to what she terms a 'higher and truer effect'" (1949–50, 72). The "thing not named" becomes for Sharon O'Brien a sign of Cather's lesbianism, giving her work "the allusive, suggestive quality we associate with modernism." O'Brien argues that "the aesthetic of indirection she espoused in "The Novel Démeublé" suggests at once the lesbian writer forced to conceal and the twentieth century writer aware of both the inadequacies and the possibilities of language" (1984, 598).

Now, it could be that there are properties in Cather's text that encourage a difficult reading. But Cather's own aesthetic statements were about "suggestion," not about "hiddenness," or "resistance," or "covert" qualities, and Cather's statements about "suggestion" and "the thing not named" seem more rooted in the aesthetics of simplicity than they are in a difficulty aesthetic and the high modern sense of the inherent fallibility of language. Further, Cather welcomed her mass audience that did not read her as a difficult writer. Instead of privileging readings that find a "deceptive simplicity" in her work, we might pay closer attention to Cather's satisfaction with her large public audience, for example, her claim that she "felt a contentment more instinctive and complete than any purely literary critic could give her" at hearing that "a former president of the Missouri Pacific" loved her writing (quoted in Peck 1996, 257). We might pay attention to her unwillingness to become part of university curricula, and we might pay more attention to Demaree Peck's reading of Cather criticism, in which Peck scrutinizes the critical presumption that readings of Cather as fundamentally cheerful and simple must be wrong, since serious art doesn't have these qualities.[15]

Robert Frost flirted with simplicity in the same way. In an interview with Richard Poirier, Frost responded to Poirier's noting that "most modern poetry is obscure and overdifficult, that this is particularly true of Pound and Eliot, but that it isn't true of you." Replied Frost: "Well, I don't want to be difficult. I like to fool—oh, you know, you like to be mischievous. But not in that dull way of just being dogged and doggedly obscure" (Frost 1963, 27). Always touchy about his relationship with intellectuals, Frost in a 1913 letter enacted the same anxieties that Norman Rockwell would a few decades later:

> there is a kind of success called "of esteem" and it butters no parsnips. It means a success with the critical few who are supposed to know. But really to arrive where I can stand on my legs as a poet and nothing else I must get outside that circle to the general reader who buys books in their thousands. I may not be able to do that. I believe in doing it—dont [sic] you doubt me there. I want to be a poet for all sorts and kinds. I could never make a merit of being caviare to the crowd the way my quasi-friend Pound does. (*Selected Letters*, 98)

To an interviewer, Frost remarked that a "poet should not include in his writing anything that the average reader will not easily understand" (quoted in Lentricchia 1994, 107).

This is not to say that Frost was above deviousness. In a letter to Louis Untermeyer, Frost wrote: "You get more credit for thinking if you restate formulae or cite cases that fall in easily under formulae, but all the fun is outside saying things that suggest formulae but won't formulate—that almost but don't quite formulate. I should like to be so subtle at this game as to seem to

> I have with me as consultant the well-known symbolist, Howard Schmitt of Buffalo, to mind my baseball slang and interpret the incidentals. The first player comes to the bat, Temple of the Redlegs, swinging two bats as he comes, the meaning of which or moral of which, I find on application to my consultant, is that we must always arrange to have just been doing something beforehand a good deal harder than what we are just going to do.
>
> But when I asked him a moment later when a ball got batted into the stands and the people instead of dogging in terror fought with each other fiercely to get and keep and were allowed to keep it, Howard bade me hold on; there seemed to be a misunderstanding between us. When he accepted the job it was orally; he didn't mean to represent himself as a symbolist in the high-brow or middle-brow sense of the word, that is as a collegiate expounder of the double entendre for college classes; he was a common ordinary cymbalist in a local band somewhere out on the far end of the Erie Canal. We were both honest men. He didn't want to be taken for a real professor any more than I wanted to be taken for a real sport.
>
> —Robert Frost, writing about the 1956 All-Star Game for *Sports Illustrated*

a casual person altogether obvious. The casual person would assume that I meant nothing or else I came near enough meaning something he was familiar with to mean it for all practical purposes. Well well well" (January 1, 1917, Frost 1964, 47). That quotation is, of course, useful for those who wish to claim an essential difficulty for Frost. But they can do so only by valuing this statement over many others that point in an opposite direction.

Since it is hard to imagine the evidence that would allow for such a privileging, it makes more sense to recognize a fundamental split in Frost's ideas, one that takes into account Frost's, and his poems', trafficking in simplicity. Perhaps we are left with nothing more exceptional than yet another instance of writers having conflicting desires—but we need to acknowledge all the aspects of that conflict, keeping all of them in play as long as possible and applying certain aspects of the conflict to where they fit most clearly. And one thing we need to acknowledge is that the works of Frost and Cather invite simple readings. They may not be the totality of readers' responses, but if the simple response is invited only in order then to show the irrelevance of those responses, then Frost and Cather are more elitist than high modern writers like Pound and Eliot—something I doubt. The best critics of Frost and Cather—Poirier, Lentricchia, Peck—acknowledge the centrality of simplicity to the aesthetic experience of reading these writers. Paradoxically, the standard difficult readings of Frost and Cather are too easy—not "too easy" for common readers, who feel a lot of anxiety in the presence of such readings, but "too easy" for academic readers, who often seem to be merely following routine, putting into play the twentieth century's default aesthetic.

The second group not generally convinced by the "deceptively simple" argument is nonprofessional readers, who often see both difficulty *and* deceptive simplicity as a self-serving attack on their own reading habits. Such distrust reveals once again how intricately difficulty is enmeshed in the social context of art's production. Consider the reactions to Lionel Trilling's famous comments on the occasion of Frost's eighty-fifth birthday celebration in March 1959. Holt, Frost's publishing house, hosted a dinner party at the Waldorf-Astoria for a hundred guests, and invited Trilling, of Columbia University, to speak. As might be expected from his assessment of Cather, Trilling did not offer blandishments to Frost, who was in the audience. Trilling at one point noted that "I have to say that my Frost is not the Frost I seem to perceive existing in the minds of so many of his admirers. He is not the Frost who confounds the characteristically modern practice of poetry by his notable democratic simplicity of utterance: on the contrary.... He is not the Frost who reassures us by his affirmation of old virtues, simplicities, pieties, and ways of feeling: anything but" (1959, 450). Trilling commented that he initially had been "alienated from Frost's great canon of work by what I saw in it, that either itself seemed to denigrate the work of the critical intellect or that gave its admirers the ground for making the denigration" (449).

Now, it's hard to know what Trilling was thinking; to present this kind of unsettled estimation on a public, celebratory occasion as large as this seems to be the kind of category mistake that only an academic could make. In any event he clearly created an awkward moment; those present noted that many of the guests were apparently "ill at ease." Frost, nodding at the head table, had apparently expected some celebration and genial bardolatry. According to his biographer, Frost "was obviously shaken and had unusual difficulty in reciting his own poetry" (Meyers 1996, 319). He clearly did not know how to respond to Trilling, who ultimately described Frost as "terrifying."[16]

One of the guests irritated by Trilling's speech was Donald Adams. Writing in his regular column in the *New York Times Book Review*, Adams described for the general public what had gone on at the celebration. Quoting extensively from Trilling's speech, Adams described (1959) it as "literary snobbery," which he characterized as "one of the most virulent forms of snobbery we have today." Castigating Trilling for turning to the work of D. H. Lawrence to explicate Frost, and for being, like Lawrence, "lost in the Freudian wood,"

Adams enjoined Trilling to "face the facts of life," and to stop being "confused," and he enjoined America in general "to recapture its earlier vision."

The reaction to Adams's article was swift; letters to the editor poured in, creating a series of responses that, in their enactment of issues discussed in this book, could have been stamped from a template. Joseph Gold (1959) was the only taker for Trilling's defense, noting that "to Mr. Adams, with his pseudo-impressionistic approach to literature, any analysis such as Lawrence's must be incomprehensible." Gold's lone letter of dissent was drowned out by the rest, which applauded Adams and vented their spleen at Trilling. Emory Neff (1959), who had been Trilling's undergraduate instructor and graduate supervisor, wrote that "Frost might have had a Nobel prize if so many New York critics hadn't gone whoring after European gods." Another reader saw Adams's article as "a fresh wind through the stale halls of the so-called 'new criticism.' This Trilling fella has had it coming to him for some time" (Rosten 1959). Another reader commented that the incident showed that "when the poets left their ivory towers, the professors moved in" (Derleth 1959). A final reader noted: "I hope Robert Frost was having a nice plate of buckwheat cakes and Vermont maple syrup as he read Mr. Adams' remarks. He couldn't have done better unless he had taken the so-called professor out to the woodshed" (Guerin 1959).

These readers, for the most part nonprofessionals, didn't like how Trilling (who, for many, was a stand-in for academia) put difficulty to work in a simple writer like Frost. But it is not just *these* readers and *Robert Frost*; in fact, common readers will *always* react strongly to the distrust of the surface of apparently simple works. The strength of such reactions partly stems from readers' distrust of the power of the critic, particularly when it seems to be directed against them. Readers don't like having their own reading experiences being seen as fundamentally wrong, and it is particularly unsettling when the "correct" reading seems to differ *in kind* from that of common readers, producing the paralyzing anxiety that their interactions with more paradigmatic high modernism also produces. In short, ordinary readers don't like being overpowered by professionals, with only their apparent love for literature to defend them. For these readers, Frost isn't deceptively simple because they haven't been deceived.

Readers have more at stake, then, than dismissing a text or a wrong reading of a text. In the first place, one must note the high emotional attachment these readers have to their aggrieved heroes. Consider again the rhetorical strategies of someone like Cyril Alington. Alington, not blind to his argumentative weaknesses, writes "No doubt there is much to be said for excellence in any pursuit; yet, after all, the amateur made no claim except that he loved that which he pursued, and the claim has surely some validity" (1923,

549). Alington undoubtedly finds the terms of his argument to be poignant. He here grants a vague something to the professionalist opinion ("much to be said for excellence in any pursuit") and opposes that to the paucity of his own position ("except that he loved that which he pursued"). Not a bad strategy: the paucity of the amateur opinion is what makes it attractive—surely speechless "love" is greater than voluble "excellence," and surely we are meant to understand and approve the hierarchy of values exhibited in the contrast between the professional "pursuit" (the careerist activity) and that which the amateur "pursued" (the romantic, amateur quest).

That is what the common reader's attachment to simplicity bases itself on: not on technical analysis, not on evidence, but on an emotional attachment, an emotional attachment congruent with a view of art as emotional expression, with pleasure as its end point. Palgrave, for example, thought that the goal of his anthology would be to teach "those indifferent to the Poets to love them, and those who love them to love them more" (1861, iv); Edward Marsh directed his 1914 *Georgian* anthology to "the lovers of poetry," and Marguerite Wilkinson found her audience in people who were "capable of sympathy and the love of beauty" (1919, 9).

For such readers, the stakes are high; common readers (or their apologists) often see the reading strategies that canonize writers like Frost and Cather to be systematic attempts to take away an author from them. Further, readers sense that in losing Frost and Cather, they lose not only literature, but their own interpretive strategies. That is why difficult readings of Frost and Cather probably create a greater crisis than the difficulty that accompanies the work of the high moderns, and why the anxiety that arises from this crisis is directed not against these writers, but their critics. In his 1955–56 Charles Eliot Norton Lectures at Harvard, Edwin Muir surveyed the triumph of difficulty and New Criticism and reached the following conclusion:

> People will read poetry for enjoyment, since that is what it is intended for; and they will not, except in a few exceptional cases, take it up as a strict methodical study. And it may be said that they will get more help, both in enjoyment and understanding, from the traditional critic who tells them what the poem means to him, than from the new one who warns them that it cannot possibly mean what it appears to mean, so that he has no choice left but to explain it. The divorce between the public audience and the poet is widened by this critical method. (1962, 77)

Advocates of Frost's and Cather's simplicity thus face a different crisis than do those who reacted strongly against *The Waste Land*. The difference between, say, Frost's and Eliot's audience is that Eliot's common readers cannot but help know the other level exists—there is no satisfactory first level. That immediate crisis is crucial to all of canonical modernism—there is no satisfactory first level, however that level might be described. With the high moderns, a surface reading is inherently dissatisfying: no one thought it a useful strategy to do a surface reading of Eliot or Joyce. The trouble with both Frost and Cather is that one could get a satisfying reading by remaining with their surface simplicity; there is no obvious need to go deeper. While reading Eliot inevitably produces anxiety, in reading Frost and Cather the anxiety needs to be produced, and to many common readers the production of difficulty seems to come from outside of the text, carried in on an agenda enmired in the politics of academia.

It is thus harder in Frost than in Eliot to see that difficulty is the *point*. "Difficult" readings of Cather and Frost seem to miss much of the texture of the experience of reading them. Difficulty is neither the first nor the obvious thing to be said about them; their difficulty is subtle, not obvious. The structures that give rise to the difficulty, and the experience of the difficulty itself, differ radically from those of classic high modern texts. The texts, unless they are seen as difficult, are much less likely to produce the vertigo and anxiety encountered in modernist difficulty. That is because there is no drive to move beyond the difficulty, the way there is in writers like Joyce and Stein. As a consequence, the readings that the general public comes up with seem to them plausible and nonproblematic, in a way that their readings of Stein and Joyce don't.

To many nonprofessional readers the subtle difficulty, as described by someone like Trilling, seems like a word game—the general public distrusts it, since it doesn't resonate with their experiences. Further, when readers doubt difficult readings of writers they think of as simple, they often are skeptical about the rewards of that kind of reading. Thus, the common op-ed reactions, as when this writer for the *New York Times* took on the literary academy, described as "a whole raft of academics" who have "created a publishing mini-industry that has lately been labeled the Bardbiz": "Did you think 'King Lear' was about a relationship between father and daughters? *Please*. It's really about 'new forms of social organization and affective relationships.' In your naïveté, did you believe the sonnets to be a great fistful of small gems, to be taken out and examined from different angles over the course of a lifetime? No, no, no. They merely 'articulate the frustration of language's indeterminacy'" ("Shakespeare for Mere Mortals" 1993, A22). So, when readers get irritated at academics who make Frost (or some other loved writer) difficult, they really don't think Frost's and Cather's work *deserves* the kind of attention, the kind of reading practices, these critics give it.

Unlike the situation that arises with classic high modern texts, with resuscitated simple moderns difficulty cannot be defined as "difficult for the average reader." It is not the case that the average reader finds difficult those things that an academic reader finds easy. In fact, the opposite occurs: the more educated, "better" reader one is, the more likely one is to see Frost and Cather as difficult; fourth-year students, for example, are less likely to chafe at difficult readings of Frost than are first-year students. This happens because the difficulty of Frost isn't obvious; it can be reached only through realizing that the seemingly effortless language is really unstable, that its "real" meaning is hidden. This form of difficulty is a socialized way of interacting with high art; in a process in which reading is slowed down and readers are made to be attentive to the subtlety of the text, people *learn* to read Frost as difficult. If the difficulty-induced vertigo comes in anything, it comes in finding that the text *actually* is difficult, not, as in Eliot's writing, in trying to understand what the difficulty means.

This anxiety separates many readers from academics, for most academics don't really expect simplicity in a work of art to which they have directed their attention. First, professional readers are disposed against the idea that language ever works at a simple level. Thus, when academics read Cather, they have a predisposition to believe that she can't be that simple; works of art must have more than just what seems to be going on in here. Second, academics don't expect simplicity because simplicity is never a subject for them. As a result, the only people who expect simplicity in Frost are ordinary readers, and they find it easily available. When told that Frost "really" is difficult, they are made anxious not by the characteristics of the difficulty (as in *The Waste Land* when readers really wonder what "Datta" means), but at *the idea* that this text is difficult.

Actual Difficulty

The question that finally needs to be asked is "what if Frost and Cather *really are* difficult?" What if Untermeyer was just wrong about Frost? The force of this question resides in the reasonable surmise that if these writers really are difficult, then while the social bifurcation that happens between general and academic readers may be regrettable, it is also just an inevitable by-product of an existing textual property. Frost and Cather are a good test case for this, for the argument about their difficulty seems a reasonable test of difficulty's range, of the inherent difficulty of aesthetic language in general. This question of Frost's and Cather's difficulty has two implications that need to be noted. First, only those who valued difficulty thought of Frost and Cather as difficult; the same was not true of a writer like Eliot, whose difficulty was universally recognized, but not universally valued. Demonstrating the actual difficulty of Frost and Cather would, it seems, be an almost infallible indication that poetic language is inherently difficult. Second, Frost's and Cather's difficulty would be a sign of difficulty's value. While for some who read the difficult high moderns and recognize them as difficult, the answer may be to turn in relief to texts that are then *not* difficult, no one makes this kind of argument for Frost and Cather, suggesting that they be jettisoned, along with the whole plague of difficult moderns, and that attention should instead be paid to writers who *really are* simple, like, say, Carl Sandburg. If Frost and Cather are difficult, difficulty is likely a more legitimate aesthetic property than if difficulty were limited to the high moderns.

The way into answering this question comes through turning to other modernist writers for whom claims of simplicity were sometimes made, but this time, writers who have a much closer relationship to classic difficult high modernism (writers who, in fact, were early and often described as difficult). Consider William Carlos Williams, whose work was described by one reviewer as having "a colossally nice simplicity" (Birch-Bartlett [1921] 1980, 68). At his most objectivist, Williams wrote poems such as the following:

POEM

As the cat
climbed over
the top of

the jamcloset
first the right
forefoot

carefully
then the hind
stepped down

into the pit of
the empty
flowerpot ([1935] 1986a, 352)

While it may, on some level, make sense to think of this poem as simple, we are a long way away from the Frost of William Morton Payne, the Frost who wrote such lines as:

Do you know me in the gloaming,
Gaunt and dusty grey with roaming?
Are you dumb because you know me not,
Or dumb because you know? (Payne [1913] 1977, 4)

Lines like these—longer than those of Williams, more sonorous and adjective-laden—begin to suggest that Frost's work doesn't present itself as simple in the way that Williams's does; it seems more allied to the simplicity one finds in Lascelles Abercrombie:

For what more like the brainless speech of a fool,—
The lives travelling dark fears,
And as a boy throws pebbles in a pool
Thrown down abysmal places? ("Hymn to Love," 1921, 3)

There are profound similarities here. As does Frost's, Abercrombie's work fits comfortably into an aesthetic in which great works of art do more than just accurately describe the world. They must do more than assert, for example, that the events depicted "really" happened; the additional work they take on has to do with a voice/speaker, which creates an emotional resonance between the voice of the poem and its subject, a resonance that gives the work its richness. (This ideal of richness underscores that simplicity is *more* than just a lack of complexity.)

Williams's poem doesn't seem rich in this way. In Williams's poetry, the simplicity doesn't support many traditional literary values: there is neither speaker nor resonance nor wisdom in the Williams poem, and it does not gesture to emotional truth. Those missing qualities, in fact, are why Williams's work (and that of other modernists such as Marcel Duchamp) is often seen as difficult. In its radical simplicity it raises questions about whether or not it is *art*.[17] As such it can be seen as *more* difficult than that of many high moderns, for it is difficult about more fundamental issues. As Babette Deutsch wrote of Williams in 1934, "People, accustomed to the passionate imagery of Yeats, to Eliot's suggestive music, to the panoplied mysticism of Hart Crane or the rich allusiveness of Pound, to name four of the more influential poets of our time, will find themselves at a loss before this stark and unashamed simplicity of statement" ([1934] 1980, 130).[18] A crisis and anxiety arise because readers cannot do what they are used to doing. Now, it may be the case that to most readers Williams's difficulty is not as obvious as that of, say, Eliot, that Williams is difficult only if you know what kinds of assertions poems usually make. But almost every reader *does* know the kinds of assertions poems usually make (the possible exception are readers radically separate from high culture, such as Esslin's San Quentin inmates). The kinds of assertions Williams's poems do not make are so basic that he is much more typically thought of as difficult than as simple, allowing someone like Harriet Monroe unproblematically to link Williams to such poets as Yvor Winters, Hart Crane, e. e. cummings, Ezra Pound, and Laura Riding—into a group Monroe characterized as the "intellectuals" (quoted in Abbott 1984, 104–5). What the work of Abercrombie and Williams shows, then, is a contrast between a hard-edged imagism versus a soft simplicity, with its penumbra of suggestion. Abercrombie's work suggests all sorts of affective human values; Williams's suggestiveness lies in what his writing implies about the nature of art.

How does this contrast play itself out in the work of Robert Frost? With the possible exception of its subject matter and diction for some of its readers, Frost's simplicity doesn't raise the "is it art" questions. (And, for academic readers, it has long stopped raising these questions, except in a perverse way, as when his poetry seems to be too simple to be art.) In Frost's

> Question—Look at this piece of sculpture. Is it a work of art?
> Witness—It is, in my opinion.
> Question—Do you have anything to do with making sculptures like this thing?
> Witness—No.
> Question—You consider it art?
> Witness—I certainly do.
> Question—Why do you?
> Witness—It pleases my sense of beauty.
> Question—So if we had a brass rail here, curved in a more or less symmetrical fashion, and highly polished, it would be a work of art?
> Witness—It might be a work of art.
> Mr. Higginbotham, who was cross examining, grinned, and several court attendants looked reminiscent, as if they remembered the kind of brass rail Mr. Higginbotham was alluding to.
> Question—Whether it was made by a sculptor or a mechanic?
> Witness—A mechanic cannot make a beautiful work.
> Question—You mean to tell me a first class mechanic could not have filed and polished up this exhibit here?
> Witness—He could not have conceived it. A mechanic cannot conceive.
> Question—If he could conceive, he would be an artist himself?
> Witness—Right.
>
> > —Partial transcript of 1927 court case to determine whether Brancusi's "Bird in Flight" was indeed a work of art, and therefore exempt from customs duty. As reported in *American Weekly*. Jacob Epstein, "celebrated sculptor," was witness for the defense.

poetry there clearly is a narrator with psychological characteristics. Further, Frost's global, moralizing statements (e.g., "and that has made all the difference," or "one could do worse than be a swinger of birches") clearly tie his work to the resonant simplicity of the early twentieth century. It may eventually shed those ties, but initially it proffers them to readers.[19]

What, then, are critics doing when they claim that Frost and Cather "really" are difficult? In deceptive simplicity are they discovering something that always existed, but just hadn't been noticed before? A profitable way into answering these questions is by noting what difficulty actually is. Difficulty is not a property of literature; it is an interaction between text and reader that is, at a fundamental level, blocked. A writer like William Carlos Williams is difficult because the things readers are used to doing don't work in the presence of his poems: there is no emotional resonance, no symbolic suggestiveness. Now, there are times when difficulty can look like a property, as when reading *The Waste Land*, which is difficult under almost any reading strategy. Readers' entrenched reading habits can suggest that this poem is inherently difficult, that it is composed of difficult properties. But the text looks like it is made up of difficult properties because of entrenched, default reading practices, such as recognizing a carefully lineated text as a poem, looking for a single lyric voice, recognizing that allusions are being made, and believing that poems are made up of syntactically complete sentences that form an organic whole. Poems like *The Waste Land*, and high modern works in general, subvert these entrenched reading habits. Our most entrenched reading practice is to read a text like *The Waste Land* as high art, and writers like Eliot and Joyce seem inevitably difficult because their works don't make sense to be read as anything but high art. There are no obvious meanings other than high art meanings that are useful, productive. But even at this level, difficulty is a matter of reading strategies, of decisions made. As for Frost and Cather, if you choose to read them in a high modern way, they are difficult (in the same way that if you choose to climb El Capitan by the north route, it is difficult). It depends on the task one values and the task undertaken. What unites the difficult texts of modernism, then, is not a peculiar property that they all share, but a reading process.[20]

When difficulty is understood as a reading practice and not an aesthetic property, one needs to acknowledge that one can perform this practice on anything, even a red dot, or a list of anthology editors, as Stanley Fish noted.[21] There is nothing that could not be difficult, given the right reading practices. Clearly, the belief that anything could be difficult ties in to current beliefs about the inherent difficulty of language and of the world. Language, then, is not so much inherently difficult as it is another item in the infinitely large list of things that can be *made* difficult. Under the right conditions, giving it a specific kind of attention, language is difficult. But under another set of protocols it isn't. While there is much to be gained from looking at language under the protocols of difficulty, it does not follow that difficulty is what language is *really* about.

And if the difficulty of language becomes a routinized academic gesture, other problems come to the fore. The protocols that can make all language difficult involve defamiliarization, slowing down the decoding process. But difficulty's defamiliarization has its dangers, for it necessarily closes down language to other protocols, such as simplicity. The more unproblematically high culture asserts that all language is difficult, the greater the likelihood that we lose the affects of a large segment of language usage (and a body of art) that does not exploit difficulty's protocols. If defamiliarization, in order to increase difficulty and its pleasures, becomes the default reading activity, it eventually gets less productive, resulting in a need for some kind of *meta*-defamiliarization, one that would involve making the defamiliarization itself strange.

Further, the assertion that all language or aesthetic language is difficult doesn't seem capable of much finesse, of acknowledging that some texts reward difficult readings more than do others. If all language is difficult, why would a critic single out Frost for special commendation, and not, say, Grace Hazard Conkling, author of the following poem:

Tampico

Oh, cut me reeds to blow upon,
   Or gather me a star.
But leave the sultry passion-flowers
   Growing where they are.

I fear their sombre yellow deeps,
   Their whirling fringe of black,
And he who gives a passion-flower
   Always asks it back. (1929, 45)

What needs to be acknowledged is that, while all literature is potentially difficult and while all language may be difficult, not all literature is equally *productively* difficult. Some things, such as, presumably, "Tampico," are difficult in not very interesting ways. Of course, someone may eventually argue for the canonization of Conkling for just such writing, but it will be, as it is with Frost, because Conkling apparently is doing something aesthetically pleasing with the inherent difficulty of language. She is recognizing this difficulty and exploiting it as an aesthetic effect, in a manner that is superior to other, less usefully difficult writers.

Yet although critics have found ways to make "difficult" readings of Frost and Cather productive, these readings are not inevitable. But they invariably are presented as inevitable; they come with an implicit value system in which those who believe these writers really are difficult tend to think that the difficult reading is the only thing to say about them, with their simple attributes being a hindrance or merely a means to a difficult end. So while in some ways it is productive to make Frost difficult, the danger lies in making difficulty what the text is "really" about. "Difficult" readings of Cather and Frost miss much of the texture of reading them.

Given the way in which difficulty is invoked in canonizing, one is left with choosing between two options. On one hand, one could evaluate each argument for canonical status on its own terms, noting in passing the coincidence that other texts that have also been canonized are also difficult. Or, using Occam's razor, one could find a less labored explanation, one that sees in these canonizing gestures the power of a single reading strategy and not first of all the properties of these texts. The second is the more believable option, and it allows literary criticism to be more conscious about its default operating principles, and therefore more likely to be capable of working outside those principles in expanding the canon.

The difficulty aesthetic that currently governs much literary criticism has significant costs on two levels. First, difficult modernism has left a situation in which the triumph of difficulty has been so complete that it is hard to recognize what it replaced as literary criticism. Members of high culture instinctively know that Marguerite Wilkinson's effusions are not the way to talk about literature. With the replacement of simplicity with difficulty, literary culture turned from one default aesthetic to another. High culture may at times not have lost that much, but it is troubling that so much of early twentieth-century aesthetic writing is unfathomable, and it is unlikely that the only thing that has been lost is a state of innocence. Second, simplicity's disappearance has left a situation in which difficulty has become the necessary condition for canonization, and the more immediate this difficulty is, the easier it is for its writer to be canonized. The high modern distrust of simplicity and the consequent valorization of difficulty, in fact, is a position so firmly entrenched that it governs current attempts to diversify the canon. Given how difficulty functioned in modern culture, Robert Frost and Willa Cather (not to mention Housman, Millay, Sandburg, Steinbeck, and even, to some extent, Hemingway and Fitzgerald) never could be more central canonical figures than T. S. Eliot, James Joyce, Gertrude Stein, Virginia Woolf, or Ezra Pound. All of modernism's canonical works are works that have a difficulty-based interpretive crisis at their heart, though what makes for that difficulty may change. It is at best debatable that noncanonical writers are best served by claiming for them all a kind of difficulty, particularly given all the activities (art as a muscular enterprise, professionalism, etc.) in which difficulty is implicated. As long as we avoid a serious examination of difficulty as an aesthetic principle (an examination that must include not just the properties of text, but also the institutions of literature), writers such as Zora Neale Hurston and Willa Cather, Robert Frost and Carl Sandburg, will never be *really* canonical. One may well ask whether, in the current context, it is indeed the art that is driving the aesthetic, or the aesthetic driving the art.

Renoir Loses His Edge

The elision of simplicity and pleasure has been widespread, moving beyond literature to other arts as well. The adventures of Auguste Renoir's reputation from the nineteenth to the late twentieth centuries reveals how completely the default aesthetic of high modernism controlled, and continues to control, high culture. Renoir's reputation as an artist, whose movement from initial ridicule to someone whose "greatness" in 1954 was described as "practically unquestioned" (Flanagan 1954, 152), initially seems different from that of Cather and Frost, for his apparent difficulty fueled his initial reputation. A key figure in the early impressionist exhibitions of the mid-1870s, Renoir and his difficulty were at the center of impressionism's initial controversies, when the difficult newness of impressionism convulsed aesthetic sensibilities.

The effects of impressionism's difficulty are nowhere more evident than in the writing of Albert Wolff, a journalist for the popular *Le Figaro*. In his commentary on an 1875 impressionist auction, which featured the work of Renoir and others, Wolff wrote: "All these pictures have had somewhat the effect on us of a painting that you must look at from fifteen paces while squinting your eyes, and certainly you need a very large apartment to be able to house these canvasses, if you wish to enjoy them even through the imagination.... The impression produced by the Impressionists is that of a cat walking on the keys of a piano, or a monkey that has got hold of a box of paints" (quoted in White 1984, 55). The next year, Wolff described an impressionist exhibition as having been put together by "five or six lunatics, one of them a woman, a group of unfortunate creatures seized with the mania of ambition." Describing the impressionists as "so-called artists" and "madmen," Wolff noted that while "some people burst out laughing in front of these things—my heart is crushed by them" (quoted in Blunden and Blunden, 1970, 110–11). Turning his attention to impressionist technique, Wolff excoriated Renoir in particular: "These self-styled artists call themselves Intransigents, Impressionists, they take some canvases, paint, and brushes, throw a few colors on at random, and sign the whole thing.... Try to explain to M. Renoir that a woman's torso is not a mass of decomposing flesh with green and purple spots that indicate the state of total putrefaction in a corpse!" (quoted in White 1984, 58). The visceral responses, the anger, the ridicule—these do the work they would later do in literary modernism, embodying an anxious response to difficulty and producing a highly dichotomized atmosphere particularly conducive to large changes in aesthetic sensibility. They are, of course, the responses of a doomed aesthetic.

Given that hostile reception, and the default critical interpretation of it, it is no surprise that modernity initially canonized Renoir in terms of his difficulty. In his role as one of the great forerunners of modernism, Renoir was difficulty's professional, developing and extending how painters approached surface and light. Herbert Read, author of the 1938 defense of difficult modernism "Obscurity in Poetry," in 1964 analyzed Renoir's reputation in professionalist terms, describing his painting as "research, experiment" (28). Similarly, Walter Pach, one of the prime movers of the Armory Show, noted of Renoir that "the simple realism of Renoir's Courbetesque beginnings developed into a further study of nature when, with Monet and the other impressionists, he made an intensive analysis of light and its rendering by color." This

> Daub three-quarters of a canvas with black and white, rub the remaining space with red and yellow, sprinkle a few red and blue spots, and you have an *impression* of spring which will send the fans into ecstasy.
>
> —Émile Cardon, *La Presse*, 1874

kind of aesthetic practice allowed for the further development of art by other artists. After Renoir, according to Pach, "the next step in art, to be made by the generation that followed, would be the use of color and form in ever-increasing independence of the object represented" ([1951] 1960, 26, 27).

This wasn't value-free valorization, of course; it had the trajectory of morality, one in which Renoir was one of the heroic leaders of a revolution in painting, the champion of difficulty's morality. Pach gave Renoir's biography the following gloss: "Though he served in the army during the war of 1870, Renoir's share in the struggle was a minor one. The real battles of his life were those of his profession" ([1951] 1960, 12). Jack Flam, writing in 1989, analyzed the initial hostile response to impressionism as occurring because the impressionists appeared "to be breaking all the laws of good painting." Moreover, Flam went on, "the philosophical values implicit in their art, with its emphasis on flux and the relativity of experience, must also have seemed to threaten the comfortable and comforting physical, moral, and social stability of the world around them" (117). Thus, when modernism was at its height, discussions of Renoir often availed themselves of difficulty's heroic language. In the late 1960s, Hans Jaffé argued that Renoir "increasingly aroused public rage" because of his "daring technique" (1969, 59–60); Colin Hayes claimed that Monet and Renoir "abandoned not only their remaining allegiance to the old order of subfuse tonality with their chromatic rendering of values, but freed themselves from the tyranny of the linear contour" (1967, 9); also grouping Monet and Renoir together, William Gaunt, a few years later, claimed that "Renoir at times went even farther in audacity than his companion" (1970, 37).

Yet while Renoir was typically seen as central to understanding impressionism and its difficulty, warning signs of his tenuous place in the canon were there early. Renoir's place in the difficult heroics of impressionism was not seamless; since the end of the nineteenth century there had been those who found his painting to be lacking in critical areas. Even George Flanagan, who was quoted earlier about Renoir's "practically unquestioned" greatness, noted that "there are some paintings that are little better than commercial 'calendar art'" (1954, 152). Renoir did not seem to have, for example, analytic rigor; he wasn't doing *research*, the way someone like Monet was.[22]

The suspicion focused on the peripheral values Renoir seemed to attach to his depictions of middle-class life, particularly optimism and pleasure. Renoir's work seemed to embody the extreme of impressionist tendencies toward these attitudes; while many impressionists celebrated bourgeois culture, Renoir outdid them all. More than anyone else, he was the pleasing, cheerful impressionist. In the 1936 edition of her ubiquitous college text *Art Through the Ages*, Helen Gardner tried to ameliorate Renoir's pleasures by framing them in terms of an inquiry into pictorial space. According to Gardner, Renoir "took sheer delight in unaffected feminine charm and frankly expressed his joy in it; but eventually he used it as a point of departure for creating abstract rhythmical designs in deep space" (669). The formal inquiry is essential; without Renoir's "point of departure" into the nature of representation, Gardner's uncertainty about the value of Renoir's pleasure would be even more pronounced.[23] As with Cather and Frost, these estimations of Renoir did not come from a vacuum, but found parallels in Renoir's own statements about art. Particularly near the end of his life, Renoir himself could make these kinds of noises, commenting to Albert André in 1919 that "Painting was intended, was it not, to decorate walls. Therefore it should be as rich as possible. For me a painting ... should be something to cherish, joyous and pretty, yes pretty!" (quoted in Distel, 1995, 127).

Consequently, defenses of Renoir often have a nervous tone. Over the course of his career Clement Greenberg, for example, had an unstable evaluation of Renoir. Writing in 1961, he noted that in Renoir "The result often verged on prettiness, but it is perhaps the most valid prettiness ever seen in modernist art" (1961b, 47).[24] A positive review of a 1998 show of Renoir's portraits begins by noting that "Renoir is not now the most universally admired of Impressionist painters." Finding much to admire in the show, the reviewer yet notes that "Less rigorous than some of his colleagues and contemporaries ... his work may seem to suffer from a dependence on charm of subject, and an evident desire to please" (Whiteley 1998, 51).

This uneasiness over Renoir had reached a head in the mid-1980s. A major retrospective at that time was the occasion for a revaluation of Renoir in which Renoir's simplicity and its accompanying qualities were seen to radically diminish his stature, driving a wedge between his great popular acceptance and his reputation with his professional audience. That popular acceptance was very much in evidence. The show was enormously popular, breaking records for attendance. At the same time, though, virtually everyone writing in response to the show had at the very least a central uneasiness about Renoir; no one had a trouble-free valorization. Even those sympathetic to Renoir knew the terms of the debate. Denys Sutton, writing in *Apollo* in 1985, somewhat bitterly noted that "Renoir is not fashionable among the intelligentsia, and the thin neurotic waifs and strays portrayed by

Schiele are at present more favoured than the plump women he depicted." Going on, Sutton analyzed Renoir's reputation in the following manner: "Now that 'serious' art is highly praised and when history painters, rather than the masters of the *fête galante*, appeal to pundits, Renoir's relaxed manner is felt to contain insufficient intellectual content" (242). William Feaver, writing in *Artnews*, noted that "Renoir's sweetness can be off-putting—especially when applied to a banker's children got up like poodles in party dresses," and that flirtation with kitsch was the reason Renoir "isn't credited with much seriousness" (1985, 45). For Renoir's skeptics, one way to handle both Renoir's popularity and one's own uneasiness was to see a liking for Renoir as evidence of an early, immature taste. Paul Tucker, reporting that in college he had initially liked Renoir, noted his own maturation: "Very soon I became convinced that Renoir was only a painter of pretty pictures, a sensualist who avoided the tougher issues of modernity in life as well as in art" (in Nochlin et al. 1986, 121).

In a symposium on the show, featured in *Art in America* in March 1986, Peter Schjeldahl was speaking for the majority when he claimed, "Renoir may be the worst artist to achieve canonical status, but this pales, for me, beside the complexity and poignance of his very badness.... How bad was he? Let me count the ways" (Nochlin et al. 1986, 107). The list was long. In the course of twenty pages, various critics and art historians argued that he was a sloppy painter, that he wasn't a deep thinker, that his nudes were adolescent fantasies, that he was too unthinking in his acceptance of the pretty and pleasurable, that he was too cheerful, and that all these qualities accounted for his popularity.

The reasons for this drastic change in evaluation have different intonations. Some of the rereadings are based on formal principles: Peter Schjeldahl complained that Renoir's colors were "tonally chaotic," and Michael Fried criticized his lack of touch. These formally based criticisms were usually tied to the idea that Renoir wasn't really an innovator, that he wasn't "really" difficult. As Carter Ratcliff wrote, Renoir was "not a radical artist, but [he is] important because he shows how easy it is to look like one, to be scorned and then revered as an 'intransigent,' while preserving the authority of standard forms and taste" (Nochlin et al. 1986, 107, 108, 111). And this awareness of Renoir's shallowness was involved in political evaluations of Renoir, particularly Renoir's relation to bourgeois culture and feminism. In an article tellingly titled "'Pleasing, Cheerful and Pretty?' Sexual and Cultural Politics at the Hayward Gallery," Lynn Nead implicated art criticism in contemporary culture's adoption of Renoir's nudes as a shallow sexual philosophy (1985, 72–74). As Walter Robinson argued, "His sunny scenes are prophetic of the modern postcard, his sensibility is common ancestor to Norman Rockwell,

Barbie and slice-of-life advertising. Renoir's painting may be trivial and obvious, but at least it's definitive" (Nochlin et al. 1986, 120).

The most obvious source of critical nervousness was the pleasure of Renoir's paintings. In the *Art in America* symposium, Robert Rosenblum noted the critical tendency to see Renoir's brain as "mushy," and that "the sugar content of his paintings could make one long for a diet of Mondrian and Seurat." "Unmitigated pleasure," Rosenblum argued, "is always suspect to certain high-minded spectators," and he went on to concede, somewhat grudgingly, that Renoir had "wrought miracles" in his ability to make "simple sensual arousal and fulfillment" believable in the modern world (Nochlin et al. 1986, 112, 116). Walter Robinson was less conflicted; writing with obvious enjoyment, Robinson noted: "Poor Renoir. There he was, leading painter of the good life in 'modern' Paris, a veritable Pollyanna with a paintbrush, recording classic scenes of idle delight with unrelenting good cheer and a shimmering dapple of rainbow-bright hues. And then look at what happens. His subjects all turn to 'kitsch'" (Nochlin et al. 1986, 120).

And that is about where things have stayed. Karen Wilkin noted in 1996 that "It's hard to believe how highly Renoir was regarded half a century ago." (48). In a 1997 article conspicuously titled "Beyond Pneumatic Nudes," Paul Jeromack interviewed Colin Bailey, chief curator of the National Gallery of Canada, about the National Gallery's show of Renoir portraits. Jeromack at one point asked, "Why do you think Renoir has become the 'Whipping boy' of impressionism?" Bailey's reply acknowledged that Renoir was often not "taken very seriously as a painter," both for his lush palette and other reasons: "He is loved so wholeheartedly by the general public that there is still something of a knee-jerk reaction to him with some scholars. More of them have more difficulty with Renoir than with any other Impressionist. Renoir is so accessible, his works do not seem as oblique or open to interpretation and his nudes have provided the grist for feminist or proto-feminist view [*sic*] that damns him. Maybe it is because you cannot make Renoir into a Modernist icon" (33).

The trajectory of Renoir's fall from grace contains within it other aspects of the difficulty aesthetic. Renoir's reception reveals that difficulty is not just a streamlined package, concerned purely with comprehension. When critics talk about pleasure or optimism, they are also, often, talking about difficulty. Difficulty is entangled in other, related issues that high culture has inherited from the moderns, particularly about seriousness, public acceptance, optimism and pleasure, and struggle.

Renoir's reputation most particularly shows the central role of habitualization and the mixed blessings of a transitory difficulty. In her standard modern reading of Renoir, Phoebe Pool notes the "ridicule" directed at

Renoir in the first impressionist exhibit, and goes on to claim that "It is a fate common to innovators in the arts, and only with the passage of time does the public come to accept, and objectively criticize, the truly new. In view of the fluorescent tones used by Pop and Op artists of today, the brilliant colours of the Impressionists, so shocking initially, seem tame" (1967, 116). This reveals a central crisis in modernism: what to do with canonical work once we have become accustomed to working with it. For many, Renoir's difficulty has disappeared, and it is no longer the first thing critics feel called upon to note about him. Indeed, the first thing to point out about him is that he isn't difficult, and that this lack presents a problem for his value. As a consequence, many art historians don't see Renoir anymore; presenting no difficulties, his work has faded into a warmish rectangular spot above innumerable college dormitory couches.

Despite this general assessment of Renoir, attempts to keep him central in the canon continue sporadically, following the predictable contours of high modern argumentation. Following Jauss's exhortations and trying to read the classic "'against the grain' of the accustomed experience to catch sight of their artistic character once again" (1982, 26), Renoir's supporters bring out the standard defense. In an article tellingly titled "The Elusive Renoir," William Feaver claimed that "Renoir's paintings aren't as easy as they look. More calculated, as a rule, than they may appear, they are also more varied than his reputation would suggest" (1985, 45). Phoebe Pool, twenty years earlier, had used a similar strategy. Acknowledging the typical criticism of Renoir, that his attitude "is that of an adolescent who glories in luscious food and plump, pink girls," Pool granted that "his sensual preferences are unsubtle and crude in comparison with the more sophisticated tastes of Manet and Degas." However, Pool went on, "the way in which Renoir painted these simple and direct subjects was far from naïve," and she went on to praise aspects of his technique as being more sophisticated than that of Pisarro or Monet (1967, 152–53). Renoir, if he is to regain some measure of his former canonical status, will be canonized with the mixed blessing of deceptive simplicity.

CONCLUSION

Modern Difficulty's Inheritance

> We have become an audience which for better or for worse is committed to the complex poem; whether as a thing to despise or as a thing to admire does not for the moment matter.
> —Mark Van Doren, 1942

In 1945, in the *American Scholar* forum "Obscurity in Modern Literature," F. W. Dupee speculated "I wonder, indeed, if a high degree of difficulty is not an aspect of the modern poetic style." After enlarging his case to include all the contemporary arts, Dupee noted that "It is not a question of individual poets and their motives, but of a general style, of which no single poet was the inventor and in which those who participate do so without necessarily having full awareness of its cultural implications" (356–57). Those cultural implications, this book has argued, are large. Modernism's difficulty seized both the canon and the principles by which the canon was formed; by midcentury its artifacts were firmly in place as the century's highest, most serious forms of literature, art, and music; and its shape and protocols continue to be ones we learn instinctively and early.

Difficulty's presence in contemporary culture was concretely brought home to me when, as a graduate student teaching literature for the first time, I opted to put Vonnegut's *Slaughterhouse-Five* on my introduction to literature syllabus. On the first day we took up the novel, a normally talkative student on whom I had come to rely remained silent, looking puzzled. On the second day, after thirty minutes of scowling and twisting (by which time my anxiety had increased as well), he querulously asked, "Are we all reading the same book?" Having heard about "teachable moments," and relentlessly sure that this *was* one, I started to make the usual noises about subjectivity in literature. But my certainty that I was having the sort of happy adventure that only seemed to happen to Stanley Fish was short-lived. Brushing my response aside, the student walked to the front of the class and thrust in my hands *his* version of *Slaughterhouse-Five*. Before turning to page 25 of the canonical *Slaughterhouse-Five*, his copy began with twenty pages of a sex education manual: *Boys and Sex*, by Wardell B. Pomeroy, which answered such questions as "What is the difference between sex and love?" and "What is a wet dream?"

It took this bright student two days of class discussion to discover that he had read the "wrong" book, and more, that what he had read didn't, apparently, mean anything. Explanations were, of course, in order. Justifying his incomprehensibly obtuse error, the student told me it took so long to realize his mistake because I had prefaced the reading assignment with the warning that its bizarre juxtapositions made *Slaughterhouse-Five* difficult (or, "difficult for first-time readers," I had somewhat patronizingly warned them). Yet he kept reading, imagining a discussion of the strenuous anxieties of male adolescent sexuality to be an ironic prelude to a book about fantasy and violence-induced disorientation—not a bad premise. Since the rest of the "real" book was accompanied by sudden juxtapositions, he assumed that the sudden transition from sex instruction manual to Billy Pilgrim fit into that structure. The characters Wardell B. Pomeroy and porn star Montana Wildhack *could* rub shoulders in the same novel. However, class discussion only increased his anxiety and eroded his confidence in his assumptions until he was so uncomfortable he spoke up.

Now, one of the things that needs to be asked at this point is whether I was just wrong about this student's brightness, self-servingly interpreting his willingness to participate in class to be a sign of intelligence. Maybe my student was actually less intelligent than I thought, and maybe his mistake was so bizarre that it's best to put this anecdote to the side, for it doesn't tell us much about high culture's aesthetic principles. But I don't think so, for such bizarre misreadings happen regularly; every time I tell this story, one of my listeners has a similar anecdote about misprint-based misreadings. This student's bizarre behavior, I believe, reveals much about how difficulty works in high culture today. It shows that people's desires for meaning are fierce, at times pushing them to find meaning where some might argue there is none. This search for meaning is also inflected by modernism's shaping of contemporary high culture: my student believed the misprint not only because he trusted the authority of a published book, but because the misprint made the work difficult. He recognized that being able to negotiate difficulty was what college was about. He also knew how to behave in the presence of difficulty; that difficulty demands respectful deference. Realizing, on the first day, that something was going on that he wasn't getting, he chose to remain silent. He was aware enough of high art and classroom protocols to know that successful students didn't express this kind of anxiety, and that one should never ask a stupid question. But it also became apparent that his anxiety was getting to be intolerable.

That anxiety, and the structures that gave rise both to it and its unsuccessful suppression, indicate how thoroughly difficult modernism came to control the cultural landscape. Its governance was sweeping; indeed, by the early 1960s, it formed part of the definition of modernity. G. S. Fraser, in his 1964 *The Modern Writer and His World*, was able to unproblematically define modernism in terms of difficulty: "Perhaps the historian of 'modern poetry'—in the sense of difficult, complex, abstruse poetry whose statements or attitudes puzzle the ordinary reader—might date its rise in England somewhere between 1910 and 1920" (33). Even difficulty's victims acknowledged its triumph. In his autobiography, Max Eastman described the "impudent war" his essay "The Cult of Unintelligibility" had waged on the high moderns: "It was a lovely war from my point of view, all weapons permitted and no holds barred." Cheerfully acknowledging that "of course I lost the war," Eastman noted that he was "carried unconscious from the field of battle," and within two years "disappeared under a cloud of awfully overwhelming language called the New Criticism" (1964, 518). Significantly less content, James Reeves, in the introduction to his 1962 anthology *Georgian Poetry*, grumbled that "The idea that a poem may be easy to understand is something that was killed along with the Georgian movement" (xv); in 1963 Patrick Howarth, the admiring author of the biography *Squire: Most Generous of Men*, called his present age "unusual, bleak and impoverished" for its inability to "enjoy" poetry. "For too long," Howarth intoned, "poetry has been written at best as an esoteric, at worst as a narcissistic, exercise," but he speculated that enjoyable poetry would inevitably "triumph over what has been done to English poetry by Eliot and Pound, their disciples and devotees" (286).

A heroic sentiment, but more than a little quixotic. By the early 1960s, high modernism had rigidly established not just its canonical texts, but difficulty itself as the default aesthetic of high culture. Further, difficulty's triumph was larger than one of stylistic strategies; modernism heightened difficulty's power by legitimizing reading processes that privileged difficulty and by bringing to the foreground those texts that were most amenable to being read as difficult and to being defended by modernism's central arguments. Modernism's difficulty also extended to how art and its audiences interact. While modern writers highlighted the idea that modernism presented a new form or language of literature, difficult modernism also put in place a new way of *relating to art*. As Harold Rosenberg argued in a review of Douglas Cooper's *The Cubist Epoch*, "Modern art doesn't begin at any identifiable point, but the modern situation of art undoubtedly begins with Cubism." What was unique about Cubism, according to Rosenberg, was that it "changed the relation of art to the public" (1975, 162).

Rosenberg's point is one that few of difficulty's initial apologists would have readily acknowledged. Yet although moderns didn't discuss this social situation comfortably, this interaction made modernism possible. Now, Rosenberg attributed the change in art's situation primarily to the "esoteric nature of Cubism" and the increasing professionalism that cubism marked (163), but the modern situation is larger than that. Difficulty is a nexus of attitudes and scripts that, to be literate in the arts, one needed—and still needs—to be able to negotiate instinctually. People admitted to the arena of high culture have become adept not so much at *solving* difficult work, but at knowing how initially to respond to the texture of the difficult experience. As soon as you know, for example, that difficult works are "serious"—and that "serious" implies a host of behaviors and attitudes, from avoiding the gaucherie of laughter or anger, to eschewing "easy," nonproblematic pleasures, to beginning one's understanding of difficult works with the assumption that difficulty is central to them and is tied up with these works' large cultural ambitions—you have entered the arena of twentieth-century high art. Difficulty, in other words, became—and continues to be—our central cultural gatekeeper.

Two central factors allowed difficulty to take on this gatekeeping role—the rise of literary criticism and the institution that housed such writing, the university. The linkage of these two to difficulty is multivalent, being not so much a direct cause and effect as what Gail McDonald calls a "symbiosis" (1993, 136), a symbiosis between institutions and art that had more than a few contradictions lurking within it (particularly brought into action by modernism's latent romanticism). If there eventually was a machine in place to ensure difficulty's survival, it was one with more than a few extraneous and competing parts. But it was astonishingly efficient and brought about enormous consequences in how high culture related to art.

Most notably, modernism changed what criticism *did*. It may be true that for the first time in history, criticism's routine activity became not to articulate affect, but to elucidate meanings that the art work obscured, and show in what manner these meanings concealed and presented themselves.[1] New Criticism was built for that job, a job that required substantial effort. It also required instant attention. Because modernism's difficulty was apparent at very basic levels of comprehension, it produced an immediate crisis in reading, one to which the necessary professional service of New Criticism responded. Difficult modernism required an expertise, a sophisticated discourse about literature (one that in addition countered the claim that difficult art was too easy to produce, a rebuttal that critics like Riding and Graves

> I'll skip over the embarrassingly bad poems I published in the high school year book—had I no shame?—well, actually, no—mentioning only briefly the word of encouragement I received from my wonderful Grade 12 English teacher, Miss Bessie Billings—"I can't understand a word of this, dear, so it must be good." ... Finally I went into English Literature at university, having decided in a cynical manner that I could always teach to support my writing habit. Once I got past the Anglo Saxon it was fun, although I did suffer a simulated cardiac arrest the first time I encountered T. S. Eliot and realized that not all poems rhymed, any more. "I don't understand a word of this," I thought, "so it must be good."
>
> —Margaret Atwood, lecture at Hay On Wye, Wales, 1995

explicitly set out to make). Indeed, that difficult modern texts merited this discourse was one of the signs that they were important, deserving of canonical status.[2]

Could any form of literary criticism other than New Criticism have interacted with difficulty to effect this change in what literary criticism set out to do? Again, without claiming an intransigent inextricability, it should be clear how New Criticism and difficult modernism were peculiarly suited for each other. As John Guillory points out, the assertion that difficulty was inherent to poetic language was central to New Critical strategies (1993, 169). Insisting on the difficulty of poetic language made difficult modernism the preferred form of modernism. But it went beyond that; New Criticism's embrace of difficulty had great range. It was not just a claim about the difficult texts of modernism, but about literature itself. As Guillory asserts, New Criticism successfully argued that literature was "a language which required *interpretation*" (1993, 172). That range made difficulty more comfortable; as a result of it, opting for difficult modernism did not mean putting to the side, say, Robert Herrick. This range could make difficult modernism seem natural, a naturalness that extended to what difficult modernism and its justifying theory considered worthy of discussion. Like all professional discourses New Criticism set the terms for what was within the pale—and what was beyond it. Clearly, simplicity and its inarticulate affect were excluded. As well, the asocial character of New Criticism excluded discussion of difficulty's social impetus and effects from discussion of its intrinsic merits.

For all its range and malleability, though, New Criticism was peculiarly suited to a certain kind of institution. In his famous 1938 essay "Criticism, Inc.," John Crowe Ransom argued that "Criticism must become more scientific, or precise and systematic, and this means that it must be developed by the collective and sustained effort of learned persons—which means that its proper seat is in the universities" (329).[3] Ransom's call for rigorous theory was particularly apt, of course, in the context of high modernism. But it wasn't just the literature, for the *type* of argument difficulty produced was made for university discourse. New Criticism gave professionals work; once it was accepted that great works of art were complex, ironic, and ambiguous, there was a great amount of scholarship to be done in precisely articulating for the first time the properties of canonical works that gave rise to these effects. Distrusting analysis and theory, simplicity's proponents, by contrast, had no effective counterargument. In his history of the rise of English as a discipline in North America, Gerald Graff notes that "Generalist manifestos were frequently no more than vapid attacks on the analytical approach to literature as such, incanting words like 'literature' in talismanic fashion, as if the power of literature were in and of itself sufficient to overcome an institutional problem" (1987, 88).

In the university setting New Critics could continue their work indefinitely, in a manner that simplicity's proponents could not, for difficulty's professionals not only had unlimited work, they were also people who could reproduce themselves. This proliferation was possible not just because of their arguments, which allowed for an infinite field of inquiry, but because their work was thought of *as* inquiry. And inquiry demanded the establishment of a system for training and certifying future practitioners; it increasingly required a Ph.D. to teach in the university. The certification of a Ph.D. could not be sustained under simplicity's terms. Having no sense of a "field" to be covered, and "methods" to teach, simplicity's advocates couldn't produce successors within the university (Graff 1987, 87–88). As it became clear that the university was where the battle for the canon was to be fought, they didn't so much *lose* an argument as not even *enter* it.

The university had functions other than the propagation of the professorate. It established a stable—and, after World War II, a large—readership. With classes being established in literary modernism, annual sales of Joyce's *Ulysses* would easily outpace the sales of the novel in its first ten years. The university also groomed, and continues to groom, neophytes. In the university setting, one's reactions to difficulty are quickly socialized: students' alienation toward it comes early in their reading practices and is quickly discarded—the classroom is a setting where one learns how to manage difficulty. Students learn that one is rewarded for finding difficulty, and that difficult works are the works that deserve study. With the rise of English studies, the university became a place where the grumbling freshman would be replaced, over four years, by the eager—or, failing that, the sullen but acquiescent—senior.

How was this dissemination of the difficulty aesthetic possible, given difficulty's visceral effects? First of all, the elitism of difficulty was alluring; it admitted one to an exclusive club. As well, criticism brought difficulty within acceptable limits. Most fundamentally, however, difficulty was *able* to be popular, easily assimilated. It's not that difficulty's exclusive club was that hard to join; as Guillory points out, "it was the notion of difficulty itself which became capable of wide dissemination, which became in a certain sense 'popular'" (1993, 169). The central assertion of the difficulty aesthetic is accessible and easily assimilated into a reflex action: what is to be valued about canonical works of literature are precisely those moments where they are hardest to understand.[4] The defenses of difficulty are similarly assimilable: as this book has argued, the basic defenses of difficulty are omnipresent and limited in number and rhetorical complexity.

Inevitably and on many levels, difficulty became domesticated—a process that began with the New Critics and continues unabated today. The university is a place to housebreak difficulty, to make it do its tricks. As Gail McDonald argues, the rise and standardization of New Criticism meant that its interpretations "could hold few surprises: every explication tended to result in celebration of a poem's controlled complexity" (1993, 194). Gerald Graff notes that due to the "convenient elasticity" of central New Critical terms such as irony and paradox, "not many poems could fail to reveal these qualities somehow, under the right kind of close inspection" (1987, 206). Concepts like irony, put through their paces an inestimable number of times, eventually tamed modernism's difficulty (and made the work of selected simple moderns alluring in very predictable ways).

Its long shelf life indicates that difficulty was able to go beyond its initial New Critical institutionalizing. And that is because those central New Critical terms—irony, complexity, ambiguity—are not the most basic allegiance of New Criticism. Difficulty is. And that basic allegiance continues to the present day, along with the lack of surprises that accrue from difficulty-based readings. The twentieth-century's default aesthetic is still running: we've only tinkered with it. For example, outside of the classroom criticism is no longer as excited about showing how the difficulties of a text like *The Waste Land* resolve themselves into a complex, final tension. That sense of final unity no longer has the attractions it once had, but the difficulty aesthetic has been merely fine-tuned. As Graff points out, "on the complexity scoreboard, an ostensible unity that unravels into a self-undoing heterogeneity naturally sets off more rockets than any merely complex unity" (1987, 242).

Indeed, difficulty has in some ways expanded its hold. A more basic tinkering has expanded a New Critical bromide—that aesthetic language is inherently difficult—to a larger assertion, that *all* language is difficult.

228   The Difficulties of Modernism

> You are an editor at an avant-garde art journal. When a piece you get in seems too readable, do you:
> A) translate all the most common words into German;
> B) insert parentheses into several words to expose the phallocentrism of language—for example: t(he);
> C) remove all the punctuation;
> D) print the whole article in the Cyrillic alphabet?
> —David Coleman and Jonathan Adler, *Vanity Fair*, 1996

Although this shift to the difficulty of all language has resulted in readings that are at times as dully domesticated as New Criticism at its most orthodox, the modulation has created a more problematic situation on a larger level. Difficulty's initial crisis, that modernism was difficult (and later, that *all* literature was difficult) worked because literary professionals convinced the public that the texts under consideration were important. It is harder to convince skeptics of the payoff of difficult readings of language in general, even if initially they seem more ambitious, for language in general is more tied up in ordinary activities than aesthetic language is. It is hard to convince that there is a large crisis here to which one *must* respond. This lack of crisis is exacerbated by a moral slippage. Availing itself both of professionalism and of romanticism's ideas of the sublime and the ineffable, modernism's argument worked partly because it had a large moral impetus. However, since it is harder to claim moral urgency and uniqueness for language in general, there isn't today as clear a sense of the special domain and urgency of difficulty. The critical task, to prove the difficulty of all language, is similar to the one performed for Frost and Cather, but without the sense that exists for literary language, that this is an important, separate, and ethically charged domain of language. It is consequently hard to get enough of a sense of urgency if *everything* is supposed to be urgent.

Today we are for the most part, then, acting out a modernist script. As the narratives that close each chapter of this book indicate, the triumph of difficulty created a default way of interacting with art, an interaction that has had tremendous staying power. That assertion may seem overgeneralized to some, for in many ways high culture has gone beyond 1960's high modernism. Texts that then were not part of the canon are now seen as crucial to it, and whole genres have become part of literary high culture. Edith Wharton has a firmer place in the canon than she did in 1960, and American mystery fiction and sensation novels are recognized objects of study. But, as

Lillian Robinson points out, membership in the canon is still governed by "'complexity' criteria" ([1983] 1997, 118). The strong hold of these complexity criteria suggests that we have not moved beyond the high modern canon in terms of how we relate to art. Certainly, postmodernism is conscious about its ideological separations from modernism, and individual postmodern texts may have a take on difficulty that is at variance with modern aesthetics. But modern difficulty's hold is not at its strongest on the production of art works, for difficulty is an even more powerful reading and social protocol than it is a stylistic property. When art is considered as a social practice, postmodernism hasn't changed high culture very much. In terms of how he is read and from a social point of view, Beckett is just modernism redone.

Most varieties of postmodern high culture share modernism's affection for difficulty and for the heroic; they share modernism's nervous relationship with the domestication of difficulty, pleasure, and what it means to "understand" a work; they share the belief that things worth doing in this century need to be professionalized, including culture; and they share modernism's moral earnestness about all of the above. Postmodernism's assertions of its difference from modernism are no more compelling than modernism's strenuous attempts to distance itself from romanticism; they sound suspiciously like Auden's claim that "Anyone who, like Mr. Brooks or myself, has ever had to teach literature, will agree that it is still necessary to combat romanticism" (1940, 187).

As an illustration of modern difficulty's hold on contemporary culture, consider the small tempest that raged in the wake of the 1993 *New York Times* obituary for Federico Fellini. The lengthy obituary clearly indicated Fellini's alliance with difficult art: "Mr. Fellini was impatient with interviewers who suggested that his films had been inspired by works he had not read and who pressed him with questions about the meanings of his imagery. 'Meaning, always meaning!' he scoffed. 'When someone asks "What do you mean in this picture?" it shows he is a prisoner of intellectual, sentimental shackles. Without his meaning, he feels vulnerable'" (Flint 1993). Going on, the writer indicated the place of Fellini in the film canon. Noting that Fellini's work "often stressed the bizarre, the garish and the grotesque," and that skeptics "variously termed the works excessive, simplistic and self-obsessed," the obituary summed up Fellini's career by noting that "the consensus was that he made brave and original movies about important issues."

Caryn James, in an article published a few days later, concurred with the obituary's assessment and called attention to the public recognition of the term "Felliniesque": "It describes that moment when you walk headlong into a scene so strange you think you're hallucinating; then it turns out to be real." Describing Fellini's works as having "gained their power from the mysterious and inexplicable," she argued that this inexplicability was true to life: "Every life, Fellini knew, is a story whose grand design can never be seen while one is in it. The plotless pattern of his movies mirrored the way life itself is composed of a string of episodes" (1993, 4).

The *New York Times* clearly meant the companion article it printed that same day to diametrically oppose James's point of view. In this piece, Bruce Weber also referred to the term "Felliniesque," giving it the same basic definition, but attaching very different values to it: "Indeed, the suffix 'esque' is often attached to his name, the lexicographical signal that we have adopted as a warning of opacity in art. Felliniesque, Pinteresque, Kafkaesque—Caution: Story not readily absorbable!" Describing himself as "thoughtfully middlebrow," Weber argued that when "the writer or movie director crosses the line in making work too hard to understand what is going on," such as in the work of Fellini, or in the film "Last Year at Marienbad," or Pynchon's *Gravity's Rainbow*, or the work of John Cage or Andy Warhol, "the audience may well become alienated, bored, irked, perplexed or some other undesirable thing." Indeed, Weber argued, in the case of Cage and Warhol, "I still hear noise and see a soup can."

Having baited the hook, the *New York Times* waited for a strike. In a letter to the paper two weeks later, the director Martin Scorsese bit. Characterizing Weber as believing that Fellini was "a film maker whose style gets in the way of his storytelling and whose films, as a result, are not easily accessible to audiences," Scorsese wrote that he found "distressing ... the underlying attitude toward artistic expression that is different, difficult or demanding." Tying Weber's attitudes to racism and xenophobia, Scorsese characterized Weber's arguments as "dangerous ... , limiting, intolerant" (1993, A26:4).

The *New York Times*' intended function for this exchange is unclear, as public spleen-ventings often are. However, if one thinks of the Fellini debate not as a consequential argument but as a ritualistic enactment of nonnegotiable principles, it comes more into focus. The exchange shows, for example, that modern difficulty's triumph, though large, has not been complete, for there are vestiges of the conservative position still left. However, these are vestiges that now occupy the margins of high culture. The public outcry against difficulty by literary establishment types has, for the most part, ceased. Few art professionals write about their own anxiety about difficult art; now, the outcry is much more from the general public and from newspaper op-ed pieces. Modern difficulty's success has been thorough enough that difficulty, for the most part, is no longer a quarrel *within* high culture, which has domesticated difficulty.

Difficulty, in fact, has become high culture's default position; during the first half of the twentieth century, Western high culture changed its default

> "A young spider knows how to spin a web without any instructions from anybody. Don't you regard that as a miracle?"
> "I suppose so," said Mrs. Arable. "I never looked at it that way before. Still, I don't understand it, and I don't like what I can't understand."
> —E. B. White, *Charlotte's Web*, 1952

aesthetic, replacing simplicity with difficulty. That is an astonishing shift, even acknowledging the residual simplicity that occasionally still surfaces. Given the bodily anxiety that it needed to manage, how did difficult modernism manage to succeed so completely? Why did so many modern artists turn to difficulty? The answer to that is a little unruly, for different writers accepted difficulty for different reasons; further, they didn't always clearly articulate those reasons, which, to make things even more amorphous, functioned more on the level of predispositions, or unarticulated instincts. But I can sketch the beginnings of an outline by turning first to the defenses put forward for difficulty: difficulty became so omnipresent because people found these arguments persuasive; on the basis of some large cultural changes, people really *did* believe, for example, that the human mind was difficult, and that difficulty was *necessary*.

That account also only gets one so far, however, and does not address the more deep-seated *attitudes* that made difficulty attractive. There was, for example, a sense of aesthetic crisis in the first quarter of the twentieth century, a crisis that made grand and powerful solutions like difficulty attractive. As well, the attractions of fashion should not be discounted: once the most interesting minds of a generation lean in one direction, there is pressure for others to follow suit. These, and more pointed attitudes, such as the modernist complicity in professionalism and its assertions of machismo and ethics, had immense persuasive force. Now, moderns were less aware of these attitudes than they were of their more logically developed defenses, but it is these attitudes that were probably more effective in making difficulty the *default* aesthetic, the aesthetic that did not need to be argued for, but that instead went without saying.

There are large consequences for difficulty's success. While difficulty's triumph still binds new texts added to the canon, it does so without the deliberateness and polemical urgency that it required near the beginning of the twentieth century. Difficulty has become "ideology" in the sense that Eagleton uses the term, a space of significant silence.[5] Its ideological function has made difficulty an intellectual safe haven; there is, for example, no great intellectual risk in working out the default position on yet another non-canonical text, claiming that a previously neglected author actually exhibits a deceptive simplicity.

Further, as the script for interacting with the difficulty of high art became more settled, some of difficulty's power was lost. It has been decades since an audience for a difficult piece of music or art show has rioted; large-scale visceral responses are now directed by the general public only at art that it feels it has some stake in, particularly publicly funded art such as *Tilted Arc* and *Voice of Fire*. Difficulty quickly became socialized; domesticated audiences soon instinctively knew what the correct responses to difficulty and simplicity ought to be. But this doesn't mean high culture has escaped modernism's difficulty; it has merely internalized it. What could still prompt difficulty's outrage and anxiety? Perhaps, as the 1989 controversy over Mapplethorpe's *X Portfolio* suggests, the moral difficulty of visual art is where difficulty still hits the larger culture.

Or, perhaps only simplicity could scandalize these days—though it would be hard to find ways to talk about it, and it would be hard for these claims to stand still. As soon as an apparently simple candidate appears under the critical lens and claims are made for its canonical status, the simplicity disappears. Consider the Norman Rockwell show of 1999–2002. While it was partly sponsored by the usual suspect, the Norman Rockwell Museum of Stockbridge, Massachusetts, it was also sponsored by the High Museum of Art in Atlanta, Georgia. Traveling to, among other places, the Corcoran in Washington and the New York Guggenheim, the show was clearly intended to assert Rockwell's canonical legitimacy, a place among the ranks of serious artists. Ned Rifkin, director of the High Museum, knew the terms that would have to be used in order to make this happen. In his catalog essay, Rifkin asserted: "Norman Rockwell clearly mastered the complexity of the human experience in the United States—his contemporary America—by making it seem and look simple. However, looking carefully at Rockwell discloses that his art is not a simple one—it only appears to be so" (1999, 20). The reflex is too easy, at times no better than a marketing ploy. A blurb for the 1999 PBS documentary *Norman Rockwell: Painting America* (2002) noted that "Insightful commentary by art experts and historians enhances one's appreciation of Rockwell's deceptively simple work."

The inevitable appearance of deceptive simplicity suggests that the advantages modern difficulty gained for art are equivocal. Modernism is neither a story in which the forces of good triumphed over conservative reactionism, nor one in which hegemonic modernism stifled good art. Modernism's advantages are more entangled than that. Expanding upon his claim that "we have become an audience which for better or for worse is committed to the complex poem," Mark Van Doren argued in 1942 that "We are committed to

> Good evening. Welcome to Difficult Listening Hour.
> The spot on your dial for that relentless and
> Impenetrable sound of Difficult Music
> [Music. . . . Music. . . . Music]
> So sit bolt upright in that straight-backed chair,
> button that top button,
> and get set for some difficult music:
> —Laurie Anderson, *Difficult Listening Hour*, 1984

it because we have it, and because we have it we know more than certain audiences have known concerning the elements of poetry. It is arguable that those elements should not be known; nor do I maintain that consciousness of them is an unmixed blessing. Many readers today for whom the complex poem is merely difficult, or merely impossible, would call it a curse" (41–42). Van Doren's mixed assessment seems right; further, it is only by beginning with this kind of measured response that we will understand the strength of the grip difficulty has on contemporary culture.

That measured response includes acknowledging difficulty's strong points. If the Western literary canon has been built around versions of inexhaustibility, difficulty exhibits central characteristics of that tradition. Alban Berg, writing in 1924 about the work of Arnold Schoenberg, noted that Schoenberg's music was "so difficult to understand" because of its "musical structure, the abundance of the artistic means everywhere employed in this harmonic style, the application of all compositional possibilities presented by music throughout the centuries—in a word: its immeasurable richness" ([1924] 1956, 458). Berg is not completely off-base: though the difficult text is typically premised not on an enriched relationship between surface and depth, but in some ways a contrast between them, it yet has affinities with traditional senses of inexhaustibility. If the central characteristic of inexhaustible works is that they have an infinite number of things to be said about them, difficulty is clearly part of that tradition. In the difficult work there is always a nub that can't be sanded down, and difficult modernism makes an awareness of further work to be done the *first* thing to be known and assented to.

A further strength of high modernism's privileging of surface difficulty is that difficulty is so spectacular, so highly expressive. From one's first interactions, modern difficulty will not leave one alone. It pushes its audience forward into a confrontation, a confrontation with several possible results. One can, presumably, successfully overcome the difficulty. Or, difficulty can raise

> Frasier: "Truth is, Dad, I—I'm not sure I can do simple."
> Father: "Well, I don't know if you can, or if you just don't want to. But you know, some of the best things in the world are simple, Frase. Just like that art gallery you took me to a couple of months ago. Do you remember? You were oohing and aahing over this painting of a big red dot."
> Frasier: "Yeah, yeah, Dad. But there is a difference between simple—and deceptively simple."
>
> —NBC's *Frasier*, January 13, 2000

an anxiety that is either partially or not resolved. One can also, of course, just walk away—but the option that the difficult text does not encourage is that of half-consciously rubbing one's eyes over hundreds of pages of text.

By refusing to let its readers go, difficult modernism brought art's viscerality to center stage; exploiting it as an embodied affect of high modernism. That is why the understanding of modernist difficulty as "crossword puzzle" difficulty was an impoverished understanding both of difficulty's resonance and its pleasures. Difficulty is more than an intellectual enterprise; it is sensuous. Even those moments in modernism that might plausibly be described as puzzle pleasures (such as the pleasure of working out the various walking routes in *Ulysses*'s "Wandering Rocks" episode) are often resonant pleasures, connecting to larger issues in the artwork as well as teasing and highlighting aspects of the nature of language or representation, or of one's strategies for making meaning. That "figuring out" is not *the* point of works like *Ulysses*, although it is one of them. The pleasures of difficult art are pleasures *because* they are resonant, not because they are single-voiced. (However, this assertion that difficulty's pleasure or value *was* single-voiced may have been inevitable, for if readers find the difficulty of a text to be beyond them, they typically conceptualize it as a single thing, the only thing that keeps them from having true pleasure. The obstacle takes over and defines the work.) The pleasures of difficulty, then, are real. To people with the right skills, works like *Ulysses* are an exhilarating ride. It makes little sense to claim that any reader's enjoyment of Gertrude Stein is inevitably a bogus, attenuated pleasure. If, for other human activities (such as sports), there is pleasure in working just at the limits of one's abilities, it makes sense that this should also be the case for art.

Further, the high modern critique of pleasure, as it was then understood, was needed. High moderns were right to see standard early twentieth-century versions of aesthetic pleasure to be an impoverished usage of art's

> In examining a work such as Peter Rabbit, it is important that the superficial characteristics of its deceptively simple plot should not be allowed to blind the reader to the more substantial fabric of its deeper motivations. In this report I plan to discuss the sociological implications of family pressures so great as to drive an otherwise moral rabbit to perform acts of thievery which he consciously knew were against the law. I also hope to explore the personality of Mr. Macgregor in his conflicting roles as farmer and humanitarian. Peter Rabbit is established from the start as a benevolent hero and it is only with the increase of social pressure that the seams in his moral fabric....
>
> —Linus, "Book Report," in Clark Gesner's *You're a Good Man, Charlie Brown*, 1967, revived 1999

range. Particularly in poetry, conservative readers tended to limit art's possible affects; it is as if they forgot about such aspects of art as the sublime. As the confrontational nature of difficulty suggests, quiet pleasure is not art's only aesthetic effect. Difficulty was peculiarly able to open up art to these other expressive effects, to do so in very powerful ways, and to indicate that these effects not only elucidated central aspects of modern experience, but they also had been, at times, part of the Western aesthetic tradition. There is great value in having the expressiveness of art be wide open, to include not only serene joy, but also terror, amazement—even, I suppose, disgust.

Finally, difficulty's implicit arguments about culture and the human mind seem to make sense. The aesthetic possibilities that Woolf and Joyce opened up in depicting the human mind are not possibilities I would willingly give up; similarly, the parallel between the disorientation of *The Waste Land* and twentieth-century culture produces, for me, a powerful aesthetic effect. It is also one that continues to find practitioners. But to value this expansion is different from asserting that the high modern position on the relationship between form and the depiction of human psychology and culture is the *only* way in which art should go. Moderns (of all persuasions) thought of difficulty as a zero sum game, which always, eventually, is a loss for art's diversity. There is no inherent prestige, no "must" to difficulty. Writing his elegant "Nothing Gold Can Stay" was not, for Frost, a way of evading life in the twentieth century. In the dichotomized suspicion that greets works whose surfaces appear simple, difficult modernism has left an ambiguous inheritance.

Modernism's difficulty, then, incurred costs that high culture continues to pay. A clear cost is found in the intensity with which the argument was

> In fact, the avant-garde has shown a remarkable robustness and longevity. Given the chance, a surprising range of people do indeed get to understand that there is a wider range of flavours to savour than the instant gratification of saccharine sweetness. People do, given the chance, get to understand that difficult things can be worthwhile.
>
> —Deyan Sudjic in the *Guardian*, 1993, responding to the controversy surrounding Rachel Whiteread's cast concrete *House*, which was later awarded the Turner Prize

conducted. Given that the difficulty argument was such a dichotomized, high-stakes argument, one that was set in motion by the anxiety surrounding difficulty, it would be extremely useful if in some of its areas there would be a clear right or wrong. For example, since difficulty does provide many with clear pleasure, it would be helpful for critics if all of difficulty's accompanying baggage were also good and clean and pure. But it's not. The morality tale that high moderns presented (in which Tennyson was the devil, surrounded by the Vices Francis Turner Palgrave, J. C. Squire, and the lazy public) was hyperbolic, overstated.

High modernism also overstated its separation from what preceded it. As many critics have argued, modernism did not completely reverse what had gone before. Its difficulty is no exception. Modernism validated difficulty not by completely overturning, but by rearranging some aesthetic values; it looked more combative than it really was. (This is no longer a surprise to scholars; what is surprising is that contemporary high culture continues to use many of these values.) The central high modern attitudes toward "understanding," "depth," and "pleasure" can be traced back to romanticism and the sublime. What modernism did was articulate these concepts in terms of difficulty and cast a professionalist and macho, ethical aura over them.

Hampered by its dichotomies and certain of the platonic rightness of its version of art, high modernism for the most part refused to deal honestly with the fact that difficult art, like all art, was a complicated social activity. High moderns tended to dichotomize literary culture, creating a culture in which those enmired in the social were opposed to the high moderns, who soared above such concerns. (In using this argument, of course, high moderns were not all that different from simplicity's advocates.) Difficulty's apologists, worried that the social conditions surrounding difficulty made it extrinsic and less valuable, worked hard both on downplaying its social context and on selling it as an intrinsic property of texts. By not working adequately with either its affect or the context for difficulty, however, high modernism did not give a complete account of difficulty's impetus and its effects, and it did not recognize that difficulty was an interaction between reader and text, and not a property of a text. And while difficult modernism did have the salutary effect of slowing down reading, it had no interest in articulating how difficulty challenged the then-dominant model of reading, a model in which the pleasures of the text were best received in a transparent reading process, in which the claims of the real world dissolved and one communicated with the literary work directly.

This lack of attention to context and affect has had numerous implications. As its macho language suggests, high modernism did not completely ignore the anxiety that came with difficulty, but it gave a very incomplete account of how difficulty was embodied and the consequences of that embodiment. Consider Gertrude Stein, who during the course of an interview in 1946 made the following comments about her work: "I took individual words and thought about them until I got their weight and volume complete and put them next to another word, and at this same time I found out very soon that there is no such thing as putting them together without sense. It is impossible to put them together without sense. I made innumerable efforts to make words write without sense and found it impossible. Any human being putting down words had to make sense out of them" ([1946] 1971, 18). But Stein, though she like most moderns was shrewd about human desires for meaning, also resembled most moderns in that she didn't deal very well with what happened when "making sense" didn't occur. She didn't articulate how one might work with the surge of anxiety that accompanied failed comprehension. She also missed the power of difficulty's awkwardness, its troubled relationship with "pure" aesthetics.

Difficulty's apologists, then, didn't adequately acknowledge the messiness of difficulty and its social situation, particularly that difficulty *is* about power and about failure: a work is difficult because some person or group of persons doesn't understand it, and further, this group that doesn't understand the difficult work recognizes that others *do* claim to understand it. As a result, while there is pleasure in difficult work, that pleasure is inherently subjective, available only to certain people who engage in a specific kind of reading practice and who bring difficulty within acceptable limits. As such, difficult modernism had trouble dealing with the commonsense observation that some things were just too hard for some people.

Difficulty thus also shows that the story of modernism, like the story of all aesthetic movements, is not just a story of the triumph of aesthetic excellence, it is a story about how to negotiate power. Consider, for example, modernism's flirtation with a semiliterate audience. On the one hand, moderns like Eliot were right to distinguish between what authors needed to know, and what their readers needed to know. This is not to say that such a distinction was unproblematic. Esslin's analysis of San Quentin might be right, that things are less difficult if you don't have the standard literary expectations, but the social consequences are dicey. Does Esslin's account imply that it is better not to educate readers? Is that also where Eliot's preference for an audience that can neither read nor write leads? Unanswered questions like these indicate that modernism was really nervous about the *point* of entry into discussions about it. Relatively at ease with their platonic ideal of a primitive audience, high moderns were more ambivalent about people who were neither primitive nor quite yet members of the aesthetic governing class, but who might aspire to it. Questions of difficulty's elitism, then, are complicated. On one hand, to its proponents, difficulty's elitism seemed initially less offensive than other aesthetic elitisms current in the first half of the past century, for it claimed to be based not on class, or wealth, or even gender, but on a willingness to work hard, a moral willingness to take literature *seriously*. On the other hand, an elitism based on what "seriousness" implied—particularly intelligence and professional credentials—is not much less insidious than an elitism based on wealth, class, or gender.

Even given difficulty's propensity to limit its audience, however, it is too simple to say that difficulty is simply elitist. Difficulty was not separate from mass culture, for central devices of mass culture, particularly professionalism and publicity, helped create its mystique and elitism. Difficulty attracted readers by presenting the allure of elitism while simultaneously proffering reading strategies that made difficulty easier to work with. In order to brace difficult modernism against the charge of elitism, difficult modernists went to a meaning that did not require knowledge, meaning beyond language, a meaning of ambiguity, resonance, suggestion. These reading strategies opened the text to a bigger group of readers and are relatively useful; it does make sense for a first-time reader to work with Conrad Aiken's claim that *The Waste Land* "has an emotional value far clearer and richer than its arbitrary and rather unworkable logical value" ([1923] 1982a, 160).[6]

Modernism also attracted a larger audience by claiming that difficulty was transitory. This assertion again has ambiguous implications. Difficulty's apologists were right to note how difficulty may lose its edge over time; transitory difficulty seems validated by the public acceptance of artists like Renoir and others, by the general sense that things become less difficult over time. As composer Elliott Carter noted in an unpublished 1955 review, "Every music student knows that Brahms was considered difficult and obscure in his time; in fact, it is only since the Second World War that his music and that of Tchaicovsky has been comparatively widely appreciated in France and Italy" (1997a, 54). Of course, by circumscribing one's sense of audience, it is easy to overstate how quickly difficulty disappears; the idea of transitory difficulty has its limitations. Twenty years after he wrote the above review, Carter claimed that some "artworks that take an imaginative effort to grasp in a serious way . . . have proved to be accessible after repeated hearings and with performers that understood the music." Turning to a specific instance, Carter claimed that: "Certainly the first American performances of the Viennese school like that of Schoenberg's Wind Quintet played by angry, loud, and somewhat uncontrolled performers at Town Hall in 1925 or of the Webern *Symphonie* a few years later left a very puzzling yet intriguing impression that has completely changed. What once seemed arbitrary, difficult, and complex now no longer presents problems, due to familiarity on the part of the performers and listeners; indeed, if anything the Schoenberg sounds, today, a little too Regerish" ([1976] 1997b, 198).

Putting to the side the questionable claim that Schoenberg "no longer presents problems," Carter leaves unresolved a further modernist assertion, one that interacts at best clumsily with the sense of transitory difficulty: the belief that difficulty is inherently valuable. Carter is not atypical; high moderns generally do not discuss at the same time two of their central assertions: both difficulty's inherent value and its transience. The two claims interact awkwardly with each other, a consequence of high modern reluctance to discuss the social context of art, as well as its inability to address how difficulty is an inherently personal experience, and, moreover, an experience that occurs on a continuum of intensity.

High modern difficulty set in motion another central uneasiness, an uneasiness about pleasure. While some versions of postmodernism employ pleasure as central to their effects, for the most part the high modern distrust continues yet today and shows up in the common practice of caricaturing pleasure as escapist and trivial. In his theory of difficulty, for example, Adorno argued that great artworks "distance themselves from the childish desire to please" (1997, 92). This attitude is easily recognized. Writing in the *London Review of Books*, Julian Bell, for example, castigates some contemporary critics for making the following kind of comment about Bloomsbury art: "These painters have made the mistake of taking Matisse's programme for an art that is 'like a good armchair' literally; they have turned something difficult and wild into mere pleasure" (2000, 22). Nancy Princenthal, reviewing a retrospective show of work by performance artist Carolee Schneeman, noted that Schneeman's *Meat Joy* has a new ability to "unsettle" viewers. According to Princenthal, "Maybe it is, simply, the shapeless, shameless celebration of pleasure, unqualified by irony, ambiguity, danger or past pain, that now proves most difficult" (1997, 108). These attitudes come from a dubious modern value structure, in which difficulty's vigorous regimen was seen as

> If previously my music had been difficult to understand on account of the peculiarities of my ideas and the way in which I expressed them, how could it happen that now, all of a sudden, everybody could follow my ideas and like them? Either the music or the audience was worthless.
>
> —Arnold Schoenberg, commenting on his sudden popularity, 1937

inherently more authentic than simplicity's pleasure. The hierarchy is both exaggerated and fundamentally off base. It's not that either difficulty or simplicity should be more authentic; high modernism's problems stem more from clinging to notions of authenticity, from making difficulty the last surviving version of authenticity (a habit that continues, as Caputo's writing shows, well into the confines of postmodernism). Authenticity, including difficulty's authenticity, is a highly problematic aesthetic.

And even when difficult modernism incorporated pleasure, the uneasiness didn't stop, revealing itself in how modernism inflected its version of pleasure. Given the inherently visceral reactions to difficulty, one's experience with difficulty is plausibly a strenuous thing. But it does not follow that difficulty should therefore be thought of as heroic, and that all other forms of aesthetic experience passively acquiesce to the numbing qualities of twentieth-century life. High culture still too easily accepts the morality of difficulty, as when Marina van Zuylen in her overview of difficulty argues that "the difficult text denies itself the comforts of mimesis" (1998, 46). It also does not follow that the moral anxiety of difficulty has large revolutionary implications. While difficulty can seem oppositional, it acquires this aura by creating anxiety, and the consequences of this anxiety are unpredictable. It does not necessarily encourage specific kinds of political change. Difficulty too quickly became the reflex action of the avant-garde.

Modernism's continuation of that moral trajectory into an argument for difficulty's health, naturalness, machismo, and vigor also leads to some odd readings of texts, particularly those of Gertrude Stein and Marianne Moore. Instead of arguing that difficulty was not perverted, but healthy, high moderns would have done better to reject (or at least scrutinize) the basis of these terms. Modernism, then, did not look closely at the consequences and implicit logic behind its major assertions about difficulty's morality. This was an important oversight, for in high modernism's language and metaphors lie the beginnings of questionable moral judgments as well as the nascent forms of social institutions. Such scrutiny may not be easy: while many of these implied arguments aren't hard to question, it may be difficult to avoid some of the tropes and conceptual metaphors that give rise to them (it would be

> Ironically the "avant-garde" no longer identifies with the new: institutionalized as it is in the universities, it has become the conservative stronghold of the current music scene, for it holds stringently to difficulty and inaccessibility as the principal signs of its integrity and moral superiority.
>
> —Musicologist Susan McClary, 1989

very difficult to avoid talking about the surface and depth of works of art, for example). However, since we can know where the linguistic alliances lie, surely it is possible to examine how they work and perhaps even walk outside of them. Without such scrutiny, these terms continued to function as default ways of valuing literature, ways that bind us.

High moderns also could have acknowledged that the aesthetic system they put in place, despite its considerable merits, was also self-serving, not so much a universal aesthetic as one peculiarly tailored for the kinds of art they produced. The reading *practice* modernism promoted, one that made all texts potentially difficult, was not value-free. James Joyce famously commented to one of his translators that he did not want to make public his schema for *Ulysses*, for "If I gave it all up immediately, I'd lose my immortality. I've put in so many enigmas and puzzles that it will keep the professors busy for centuries arguing over what I meant, and that's the only way of ensuring one's immortality" (quoted in Ellmann 1982, 521). Carl Van Vechten also noted the connection between the scandal of difficulty and its profitability. Commenting on Stein's literary portraits of painters, Van Vechten noted that "these portraits, the earliest examples of Gertrude Stein's 'difficult' work to reach the public were much commented on and satirized." Their potential was spotted early. Reports Van Vechten: "Stieglitz told me that he had accepted them for publication as soon as he had looked them over, principally because he did not understand them" (quoted in Stein 1962, 328). Literary professionals need to take the step that high modernism didn't take, to squeamishly acknowledge both that difficulty is a wonderful aesthetic *and* that it sells texts and provides employment.

This modernist understanding of art still drives contemporary high culture; difficulty has become too integral and unexamined a part of our reading as critics. To those whose principal activity it is to explicate literature or other cultural artifacts, it has become hard not to think of difficulty as an inherent good. There is *still* a great impulse to make one's reading practices inevitable: it is not enough just to say that a difficult reading of a noncanonical author is one way among many; the difficulty has to be crucially *in* the text. Difficulty also drives how critics expand the literary canon and ground this expansion on a shaky principle, for we look for the devices of difficulty in works that weren't built to run on that aesthetic. This to a large degree comes about because literary professionals are trained to expect disruptions to their expectations: the unexpected is what we expect, and the more we read, the less we are truly shocked. Those disruptions have become, in a sense, domesticated, resulting in the odd situation in which it is too easy to make Frost difficult.

Now, all these problems with modern difficulty may suggest that it is difficulty that created the apparent loss of an audience for high art. Such a suggestion would be partly right and partly wrong.[7] The best modernist analysis of the more complicated relationship that actually exists was put forward by Randall Jarrell. In "The Obscurity of the Poet," Jarrell argued that while sometimes a poet "is unread because he is difficult," or "difficult *because* he is not read," more often the situation is more complicated. The difficulty of poetry and the lack of an audience for it, Jarrell asserted,

> are no more than effects of that long-continued, world-overturning cultural and social revolution (seen at its most advanced stage here in the United States) which has made the poet difficult and the public unused to any poetry exactly as it has made poet and public divorce their wives, stay away from church, dislike bull-baiting, free the slaves, get insulin shots for diabetes, or do a hundred thousand other things, some bad, some good, and some indifferent. It is superficial to extract two parts from this world-high whole, and to say of them: "This one, here, is the cause of that one, there; and that's all there is to it."
>
> If we were in the habit of reading poets their obscurity would not matter; and once we are out of the habit, their clarity does not help. (1953a, 3–4)

The contemporary situation, Jarrell caustically observed, was not flattering; according to Jarrell, "people who have inherited the custom of not reading poets justify it by referring to the obscurity of the poems they have never read—since most people decide that poets are obscure very much as legislators decide that books are pornographic: by glancing at a few fragments someone has strung together to disgust them." There is some large-scale cultural duplicity going on, one that points to a general cultural move away from the products of high culture:

> When a person says accusingly that he can't understand Eliot, his tone implies that most of his happiest hours are spent at the fireside among worn copies of the *Agememnon*, *Phèdre*, and the Symbolic Books of William Blake; and it is melancholy to find, as one commonly will, that for months at a time he can be found pushing eagerly through the pages of *Gone with the Wind* or *Forever Amber*, where *with head, hands, wings, or feet* this poor fiend *pursues his way, and swims, or sinks, or wades, or creeps, or flies*; that all his happiest memories of Shakespeare seem to come from a high school production of *As You Like It* in which he played the wrestler Charles; and

that he has, by some obscure process of free association, combined James Russell, Amy, and Robert Lowell into one majestic whole: a bearded cigar-smoking ambassador to the Vatican who, after accompanying Theodore Roosevelt on his first African expedition, came home to dictate on his deathbed the "Concord Hymn." Many a man, because Ezra Pound is too obscure for him, has shut forever the pages of *Paradise Lost*; or so one would gather, from the theory and practice such people combine. (Jarrell 1953a, 9–10)

Now, few would argue that high art *hasn't* lost much of its audience. But Jarrell's insightful contribution is that people have turned away from high art for lots of reasons other than difficulty, perhaps the most pressing of which is that culture has found more instantly available pleasures that look even more gratifying when set next to a difficult artwork. Another part of the reason is that difficulty has become a familiar aesthetic strategy. Difficulty has become so familiar that, once we see difficulty coming, it is much easier to disengage than it used to be. Perhaps culture today has taken up what was for modern readers a less dominant reaction to difficulty: boredom.

The way out of these entanglements is not clear, but I can suggest a beginning, one that starts with the recognition that early twentieth-century attacks on difficulty have their limitations. Believing what I do about difficulty's problems, I still have to say that attacks like those of Untermeyer don't attract me all that much (although at times I admire the wit of the parodies). My dissatisfaction with difficulty has limits; I cannot go all the way back and say high culture ought to return to simplicity as it was understood at the beginning of the twentieth century. Not only was such an understanding based on an impoverished notion of art's expressive capabilities, its weaknesses as argumentation meant that modern difficulty's opponents could not form a useful rebuttal of difficulty. Once modernism opened aesthetic discussion to evidentiary, logically developed arguments based on close reading, there was no going back. Further, many of these readings, and the texts upon which they are based, have provided me with resonant, significant pleasures. But at the same time, to read every text as if its essence were difficult is a mind-numbing exercise. While every text can be made difficult, it is not the case that every text can be made difficult in equally rich and compelling ways that are central to the effects of the text. Further, as long as literary criticism makes its central activity the honing of critical skills on principles of difficulty, it will remove itself further from the general public as the entry point to high art gets more arduous.

A further constraint imposed by difficulty is that, regardless of the positive or negative values we attach to it, some of difficulty's inheritance will never change. Even though in the future readers might become more accustomed to difficulty, or culture's sense of what makes for difficulty might change, there is no way to change the bodily basis of the dramatic responses to difficulty.

When for an individual difficulty becomes too great to manage, either flight or anxiety will result. This realization acknowledges that much of difficulty—its pleasures and its anxiety—is affect-based. And because it is affect-based, there is always going to be a continuum of reactions to difficult texts.

Now, that argument may seem modest, for instead of giving some principled objection to or defense of difficulty, it brings in an ad hoc principle, one that cannot be verified solely by a work's properties, for it is personally determined. But the seeming modesty hides an important principle: difficulty is an excess that is not a property of the difficult work at hand, but a reading protocol that is radically affect-based. The line between pleasure and unmanageable anxiety is personally determined, occurring in an interaction between reader and text. For some, the difficult text is just too far along the curve; the argument about difficulty turns out to be one about whether there is *too much* difficulty. Acknowledging that subjectivity and that the pleasures of high modern difficult texts are real pleasures for some and terrifying for others, high culture should recognize that the audience for difficult art will always be small, and will always need to be supported by the university classroom or some institution like it. A two-tiered audience for the products of art is just one of difficulty's consequences, and it is not completely negative. While perhaps not an ideal cultural situation, the presence of difficulty among an elite audience is not the horribly irresponsible thing that critics like Russell Jacoby have portrayed. At the same time, however, literary professionals need to move away from privileging difficulty as the central and highest paradigm of what art ought to do. Difficulty's effects are not the *only* effects of art, and at times high modernism made it seem like they were. In response to this, high culture need not return en masse to simplicity. But it should be open to alternate aesthetic systems and to finding ways to discuss those systems, so that difficulty isn't inevitable. Modernism's difficulty is just one form of attention that can be brought to bear on art. On that level at least, when he argued that "poets in our civilization, as it exists at present, must be *difficult*," Eliot was just wrong.

Notes

Chapter 1

1. The term "modern," of course, has a wider range than just the difficult texts of high modernism; Harriet Monroe of *Poetry* (with her promotion of home-grown, democratic writers), Harold Monro (of the *Georgian* anthologies), and a host of writers of, say, the Harlem renaissance all rightly saw themselves as responding to the conditions of modernity. For the sake of clarity in this book, if the term "modern," left unmodified, would have an unclear referent, I will modify it with terms like "high" modernism, "difficult" modernism, or "populist" modernism. The term "modernist," in this book, is always used to refer to difficult modernism.
2. Pamela McCallum (1993), Marina van Zuylen (1998), and William Christie (2000) offer overviews of historical discussions of difficulty. Major book-length studies of aspects of difficulty can be found in Marina van Zuylen (1994), Allon White (1981), James Wilhelm (1982), and Malcolm Bowie (1978). These are not works, however, that derive their energy from the social context of difficulty. More contextually based discussions of the peculiar situation of modern difficulty can be found in Vernon Shetley (1993) and Bob Perelman (1994). George Steiner's (1978) essay "On Difficulty" provides a useful taxonomy of the types of difficulty. The essays in Purves's collection *The Idea of Difficulty in Literature* (1991) make a valuable contribution in noting that difficulty is not so much a property of an art work as it is something that occurs in an interaction between readers and texts. Other works that I have found particularly useful are James Elkins's (1999) *Why Are Our Pictures Puzzles?*, Jeremy Gilbert-Rolfe's (1993) "Seriousness and Difficulty in Contemporary Art and Criticism," Susan McClary's (1989) "Terminal Prestige," Constance Perin's (1994) "The Reception of New, Unusual, and Difficult Art," Joseph Aimone et al.'s (1995) "Obscurity: An Internet Dialogue," and Richard Poirier's (1992) "The Difficulties of Modernism and the Modernism of Difficulty."
3. The *Times Literary Supplement* about that time had a circulation of 23,000; the *Dial* reached 9,000.

4. Of course, the situation was not quite as dichotomized as many portrayed it at the time, although it was useful and perhaps therapeutic to have a clear enemy. Squire, for example, had thought well of Ezra Pound's first books of poetry, and he supported the sculptor Jacob Epstein, whose work was frequently the butt of traditionalist fervor. Further, writers on both sides of the difficulty argument were steeped in romantic aesthetic attitudes. And, there were a few writers who were ambivalent about specific instances of difficult writing. (The more explicitly one held to romantic ideals of art, the more likely it was that one would dislike one instance of difficulty, but like another.) Yet for the most part, discussion about difficult writing attracted polarized and extreme reactions, and most of those involved in literary politics enjoyed seeing it as a battleground on which the lines were clearly drawn. (Its military metaphors are a central characteristic of early twentieth-century literary discussion.)

5. My research has discovered over eight hundred sources (approximately one hundred of which are poetry anthologies) that during the years 1910 to 1950 comment on difficulty in a given text or group of texts (and, more than five hundred from after 1950 comment on difficulty in either modernism or contemporary high culture). These early readers also knew that comments on difficulty were a common reaction to modernism: about one in five of them chose to contextualize their comments by noting that difficulty was prevalent, even fashionable in modernism (often adding even one more turn: noting how common it was to comment on modernism's difficulty).

   I have discovered more than seventy-five books written before 1950 that comment on the difficulty of a given modern text or modernism in general; of these, many devote entire chapters to difficulty, and twenty-nine specifically discuss the prevalence of difficulty in modernism. Several early critics (Cleanth Brooks, Robert Graves, Edith Sitwell, and Yvor Winters) also choose to *begin* a major work about modernism with the claim that difficulty is everywhere. This list of major sources does not include writers published in mass circulation magazines, such as Randall Jarrell in the *Nation*, Sinclair Lewis in *Esquire*, Max Eastman in *Harper's*, and a 1945 symposium in the *American Scholar*. My research shows that about half of those writers who comment on difficulty in twentieth-century art or music also claim that difficulty is fashionable.

   An historical note: John Guillory in *Cultural Capital* argues that "the notion of difficulty circulated between the wars as a negative criterion of judgement" (1993, 169). My study suggests that the contestation over how difficulty was to be defined was undertaken much earlier than Brooks's 1939 *Modern Poetry and the Tradition*, although I agree with Guillory that the ascendancy of New Criticism in the university was the occasion for difficulty's triumph.

6. Eliot's short comment is quoted in its entirety, or its phrasing precisely referred to, in thirty-one of my sources. His later comment, that "genuine poetry can communicate before it is understood" ([1929] 1975, 206), though less frequently cited, is nevertheless also more often noted than any other comment about difficulty by any other critic. In addition, in discussions of influential writers, early

modern readers mention Eliot's influence on poetry and literature in general (and Joyce's influence on fiction) far more often than any other writer, and he is acknowledged as influential by readers and critics of highly divergent attitudes toward difficult modernism.

7. For example, *all* the initial reviewers of Eliot's (1922) *The Waste Land* (about twenty) mention some form of difficulty as central to their response. Such claims are made not only about all the canonical international modernists, but also of many others more at the edges, including Marianne Moore, Mina Loy, Laura Riding, William Carlos Williams, Wallace Stevens, and W. H. Auden. Such comments are also typical about modern music and art. My research shows that about half of those writers who comment on difficulty in twentieth-century art or music also claim that difficulty is fashionable. Further, many readers of modernism would reach to other arts to comment on difficulty in literature. That reaching was important, for those works that could most easily sustain interarts and more general cultural comparisons were most often claimed as central to modernism.
8. With painting and music, the increase in difficulty as a social phenomenon was often perceived to have begun earlier than in literature, as early as the mid-1800s.
9. The Chicago *Record-Herald*, on the occasion of the arrival of the 1913 Armory Show, connected its arrival with Stein's "Portrait of Mabel Dodge," "a real, thrilling bit of cubist literature that was made public yesterday" ("Director French," 1913).
10. About one in five of my sources either responds with this kind of emotion, or notes that such responses are common. While such extreme responses are, of course, more a part of attacks on modernism than of defenses of it, even a positive reviewer of Faulkner, after claiming that *Absalom, Absalom!* was Faulkner's "master work," articulated his anxiety at the work's difficulty: "It is, by its very genius, the hardest to read. I confess at the outset that many times I was lost and terrified in the shadows and thunders of his involved prose, lost and annoyed in his ramifications of chronology and ancestry" (Shipp [1936] 1995, 151). These reactions were so frequent that writers of the time routinely commented on how typical it was for difficulty to elicit such responses.
11. While difficulty had as many published proponents as detractors, more than two-thirds of the time its omnipresence was seen as a negative thing, pointed out by those who disliked what became the high modern canon. Particularly in the early years of modernism, favorable readers didn't often use as their central defense the claim that difficulty is everywhere. Even Brooks, who begins his 1939 account of modernism with the observation that difficulty is everywhere, does not present difficulty's prevalence as a sign of its value; rather, he presents difficulty as an uncomfortable aspect of modernism that needs explanation. (According to Brooks, difficulty's upsurge did not come about for the sorts of reasons that cause fashions to change, but because of cultural necessity.) While difficulty did triumph and come to be a central characteristic of the modern canon, the claim that difficulty is everywhere is, consequently, primarily a story about losers,

people who once were major voices on the literary scene, but who until recently have been at best barely visible: J. C. Squire, Harriet Monroe, Louis Untermeyer, John Sparrow, Max Eastman, Herbert Palmer, F. L. Lucas.

12. The term "cult" is a common pejorative for modernism's difficulty. My research covering the 1920s and 30s, for example, discovered at least forty-five writers who use the term. When readers characterized difficulty as a cult, they generally asserted that it had a strong leader (either such writers as Eliot, Stein, Joyce, or Faulkner, or seductive difficulty itself), and that there was an unthinking obedience, on the part of weak writers, to the cult's principles. Those outside the cult, of course, congratulated themselves on their own clear-headed refusal to join.

13. About 10 percent of my sources use this argument in a negative way, and negative readers are ten times more likely to use this argument than are positive readers. A typical argument that separates modern difficulty from earlier forms of difficulty is that modern difficulty is technical, and therefore unlike some earlier forms of difficulty (that of Dante, for example). Further, unlike earlier forms of difficulty, modern difficulty is also opposed to emotional expression.

14. Being influenced was a weak and dangerous characteristic to have, for modern readers on all sides of the difficulty argument tended to value most highly the authentic innovator and to see those who came afterward, doing similar work, as lesser writers. Readers publicly wrung their hands worrying that difficulty irresistibly tempted those most susceptible to fashion and the instant status it confers the young. Critic after critic made this point, which allowed them to attack the weak users of difficulty without ever naming them.

    These easily influenced writers were often described as the prey of those critics who promote difficult work, critics referred to by one writer as "our truly capable cognoscenti" (Rehm [1922] 1970, 212). Louis Untermeyer, probably the most influential anthologist of the past century, complained about those critics whose "emphatic reiterations" were attracting the "younger cerebralists" and whose writings were "attempting to do for Mr. Eliot what 'Ulysses' did for Mr. Joyce" ([1923] 1982, 151).

15. This clump of complementary attitudes is summed up by the anonymous reviewer of Faulkner who grumbled that the technical feats of *Absalom, Absalom!* are corrupt, since "Such devices should draw only the contempt of an honest writer, for they give him a means whereby he can perpetuate bad writing and slovenly thinking under the guise of profundity, and at the same time gain the adulation of weakish ladies and gentlemen who adore anything they can't understand" (M.L. [1937] 1995, 162).

16. See J. K. Newman's appendix "Alexandrianism in Modern English Poetry," in his *Augustus and the New Poetry* (1967). For a detailed look at how one reader connected Alexandrianism to modernism, see "Joyce and Alexandria," in Francis Russell's *Three Studies in Twentieth Century Obscurity* (1954, 1–43).

17. Fewer would claim this sort of difficulty for Jacobean writers (who would more typically be seen as employing an exaggerated use of Elizabethan techniques).

18. Although modern difficulty is recognized as encompassing all the arts, the historical narrative about difficult literature primarily deals with poetry, and not with

the novel (Meredith and James are the two main exceptions). To a large degree because of fiction's clearer ties to mass culture, most modern readers did not think pre-twentieth-century fiction was as good an example of high art as was poetry.

19. As a modern poet, Yeats did not always fare so well in historical assessments. A 1930 *Times Literary Supplement* review of Yeats's *The Winding Stair* argues that "one cannot understand the meaning of Mr. Yeats's lines in the same way as, for example, a poem by Donne. Donne may require a great deal of reading and rereading before one can understand his notions, but one knows from the start that Mr. Yeats's knots can never be untied in the same way" (Review of *The Winding Stair* [1930] 1977, 301).

20. This was an important point for Squire. As he had argued a few years earlier:

> Not all the technical experiments of modern intellectual artists (akin to experiments in new media) may be fruitful, but at the centre of most movements, however extravagant, may be found an original artist who has either a peculiar way of looking at the world (El Greco is an example) or desires to experiment with some method in order to find out what results may accrue from it. But it is not a good thing to base a theory on the mannerisms of an original artist; it is still worse to build a convention on his unsuccessful experiments; and worst of all, perhaps, for an artist to paint not what he sees as he sees it through the medium of his temperament, but what some philosophical critic, with a distaste for both Nature and humanity, tells him to paint. (1920, 386)

21. For an account of Untermeyer's anthologies, as well as those of Marguerite Wilkinson and Harriet Monroe, and their relationship to the rising of academic New Critics, *see* Craig Abbott's (1990) "Modern American Poetry." Also see Abbott's (1988) "Untermeyer on Eliot" for an account of Untermeyer's gradually changing estimation of Eliot.

    This distinction between lesser and greater difficult writers was also congenial to many promoters of modernism. When they conceded that some instances of modern difficulty were merely fashionable forms of the really good work, they granted the awfulness of many writers in order to preserve the greatness of a few. Consider Ezra Pound on T. S. Eliot:

> It would be possible to point out his method of conveying a whole situation and half a character by three words of a quoted phrase; his constant aliveness, his mingling of a very subtle observation with the unexpectedness of a backhanded cliché. It is, however, extremely dangerous to point out such devices. The method is Mr. Eliot's own, but as soon as one has reduced even a fragment of it to a formula, someone else, not Mr. Eliot, someone else wholly lacking in his aptitudes, will at once try to make poetry by mimicking his external procedure. And this indefinite "someone" will, needless to say, make a botch of it. ([1917] 1982, 77)

22. Readers argued that history also shows that technical difficulty has had some unfortunate consequences for its readership. As the poet Randall Jarrell claimed,

the modern poet's "erudition and allusiveness (compare the Alexandrian poet Lycophron) consciously restrict his audience to a small, highly specialized group; the poet is a specialist like everyone else" (1942, 224). Jarrell's comments about the fashionability of technical difficulty and about its audience are not just comments about the formal properties of difficult works. Technically difficult art is almost always described in the context of a cultural situation that allows it to come to life. For Jarrell, poetry produced under this schema is a diminished thing, both in terms of the kind of writing it produces and the kind of audience it attracts.

23. As chapter 3 will discuss, this use of difficulty as an inherent property of good writing is tied to the institutionalization of modernism by New Criticism. I will also discuss later the pro-modernist claim that the twentieth century is a totally new time, breaking with all previous history, a time that consequently *demands* difficulty.

24. Some of the poets called up to prove that all poetry is difficult are less startling than others. For both negative and positive readers Baudelaire, Rimbaud, Mallarmé, Donne, Blake, and Browning are always seen as difficult.

25. In 1931 Thomas McGreevy published *Thomas Stearns Eliot*, a seventy-one-page introductory analysis of Eliot's work.

26. For another major work that linked Donne and difficult modernism, see the 1931 collection of essays *A Garland for John Donne*, which includes an essay by Eliot.

27. When one argues that *all* good poetry is difficult, the sense of which writers influenced modern difficulty needs to be sharpened. To designate *all* good writers an influence on modernism makes the "influence" story either totally uninteresting (because everybody is an influence) or nonexistent. But difficulty's influence story was told in specific and predictable ways. The narrative points to a *kind* of difficulty being influential in modernism, and the list of influences is short: Donne and the metaphysicals, the French symbolists (Mallarmé, Baudelaire, and Rimbaud in particular), Browning, James, and (to a lesser degree) Hopkins. These writers are influential not just because they are difficult, but because of the particular forms of their difficulty: the suggestiveness of meaning that hovers just beyond language, the yoking together of dissimilarities, and an accurate rendering of the human mind, a rendering which Eliot called "a fidelity to thought and feeling" ([1921] 1975b, 62).

28. For many modernists, not only were general audiences unnecessary for great art, such audiences could also be just wrong, making initial judgments about difficulty that time showed to be inadequate. Ford Madox Ford, author of the central modernist novel *The Good Soldier*, gives a thumbnail history lesson in his defense of Joyce's *Ulysses*. While arguing his "improbable" claim that *Ulysses* will one day be read by a wide audience, Ford writes that "it should be remembered that there was once a time when the works of Alfred Tennyson were hailed as incomprehensible." For Ford, the fact that someone as easily digestible as Tennyson could once have been considered difficult ought to be more instructive to modernism's readers than it is; Ford notes that these "strange revolutions ... are conveniently ignored, as a rule" (1922, 541).

This comparison is echoed by May Sinclair, in a review of Eliot's "The Love Song of J. Alfred Prufrock": "But there was a time when the transparent Tennyson was judged obscure; when people wondered what under heaven the young man was after; they couldn't tell for the life of them whether it was his 'dreary gleams' or his 'curlews' that were flying over Locksley Hall" ([1917] 1982, 86).

29. For Rodman, as for many readers, Shakespeare was the last real hero: "Long before Goethe's day, however, the poet was on his way to becoming a specialist. Shakespeare was the last great writer of modern times who found it possible to interpret the whole of life for an audience of common men without raising his voice—or lowering it. Through him, for the last time, poetry spoke 'publicly' without sacrificing any of the richness of language, ambiguity, and associative 'magic' which must always serve to distinguish it from 'prose.' After Shakespeare, poets were obliged to make the unnatural choice between poetry and communication" (1949, vii).

30. There are other scattered references to theories of difficulty, such as Bernard Bosanquet ([1915] 1963, 49) or Selden Rodman on Aristotle (1938, 32–33; 1946, xxxv), or Arnold Stein on Gascoigne (1946, 98, 109). However, I have found no further references to these figures and difficulty, while the references to Johnson and Coleridge are common.

31. Romanticism, seemingly the least likely poetic movement for which one could claim difficulty, was at times seen by conservatives as promoting a very specific form of difficult writing that was available only to a select few: the sublime. For these readers this distinction was important: unlike with modernist difficulty, entry into the incommunicable sublime was not on professionalist terms; it was spiritual, authentic.

32. Most disastrous of all, many moderns believed, was Tennyson—the poet high moderns most loved to hate. Leavis closed the book on the nineteenth century with this quip: "Tennyson did his best" ([1932] 1960, 14). On the other hand, Tennyson was the last bastion of defense for conservative readers. One anthologist claimed that in the first two decades of the twentieth century there had been a resurgence of "ordinary reader" interest in poetry: "It is a salutary omen that Shelley is selling better to-day than he ever sold; and that Alfred Noyes, through his courses at Princeton, has driven many a young man to Tennyson. It has been made clear that poetry is not 'difficult'; that the best of it, as in all art, is understandable to the multitude; that it can be made a very portion of ourselves" (Towne, 1923, viii). Leavis probably would have liked the idea of a young man being "driven to Tennyson" by Alfred Noyes, who called *Ulysses* "the foulest book that has ever found its way into print," an instance of "literary Bolshevism" ([1922] 1970, 274, 275).

33. While proponents of difficulty might grant that at its extremes difficult writing may be fraudulent, they much more typically argued that a particularly extreme example of difficulty just wasn't very good.

34 Two and a half years earlier, Pollock's great champion, Clement Greenberg, had published a piece in the *Saturday Evening Post*'s series "Adventures of the Mind," an article titled "The Case for Abstract Art." Greenberg began his essay with the following description of the contemporary art situation:

Many people say that the kind of art our age produces is one of the major symptoms of what's wrong with the age. The disintegration and, finally, the disappearance of recognizable images in painting and sculpture, like the obscurity in advanced literature, are supposed to reflect a disintegration of values in society itself. Some people go further and say that abstract, non-representational art is pathological art, crazy art, and that those who practice it and those who admire and buy it are either sick or silly. The kindest critics are those who say it's all a joke, a hoax and a fad, and that modernist art in general, or abstract art in particular, will soon pass. This sort of thing is heard or read pretty constantly, but in some years more often than others. (1959, 18)

Chapter 2

1. Writers who adopt this strategy include Richard Aldington, Ezra Pound, Laura Riding and Robert Graves, C. Day Lewis, Michael Roberts, Conrad Aiken, T. S. Eliot, Elizabeth Drew, and F. R. Leavis. This strategy has not disappeared in today's more rigorous theoretical climate. Alan Williamson, writing in the *American Poetry Review* in 1995, comments that "what worries most, at the moment, is my sense that the densely textured, splendid—call it the 'difficult'—poem is becoming an endangered species" (51). Or, consider Jerome McGann's comments on Charles Bernstein's poem "The Klupzy Girl": "Though 'difficult' in certain respects, the poem is structurally quite simple" (1993, 149).

   Jacques Ehrmann writes that quotation marks "serve to isolate a word, an expression, a text by placing it at a distance (is 'esthetic distance' anything close?). The 'writer' refuses to accept them as they are given to him. This gesture is quite the opposite of an appropriation! However, he also calls them to himself because he incorporates them in his discourse, because he makes of them the subject matter of his discourse" (1971, 37, 38). John Taylor, in his *Linguistic Categorization*, discusses such conceptualizing strategies as "hedges," a recognition of the awkwardness of a given term's membership in a category (1995, 75–80).

2. Over 90 percent of my sources who put one of difficulty's terms in quotation marks are writers who overtly favor the supposedly difficult text or movement under discussion.

3. This shorthand way of analyzing contemporary culture was not limited to the idea of difficulty. It was fairly common early in modernism for skeptical writers to question modernism's existence in the same way. In his 1931 *The Poetic Way of Release*, Bonaro Wilkinson gave the following analysis of modernism: "It appears that most of those whom we may call 'modernistic poets' have fairly lost sight of the fact that truly significant poetry is more intelligible than experience itself, not less intelligible" (212).

4. I use "difficulty" in two senses throughout this chapter. Usually, I present *difficulty* as a category, consisting of several different lexical terms (I will announce this usage through italics). At other times, I present "difficulty" as a lexical term (indicated by quotation marks), a member of the category *difficulty*. Additionally, when I refer to a member of *difficulty*, I often refer to a lexical term, such as "eru-

dition." However, such terms also have an implied content that slips around a bit, but which *basically* attaches these terms to generally understood definitions. The terms and the slippery, implied content both point to *difficulty*, and together are members of the category. Usually, I will employ the lexical term as a shorthand way of referring to an amalgam of the term and its implied meaning.

5. The shape of Eliot's argument about difficulty is similar to the shape of his other famous arguments, such as his claims about the objective correlative. With his argument against the mimetic fallacy, Yvor Winters vigorously contested Eliot's idea that form must mimic content. But then, as now, Winters was a fairly lonely dissenting voice.

6. For a literary history that uses a similar argument to make a case for the shape of the American literary canon, see Timothy Morris's *Becoming Canonical in American Poetry*, which posits for a "poetics of presence" the same function that I ascribe to difficulty.

    Not surprisingly, there is no clear narrative to be constructed of the development of difficulty as a concept; there are few *influential* texts (other than Eliot's quip). There are no critical texts that have more than an incidental importance in the *development* of an argument about difficulty (although there are some spectacular moments in publishing history, such as Max Eastman's *The Literary Mind*).

7. Mark Turner delineates two forms of entrenchment: use entrenchment and generative entrenchment. Use-entrenched concepts occur most frequently: we memorize a phone number because we use it a lot. But some use-entrenched concepts are also generative, that is, they govern how people think about several areas of life, such as our concept of time as linear (1991, 156; see also 123ff, 140ff). As Turner argues, a generatively entrenched concept "resists disturbance because to disturb it is to disturb all the conceptual forms that depend on it" (156). And such wide changes are not just intellectually, but also emotionally resisted.

8. As I will argue later, difficulty is more accurately described as an interaction between text and reader, but the common understanding of it as a property had important consequences for the rise of high modernism.

9. For a similar reading of modernist difficulty, see D. Powell (1934, 87–88).

10. The major works I rely on are George Lakoff, *Women, Fire, and Dangerous Things*; George Lakoff and Mark Turner, *More than Cool Reason: A Field Guide to Poetic Metaphor*; George Lakoff and Mark Johnson, *Metaphors We Live By*; Mark Turner, *Reading Minds: The Study of English in the Age of Cognitive Science* and *The Literary Mind*.

11. The organization of a radial category thus is not from general to specific. The noncentral members of a radial category are members not because they equally share certain general characteristics and are differentiated by more specific, unshared characteristics; rather, they are members of this category by certain principles of extension, principles of inclusion that Lakoff describes as *motivated*, neither inevitable nor arbitrary. That is, one could not predict that there ought to be a member of the category of *difficulty* that does the work that "erudition" does, but neither is it the case that there are no reasons for its inclusion.

Although it appears early in people's lexicons, "difficulty" is *not* at the center by virtue of its being simply the most general of the category *difficulty's* terms. In the first place, critics typically have specific effects in mind when they use the term "difficulty," effects as specific as those typically claimed by such terms as "incoherence," for example. Second, some writers claim one or other of the category's noncentral terms as being *opposed* in some crucial way to the term "difficulty," and both "difficulty" and this other term have the same specificity of reference.

12. "Difficulty" and "obscurity" are each used about twice as often as the other terms in the category. "Difficulty" and "obscurity" are each used by approximately two hundred of the roughly eight hundred sources that comment on difficulty; "complexity" by about ninety; "unintelligible" by about fifty-five; with "erudition," "nonsense," "esoteric," "opacity," and "incoherence" all having significantly fewer citations. These terms occur with similar proportions in writing about modern music and art.

13. The term "hard" probably enters people's lexicons earlier than does "difficulty," but readers do not turn to it very often in describing the properties of modern texts. "Difficulty" has many of the characteristics and attractiveness of what cognitive linguists call a basic-level term. While Lakoff analyzes basic-level terms in terms of *entities*, many of the functions of basic-level terms also apply to an abstraction like "difficulty."

14. "Fathom," a verb meaning "to measure the depth of water," relates to conceptualizings of understanding that see understanding in terms of depth.

15. For analysis of this particular metaphor, *see* Lakoff and Turner (1989). For a more general discussion of conceptual metaphors, *see* Lakoff and Johnson (1980).

16. Zoltán Kövecses, looking at the relationship between conceptual metaphors and emotion, spends a little time discussing the submetaphor DIFFICULTIES ARE IMPEDIMENTS TO MOTION (2000, 54). Other than that, however, research in cognitive linguistics has worked with metaphors based on comprehension rather than noncomprehension.

17. Metaphors of "above" and "beyond" are not dominant in twentieth-century understandings of difficulty. In literary history, they show up tellingly in the early reception of John Donne, particularly the commendatory verses to the 1633 edition of his *Poems*. There, Jasper Mayne writes that Donne's writing is "so farre above its Reader, good, That wee are thought wits, when 'tis understood" (7–8). Mayne goes on to claim:

> Hadst thou beene shallower, and not writ so high,
> Or left some new way for our pennes, or eye,
> To shed a funerall teare, perchance thy Tombe
> Had not beene speechlesse, or our Muses dumbe; (393–94)

Similarly, Arthur Wilson writes that Donne

> dost not stoope unto the vulgar sight,
> But, hovering highly in the aire of Wit,

>Hold'st such a pitch, that few can follow it;
>Admire they may. (397)

At the end of the 1600s, as Donne's reputation diminishes, the dominant metaphors change to ones of twisting and entanglement.

18. Some of *difficulty*'s terms, though they could go with visual metaphors, are based on the idea of strain: the terms "hard" and "tough" go both ways, seeing the difficult text as formidable, challenging. This makes sense, given the visceral language surrounding difficulty, and I will take up this idea in chapter 4. Though some terms, like "incoherence," can fit into the dominant conceptual metaphor, they more clearly are related to the idea of a "normal" work of art as a purposeful collection of parts, and the difficult text as one that does not have this purposeful structure. Thus, according to some readers of *The Waste Land*, the text does not "cohere," it is a "kaleidoscope," it "falls apart," it is a "mad medley." Readers may see clearly, but the text is incoherent.

19. They had their work cut out for them, for these tropes and metaphors did not spring fully formed from the heads of twentieth-century readers; they had been used throughout Western culture. Raymond Gibbs notes "the tendency in Indo-European languages to borrow concepts and vocabulary from the more accessible physical and social world to refer to the less accessible worlds of reasoning, emotion, and conversational structure." Gibbs uses as his example the relationship between seeing and knowing: "With few exceptions, words in Indo-European languages meaning *see* regularly acquire the meaning *know* at widely scattered times and places" (1994, 158–59). In his *Metaphor: A Practical Introduction* (2002), Zoltán Kövecses addresses the universality of conceptual metaphors, finding individual metaphors to exist not just across related languages, but also across unrelated languages (such as Hungarian, English, and Chinese). Kövecses attributes this universality to two things: one is that many of these metaphors (such as ANGER IS HEAT) are rooted in physiology; others are rooted in general human experience (such as the Event Structure metaphor) (163–77).

The tradition of Western aesthetics is no exception to this linguistic/conceptual structure. While it would take me too far afield to go into much detail, I would like to sketch out its parameters. Augustine, in his *On Christian Doctrine*, notes that "many and varied obscurities and ambiguities deceive those who read casually"; indeed, the ambiguities can increase so much that eventually all comprehension stops, "so obscurely are certain sayings covered with a most dense mist." For Augustine, the value of this situation lies in God's wish "to conquer pride by work and to combat disdain in our minds, to which those things which are easily discovered seem frequently to become worthless" (1958, 37; 2.6.7). As it would be in the twentieth century, here difficulty is seen as an obscuring of a surface, and the overcoming of it is seen as a moral virtue.

The idea of understanding as following is also seen much earlier than in modernism. Petrarch, for example, after quoting Augustine and Gregory on the uses of scriptural obscurity, goes on to claim: "Among poets ... a majesty and dignity of style are maintained, not so that those who are worthy may be prevented from understanding, but so that, a sweet labor having been presented to them, they may be benefited at once in memory and delight; for those things which we seek with difficulty are dearer to us and more carefully heeded. And for those who are unworthy it is proved that, lest they exhaust themselves in vain on the surfaces of these things, if they are wise, they are discouraged from approaching them" (quoted in Robertson 1958, xvi).

As they did in modernism, such uses of language came with values attached to them. Aristotle, in his *Rhetoric*, uses the idea of distance and the unexpected to argue for difficulty's virtues: "one should make the language unfamiliar, for people are admirers of what is far off, and what is marvelous is sweet. Many [kinds of words] accomplish this in verse and are appropriate there; for what is said [in poetry] about subjects and characters is more out of the ordinary, but in prose much less so; for the subject matter is less remarkable " (1991, 221–22 [3.2 1404b]). For Aristotle, it is the unknown, the difficult, that is behind the pleasures of learning. In *Metaphysics*, he notes that "it is owing to their wonder that men both now begin and at first began to philosophize.... And a man who is puzzled and wonders thinks himself ignorant (whence even the lover of myth is in a sense a lover of Wisdom, for the myth is composed of wonders)" (Aristotle 1941, 692 [982b 12–19]). The pleasures also have, for Aristotle, a sense of wonder, of marvel, of amazement (see his *Poetics* [1997] §63, 64). And this valuation and understanding of difficulty, of course, would eventually lead to the sublime, which also uses some of the standard language of difficulty. In an early statement of the sublime, Plotinus noted that "This is the effect that Beauty must ever induce, wonderment and a pleasant astonishment, longing and love and a dread that is pleasurable" (quoted in Cunningham 1976, 60). As we will see, this central recurring language about anxiety and terror is even more useful in explicating difficulty's social function.

20. See Modris Eksteins's *Rites of Spring* (1989) for an account of the Ballets Russes and of the first performance of *Sacre du printemps*. Of course, Stravinsky's supporters were not moved to anger or laughter by the work's difficulty, but by the negative reaction to it. Yet there is a congruity between their reactions and those that vilified the work. For Stravinsky's supporters, the work demanded a strong reaction, based on large claims (and perhaps, based on a wish to counter the protestors with an equally forceful reaction). Hearing the work in a London performance some years later, T. S. Eliot claimed that Stravinsky "has been the greatest success since Picasso": "Whether Strawinsky's [sic] music be permanent or ephemeral I do not know; but it did seem to transform the rhythm of the steppes into the scream of the motor horn, the rattle of machinery, the grind of wheels, the beating of iron and steel, the roar of the underground railway, and the other barbaric cries of modern life; and to transform these despairing noises into music" (Eliot 1921a, 452, 453).

21. For another historical example, consider the big lurch in the visual arts toward modernity, the famous *Salon des Refusés* of 1874 (which launched impressionist art, and signaled the beginning of the end of academic art). Like many controversial, difficult shows this one was accompanied by anger and ridicule, as well as extremely physical responses. The editor of *Le Figaro* reported that a member of

the lower classes was arrested after viewing the *Salon des Refusés* because "he began biting everyone in sight" (quoted in Dunlop 1972, 81).
22. Writing of Pound's *Cantos* in 1931, Dudley Fitts noted: "Confronted by this array of scenes and allusions exhumed from dead mythologies and forgotten literatures, of references to experience whose interest is limited to a contemporary few, the thoughtless reader will throw up his hands and exclaim, 'But what is it all *about*? I don't *know* enough to be able to understand this poem'" ([1931] 1972, 251).
23. For an overview of research in this area, see Gardner (1985, 26), and my "Reading Nonsense" (1991). For other formulations of this idea, see also Rumelhart, who argues that "perception is goal directed" (1980, 51) and Mayer (1983, 7). For specific studies of sentence comprehension and what contributes to a lack of comprehension, see Huggins and Adams (1980) and Adams (1980).
24. For a romanticized *modernist* history of these subverted expectations, consider this comment made by Mark Van Doren in 1930: "A reader, then or now, who had been brought up on the poetry familiar to his parents, the household poetry, shall we say, of late nineteenth-century America, the poetry which millions of school children had memorized and politicians had quoted in their speeches, the poetry of Victorian England and of Victorian America, the poetry of Tennyson, Longfellow, and Swinburne (but chiefly of their innumerable and indistinguishable followers)—such a reader had every right to be bewildered a decade and a half ago." The new poetry presented a crisis, one in which bewilderment turned to resentment. Van Doren continues with his description of his common reader: "He frequently, indeed, resented the kind of poetry then coming upon the scene; or he refused to call it poetry at all. And no wonder. For the new poets were trying their best not to write like the new poets he had known; they were getting as far away from the usual thing as paper and ink could take them. They had declared war upon the current conceptions of poetry" (1930a, 10).
25. Because one's understanding of what difficulty is depends on metaphors of successful perception, that dependence is another factor that makes difficulty work as a "marked" category. For a discussion of default settings, see Turner (1991, 24, 25–27).
26. For an overview of the processes involved in fear and anxiety, and its relationship to threat, see Arne Öhman (1993) as well as Harmon-Jones (2000).
27. Working out of the findings of Gray (1971), researchers on emotion and thought have shown how anxiety makes people unable to focus on details, or that they seize on the wrong details. That inability has an important correlation in modernism's difficulty; for many readers, the difficult text is one in which one is distracted: things that should go without saying do not go without saying; one is bombarded with details. All this leads to anxiety. Note the following review of Faulkner's *Absalom, Absalom!*, in which the writer claims that the novel is Faulkner's "master work," and goes on to argue that "It is, by its very genius, the hardest to read. I confess at the outset that many times I was lost and terrified in the shadows and thunders of his involved prose, lost and annoyed in his ramifications of chronology and ancestry" (Shipp [1936] 1995, 151).

28. The shape of the Berlyne curve, then, is like an asymmetrical bell curve:

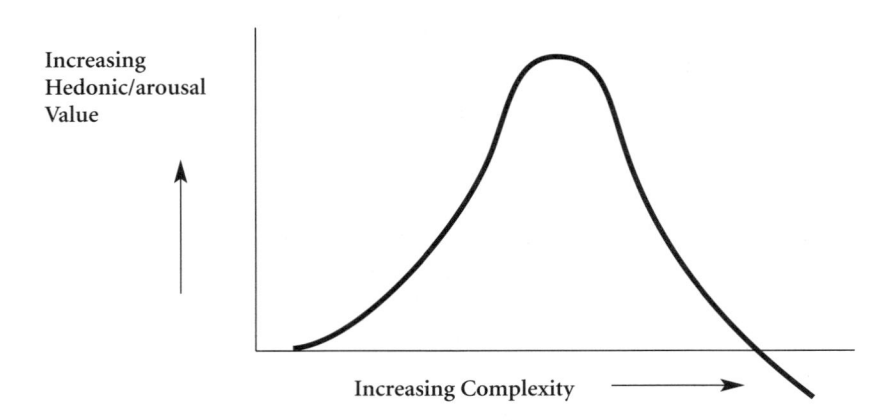

Increasing Hedonic/arousal Value

Increasing Complexity →

29. See also Perin's comment: "Small differences the brain experiences as pleasurable stimulations; large differences, as fearful" (1994, 178). Richard Mayer is typical in showing that productive new knowledge is based on a *manageable* degree of new information. Using a Piagetian model, Mayer argues that new knowledge must be slightly different from what we already know (1983, 260ff).
30. Ibsch also gives a useful catalogue on the types of conditions that lead viewers to reject a work as too difficult:

> (a) if the reader is in peril of life or in threatening circumstances as a result of which all his attention is concentrated on the exigencies of his lifeworld; in that case—if he would turn to literature at all—he would search for identification instead of estrangement; (b) if the reader has not internalized the relative autonomy of the literary system; (c) if the thematic relevance of a literary work pertains to the core of the lifeworld of the reader with the result that he cannot effect a playful suspension of fixed beliefs . . . ; (d) if the thematic relevance is rather slight, so that the reader's frame of reference has no affinity to that of the text . . . ; (e) if the reader scores high on the scale of dogmatism or rigidity (here a personality-theory comes into play). (1986, 45)

See also Martindale (1990, 40–43). Martindale also argues that "Because artists are exposed to art more or less continually, they are always ahead of whatever audience they do have. Artistic innovations are almost always met with some shock, outrage, and resistance" (52).
31. As I present it here, the reaction to difficulty is primarily a physiological reaction. But this physiological reaction also has an intellectual heritage, found in romantic conceptions of the sublime. Edmund Burke, in his discussion of the sublime, cites its primary affects as being terror and astonishment. These affects are brought into play by such qualities as obscurity, displays of power, privation (lack), infinitude and vastness, and difficulty of creation. In an evocative phrase,

Burke argues that "the sublime is an idea belonging to self-preservation" ([1759] 1968, 86).

32. Duyckinck's view is closely tied to Wordsworth's view of simplicity: "In the higher poetry, an enlightened Critic chiefly looks for a reflection of the wisdom of the heart and the grandeur of the imagination. Wherever these appear, simplicity accompanies them; Magnificence herself, when legitimate, depending upon a simplicity of her own, to regulate her ornaments" ("Essay" [1841] 1974, 194).

33. See also Theobald's famous attack on Donne in his preface to Shakespeare:

> Now, the Age, in which *Shakespeare* liv'd, having, above all others, a wonderful Affection to appear Learned, They declined vulgar Images, such as are immediately fetch'd from Nature, and rang'd thro' the Circle of the Sciences to fetch their Ideas from thence. But as the Resemblances of such Ideas to the Subject must necessarily lie very much out of the common Way, and every piece of Wit appear a Riddle to the Vulgar; This, that should have taught them the forced, quaint, unnatural Tract they were in, (and induce them to follow a more natural One,) was the very Thing that kept them attach'd to it. The ostentatious Affectation of abstruse Learning, peculiar to that Time, the Love that Men naturally have to every Thing that looks like Mystery, fixed them down to this Habit of Obscurity. Thus became the poetry of DONNE (tho' the wittiest Man of that Age,) nothing but a continued Heap of Riddles. And our *Shakespeare*, with all his easy Nature about him, for want of the Knowledge of the true Rules of Art, falls frequently into this vicious Manner. (1740, n.p.)

34. As in the obscenity trials, the common reader was the nub. By those opposed to difficult modernism, the common reader was invoked as the standard by which to judge difficulty and morality. (Similarly, the test of obscenity, under law, was that of the average reader, not the professional.) Reviewer Joseph Collins based his attack on *Ulysses* on the "bewilderment and a sense of disgust" that the novel caused in "the average intelligent reader" ([1922] 1970, 222). For those more favorably disposed to difficult modernism, the common reader was not the pertinent criterion. Edwin Muir, reviewing Ezra Pound's *Hugh Selwyn Mauberley* in 1922, argued that Pound "has made sure beforehand that the bourgeoisie would not applaud, dreading their approbation, justly, more than their resentment. There is no doubt that he is right; it may be, too, that Philistia is more deeply wounded by something which puzzles it than by something which hits it palpably" ([1922] 1972, 194, 195).

35. The linkage even shows up in the novel's censorship trials, after it had been seized by the American Post Office or the New York Society for the Suppression of Vice. The standard defense was that *Ulysses*' difficulty made the pornography impossible. (For a complete account of the relationship between obscenity and difficulty in the *Ulysses* obscenity trial, see Vanderham (1998, 87–131].) The bewilderment, then, runs over, erases any other possible affective responses. Basing his defense of *Ulysses* on the triumph of high culture, Valéry Larbaud argued that "It is

implausible that people cultivated enough to savour a writer this difficult mistake a work of pornography for a work of literature" (quoted in Vanderham 1998, 74).

36. The relationship between morality and difficulty goes even further, particularly in contemporary visual art, where unsettling difficulty does not just arise from problems with basic comprehension; it also arises via some works' involvement with moral issues. There, instead of following modernism's skeptics in arguing that difficult works are immoral, proponents claim that morally risky works are difficult, that works like Robert Mapplethorpe's *X Portfolio* and Nan Goldin's *The Ballad of Sexual Dependency* are more clearly a part of the tradition of difficulty and therefore of high art than they are of the tradition of obscenity.

   To call these artists' work difficult may seem wrong-headed, for both artists' work is in important ways easily understandable, neither aesthetically nor intellectually difficult. Yet, works like Goldin's and Mapplethorpe's are difficult in ways similar to difficult intellectual art, such as Joyce's *Finnegans Wake*. In both artists' works audiences feel uncertain how to proceed effectively and safely. These are risky works: one violates intellectual codes of denotation and syntax; the other violates moral codes of propriety. Both attempt to change the usual categories of what counts as art. Further, the moral and the intellectual are inextricable at times. Mapplethorpe's representations of the taboo, because they challenge gender constructions and definitions of obscenity or art itself, are intellectual challenges. And, in both his and Joyce's work choices about what is appropriate, allowable, or legitimate to represent are also aesthetic issues. (Further, for some viewers Joyce's work too seemed morally outrageous, a lazy avoidance of the real work of art.)

37. Dale Jacquette makes this kind of point when he argues, in the context of discussing Bernard Bosanquet's 1915 concept of "difficult beauty," that "To the extent that an object is found difficult by a subject, to that extent the difficulty of appreciating its beauty must have already been removed, resolved, or overcome. The object is never both beautiful and difficult at once" (1984, 82).

38. William Empson's *Seven Types of Ambiguity* (1930) may be the lone exception to this rule, but it tends to present *all* forms of difficulty as good.

39. There is a modulation in texture of reference when one goes from a lexical term that for a given reader describes a good form of difficulty to a term that describes a bad form, for the bad is often seen as an extreme, and therefore deliberate, version of the good. For example, Donald Stauffer complained that "Eliot, the early Auden, and the later Yeats, seem to strive for a complexity which to uninitiated readers verges on willful obscurity and bewilderment" (1946, 154–55).

40. All quotations in the following pages are taken from *Voices of Fire: Art, Rage, Power, and the State* (Barber, Guilbaut, and O'Brian 1996), a valuable collection of original documents from the controversy, as well as analytical essays about it.

Chapter 3

1. As this chapter will make clear, while the polarity that I establish (romantic-professional) both has ties to and is less common than the traditional polarity attached to modernism (that between classicism and romanticism), the use of

professionalism gives a social grounding to modernism that is not as available in turning to classicism and that was essential to understanding how the modern canon was established.
2. Both Beckett's biographer and the director of the Miami production report that the New York production was successful, although it did receive more than a few hostile reviews (Knowlson 1996, 180; Schneider 1993, 74). Esslin's assertions to the contrary, the print record suggests that *Godot* was contested; it was not universally condemned.
3. Surely the morality is overstated, taking an audience's education and attaching moral weight to the almost inevitable consequences of that education. It would be inevitable that a moderately skilled audience would feel the classic anxieties of difficulty, but that a less-skilled audience, not knowing the tasks that "typical" art demanded of its audience, would not have such anxiety. Why didn't Miami audiences have the San Quentin reaction? It is because they had more at stake in seeing the conventions of drama remaining undisturbed.
4. Slightly over 95 percent of my sources who believe modern difficulty to be deliberate note it as a negative characteristic of the works in question.
5. Selden Rodman, in his *A New Anthology of Modern Poetry*, lists Lewis's *A Hope for Poetry* in his "short list of the best studies of modern poetry" (1946, xxxvii). Babette Deutsch, in her *This Modern Poetry*, also commends Lewis's "penetrating essay" (1935, 253).
6. There were, of course, critics who would speak favorably of one text's difficulty, while being less sanguine about the difficulty of another text. The most notable are Richard Aldington, David Daiches, and Virginia Woolf. (Daiches is a particularly interesting case, since his opinion of difficulty takes a markedly more positive tone in his 1940 *Poetry and the Modern World* than in his 1935 *The Place of Meaning in Poetry*.) Generally, the more one was allied with romantic values of the sublime, the more likely one was to make distinctions and have changing attitudes to different forms of difficulty. But these differing assessments do not often display original thinking about difficulty. When such writers approved of the difficulty of a given work, they tended to make the standard arguments supporting difficulty, and when they disliked another work, they made the standard arguments against it.
7. It is the avant-garde that would, at times (and particularly later in the twentieth century), note its deliberate difficulty as a positive thing. John O'Brian, speaking on CBC radio in 1997, asserted that the idea of deliberate difficulty as a virtue is peculiar to the avant-garde: "The avant-garde as a formation, which is a social formation, is one that wishes to produce an art that is not accessible, that affronts viewers, that contests those aspects of society that the artists are in disagreement with. And that art, by its very nature, is going to be difficult for a large number of viewers because it's meant to be. It's meant to be that, amongst other things" (quoted in Sinclair 1997).
8. This understanding of professions has more than a few congruencies with the work of Pierre Bourdieu, who argues that criticism in the field of restricted production (that is, of artists writing for other artists), "placed itself unconditionally

at the service of the artist, while paradoxically excluding the public of non-producers from the entire business by attesting, through its 'inspired' readings, the intelligibility of works which were bound to remain unintelligible to those not sufficiently integrated into the producers' field" (1993, 116). The major analyses of professionalism in art are: Bledstein (1976), Larson (1977), Menand (1987), Strychacz (1993), and Robbins (1993). There is also a sizable body of scholarship on the relationship between professionalism and the academy. See Fish (1985), Ohmann (1976), Graff (1987), Weber (1982, 1990), Bledstein (1976), McRae (1990), Warner (1985).

9. The contemporary commentary on the rise of professionalism within modernism is extensive. I have found over 125 different sources that, before 1950 and as part of their argument about difficulty and modern culture, comment on the professionalization of modernism.

10. Louis Menand sees this emphasis as a central strategy of professionalism in general: "to isolate the one feature of an activity that is most likely to require full-time attention, to make that feature the chief criterion of whether the activity is done well or not, and then to argue that every previous worker has historically taken the isolated characteristic to be the most important one as well" (1987, 129).

11. See Brooker and Bentley (1990, 53) for a reading of this quotation.

12. This sense of development could also discredit some works of high modernism. Adrienne Monnier, Joyce's enthusiastic patron during the writing of *Ulysses*, cast an increasingly jaundiced eye on the installments of *Finnegans Wake* appearing in literary journals. Questioning whether Joyce's narrative technique was "an appreciable literary gain," she responded: "No, on reflection, for if it registers completely the cerebral mechanism, its value is purely a scientific one; if it means a new convention, there is no reason why it should be preferred to ordinary analytic methods" ([1940] 1970, 464).

13. See Eliot's "A Brief Treatise on the Criticism of Poetry" (1920) "The Function of a Literary Review" (1923b) and "The Function of Criticism" (1923a).

14. More than a few writers tried to negotiate a relationship between this exactitude and romantically derived notions of inspiration. Carl Sandburg, for example, approvingly quoting Pound's phrase on poetry and "inspired mathematics," came to the following wobbly approximation: "while he [Pound] is an ignorant barbarian on the sources of his inspiration and the power by which he works out his inward flashes, once the urge and blaze is on him he works by rules, measurements, formulae and data as strict and definite as any worker who uses exact science, and employs fractions of inches, and drills in steel by thousandths of millimeters" ([1916] 1972, 113).

15. One also regularly heard the argument that ordinary readers didn't need the knowledge that professionals had, they didn't need the technical sense of what was going on, and they didn't even need to "understand" in the traditional sense. There is a different kind of understanding that the ordinary reader achieves, the understanding that Esslin describes as "immediate." That claim for immediacy is an argument this chapter will turn to later.

16. Thus, the thesis put forward by John Carey in *The Intellectuals and the Masses* (1992) is too simple, based on a single-voiced opposition between high modernism and the general public. The attitude that this chapter tries to articulate is one more in keeping with the understanding of modernism propounded by Lawrence Rainey in his 1998 *Institutions of Modernism: Literary Elites and Public Culture*, and one that uses a sense of aesthetic value in keeping with Pierre Bourdieu's (1993) work on cultural capital and John Guillory's 1993 *Cultural Capital: The Problem of Literary Canon Formation*.
17. Refusal to participate in movements was one reason for Frost's early acceptance by literary conservatives. One reviewer noted: "At the same time, it [the book] is extraordinarily free from a young man's extravagances; there is no insistent obtrusion of self-strain after super-things. Neither does it belong to any modern 'school,' nor go in harness to any new and twisted theory of art. It is so simple, lucid, and experimental that, reading a poem, one can see clearly with the poet's own swift eye, and follow the trail of his glancing thought" ([1913] 1977, 5).
18. See also Edward Rothschild's "The Meaning of Unintelligibility in Modern Art":

    Because the artist has an isolated position in the division of labor applied to the culture of modern society, he is unintelligible like the occupants of the other compartments; but because he has no practical or functional contact with society at large, his unintelligibility constitutes a greater barrier than it does elsewhere. This view can be supported by reference to modern architecture and applied design (furniture, textiles, ceramics, clothing and millinery, etc.), where the artistic idiom is distinctly parallel to that of painting and sculpture, but where the products are much more readily acceptable because of the addition of obvious utility. It is a situation similar to the situation in science and industry where the unintelligibility of science is mitigated by practical, industrial utility. ([1934] 1972, 31)

19. The claims for the psychological accuracy of difficulty were quite prevalent. In my research I have come across more than 120 different sources from 1950 or earlier that make a specific equation between difficulty and the accurate presentation of human psychology. For typical articulations of this position, see Conrad Aiken, "Divers Realists" ([1917] 1982b); Clive Bell, "Woolf's Painterly Vision" ([1924] 1975); and Rachel Taylor, Review of *To the Lighthouse* ([1927] 1975).

    This type of psychological accuracy was a discovery many attributed to Donne. In 1938 Herbert Read, for example, credited Donne's "difficulty" to the fact that in Donne we "find the first consciousness of felt thought" (1938a, 76).
20. While many conservative readers would grant that modern difficulty seemed to be about the subconscious, conservative readers often would not grant it aesthetic validity. J. C. Squire argued that in *Ulysses* Joyce "has sunk a shaft down into the welter of nonsense which lies at the bottom of the mind, pumped up this stuff and presented it as criticism of life" (Squire [Affable Hawk] 1923, 775). This kind of description peaks in reviews of *Finnegans Wake*.

21. Pound's description of Marianne Moore and Mina Loy's poetry as "logopoeia" (poetry "which is a dance of the intelligence among words and ideas") is yet another version of this understanding of the human mind (1918, 57).
22. The commentary on the relationship between difficulty and modern culture is extensive. In my research I have discovered more than 110 sources from 1950 or earlier that connect difficulty and the accurate representation of modern culture. For typical articulations of this position, see Sharon Brown (1928); Evans and Lawson (1949); and Allen Tate (1959).
23. For other examples of such an understanding of Donne, see Spencer (1931a, 180); Sharp (1934, 499).
24. In my research I have discovered sixteen sources from before 1950 that, in their arguments about difficulty and modern culture, either directly quote the phrase or clearly paraphrase it. Eliot's argument is still the defense of difficulty most people reach to, with an additional thirteen sources since 1950 that either quote it or directly refer to it.
25. The argument about social mimesis takes up an issue that this book has touched on in chapter 1, the question of exactly how unique the twentieth century was. For many, the early twentieth century was a time unlike any other, and its uniqueness demanded an appropriate form. Eliot, reflecting on the London premiere of *Sacre du printemps* (which apparently he gave a standing ovation), approvingly noted that Stravinsky's music gave its hearers "the sense of the present": "Whether Strawinsky's music be permanent or ephemeral I do not know; but it did seem to transform the rhythm of the steppes into the scream of the motor horn, the rattle of machinery, the grind of wheels, the beating of iron and steel, the roar of the underground railway, and the other barbaric cries of modern life; and to transform these despairing noises into music" (1921b, 453). Yet there was a profound uncertainty in modernism about the relationship between modernism and the canon. For, if modernism was unlike any period before it, how was modern aesthetic expression to link up with what had preceded it? Some answered that it could not and reveled in the rupture, claiming for the modern artist the status of a revolutionary. Others wanted to stake the claim about modernism's greatness on its equivalence to other literature.
26. As far as Eliot went, Williams was not one to pull his punches, at one point calling Eliot the "archbishop of procurers to a lecherous antiquity" and *The Waste Land* "the great catastrophe to our letters" (1967, 146).
27. Monroe's anthology is extensively described in Abbott (1984). Abbott notes that there were probably at least twelve thousand copies printed of the 1917 edition of *The New Poetry*. Golding notes the anthology's "three editions through 1932 and multiple printings through 1946" (1995, 22).
28. So far as I can tell, Monroe's science prize was never awarded.
29. While it is difficult to accurately assess the cultural weight of this anthology, whose history is undocumented, apparently, there was some call for it; it was reprinted or revised in 1931, 1935, and 1936.
30. The strongest voice opposing this inherent relationship between form and content was that of Yvor Winters. Winters argued that literary modernism had

resulted in a social context in which lesser poets took on difficulty as a technique since "If one cannot be profound, it is always fairly easy to be difficult." *That* belief, Winters argued was "a form of group hypochondria" (1937, 90). In a later essay, after quoting Eliot's famous comment from "The Metaphysical Poets," and acknowledging how frequently it is invoked, Winters took to task the idea that modern poetry demanded new forms because of the unique "social conditions" of modernism (1943, 136–37).

31. This articulation of newness, difficulty, and aesthetic value finds a close relationship in reception theory as articulated by Hans Robert Jauss, who in his seminal *Toward an Aesthetic of Reception* claims that an "important work ... indicates a new direction in the literary process" (1982, 12).

32. One way of expressing this urgency was that difficult modernism freshened what had become a stale or dead language. William Carlos Williams, reviewing the work of Stein and Pound, exhorted "It's the words, the words we need to get back to, words washed clean." Williams found the difficulty of Pound's and Stein's writing to be necessary, for, he argued, "Until we get the power of thought back through a new minting of the words we are actually sunk" ([1935] 1969, 163). While the necessity of a fresh language was a central argument in modernism, it was not a big part of most difficulty arguments, except implicitly, as in the argument about newness.

33. Thus, a high modern like Virginia Woolf recognized as real the crisis to which modernism responded, but she was ambivalent about whether *revolution* was necessary: "The literary convention of the time is so artificial ... that, naturally, the feeble are tempted to outrage, and the strong are led to destroy the very foundations and rules of literary society. Signs of this are everywhere apparent. Grammar is violated; syntax disintegrated; as a boy staying with an aunt for a week-end rolls in the geranium bed out of sheer desperation as the solemnities of the sabbath wear on. The more adult writers do not, of course, indulge in such wanton exhibitions of spleen" ([1924] 1966, 112–13).

34. Many doubted whether difficulty, particularly in its extremes, could be useful in the service of a revolution. John Middleton Murry wrote this of Joyce and his *Ulysses*: "His intention, so far as he has any social intention, is completely anarchic. But in order to be a successful anarchist you must work within the comprehension of society. You have to use the time-tables and the language of ordinary men. By the excess of his anarchy, Mr. Joyce makes himself socially harmless" ([1922] 1970, 196). More overtly in favor of drastic social change, this reviewer of Joyce's *Work in Progress* raised similar concerns:

> A writer produces a book that the initiated alone may evaluate. Many admirers of James Joyce will find the Fascist "Leader" idea right after their own hearts.... The revelation of men in relation to the outside world, in relation to the past and the future, is undesirable from the bourgeois point of view. If light must be cast, then let it be the light of a projector, which does not illuminate but blinds. In this way Joyce acquires social significance. He promises his audience that he will lead them to the depths that they long to fathom,

but he excludes those things the penetration of which might lead to the revolution. (Gertsfelde [1934] 1970, 617)

35. Shklovsky's formalism is central to his thought; at one point in his essay he argues that "*Art is a way of experiencing the artfulness of an object; the object is not important*" ([1917] 1965, 12; italics in the original). Now, in current theory's exploration of the social consequences of difficulty, Shklovky's formalism has not been completely shed. Difficulty's social consequences arrive via a curious route. Theorists for the most part believe that difficulty is a property of a work and so turn to formal aspects of artworks to account for their difficulty. Such characteristics, in turn, result in certain affects, such as defamiliarization or alienation, which may have consequences for behavior. Thus, defenses of difficulty are affect-based in an idiosyncratic way: for most theorists, difficulty is a property that, when one views it as estrangement, inherently produces a specific affect. Difficulty is a property the text brings to you, not a reading practice you bring to the text.
36. Simon Jarvis notes that this idea of art as a separate realm was earliest expressed by Immanuel Kant, who separated the ability for aesthetic judgment from other cognitive abilities. In the *Critique of Judgement* Kant argued that "Fine art must be free art in a double sense: it must be free in the sense of not being a mercenary occupation and hence a kind of labor, whose magnitude can be judged, exacted or paid for according to a certain standard; but fine art must also be free in the sense that, though the mind is occupying itself, yet it feels satisfied and aroused (independently of any pay) without looking to some other purpose" (§8, 59; quoted in Jarvis 1998, 94). As Jarvis notes, this position is strikingly similar to that of Adorno.
37. Helen Elam argues that "Difficulty opposes itself to ideology because in an ultimate sense it is synonymous with a conflict for which no solution can be posited, with a contradiction that attends every attempt at understanding." According to Elam, part of the reason that recent critical theory has been difficult is that it is a "deliberate attempt to break the illusion of lucidity, the illusion that language is a transparent entity and that we are in control of it" (1991, 80).
38. Note the similarity of Nietzsche's position to Augustine's claim: "Although we select certain examples of eloquence from their writings [of the writers of Scripture] which may be understood without difficulty, nevertheless we should not think that we must imitate them in that which they have spoken with a useful and healthful obscurity for the purpose of exercising and sharpening, as it were, the minds of the readers and of destroying fastidiousness and stimulating the desire to learn, concealing their intention in such a way that the minds of the impious are either converted to piety or excluded from the mysteries of the faith." While Augustine grants this exclusionary ability to writers of scripture, he is much more dubious about the writings of lesser mortals. He continues:

> But their expositors should not for this reason so speak that they, having a similar authority, offer themselves for interpretation. But in all their utterances they should first of all seek to speak so that they may be understood,

speaking in so far as they are able with such clarity that either he who does not understand is very slow or that the difficulty and subtlety lie not in the manner of speaking but in the things which we wish to explain and show, so that this is the reason why we are understood less, or more slowly. (1958, 132–33)

Nietzsche's comment is also similar to a small but significant body of modernism that ties difficulty to an interest in the occult. Writers such as Demetres Tryphonopoulos in his 1992 *The Celestial Tradition: A Study of Ezra Pound's The Cantos*, and Leon Surette in his 1993 *Birth of Modernism: Ezra Pound, T. S. Eliot, W. B. Yeats and the Occult* establish linkages between the occult and such writers as Ezra Pound, William Butler Yeats, and H. D.

39. For a more contemporary formulation of this position, see Arnold Hauser's *The Sociology of Art*. There, Hauser argues that "High, serious, uncompromising art has a disturbing effect, often distressing and torturing; popular art, on the other hand, wants to soothe, distract us from the painful problems of existence, and instead of inspiring us to activity and exertion, criticism and self-examination, moves us on the contrary to passivity and self-satisfaction" (1982, 582).

40. Now, it is not that difficulty has never been associated with pleasure. In *On Christian Doctrine* Augustine notes that "what is sought with difficulty is discovered with more pleasure" (1958, 38 2.6.8). Augustine is not unequivocal in his support of difficult pleasures. He argues for a balance between easy and difficult writing, noting that scripture provides such a model. As for contemporary critical theory, I realize that there are exceptions to the distrust of pleasure, such as the Roland Barthes of *S/Z*. I am also not the only person to note this uneasiness with pleasure on the part of much contemporary critical theory. Wendy Steiner, in *The Scandal of Pleasure*, notes "The deconstructive scholarship that de Man inspired flees artistic pleasure as if it were a mortal danger. Its prose is often so convoluted as to empty the critical act of pleasure altogether, its appeal to the reader of that barbed-wire masochism encircling a fellowship of unerring ascetics" (1995, 206).

41. Further, despite its significant merits, Adorno's analysis is not congruent with modernism's social practice, which, critics are increasingly discovering, was more implicated in the practices of a deadening consumer culture than moderns thought. Among other things, modernism provided models for how mass culture might package difficulty. Among other works that discuss this phenomenon, see Rainey's *Institutions of Modernism* (1998).

42. The relationship of this claim to modernism's sense of literary history was discussed in chapter 1. In my research I have discovered more than sixty sources from 1950 or earlier that argue that difficulty is transitory. For typical articulations of this position, see Ernst Curtius, "Technique and Thematic Development of James Joyce" ([1929] 1970); Kenyon Cox, "The 'Modern' Spirit in Art" (1913); Louis MacNiece, *Modern Poetry*, ([1938] 1968, 163).

43. William Van O'Connor was one of the few who would actually specify this audience: "A part of our hesitancy to accept such language [as in Donne's sermons] may not rest so much in our being baffled by the obscurity of it as in our

inherited fear of metaphors and our lack of practice in perceiving their implications. A good deal of modern poetry that was once held obscure is now easily read by those who are practiced in such reading" (1948, 231).

44. While Moore seems to suggest that formal meanings are capable of being *enjoyed* by anyone, when formal values were recruited in an *understanding* of the work, such meaning was commonly seen to be available only to professionals. Composer Arnold Schoenberg, for example, argued that J. S. Bach wrote "music of a kind which in its real values only the expert is capable of understanding" (1950, 184). According to Schoenberg, later composers had a more skittish relationship with professionals: "I would not contend that later composers consciously gave in to these popular demands for comprehensibility—demands which do not correspond entirely to the demands of higher art. But there is no doubt that much in Schubert's melodic construction—his juxtaposition of motives, which are only melodically varied, but rhythmically very similar—accommodated, probably instinctively, to the popular feeling" (184).

45. I. A. Richards ([1935] 1960, 214) puts the same Coleridge quotation to the same use. As it is for Coleridge, for Eliot the imperfect understanding is the source of pleasure. See also Eliot's "The Music of Poetry": "It is not necessary, in order to enjoy the poem [the *Blue Closet* of William Morris], to know what the dream means" (1942, 456).

While in some ways Aristotelian wonder, as an affect, looks much like romantic ideas of the sublime, its motivation is given a much more specific location than is typically given for the sublime. The relevant passage lies in Aristotle's *Poetics* (1997, §34, 53, 63–64), in which Aristotle argues that artists "should choose [to render] things that are impossible but [will look] plausible, rather than things that are possible but [look] unbelievable" (133). The effect of such rendering will be wonder, or amazement. The sublime and wonder are obvious precedents for some high modern discussion of difficulty, but they have some key difficulties in being effortlessly translated into the modern context. In the first place, Aristotle's comments, while they have intriguing relationships to the anxiety effects of difficulty, deal mainly with plot. In the second place, wonder and the sublime are not as heavily reliant on *resistance* as are most modernist notions of difficulty. For a historical overview of Aristotle's idea of wonder, see J. V. Cunningham (1976).

46. The most strenuous opponent to Eliot's formulation was Yvor Winters, who argued: "It is possible, of course, as Eliot somewhere else remarks, to admire a poem deeply without wholly understanding it; but such admiration must rest on an understanding at least imperfect, and the idea that this admiration is adequate as compared with that which comes with full understanding is mere nonsense. . . . If the meaning is important in the creation of the poem, at any rate, it is foolish to suppose that one can dispense with it in reading the poem or that the poet did not take his meaning seriously" (1943, 47).

47. In fact, Eliot, in reviewing Pound's work, came to a formulation quite close to that of Friedlaender: "no word is ever chosen merely for the tinkle; each has always its part in producing an impression which is produced always through language. Words are perhaps the hardest of all material of art: for they must be

used to express both visual beauty and beauty of sound, as well as communicating a grammatical statement" ([1917] 1965, 171).

48. In my research, I have discovered over ninety sources from before 1950 that use some version of emotional expression to talk about difficulty. For some typical expressions of this defense (including its tensions), see Ezra Pound, *Spirit of Romance* ([1910] 1952, 14); Gilbert Seldes ([1922] 1982, 149); Edmund Wilson (1924, 102).

49. Eliot argued that although the initial impression of a work of art may be imperfect, this did not mean that precision was never to be arrived at. Writing about Dante, he claimed: "The impression can be verified on fuller knowledge; I have found with Dante and with several other poets in languages in which I was unskilled, that about such impressions there was nothing fanciful. They were not due, that is, to *mis*understanding the passage, or to reading into it something not there, or to accidental sentimental evocations out of my own past. The impression was new, and of, I believe, the objective 'poetic emotion'" ([1929] 1975a, 206).

50. This "specialized" knowledge could be notoriously vaguely defined. For many reviewers it seems to have meant nothing more than specialized knowledge that a given reviewer or anthologist did not have (and was not embarrassed to reveal to his or her readers). In his defense of the difficulty of Pound, Eliot was particularly clever at pointing this out: "Very few people know the Arthurian legends well, or even Malory...; but no one accuses Tennyson of needing footnotes, or of superciliousness toward the uninstructed. The difference is merely in what people are prepared for; most readers could no more relate the myth of Atys correctly than they could give a biography of Bertrand de Born. It is hardly too much to say there is no poem in these volumes of Mr. Pound which needs fuller explanation than he gives himself" ([1917] 1965, 166). Eliot was not prepared to go on to claim that Pound's work was easy; what he did go on to argue was that the difficulty was of a different kind than one based on knowledge: "What the poems do require is a trained ear, or at least the willingness to be trained" (166, 67).

51. For other uses of this trope, see, for example Munson ([1924] 1982, 206), Nichols ([1920] 1972, 166), and Powell ([1923] 1982, 194). A large number of readers, in looking at the difficulty of modernism and the apparent knowledge required, described these works as being "chaotic," a term that suggested that there was no way *in to* the difficult text. It's not that the difficult work's structuring principles, or principles for reading it, were clear, and that readers just had trouble completing the reading process at the highest level. This is an assertion that few today are willing to make: of the approximately one hundred sources that I have read that describe a given difficult work as chaos, eighty-five or more come from 1950 or earlier. Claims that a given difficult work was nothing but chaos were made primarily in the first stages of the reception history of modernism.

52. Dudley Fitts noted that the problem with the notes to *The Waste Land* was that "Mr T. S. Eliot, by appending apparently 'explanatory' notes to the text of 'The Waste Land', obscured what was otherwise perfectly clear because he seemed to suggest that participation in his erudition was essential for the 'understanding' of

his poetry" ([1931] 1972, 252). Note, though, that despite Fitts's quotation marks, Eliot himself never made such claims for his notes. He wrote that they were probably less helpful than Weston's *From Ritual to Romance*, a work which he vaguely claimed would "elucidate the difficulties of the poem much better than my notes can do" ([1922] 1969, 47).

53. To make this assertion work would require a change in reading practices, since that is not how the general public had been taught to read. It took some work to claim difficulty for Shakespeare, for instance. Drew would a few pages later comment: "There have always been 'difficult' poets. Shakespeare is the most difficult of all, and it is only because he appeals at so many different levels to so many different types of audience and reader that his difficulty has escaped much comment. There is so much else to say about him!" (1933, 82). With great difficult writers, then, one could go on to more difficult levels of meaning.

54. For examples of this approach, see Riding and Graves (1927, 9); Leavis (1931, 347), Richards ([1935] 1960, 197–98); Brooks (1947, 67). In his *Wallace Stevens and Literary Canons*, John Timberman Newcomb notes that in this articulating of a universal difficulty a writer like William Empson, in his *Seven Types of Ambiguity*, domesticates difficulty by making it resolvable. The ambiguity described by Empson is "tamed into the pleasant savoring of multiple, perhaps paradoxical, but knowable properties within a range of contemplative meaning" (1992, 94).

For accounts of the rise of New Criticism and its relation to these values, see Guillory (1993, 134–75); McDonald (1993, 176–210); Bush (1948); Golding (1995, 75ff); Graff (1987, 145ff); Searle (1994); Strychacz (1993, 35, passim).

55. In 1940, this assertion awkwardly surfaced at an odd moment, in a review of *Finnegans Wake*: "It is not to be wondered that the book is unknown to otherwise voracious consumers of the fiction market. The reviewers have told them it is unintelligible. That the reading of *Finnegans Wake* is plenty tough is undeniable. That it is unintelligible is not true" (Rybert [1940] 1970, 731–32).

56. Weyergraf-Serra and Buskirk's book is a collection of documents about the *Tilted Arc* controversy, printing letters, citations, petitions, testimony, and legal documents. It regrettably does not have the complete testimony of people from the three-day hearings, and it does at times nudge readers along: for example, while the complete list of names and professional qualifications are given of those who testified for the work, there is no such list for those who testified against it.

Chapter 4

1. For some earlier comments on the rise of Eliot's influence, see Day Lewis and Strong ([1924] 1941, xix); Untermeyer (1924, 350); Tate (1922, 100); Seldes ([1922] 1982, 145).
2. For a contemporary discussion on this aspect of reading, see Sven Birkert's *The Gutenberg Elegies* (1994).
3. See Abbott (1990) for an account of the battle between the canon as given in democratic, native anthologies and the canon that was coming into being with the rise of the study of modern literature in the university.

4. But, in addition to being a way to handle difficulty, this passivity also was important because it was yet another way to imply that with great (and difficult) art you are outside of yourself and culture, in an atemporal, asocial realm. It is a Kantian realm in which art, having been removed from the social, is self-subsistent, answerable, and referring only to itself.
5. See James Elkins, *Why Are Our Pictures Puzzles?* (1999) for a look at the relationship between puzzles and twentieth-century high art criticism. For other uses of this trope, see Roosevelt (1913); "Eclipse of the Highbrow" (1941); Yust ([1929] 1995).
6. For other representative writers who use the term "clever" to characterize difficult modernism, see Courtney ([1922] 1975); Untermeyer (1920, 382); Nichols ([1920] 1972, 167); Waugh (1919, 3). William Empson is one of the very few pro-difficulty moderns who accepted the terms of the "game" argument. Empson, commenting on the notes he published with a book of his poetry, argued:

> they are meant to be like answers to a crossword puzzle; a sort of puzzle interest is part of the pleasure that you are meant to get from the verse, and that I get myself when I go back to it. It is clear that you try to guess the puzzle before you turn to the answer; but you aren't offended with the newspaper for publishing the whole answer, even when you had guessed it. There would be no point in publishing a puzzle in a newspaper, if it were admittedly so simple that there was no need to publish the answer. And the comparison is not quite a random one; the fashion for obscure poetry, as a recent development, came in at about the same time as the fashion for crossword puzzles; and it seems to me that this revival of puzzle interest in poetry, an old and natural thing, has got a bad name merely by failing to know itself and refusing to publish the answers." (1940, 55)

Accepting the characterization of his poetry as being similar to crossword puzzles, Empson adroitly maneuvered through the minefield of ensuing issues by claiming that this kind of difficulty was both natural and traditional. Empson's position is given additional expansion in Adorno's comments on pleasure: "Every artwork is a picture puzzle, a puzzle to be solved, but this puzzle is constituted in such a fashion that it remains a vexation, the preestablished routing of its observer. The newspaper picture puzzle recapitulates playfully what artworks carry out in earnest" (1997, 121).

7. Their thinking on this wasn't crystalline: while it was often described as an effect, vigor could also be seen as an aesthetic property, in the same way that pleasure was: the statement "this is a pleasurable text" often meant "this is a text that produces pleasure."
8. Characterizations of the machismo of modern difficulty (both appreciative and dismissive) were frequent. In my research I have come across over 130 different sources from 1950 or earlier that, both for and against, make a specific equation between difficulty and vigorousness or virility. For typical articulations of this linkage, see Dudley ([1924] 1977); Rothschild ([1934] 1972, 9); Vern ([1936] 1995).

9. There is a large body of scholarship on the claims for the virility of modernism, which I do not here retrace. This book looks at those claims more selectively, noting where they overlap (as they often do) with assertions about modernism's difficulty.
10. John Sparrow was perhaps the first of modernism's skeptics to explicitly note the relationship between difficulty and morality: "Mallarmé and his followers deserted intelligibility in various ways and for various reasons, but with all of them the predominant aim was to create a new kind of aesthetic pleasure; they neglected intelligibility in the interests of art. The modern poet who claims to be an inheritor of their tradition writes nonsense not for art's sake, but for the sake of truthfulness; nothing more radically opposed to the creed of *l'art pour l'art* than the moralistic theory which he would seek to justify his method" (1934, xv). For a more recent analysis of this moral strain in modernism, see Carol Duncan's *Civilizing Rituals* (1995, 108–9).
11. See Andreas Huyssen's *After the Great Divide* for his analysis of the high modern tendency to equate mass culture, pleasure, and the feminine (1986, 44–62).
12. See the opening of Bruce Robbins's *Secular Vocations* (1993) for a description of the divide between professionals and pleasure.
13. Sinclair was almost certainly referring to a review in the *New Statesman*, which had appeared a few months before. There, the reviewer availed him- or herself of the same conceptual metaphor, but came to a different conclusion. Recognizing the ambitious claims made for Eliot, the reviewer began, "Mr. Eliot may possibly give us the quintessence of twenty-first century poetry. Certainly much of what he writes is unrecognisable as poetry at present, but it is all decidedly amusing, and it is only fair to say that he does not call these pieces poems. . . . We do not pretend to follow the drift of 'The Love Song of J. Alfred Prufrock.'" The reviewer instead chose to quote "The Boston Evening Transcript," describing it as "Mr. Eliot's highest flight, and we shall treasure it" (Review of *Prufrock* [1917] 1982b, 75).
14. L. A. G. Strong similarly noted that great poetry was not "an amiable soporific," that much of it was difficult because of "the speed with which a great poet's imagination leaps from point to point." Strong continued, "In a flash, the kindled mind apprehends a series of conclusions, and has sped across them to a new peak while the pedestrian reader is boggling at the preliminaries to the first leap" (1931, 156).

Chapter 5

1. For an account of Palgrave's anthology, see Lentricchia's *Modernist Quartet*, which also lists as its major competitors the equally conservative "F.L. Knowle's *Golden Treasury of American Songs and Lyrics* (1898) [which] saw seven editions in about fifteen years, and Jessie Belle Rittenhouse's 1912 *Little Book of Modern Verse*—[which] sold 100,000 copies in its first edition" (1994, 59). See also Perloff (1985, 176–79).
2. In this essay, it should be noted, Tietjens was restricting her comments to lyric poetry, and not dramatic or narrative. But it is also clear from her essay that

Tietjens, like Palgrave, thought of the lyric as the greatest form of poetry, the litmus test for great art.

3. The simple text gives pleasure because it returns one to things that are familiar, that have always been known. A 1916 review of Robert Frost notes that Frost is popular "because American readers have discovered that they can understand and enjoy poetry which deals veraciously with the life and the people they know—poetry which is written in a language they can understand and enjoy, because it is the language they speak, vibrant with the feeling and force and form of the familiar spoken sentence" (Browne [1916] 1977, 36).

4. These comments are cited by Craig Abbott in his article "Modern American Poetry: Anthologies, Classrooms, and Canons" (1990, 217). Abbott there similarly notes that Wilkinson's use of "simply" closes off inquiry.

5. Lentricchia makes basically the same point for lyric poetry, arguing that Palgrave's introduction defined lyric as exclusion: "No narrative allowed, no intellect at mediation, no description of local reference, no didacticism, no personal, occasional, or religious material, no humor, . . . no dramatic textures of blank verse" (1994, 57).

6. This is *Dial* under old management, before it was retooled as a forum for modernist apologetics.

7. For a discussion of a similar ground-shift in modern painting, see James Elkins's *Why Are Our Pictures Puzzles?* (1999).

8. For some standard announcements of Frost and Cather's uncertain place in the modern canon, see Poirier (1977, ix–xiii, 226–76); O'Brien (1988, 110); and Middleton (1990, 19–21). Joan Acocella's *Willa Cather and the Politics of Criticism* (2000) gives a recent and highly charged reading of Cather's reception history.

9. For a discussion of the pivotal role of Jarrell's "Other Frost" essay, see Pritchard (1984) and Shetley (1993, 32).

10. For a discussion of inexhaustibility, see Trevor Ross, *The Making of the English Literary Canon: From the Middle Ages to the Late Eighteenth Century* (Montreal and Kingston: McGill-Queens, 1998).

11. Modernism's readers variously described the surface of a work of art as its sensory aspect, its allusions, its realism, and its narrative. But such ideas of the surface weren't stable, fixed. The surface wasn't *always* narrative, for example. "Surface," then, needs to be understood anew each time in the context of the work to which it refers.

12. Several critics have noted this point, including Pritchard (1984, 97), Lentricchia (1994, 70–71), and Perelman (1994, 1).

13. The importance of this book, and particularly the essay *The Novel Démeublé* in the critical understanding of Cather's art cannot be overestimated. See, in particular, Trilling (1936); Stewart (1966); O'Brien (1984).

14. For an analysis of the beginnings of difficulty in nineteenth-century fiction, see Marina van Zuylen's 1994 *Difficulty as an Aesthetic Principle: Realism and Unreadability in Stifter, Melville, and Flaubert*. Arguing that the roots of high modern difficulty can be found in these three central novelists, van Zuylen finds their difficulty in, among other things, their unwillingness to simplify the world,

to remove its confusing details. In the work of Stifter, van Zuylen argues, the reader "is asked to puzzle and to probe, until the thick-skinned surface yields a literary meaning" (19).

15. See especially 257–78. Peck ties in the wish for Cather to be difficult with academic critical practices: "The early, relatively unsophisticated criticism of Cather during the 1920s, 1930s, and 1940s most transparently responds to Cather's fictional myth of conquest and individual power.... More recent criticism of Cather in the 1960s, 1970s and 1980s has been less willing to acknowledge the primal fantasy of power. Critics of this period, eager to secure Cather's reputation as a serious and important writer, have worked hard to deny her simplicity, emotionalism, and optimism, as if those qualities would diminish her literary status. One reason for their discomfort is that they have inherited the assumptions of New Criticism, with its modernist demands for psychological complexity, conflicting thematic threads, moral ambiguity and stylistic density" (1996, 269).

16. For a discussion of this speech and the ensuing controversy, see Meyers (1994, 318–20); Poirier (1977, 3–5); Burnshaw (1986, 101–8); and O'Hara (1988, 142–46). In addition to the contemporary accounts I cite in these pages, consult the following: M. L. Rosenthal, "The Robert Frost Controversy," *Nation* 188 (June 20, 1959): 559–61; *Newsweek* 54, no. 27 (July 27, 1959); and "The Art of Poetry II: An Interview with Robert Frost," *Paris Review* 24, no. 2 (Summer-Fall 1960): 88–120.

17. Williams's peculiar brand of difficulty is the difficulty that George Steiner characterizes as "modal difficulty," a difficulty that arises when one is uncertain why a given text, object, or act is being presented as art (1978, 27–29ff).

18. See also Conrad Aiken on Williams's work: "Mr. Williams too seldom goes below the surface. He restricts his observations almost entirely to the sensory plane. His moods, so to speak, are nearly always the moods of the eye, the ear, and the nostril. We get the impression from these poems that his world is a world of plane surfaces, bizarrely coloured, and cunningly arranged so as to give an effect of depth and solidity; but we do not get depth itself" ([1919] 1980, 57–58).

19. George Santayana, in his *The Sense of Beauty*, noted that "there must always remain a penumbra and fringe of suggestion if the most explicit representation is to communicate a truth. When there is real profundity ... there will accordingly be felt inadequacy of expression, and an appeal to the observer to piece out the imperfections with his thought" (quoted in van Zuylen 1998, 45).

20. As Alan Purves argues, *The Waste Land* "is complex because a group of readers has established the ground rules for complexity; if they were to take a more impressionistic view of how the poem is to be read, its complexity diminishes" (1991a, 167). All of the authors in the collection from which this quotation is taken argue some version of this thesis about difficulty, that "difficulty of text is not simply a matter of textual qualities but more importantly of the relationship of those qualities to the demands placed upon the reader" (Purves 1991b, 4).

21. "How to Recognize a Poem When You See One," in *Is There a Text in This Class?* (Cambridge: Harvard, 1980), 322–37. Jerome McGann's "The Alice Fallacy" (1997) plays with these issues in its rereading of Brooks's and Warren's reading of Joyce Kilmer's "Trees."

22. See Stafford (1998) for an assessment of Renoir's reputation along these lines.
23. By the mid-1980s it was possible for Fred Orton to characterize Renoir's reputation in the following terms: "We might say that of all the Artists we read about in the History of Impressionism it's Renoir who causes the Modernist most problems in the terms of the value to be placed on his paintings" (1985, 28).
24. In an article on Greenberg's changing estimations of Renoir, Karen Wilkin notes Greenberg's 1946 comment that Renoir was "flaccid at times." Later, though, in 1950, Greenberg enthused "What a profusion of pleasure there is: a foaming, pouring, shimmering profusion like nothing else in painting; pictures that are spotted and woven with soft, porous colors, and look in themselves like bouquets of flowers (so that whenever the actual image of a bouquet appears it tends to be a supererogatory presence); pictures whose space is handled like a fluid that floats all objects to the surface; pictures in which our eyes swim with the paint and dance with the brushstroke" (Wilkin, 1996, 46–47).

Conclusion
1. For another version of this argument, see Chris Baldick's *Criticism and Literary Theory* (1996, 60).
2. For other statements of this position, see Travis (1998, 26); Golding (1995, 75–78); McDonald (1993, 136–37).
3. Guillory similarly asserts that New Criticism believed that because literature was inherently difficult, "it needed to be studied *in the university*" (1993, 172).
4. Vernon Shetley makes essentially the same point about poets after World War II. According to Shetley, these poets "found a new audience, one accustomed to making sense of modernist 'difficulty' and fitted with habits of reading and standards for judgment that enabled them to grasp and respond to the witty, paradoxical, erudite, and fragmented constructions typical of high modernism" (1993, 12).
5. This is partly indicated by critical unwillingness, once the high modern canon seemed firmly established, to discuss difficulty as central to high modernism. Starting in the 1960s, comments on the omnipresence of difficulty in modernism fall off sharply and become an observation made by those outside of the academy.
6. For an account of how Eliot put this strategy into practice, see my "'I Can Have More than Enough Power to Satisfy Me:' T. S. Eliot's Construction of His Audience" (1996).
7. For a discussion of the loss of a public audience for poetry, see Shetley (1993) and Aimone (1995).

Works Cited

Abbott, Craig S. 1984. "Publishing the New Poetry: Harriet Monroe's Anthology." *Journal of Modern Literature* 11, no. 1: 89–108.

———. 1988. "Untermeyer on Eliot." *Journal of Modern Literature* 15, no. 1: 105–19.

———. 1990. "Modern American Poetry: Anthologies, Classrooms, and Canons." *College Literature* 17: 209–21.

Abercrombie, Lascelles. 1921. "Hymn to Love." In *An Anthology of Modern Verse*, edited by A. Methuen (3–4). London: Methuen and Company.

Acocella, Joan. 2000. *Willa Cather and the Politics of Criticism*. Lincoln and London: University of Nebraska.

Adams, Hazard. 1991. "The Difficulty of Difficulty." In *The Idea of Difficulty in Literature*, edited by Alan C. Purves (23–50). Albany: State University of New York Press.

Adams, J. Donald. 1959. "Speaking of Books." *New York Times Book Review* (April 12): 2.

———. 1970. Review of *Finnegans Wake*. In *James Joyce: The Critical Heritage* (Vol. 2, 754–55). London: Routledge and Kegan Paul. First published in *New York Times* (January 26, 1941): 2.

Adams, Marilyn Jager. 1980. "Failures to Comprehend and Levels of Processing in Reading." In *Theoretical Issues in Reading Comprehension: Perspectives from Cognitive Psychology, Linguistics, Artificial Intelligence, and Education*, edited by Rand J. Spiro, Bertram C. Bruce and William F. Brewer (11–32). Hillsdale, N.J.: Lawrence Erlbaum Associates.

Adorno, Theodor and Max Horkheimer. 1972. *Dialectic of Enlightenment*. Translated by John Cumming. New York: Seabury Press.

———. 1997. *Aesthetic Theory*. Translated by Robert Hullot-Kentor. Edited by Greta Adorno and Rolf Tiedemann. Vol. 88, *Theory and History of Literature*. Minneapolis: University of Minnesota.

Aiken, Conrad. 1980 [1919]. "Scepticisms: Notes on Contemporary Poetry." In *William Carlos Williams: The Critical Heritage* (57–58). London: Routledge and Kegan Paul.

———. 1982a. "An Anatomy of Melancholy." In *T. S. Eliot: The Critical Heritage* (Vol. 1, 156–62). London: Routledge and Kegan Paul. First published in *New Republic* 33 (February 7, 1923): 294–95.

———. 1982b. "Divers Realists." In *T. S. Eliot: The Critical Heritage* (Vol. 1, 80–81). London: Routledge and Kegan Paul. First published in *Dial* 43 (November 8, 1917): 454–55.

Aimone, Joseph, Alfred Corn, Gerald Harnett, Fred Muratori, Stephen Ramsay, Rusty Rushton, and Mark Seidl. 1995. "Obscurity: An Internet Dialogue." *Hellas: A Journal of Poetry and the Humanities* 6, no. 2: 81–100.

Aldington, Richard. 1924. *Literary Studies and Reviews*. London: George Allen and Unwin.

———. 1970. Review of *Finnegans Wake*. In *James Joyce: The Critical Heritage* (Vol. 2, 690). London: Routledge and Kegan Paul. First published in *Atlantic Monthly* 163 (June 1939): n.p.

Alington, Cyril. 1923. "A Plea for Lucidity." *English Review* (June): 545–49.

Amis, Martin. 1996. *The Information*. New York: Random House.

Anderson, Laurie. 1984. "Difficult Listening Hour." In *United States* (n.p.). New York: Harper and Row.

Anderson, Sherwood. 1922. "Four American Impressions." *New Republic* (October 11): 171–73.

———. 1986. Reprint Gertrude Stein, *Geography and Plays* (New York: Haskell House, 1967 [1922]), 5–8. In *Critical Essays on Gertrude Stein* (39–41) Boston: G. K. Hall.

Announcement of *Dial* Prize. In *T. S. Eliot: The Critical Heritage* (Vol. 1, 136–38). London: Routledge and Kegan Paul. First published in *Dial* 73 (1922): 685–87.

Aramis. 1970. *James Joyce: The Critical Heritage* (Vol. 1, 192–94). London: Routledge and Kegan Paul. First published in *Sporting Times* (April 1, 1922): 4.

Aristotle. 1941. *The Basic Works of Aristotle*. Edited by Richard Peter McKeon. New York: Random House.

———. 1991. *On Rhetoric: A Theory of Civic Discourse*. Edited by George Alexander Kennedy. New York: Oxford University Press.

———. 1997. *Aristotle's Poetics*. Edited by George Whalley, John Baxter, and Patrick Atherton. Montreal and Buffalo: McGill-Queen's University Press.

"Artists Give Cubist Play." 1913. *Chicago Daily Tribune* (March 27), 1.

Ashbery, John. 1990. "An Interview with John Ashbery by Paul Munn." *New Orleans Review* 17, no. 2: 59–63.

Atkins, Elizabeth. 1936. *Edna St. Vincent Millay and Her Times*. Chicago: University of Chicago Press.

Atwood, Margaret. 1995. Waterstone's Poetry Lecture [webpage]. Retrieved March 21 2001, from http://www.web.net/owtoad/lecture.html.

Auden, W. H. 1940. "Against Romanticism." *New Republic* (February 5): 187.

Augustine. 1958. *On Christian Doctrine*. Translated by D. W. Robertson Jr. Indianapolis: Bobbs-Merrill.

Babbitt, Milton. 1966. "Who Cares if You Listen?" In *The American Composer Speaks: A Historical Anthology, 1770–1965* (235–44). Baton Rouge: Louisiana State University Press. First published in *High Fidelity Magazine* 8, no. 2 (February 1958).

Bair, Deirdre. 1978. *Samuel Beckett*. New York: Harcourt Brace Jovanovich.
Baldick, Chris. 1996. *Criticism and Literary Theory: 1890 to the Present*. New York: Longman.
Barber, Bruce, Serge Guilbaut, and John O'Brian. 1996. *Voices of Fire: Art, Rage, Power, and the State, Theory/Culture*. Toronto: University of Toronto Press.
Barker, Ronald. 1993. "Waiting for Godot." In *Critical Essays on Samuel Beckett* (22–23). Aldershot, Eng.: Scolar Press. First published in *Plays and Players* (September 1955): 18–19.
Bell, Clive. 1982. "T. S. Eliot." In *T. S. Eliot: The Critical Heritage* (Vol. 1, 186–91). London: Routledge and Kegan Paul. First published in *Nation and Athenaeum* 33 (September 1923): 772–73.
———. 1975. "Woolf's Painterly Vision." In *Virginia Woolf: The Critical Heritage* (138–47). London: Routledge and Kegan Paul. First published in *Dial* (December 1924).
Bell, Julian. 2000. "Unreal Food Uneaten." *London Review of Books* 13 (April): 22–23.
Benét, William Rose. 1982. "Poetry Ad Lib." In *T.S. Eliot: The Critical Heritage* (Vol. 1, 192–93). London: Routledge and Kegan Paul. First published in *Yale Review* 13 (October 1923): 161–62.
Bennett, Arnold [Jacob Tonson, pseud.]. 1910. "Books and Persons." *New Age* (December): 135–36.
Bentley, Eric. 1993. "The Talent of Samuel Beckett." In *Critical Essays on Samuel Beckett* (37–40). Aldershot, Eng.: Scolar Press. First published in *New Republic* (May 14, 1956): 20–21.
Berg, Alban. 1956 [1924]. "Why Is Schoenberg's Music So Hard to Understand?" In *Composers on Music: An Anthology of Composers' Writings from Palestrina to Copland* (458–60). New York: Pantheon. Reprint in Reich, Willi. *Alban Berg*. Vienna: Reichner, 1937.
Berlyne, D. E. 1971. *Aesthetics and Psychobiology*. Edited by Lindzey Gardner, Kenneth MacCorquodale, and Kenneth E. Clark. The Century Psychology Series. New York: Appleton-Century-Crofts.
Bettany, Lewis. 1975. "Middle Aged Sensualists." In *Virginia Woolf: The Critical Heritage* (98). London: Routledge and Kegan Paul. First published in *Daily News* (October 27, 1922).
Birch-Bartlett, Helen. 1980. Review of *Kora in Hell: Improvisations*. In *William Carlos Williams: The Critical Heritage* (67–68). London: Routledge and Kegan Paul. First published in *Poetry* 17, no. 6 (March 1921): 330–32.
Birkerts, Sven. 1994. *The Gutenberg Elegies: The Fate of Reading in an Electronic Age*. New York: Ballantine.
Bishop, John Peale. 1972. "The Intelligence of Poets." In *Ezra Pound: The Critical Heritage* (207–8). London: Routledge and Kegan Paul. First published in *Vanity Fair* (January 17, 1922): 13–14.
Blackmur, R. P. 1936. "The Instincts of a Bard." *Nation* (June 24): 817–19.
Bledstein, Burton. 1976. *The Culture of Professionalism: The Middle-Class and the Development of Higher Education in America*. New York: Norton.
Bloom, Edward A., and Lillian D. Bloom. 1949–50. "Willa Cather's Novels of the Frontier: A Study in Thematic Symbolism." *American Literature* 21: 71–93.

Blunden, Maria, and Godfrey Blunden. 1970. *Impressionists and Impressionism.* New York: World Publishing.
Boccioni, Umberto, Carlo Carrà, Luigi Russolo, Giacomo Balla, and Gino Severini. 1973. "Manifesto of the Futurist Painters 1910." In *Futurist Manifestos* (24–27). New York: Viking. First published in *Poesia* (Milan), (February 1, 1910).
Bodenheim, Maxwell. 1972. "The Isolation of Carved Metal." In *Ezra Pound: The Critical Heritage* (203–6). London: Routledge and Kegan Paul. First published in *Dial* 72 (January 1922): 87–91.
Bosanquet, Bernard. 1963. *Three Lectures on Aesthetic.* London: Macmillan, 1915; New York: Bobbs-Merrill, 1963.
Bourdieu, Pierre. 1993. *The Field of Cultural Production: Essays on Art and Literature.* Edited by Randal Johnson. New York: Columbia University Press.
Bowie, Malcolm. 1978. *Mallarmé and the Art of Being Difficult.* Cambridge: Cambridge University Press.
Brenner, Rica. 1930. *Ten Modern Poets.* New York: Harcourt, Brace and Company.
Brickell, Herschell. 1927. "The Literary Landscape." *North American Review* 224: advertising section.
Brooker, Jewel Spears, and Joseph Bentley. 1990. *Reading the Waste Land: Modernism and the Limits of Interpretation.* Amherst: University of Massachusetts Press.
Brooks, Cleanth. 1939. *Modern Poetry and the Tradition.* Chapel Hill: University of North Carolina Press.
———. 1947. *The Well Wrought Urn: Studies in the Structure of Poetry.* New York: Harcourt, Brace, and World.
Brooks, Cleanth, and Robert Penn Warren. 1938. *Understanding Poetry: An Anthology for College Students.* New York: H. Holt and Company.
Brooks, Van Wyck. 1972. "Reviewer's Notebook." In *Ezra Pound: The Critical Heritage* (186–89). London: Routledge and Kegan Paul. First published in *Freeman* (June 16, 1920): 334–35.
Brown, Milton W. 1963. *The Story of the Armory Show.* New York: Joseph H. Hirshhorn Foundation.
Brown, Sharon. 1928. "Introduction." In *Poetry of Our Times*, edited by Sharon Brown (21–56). Chicago: Scott, Foresman and Company.
Browne, George H. 1977. "Robert Frost, A Poet of Speech." In *Robert Frost: The Critical Reception* (36–38). New York: Burt Franklin. First published in *Independent* (May 22, 1916): 283–84.
Bryher, Winifred. 1922. "A Symposium on Marianne Moore." *Poetry* 19, no. 4 (January): 208–17.
Buckle, Richard. 1971. *Nijinsky.* London: Weidenfeld and Nicolson.
Bürger, Peter. 1984. *Theory of the Avant-Garde.* Translated by Michael Shaw. Minneapolis: University of Minnesota Press.
Burke, Edmund. 1968 [1759]. *A Philosophical Enquiry into the Origin of Our Ideas of the Sublime and Beautiful.* 1st paperback ed. Ed. James T. Boulton. Notre Dame, Ind.: University of Notre Dame Press.
Burke, Kenneth. 1986. "Engineering with Words." In *Critical Essays on Gertrude Stein* (42–45). Boston: G. K. Hall. First published in *Dial* 74 (April 1923): 408–12.

Burnshaw, Stanley. 1986. *Robert Frost Himself.* New York: George Braziller.
Bush, Douglas. 1945. *English Literature in the Earlier Seventeenth Century, 1600–1660.* London: Oxford University Press.
———. 1948. *The New Criticism: Some Old-Fashioned Queries* (MLA Presidential Address).
Bynner, Witter. 1913. "Lines to W.B." *Poetry* 2, no. 3 (June): 113–14.
Caputo, John D. 1987. *Radical Hermeneutics: Repetition, Deconstruction, and the Hermeneutic Project.* Bloomington: Indiana University Press.
Carey, John. 1992. *The Intellectuals and the Masses: Pride and Prejudice among the Literary Intelligentsia, 1880–1939.* London: Faber and Faber.
Carlin, Deborah. 1992. *Cather, Canon, and the Politics of Reading.* Amherst: University of Massachusetts Press.
Carter, Elliott. 1997a. "The Agony of Modern Music in America, 1955." In *Collected Essays and Lectures, 1937–1995,* edited by Jonathan W. Bernard (53–57). Rochester, N.Y.: University of Rochester.
———. 1997b. "To Think of Milton Babbitt." In *Collected Essays and Lectures, 1937–1995,* edited by Jonathan W. Bernard (197–99). Rochester, N.Y.: University of Rochester. First published in *Perspectives of New Music* 11:1 (Fall–Winter 1972): 3–5.
Cather, Willa. 1936. *The Novel Démeublé: Not under Forty.* New York: Alfred A. Knopf.
———. 1966. *The Kingdom of Art: Willa Cather's First Principles and Critical Statements, 1893–1896,* edited by Bernice Slote. Lincoln: University of Nebraska Press.
Chafe, Wallace. 1991. "Sources of Difficulty in the Processing of Written Language." In *The Idea of Difficulty in Literature,* edited by Alan C. Purves (7–22). Albany: State University of New York Press.
Child, Harold. 1972. Review of *Ripostes,* by Ezra Pound. In *Ezra Pound: The Critical Heritage* (94–95). London: Routledge and Kegan Paul. First published in *Times Literary Supplement* (December 12, 1912): 568, 570.
Christie, William. 2000. "A Recent History of Poetic Difficulty." *ELH* 67: 539–64.
Ciardi, John. 1962. "Robert Frost: American Bard." *Saturday Review* (March 24): 15–17, 52–54.
Clutton-Brock, A. 1922. "On Some Perversities of Criticism." *London Mercury* 2, no. 3: 628–34.
Coleman, David, and Jonathan Adler. 1996. "Intro to Glossies 101." *Vanity Fair* (September): 264.
Coleridge, Hartley. 1992 [1827]. "He Lived Amidst Th'Untrodden Ways." In *Romantic Parodies, 1797–1831,* edited by David A. Kent and D. R. Ewen. Rutherford N.J., London; Cranbury, N.J.: Fairleigh Dickinson University Press/Associated University Presses.
Coleridge, Samuel Taylor. 1983 [1817]. *Biographia Literaria.* Edited by James Engell and Walter Jackson Bate. *The Collected Works of Samuel Taylor Coleridge.* Vol. 7 parts 1 and 2. Princeton, N.J.: Princeton University Press.
Coleridge, Samuel Taylor, and Ernest Hartley Coleridge. 1895. *Anima Poetae, from the Unpublished Note-Books of Samuel Taylor Coleridge.* Edited by Ernest Hartley Coleridge. Boston and New York: Houghton Mifflin and Company.

Coleridge, Samuel Taylor, and Henry Nelson Coleridge. 1967. *The Literary Remains of Samuel Taylor Coleridge*. New York: AMS Press.

Collins, Joseph. 1970. "James Joyce's Amazing Chronicle." In *James Joyce: The Critical Heritage* (Vol. 1, 222–26). London: Routledge and Kegan Paul. First published in *New York Times Book Review* (May 28, 1922): 6, 17.

Conkling, Grace Hazard. 1929. "Tampico." In *New Voices: An Introduction to Contemporary Poetry* (45). New York: Macmillan.

Copland, Aaron. 1957 [1939]. *What to Listen for in Music*. Rev. ed. New York: McGraw-Hill.

Courtney, W. L. 1975. Review of *Jacob's Room*. In *Virginia Woolf: The Critical Heritage* (103–5). London: Routledge and Kegan Paul. First published in *Daily Telegraph* (November 10, 1922).

"The Cover." 1962. *The Saturday Evening Post* (January 13 1962): 3.

Cox, Kenyon. 1913. "The 'Modern' Spirit in Art: Some Reflection Inspired by the Recent International Exhibition." *Harper's Weekly* (March 15): 165–68.

Crimp, Douglas. 1988. "Testimony." In *Richard Serra's Tilted Arc* (73–74), ed. Clara Weyergraf-Serra and Martha Buskirk. Eindhoven: Van Abbemuseum.

"Cubist Art Is Here: As Clear as Mud." 1913. *Chicago Record-Herald* (March 20), 1.

cummings, e. e. 1992. "The New Art." In *Critical Essays on American Modernism* (20–24). New York: G. K. Hall. First published in *Harvard Advocate* (June 24, 1915): 154–56.

Cunningham, J. V. 1976. *The Collected Essays of J. V. Cunningham*. Chicago: Swallow Press.

Curtius, Ernst R. 1973. [1927]. "T. S. Eliot." In *Essays on European Literature* (355–71). Princeton, N.J.: Princeton University Press.

———. 1970. "Technique and Thematic Development of James Joyce." In *James Joyce: The Critical Heritage* (Vol. 2, 466–70). London: Routledge and Kegan Paul. First published in *Neue Schwiezer Rundschau* (January 1929), translated by Eugene Jolas in *transition*, no. 16–17 (June 1929): 310–25.

Daiches, David. 1935. *The Place of Meaning in Poetry*. London: Oliver and Boyd.

———. 1940. *Poetry and the Modern World: A Study of Poetry in England between 1900 and 1939*. Chicago: University of Chicago Press.

———. 1951. *Willa Cather: A Critical Introduction*. Westport, Conn.: Greenwood.

Day Lewis, Cecil. 1934. *A Hope for Poetry*. Oxford: Basil Blackwell.

Day Lewis, Cecil, and L. A. G. Strong. "Introduction." In *A New Anthology of Modern Verse 1920–1940*, edited by Cecil Day Lewis and L. A. G. Strong (xiii–xxiv). London: Methuen and Company.

De Duve, Thierry. 1996. "Vox Ignis Vox Populi." In *Voices of Fire: Art, Rage, Power, and the State*, edited by Bruce Barber, Serge Guilbaut, and John O'Brian (81–95). Toronto: University of Toronto Press.

de Man, Paul. 1989. *Critical Writings, 1953–1978*, edited by Lindsay Waters. Vol. 66, *Theory and History of Literature*. Minneapolis: University of Minnesota Press.

De Voto, Bernard. 1995. "Witchcraft in Mississippi." 4. In *William Faulkner: The Contemporary Reviews* (144–49). Cambridge: Cambridge University Press. First published in *Saturday Review of Literature* 15 (October 31, 1936): 3–4, 14.

Dell, Floyd. 1972. Review of *Provença*. In *Ezra Pound: The Critical Heritage* (70–72). London: Routledge and Kegan Paul. First published in *Chicago Evening Post* (January 6, 1911): 5.

Derleth, August. 1959. "Letter to the Editor." *New York Times Book Review* (May 3): 24.

Deutsch, Babette. 1935. *This Modern Poetry*. New York: W. W. Norton.

———. 1980. Review of *Collected Poems 1921–1931*. In *Willliam Carlos Williams: The Critical Heritage* (130–31). London: Routledge and Kegan Paul. First published in *New York Herald Tribune Books* (April 1, 1934): 16ff.

Dickens, Charles. 1981. *David Copperfield*. Edited by Nina Burgis. Oxford, New York: Oxford University Press.

Dickinson, Emily. 1999. *The Poems of Emily Dickinson*. Edited by R. W. Franklin. Cambridge, Mass.: Belknap Press.

Diepeveen, Leonard. 1991. "Reading Nonsense: The Experience of Contemporary Poetry." *Genre* (Spring): 25–43.

———. 1996. "'I Can Have More than Enough Power to Satisfy Me:' T. S. Eliot's Construction of His Audience." In *Marketing Modernisms*, edited by Stephen Watt and Kevin J. H. Dettmar (37–60). Ann Arbor: University of Michigan Press.

"Director French Flees Deluge of Cubist Art." 1913. *Chicago Record-Herald* (March 21): 1.

Distel, Anne. 1995. *Renoir: A Sensuous Vision*. New York: H. N. Abrams.

Dobrée, Bonamy. 1929. *The Lamp and the Lute*. Oxford: Oxford University Press.

Dodge, Mabel. 1913. "Speculations, or Post-Impressionism in Prose." *Arts and Decoration* 3 (March 1913): 172–74.

Donne, John. 1633. *Poems, by J. D. with Elegies on the Authors Death*. London.

———. 1967. *The Complete Poetry of John Donne*. Edited by John T. Shawcross. Garden City, N.Y.: Doubleday Anchor.

Drew, Elizabeth. 1933. *Discovering Poetry*. New York: Norton.

Dubreuil-Blondin, Nicole. 1996. "Tightrope Metaphysics." In *Voices of Fire: Art, Rage, Power, and the State*, edited by Bruce Barber, Serge Guilbaut, and John O'Brian (153–64). Toronto: University of Toronto Press.

Dudley, Dorothy. 1977. "The Acid Test." In *Robert Frost: The Critical Reception* (65–76). New York: Burt Franklin. First published in *Poetry* 23 (March 1924): 328–35.

———. 1980. "A Small Garden Induced to Grow in Unlikely Surroundings." In *Willliam Carlos Williams: The Critical Heritage* (54–57). London: Routledge and Kegan Paul. First published in *Poetry* 12, no. 1 (April 1918): 38–43.

Duncan, Carol. 1995. *Civilizing Rituals: Inside Public Art Museums*. Edited by Jon Bird and Lisa Tickner, Re Visions: Critical Studies in the History and Theory of Art. London and New York: Routledge.

Dunlop, Ian. 1972. *The Shock of the New: Seven Historic Exhibitions of Modern Art*. New York: American Heritage Press.

Dupee, F. W. 1945. "Difficulty as Style." *American Scholar* 14, no. 3: 355–57.

Duyckinck, Evert Augustus. 1975. "Dr Donne." In *John Donne: the Critical Heritage* (384–87). London and Boston: Routledge and Kegan Paul. First published in *Arcturus, A Journal of Books and Opinions* (June 1841): 19–26.

Eastman, Max. 1913. *Enjoyment of Poetry*. New York: Charles Scribner's Sons.

———. 1929. "The Cult of Unintelligibility." *Harpers* (April): 632–39.

———. 1931. *The Literary Mind: Its Place in an Age of Science*. New York: Charles Scribner's Sons.

———. 1939. "Foreword." In *Anthology for the Enjoyment of Poetry*, edited by Max Eastman (ix–xvi). New York: Charles Scribner's Sons.

———. 1964. *Love and Revolution: My Journey through an Epoch*. New York: Random House.

———. 1970. "Poets Talking to Themselves." (Interview). In *James Joyce: The Critical Heritage* (Vol. 2, 416–19). London: Routledge and Kegan Paul. First published in *Harper's* no. 977 (October 1931): 563–74.

"Eclipse of the Highbrow." 1941. *New York Times* (March 25): 5.

Editors. 1927. "Introduction." *transition* (April): 135–38.

Ehrmann, Jacques. 1971. "The Death of Literature." *New Literary History* (Autumn): 31–47.

Eksteins, Modris. 1989. *Rites of Spring: The Great War and the Birth of the Modern Age*. Toronto: Lester and Orpen Dennys.

Elam, Helen Regueiro. 1991. "The Difficulty of Reading." In *The Idea of Difficulty in Literature*, edited by Alan C. Purves (73–89). Albany: State University of New York Press.

Eliot, T. S. 1918. "Professional, Or . . . " *Egoist* 5, no. 4: 61.

———. 1920. "A Brief Treatise on the Criticism of Poetry." *The Chapbook* (March): 1–10.

———. 1921a. "London Letter." *Dial* 70, no. 6 (June): 686–91.

———. 1921b. "London Letter." *Dial* 71, no. 4 (October): 452–55.

———. 1923a. "The Function of Criticism." *Criterion* (October): 31–42.

———. 1923b. "The Function of a Literary Review." *Criterion* (July): 421.

———. 1923c. "John Donne." *Nation and Athenaeum* (June 9): 331–32.

———. 1935. "Introduction." *Selected Poems by Marianne Moore* (vii–xiv). New York: Macmillan.

———. 1942. "The Music of Poetry." *Partisan Review* (November–December): 450–65.

———. 1964 [1933]. *The Use of Poetry and the Use of Criticism*. London: Faber and Faber.

———. 1965 [1917]. "Ezra Pound: His Metric and His Poetry." In *To Criticize the Critic and Other Writings* (162–82). London: Faber and Faber.

———. 1969 [1922]. "The Waste Land." In *Complete Poems and Plays of T. S. Eliot*. London: Faber and Faber.

———. 1969. *Complete Poems and Plays of T.S. Eliot*. London: Faber and Faber, 1969.

———.1975a [1929]. "Dante." In *Selected Prose of T. S. Eliot* (205–30). New York: Harcourt Brace Jovanovich, Farrar, Straus and Giroux.

———. 1975b. "The Metaphysical Poets." In *Selected Prose of T. S. Eliot* (59–67). New York: Harcourt Brace Jovanovich, Farrar, Straus and Giroux. First published in *Times Literary Supplement* (October 20, 1921): 669–70.

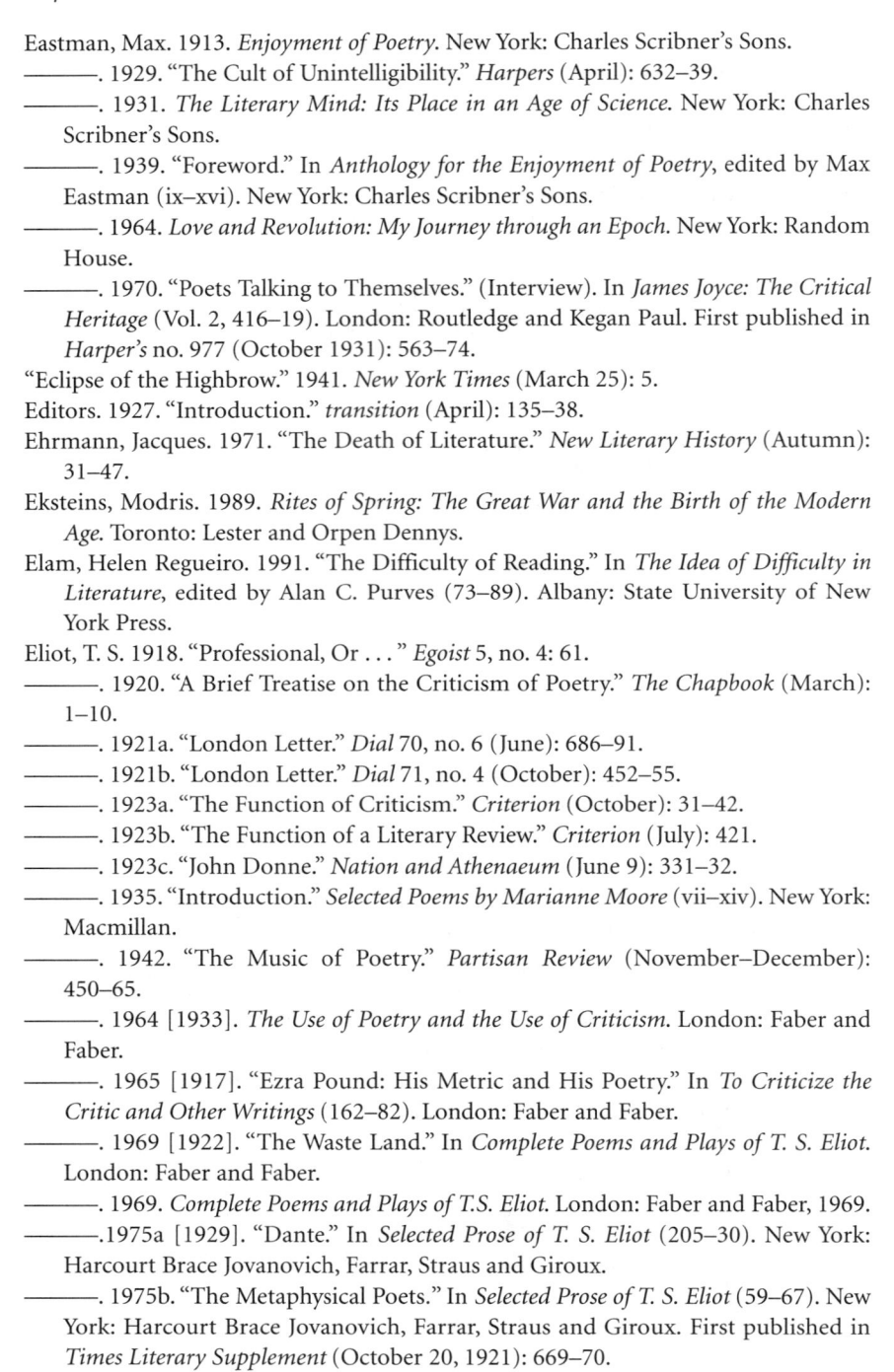

———. 1975c. "Philip Massinger." In *Selected Prose of T. S. Eliot* (153–60). New York:

Harcourt Brace Jovanovich, Farrar, Straus and Giroux. First published in *Times Literary Supplement* (May 27, 1920).

———. 1975d. "*Ulysses*, Order and Myth." In *Selected Prose of T. S. Eliot* (175–78). New York: Harcourt Brace Jovanovich Farrar, Straus and Giroux. First published in *Dial* 75 (November 1923): 480–83.

———. 1988. *The Letters of T. S. Eliot.* Vol. 1. Edited by Valerie Eliot. London: Faber and Faber.

Elkins, James. 1999. *Why Are Our Pictures Puzzles?: On the Modern Origins of Pictorial Complexity.* New York: Routledge.

Ellmann, Richard. 1982. *James Joyce.* 2nd ed. Oxford: Oxford University Press.

Ellsworth, William Webster. 1928. "Interlude." In *Readings from the New Poets*, edited by William Webster Ellsworth (157). New York: Macmillan.

Elton, Lord. 1941. *Notebook in Wartime.* London: Collins.

Empson, William. 1930. *Seven Types of Ambiguity.* London: Chatto and Windus.

———. 1940. *The Gathering Storm.* London: Faber and Faber.

Enright, D. J. 1984 [1955]. *Academic Year.* London: Buchan and Enright.

Esslin, Martin. 1969. *The Theatre of the Absurd.* Rev. ed. London: Doubleday.

Evans, M., and K. C. Lawson. 1949. "Foreword." In *Contemporary Verse: An Anthology*, edited by M. Evans and K. C. Lawson (v–vii). London and New York: Longmans, Green and Company.

Fadiman, Clifton. 1937. "Review of *Nightwood*, by Djuna Barnes." *New Yorker* (March 13): 83–85.

"Famous Cubists' Collection Here." 1913. *Chicago Daily Tribune* (March 22): 3.

Fausset, Hugh l'Anson. 1931. "The Poet and His Vision." *Bookman*: 341–42.

Feaver, William. 1985. "The Elusive Renoir." *Artnews* (December): 44–48.

Feger, Lois. 1970. "The Dark Dimension of Willa Cather's *My Antonia*." *English Journal* (September): 774–79.

Firkins, O. W. 1977. "Poets of the Day." Review of *A Boy's Will*, by Robert Frost. In *Robert Frost: The Critical Reception* (8–9). New York: Burt Franklin. First published in *The Nation* 101 (August 18, 1915): 228.

Fish, Stanley. 1980. "How to Recognize a Poem When You See One." In *Is There a Text in This Class?* (322–37). Cambridge: Harvard University Press.

———. 1985. "Anti-Professionalism." *New Literary History* (Autumn): 89–108.

Fitts, Dudley. 1972. "'Music Fit for the Odes.'" In *Ezra Pound: The Critical Heritage* (246–55). London: Routledge and Kegan Paul. First published in *Hound and Horn* 4 (Winter 1931): 278–89.

Flam, Jack. 1989. "In a Different Light." *Artnews* (Summer): 113–17.

Flanagan, George A. 1954. *How to Understand Modern Art.* New York: Studio Publications; Thomas Y. Crowell.

"Flat Prose." 1986. In *Critical Essays on Gertrude Stein* (38–39) Boston: G. K. Hall. First published in *Atlantic Monthly* 114 (September 1914): 431–32.

Fletcher, John Gould. 1985. "The Revival of Aestheticism." In *Wallace Stevens: The Critical Heritage* (46–47). London and Boston: Routledge and Kegan Paul. First published in *Freeman* 8 (December 19, 1923).

Flint, F. S. 1977. Review of *A Boy's Will*. In *Robert Frost: The Critical Reception* (3–4).

New York: Burt Franklin. First published in *Poetry and Drama*, 1 (June 1913): 250.

Flint, Peter B. 1993. "Federico Fellini, Film Visionary, Is Dead at 73." *New York Times* (November 1): A1, D10.

Ford, Ford Madox. 1922. "'Ulysses' and the Handling of Indecencies." *English Review* 35: 538–48.

Foucault, Michel. 1996. Interview with Raymond Bellour. In *Foucault Live* (19–32). New York: Semiotext(e). First published in *Les lettres française* (June 15, 1967). Reprint in *Le livre des autres* (Paris: UGE, 1978).

Fraser, G. S. 1964. *The Modern Writer and His World*. Rev. ed. Harmondsworth: Penguin.

Freeman, John. 1925. "Literary History and Criticism—II." *London Mercury* 11, no. 66 (May): 662–64.

Friedlaender, Marc. 1945. "Poetry and the Common Store." *American Scholar* (Summer): 362–65.

Frijda, Nico H. 1986. *The Emotions, Studies in Emotion and Social Interaction*. Cambridge; New York: Cambridge University Press; Paris: Editions de la Maison des sciences de l'homme.

Fromm, Harold. 1987. "Public Worlds/Private Muses: Criticism, Professionalism, and the Audience for the Arts." *Massachusetts Review* (Spring): 13–29.

Frost, Robert. 1956. "'Perfect Day—a Day of Prowess'." *Sports Illustrated* 5, no. 4 (July 23): 51–53.

———. 1963. "Interview by Richard Poirier." In *Writers at Work: Second Series*, edited by George Plimpton (9–34). New York: Penguin.

———. 1964. *Selected Letters of Robert Frost*. Edited by Lawrance Thompson. New York: Holt, Rinehart and Winston.

Fry, Roger. 1921. *Vision and Design*. London: Chatto and Windus.

Gablik, Suzi. 1984. *Has Modernism Failed?* New York: Thames and Hudson.

Gardner, Helen. 1936. *Art through the Ages*. New York: Harcourt, Brace.

Gardner, Howard. 1985. *The Mind's New Science: A History of the Cognitive Revolution*. New York: Basic Books.

Gaunt, William. 1970. *Impressionism: A Visual History*. New York: Praeger.

Geismar, Maxwell. 1943. *The Last of the Provincials: The American Novel, 1915–1925*. New York: Hill and Wang.

Gertsfelde, V. 1970. "A Communist on Joyce." In *James Joyce: The Critical Heritage* (Vol. 2, 616–18). London: Routledge and Kegan Paul. First published in *Living Age* 347 (November 1934): 268–70.

Gesner, Clark. 1967. *You're a Good Man, Charlie Brown*. New York: Random House.

Gibbs, Raymond W., Jr. 1994. *The Poetics of Mind: Figurative Thought, Language, and Understanding*. Cambridge: Cambridge University Press.

Gilbert, Stuart. 1970. "The Growth of a Titan." In *James Joyce: The Critical Heritage* (Vol. 2, 537–41). London: Routledge and Kegan Paul. First published in *Saturday Review of Literature*, 7 (August 2, 1930): 17–19.

Gilbert, W. S. 1986. From "Patience." In *The Norton Anthology of English Literature*. 5th ed. 2 vols. (Vol. 2, 1604–6). New York: W. W. Norton.

Gilbert-Rolfe, Jeremy. 1993. "Seriousness and Difficulty in Contemporary Art and Criticism." In *Theories of Contemporary Art*, edited by Richard Hertz (141–55). Englewood Cliffs, N.J.: Prentice-Hall.

Gilfillan, George. 1975. "Specimens with Memoirs of the Less-Known British Poets," 1860 Vol. 1, In *John Donne: The Critical Heritage* (420–24). London and Boston: Routledge and Kegan Paul.

Gillet, Louis. 1970. "A Propos de Finnegans Wake." In *James Joyce: The Critical Heritage* (Vol. 2, 724–30). London: Routledge and Kegan Paul. First published in *Babel* I (1940): 101–13. Translated by D. D. Paige as "Joyce's Treatment." *Quarterly Review of Literature* I, no. 2 (Winter 1944): 87–99.

Glare, P. G. W. 1990 *Oxford Latin Dictionary*. Oxford: Clarendon Press.

"'Godot' Gets Around." 1958. *Theatre Arts* (July): 73–74.

Gogarty, Oliver. 1970. "They Think They Know Joyce." In *James Joyce: The Critical Heritage* (Vol. 2, 764–65). London: Routledge and Kegan Paul. First published in *Saturday Review of Literature* 33 (18 March 1950): 8, 9, 36, 37.

Gold, Joseph. 1959. "Letter to the Editor." *Times Book Review* (May 3): 24.

Goldensohn, Barry. 1985. "Poetry Anthologies and the Canon." *Yale Review* 74, no. 3: 404–14.

Golding, Alan. 1995. *From Outlaw to Classic: Canons in American Poetry*. Madison: University of Wisconsin Press.

Gordon, Margery, and Marie B. King. 1923. "Foreword." In *Verse of Our Day: An Anthology of Modern American and British Poetry*, edited by Margery Gordon and Marie B. King (xi–xiii). New York: D. Appleton and Company.

Gorman, Herbert. 1929. "Experimentalism—and Experimentalists." *Modern Quarterly* 5, no. 3: 292–93.

Graff, Gerald. 1987. *Professing Literature: An Institutional History*. Chicago: University of Chicago Press.

Granville, Charles. 1972. "Modern Poetry." In *Ezra Pound: The Critical Heritage* (77–80). London: Routledge and Kegan Paul. First published in *Eye-Witness* (August 10, 1911): i, 247–48.

Graver, Lawrence, and Raymond Federman. 1979. "Introduction." In *Samuel Beckett: The Critical Heritage*, edited by Lawrence Graver and Raymond Federman (1–38). London: Routledge and Kegan Paul.

Gray, Jeffrey Alan. 1971. *The Psychology of Fear and Stress*. New York: McGraw-Hill.

Greenberg, Clement. 1959. "The Case for Abstract Art." *The Saturday Evening Post* (August 1): 18, 69–72.

———. 1961a. "T. S. Eliot: A Book Review." In *Art and Culture: Critical Essays* (239–44). Boston: Beacon.

———. 1961b. "Renoir." In *Art and Culture: Critical Essays* (46–49). Boston: Beacon.

Grierson, Herbert J. C. 1912. "Introduction." In *The Poems of John Donne*, edited by Herbert J. C. Grierson (v–cliii). London: Oxford University Press.

———. 1921. "Introduction." In *Metaphysical Lyrics and Poems of the Seventeenth Century: Donne to Butler*, edited by Herbert J.C. Grierson (xiii–lviii). Oxford: Oxford University Press.

Grigson, Geoffrey. 1972. "The Methodism of Ezra Pound. . In *Ezra Pound: The Critical Heritage* (259–64). London: Routledge and Kegan Paul. *New Verse* 5 (October 1933): 17–22.

Guerin, T. M., Jr. 1959. "Letter to the Editor." *New York Times Book Review* (May 3): 24.

Guillory, John. 1993. *Cultural Capital: The Problem of Literary Canon Formation.* Chicago: University of Chicago Press.

Gupta, Suman. 1993. "A Random House Advertisement." *James Joyce Quarterly* 30–31, no. 4–1: 861–68.

Habermas, Jürgen. 1976. "Systematically Distorted Communication." In *Critical Sociology*, edited by P. Connerton. Harmondsworth: Penguin.

Hansson, Gunnar. 1991. "Kinds of Understanding, Kinds of Difficulties in the Reading of Literature." In *The Idea of Difficulty in Literature*, edited by Alan C. Purves (93–115). Albany: State University of New York Press.

Harmon-Jones, Eddie. 2000. "A Cognitive Dissonance Theory Perspective on the Role of Emotion in the Maintenance and Change of Beliefs and Attitudes." In *Emotions and Beliefs: How Feelings Influence Thoughts*, edited by Nico H. Frijda, Antony S. R. Manstead and Sacha Bern (185–211). Cambridge: Cambridge University Press.

Harris, Michael. 1957. "'Godot' Presented at Quentin: Theme Not New to Cons." *San Francisco Chronicle* (November 24): 23.

Hauser, Arnold. 1982. *The Sociology of Art.* Chicago: University of Chicago Press.

Hayes, Colin. 1967. *Renoir.* London: Paul Hamlyn.

Heyward, Michael. 1993. *The Ern Malley Affair.* London: Faber and Faber.

Horowitz, Gregg M. 1996. "Public Art/Public Space: The Spectacle of the *Tilted Arc* Controversy." *Journal of Aesthetics and Art Criticism* 54: 8–14.

Housman, A. E. 1933. *The Name and Nature of Poetry.* Cambridge: Cambridge University Press.

"How to Enjoy James Joyce's Great Novel *Ulysses*." 1934. *Saturday Review of Literature* (February 10): 474–75.

Howarth, Patrick. 1963. *Squire: Most Generous of Men.* London: Hutchinson.

H. S. C. 1970. Review of *Ulysses*. In *James Joyce: The Critical Heritage* (Vol. 1, 242–46). London: Routledge and Kegan Paul. First published in *Carnegie Magazine* 7, no. 2 (February 1934): 279–81.

Huggins, A. W. F., and Marillyn Jager Adams. 1980. "Syntactic Aspects of Reading Comprehension." In *Theoretical Issues in Reading Comprehension: Perspectives from Cognitive Psychology, Linguistics, Artificial Intelligence, and Education*, edited by Rand J. Spiro, Bertram C. Bruce, and William F. Brewer (87–112). Hillsdale, N.J.: Lawrence Erlbaum Associates.

Huxley, Aldous, ed. 1933. *Texts and Pretexts: An Anthology with Commentaries.* New York: Harper.

Huyssen, Andreas. 1986. *After the Great Divide: Modernism, Mass Culture, Postmodernism.* Bloomington: Indiana University Press.

Hynds, Susan. 1991. "Questions of Difficulty in Literary Reading." In *The Idea of Difficulty in Literature*, edited by Alan C. Purves (117–39). Albany: State University of New York Press.

Ibsch, Elrud. 1986. "Reception Aesthetics Versus Emperical Research of Reader's Response." *Cahiers Ruomains d'Etudes Litteraires* 3: 38–48.
Jackson, Holbrook. 1970. "Ulysses à la Joyce." In *James Joyce: The Critical Heritage* (Vol. 1, 198–200). London: Routledge and Kegan Paul. First published in *To-Day* 9 (June 1922): 47–49.
Jacoby, Russell. 1994. *Dogmatic Wisdom: How the Culture Wars Divert Education and Distract America*. New York: Doubleday.
Jacquette, Dale. 1984. "Bosanquet's Concept of Difficult Beauty." *Journal of Aesthetics and Art Criticism* 43: 79–87.
Jaffé, Hans L. C. 1969. *The World of the Impressionists: The Artists Who Painted with Delight in Being Alive*. Maplewood, N.J.: Hammond.
James, Caryn. 1993. "Fellini's World Was So Real It Was Bizarre." *New York Times* (November 7): sec. 2, p. 26.
Jameson, Frederic. 1971. *Marxism and Form*. Princeton, N.J.: Princeton University Press.
Jarrell, Randall. 1942. "The End of the Line." *Nation* (February 21): 222–28.
———. 1953a. "The Obscurity of the Poet." In *Poetry and the Age* (3–25). New York: Vintage.
———. 1953b. "The Other Frost." In *Poetry and the Age* (26–33). New York: Vintage.
Jarvis, Simon. 1998. *Adorno: A Critical Introduction*. New York: Routledge.
Jauss, Hans Robert. 1982. *Toward an Aesthetic of Reception*. Vol. 2, *Theory and History of Literature*. Translated by Timothy Bahti. Minneapolis: University of Minnesota Press.
Jeromack, Paul. 1997. "Beyond Pneumatic Nudes." *Art Newspaper* 72: 33.
J. M. 1982. Review of *The Waste Land*. In *T.S. Eliot: The Critical Heritage* (Vol. 1, 170–72). London: Routledge and Kegan Paul. First published in *Double Dealer* 5 (May 1923): 173–74.
Johnson, Samuel. 1967. *Lives of the English Poets*. Edited by George Birkbeck Norman Hill. New York: Octagon Books.
Jolas, Eugène, Hans Arp, Samuel Beckett, Carl Einstein, Thomas McGreevy, Georges Pelorson, Theo Rutra, James J. Sweeney, Ronald Symond. 1932. "Poetry Is Vertical." *transition* (March): 148–49.
Jung, Carl. 1970. "*Ulysses*: ein Monolog." In *James Joyce: The Critical Heritage* (Vol. 2, 584–85). London: Routledge and Kegan Paul. First published in *Collected Works of C. G. Jung*. Vol. 15 (*The Spirit in Man, Art and Literature*) (1966). Translated by R. F. C. Hull (109–32).
Kazin, Alfred. 1942. *On Native Grounds: An Interpretation of Modern American Prose Literature*. New York: Harcourt, Brace and World.
Knowlson, James. 1996. *Damned to Fame: The Life of Samuel Beckett*. New York: Simon and Schuster.
Kövecses, Zoltán. 2000. *Metaphor and Emotion: Language, Culture, and Body in Human Emotion*. Studies in Emotion and Social Interaction. Cambridge: Cambridge University Press.
———. 2002. *Metaphor: A Practical Introduction*. New York: Oxford University Press.
Krenek, Ernst. 1966. "The Ivory Tower." In *Exploring Music* (155–65). London: Calder and Boyars.

Kronenberger, Louis. 1975. Review of *To the Lighthouse*. In *Virginia Woolf: The Critical Heritage* (195–98). London: Routledge and Kegan Paul. First published in *New York Times* (May 8, 1927): 2.

Lakoff, George. 1987. *Women, Fire, and Dangerous Things: What Categories Reveal About the Mind.* Chicago: University of Chicago Press.

Lakoff, George, and Mark Johnson. 1980. *Metaphors We Live By.* Chicago: University of Chicago Press.

Lakoff, George, and Mark Turner. 1989. *More Than Cool Reason: A Field Guide to Poetic Metaphor.* Chicago: University of Chicago Press.

Landon, Herman. 1913. "Hark! Hark! The Critics Bark! The Cubists Are Coming." Chicago Sunday *Record-Herald* (March 23): 2.

Larson, Magali Sarfatti. 1977. *The Rise of Professionalism.* Berkeley: University of California Press.

Leavis, F. R. 1931. "The Influence of Donne on Modern Poetry." *Bookman*: 346–47.

———. 1960 [1932]. *New Bearings in English Poetry: A Study of the Contemporary Situation.* Ann Arbor: University of Michigan Press.

Leavis, Q. D. 1965 [1932]. *Fiction and the Reading Public.* London: Chatto and Windus.

Lentricchia, Frank. 1994. *Modernist Quartet.* Cambridge: Cambridge University Press.

Leslie, Shane. 1970. "*Ulysses.*" In *James Joyce: The Critical Heritage* (Vol. 1, 206–11). London: Routledge and Kegan Paul. First published in *Quarterly Review* 238 (October 1922): 219–34.

Lewis, Sinclair. 1938. "The Greatest American Novelist." *Newsweek* (January 3): 29.

———. 1945. "Obscenity and Obscurity." *Esquire* (July): 51, 140.

Lewis, Wyndham. 1970 [1927]. "Time and Western Man." In *James Joyce: The Critical Heritage* (Vol. 1, 359–65). London: Routledge and Kegan Paul.

"A Line-O' Type or Two." 1913. *Chicago Daily Tribune* (March 22): 6.

Lipman, Samuel. 1982. "American Opera: Honors and Performances." *New Criterion*: 57–60.

Lowell, Amy. 1977. Review of *North of Boston*. In *Robert Frost: The Critical Reception* (17–21). New York: Burt Franklin. First published in *New Republic* 2 (February 20, 1915): 81–82.

Lucas, F. L. 1936. *The Decline and Fall of the Romantic Ideal.* Cambridge: Cambridge University Press.

———. 1982. Review of *The Waste Land*. In *T. S. Eliot: The Critical Heritage* (Vol. 1, 195–99). London: Routledge and Kegan Paul. First published in *New Statesman* 22 (3 November 1923): 116–18.

Lyall, Mary Mills. 1913. *The Cubies' ABC.* New York: G. P. Putnam's Sons.

Lynd, Robert. 1939. "Preface." In *Modern Poetry*, edited by Robert Lynd (v–ix). London: Thomas Nelson and Sons Ltd.

MacDougall, Curtis D. 1940. *Hoaxes.* New York: Macmillan.

MacNeice, Louis. 1968 [1938]. *Modern Poetry: A Personal Essay.* 2nd ed. Oxford: Oxford University Press.

Marcus, Jane. 1991. "Mousemeat: Contemporary Reviews of *Nightwood.*" In *Silence and*

Power: A Reevaluation of Djuna Barnes, edited by Mary Lynn Broe (195–204). Carbondale, Ill.: Southern Illinois University Press.

Marsh, Edward. 1914. "Prefatory Note." In *Georgian Poetry 1911–1912*, edited by Edward Marsh (n.p.). London: The Poetry Bookshop.

Martindale, Colin. 1990. *The Clockwork Muse: The Predictability of Artistic Change*. New York: Basic Books.

Mason, William. 1975. Note to *Religio Clerici*, 1796. In *John Donne: The Critical Heritage* (201–2). London and Boston: Routledge and Kegan Paul.

Matthiessen, F. O. 1947. *The Achievement of T. S. Eliot: An Essay on the Nature of Poetry*. New York and London: Oxford University Press.

Mayer, Richard E. 1983. *Thinking, Problem Solving, Cognition*. New York: W. H. Freeman.

McCallum, Pamela. 1993. "Obscurity." In *The New Princeton Encyclopedia of Poetry and Poetics*, edited by Alex Preminger and T. V. F. Brogan (849–51). Princeton, N.J.: Princeton University Press.

McCarthy, Desmond. 1945. "The Art Quake of 1910." *Listener* (February): 123–24, 29.

———. 1982. "New Poets, T. S. Eliot." In *T. S. Eliot: The Critical Heritage* (Vol. 1, 111–17). London: Routledge and Kegan Paul. First published in *New Statesman*. 16 (January 8, 1921): 418–20.

McClary, Susan. 1989. "Terminal Prestige: The Case of Avant-Garde Music Composition." *Cultural Critique* 12: 57–81.

McDonald, Gail. 1993. *Learning to Be Modern: Pound, Eliot, and the American University*. Oxford and New York: Oxford University Press.

McDowall, A. S. 1975. "The Enchantment of a Mirror." In *Virginia Woolf: The Critical Heritage* (95–97). London: Routledge and Kegan Paul. First published in *Times Literary Supplement* (October 26, 1922).

McGann, Jerome. 1993. *Black Riders: The Visible Language of Modernism*. Princeton, N.J.: Princeton University Press.

———. 1997. "The Alice Fallacy; or, Only God Can Make a Tree: A Dialogue of Pleasure and Instruction." In *Beauty and the Critic: Aesthetics in an Age of Cultural Studies*, edited by James Soderholm (46–73). Tuscaloosa: University of Alabama Press.

McGreevy, Thomas. 1931. *Thomas Stearns Eliot*. London: Chatto and Windus.

McRae, Brian. 1990. *Addison and Steele Are Dead: The English Department, Its Canon, and the Professionalization of Literary Criticism*. Newark: University of Delaware Press.

Mégroz, R. L. 1936. "Introduction." In *A Treasury of Modern Poetry: An Anthology of the Last Forty Years*, edited by R. L. Mégroz (vii–xiii). London: Sir Isaac Pitman and Sons.

Mellers, Wilfrid. 1947. *Studies in Contemporary Music*. London: Dennis Dobson.

Mellow, James R. 1974. *Charmed Circle: Gertrude Stein and Company*. New York: Praeger.

Menand, Louis. 1987. *Discovering Modernism: T. S. Eliot and His Context*. New York: Oxford University Press.

Meyers, Jeffrey. 1996. *Robert Frost: A Biography*. Boston and New York: Houghton Mifflin.

Middleton, Jo Ann. 1990. *Willa Cather's Modernism: A Study of Style and Technique*. Rutherford, N.J.: Fairleigh Dickinson University Press.

M. L. 1995. "Cult of Infantilism." In *William Faulkner: The Contemporary Reviews* (161–63). Cambridge: Cambridge University Press. First published in *American Spectator* (February–March 1937): 13–14.

Monnier, Adrienne. 1970. "L'Ulysse de Joyce et le Public Francais." In *James Joyce: The Critical Heritage* (Vol. 2, 462–65). London: Routledge and Kegan Paul. First published in *La Gazette des Amis des Livres* 3, no. 10 (May 1940): 50–64. Translated by Sylvia Beach in *Kenyon Review* 8 (Summer 1946): 430–44.

Monro, Harold. 1920a. "Introduction." In *An Anthology of Recent Poetry*, edited by L. D'O. Walters (v–xxiii). New York: Dodd, Mead and Company.

———. 1920b. *Some Contemporary Poets*. London: Leonard Parsons.

———. 1982. "Notes for a Study of 'The Waste Land': An Imaginary Dialogue with T. S. Eliot." In *T. S. Eliot: The Critical Heritage* (Vol. 1, 162–66). London: Routledge and Kegan Paul. First published in *The Chapbook* 34 (February 1923): 20–24.

Monroe, Harriet. 1917. "Introduction." In *The New Poetry: An Anthology of Twentieth-Century Verse in English*, edited by Harriet Monroe and Alice Corbin Henderson (v–xiii). New York: Macmillan.

———. 1922. "A Symposium on Marianne Moore." *Poetry* 19, no. 4 (January): 208–17.

———. 1923. "A Contrast." *Poetry* 21, no. 6 (March): 325–31.

———. 1927. "Wanted—a Theme." *Poetry* 31, no. 2 (November): 86–91.

Moore, Marianne. 1986a. "The Cantos." Review of *A Draft of XXX Cantos*, by Ezra Pound. In *The Complete Prose of Marianne Moore* (268–77). New York: Viking. First published in *Poetry* (October 1931): 37–56.

———. 1986b. "Feeling and Precision." In *The Complete Prose of Marianne Moore* (396–402). New York: Viking. First published in *Sewanee Review* 52 (Autumn 1944): 499–507.

———. 1986c. "A Note on T. S. Eliot's Book." Review of *Prufrock and Other Observations*. In *The Complete Prose of Marianne Moore* (35). New York: Viking. First published in *Poetry* 12 (April 1918): 36–39.

———. 1986d. Review of *Collected Poems, 1921–1931*, by William Carlos Williams. In *The Complete Prose of Marianne Moore* (325–27). New York: Viking. First published in *Poetry* 44 (May 1934): 103–6.

Moorman, Margaret. 1985. "Arc Enemies." *Artnews* (May): 13, 156.

Morgan, Louise. 1982. "The Poetry of Mr. Eliot." In *T. S. Eliot: The Critical Heritage* (Vol. 1, 219–22). London: Routledge and Kegan Paul. First published in *Outlook* 57 (February 20, 1926): 135–36.

Morley, Chistopher. 1926. "Every Tuesday." In *The Romany Stain* (205–10). Garden City, N.Y.: Doubleday, Page.

Morris, Timothy. 1995. *Becoming Canonical in American Poetry*. Urbana and Chicago: University of Illinois Press.

Morton, David. 1923. "Promise and Achievement." *Bookman* (February): 765–66.

Moscato, Michael, and Leslie LeBlanc, eds. 1984. *The United States of America V. One Book Entitled Ulysses by James Joyce*. Frederick, Md.: University Publications of America.

Muggeridge, Malcolm. 1970. Review of *Finnegans Wake*. In *James Joyce: The Critical Heritage* (Vol. 2, 683–84). London: Routledge and Kegan Paul. First published in *Time and Tide* (May 20, 1939): 654–55.

Muir, Edwin. 1962. *The Estate of Poetry, The Charles Eliot Norton Lectures 1955–56*. Cambridge: Harvard University Press.

———. 1972. Review of *Hugh Selwyn Mauberley*. In *Ezra Pound: The Critical Heritage* (194–95). London: Routledge and Kegan Paul. First published in *New Age* 31 (October 5, 1922): 288.

———. 1975. Review of *To the Lighthouse*. In *Virginia Woolf: The Critical Heritage* (209–10). London: Routledge and Kegan Paul. First published in *Nation and Athenaeum* (July 2, 1927): 450.

Munson, Gorham. 1980 [1928]. *Destinations: A Canvass of American Literature since 1900*. In *William Carlos Williams: The Critical Heritage* (93–108). London: Routledge and Kegan Paul.

———. 1982. "The Esotericism of T. S. Eliot." In *T. S. Eliot: The Critical Heritage* (203–12). London: Routledge and Kegan Paul. First published in *1924* (July 1, 1924): 3–10.

Munson-Williams-Proctor Institute, Henry Street Settlement (New York, N.Y.), and Association of American Painters and Sculptors New York. 1963. *1913 Armory Show; 50th Anniversary Exhibition, 1963*. Utica.

Murphy, Gwendolen. 1938. "Introduction." In *The Modern Poet*, edited by Gwendolen Murphy (xv–xx). London: Sidgwick and Jackson.

Murphy, John J. 1984. *Critical Essays on Willa Cather*. Boston: G. K. Hall.

Murry, J. Middleton. 1970. Review of *Ulysses*. In *James Joyce: The Critical Heritage* (Vol. 1, 195–98). London: Routledge and Kegan Paul. First published in *Nation and Atheneum* 31 (April 22, 1922): 124–25.

———. 1977. Review of *Wild Swans at Coole*. In *W. B. Yeats: The Critical Heritage* (216–20). London: Routledge and Kegan Paul. First published in *Anthenaeum* (April 4, 1919).

———. 1983. *The Letters of John Middleton Murry to Katherine Mansfield*. Edited by C. A. Hankin. London: Constable.

Nabokov, Vladimir. 1973. "Interview." In *Strong Opinions* (9–19). New York: Vintage International.

Nead, Lynn. 1985. "'Pleasing, Cheerful and Pretty?' Sexual and Cultural Politics at the Hayward Gallery." *Oxford Art Journal* 8, no. 1: 72–74.

Neff, Emory. 1959. "Letter to the Editor." *New York Times Book Review* (May 3): 24.

New Books in Nineteenth-Century Studies. 2002. University of Southern California Department of English. Retrieved February 11, 2002, from http://www.usc.edu/dept/LAS/english/19c/books/book-0–312–22318–8.html.

Newcomb, John Timberman. 1992. *Wallace Stevens and Literary Canons*. Jackson: University Press of Mississippi.

Newman, J. K. 1967. *Augustus and the New Poetry.* Vol. 88, *Collection Latomus.* Bruxelles, Berchem: Latomus revue d'études latines.

Nichols, Charles H. 1995. "The Achievement of William Faulkner." In *William Faulkner: The Contemporary Reviews* (360–61). Cambridge: Cambridge University Press. First published in *Phylon* 15 (2nd Quarter 1954): 209–10.

Nichols, Robert. 1972. "Poetry and Mr. Pound." In *Ezra Pound: The Critical Heritage* (165–67). London: Routledge and Kegan Paul. First published in *Observer* (January 11, 1920): 6.

Nicholson, Harold. 1970. "The Significance of James Joyce." In *James Joyce: The Critical Heritage* (Vol. 2, 560–63). London: Routledge and Kegan Paul. First published in *Listener* (December 16, 1931): 1062.

Nietzsche, Friedrich. 1960 [1886]. *Joyful Wisdom.* New York: Frederick Ungar.

Nochlin, Linda, Peter Schjeldahl, Charles Stuckey, Gary Stepeh, Michal Fried, Carter Ratcliff, Robert Rosenblum, Mel Bochner, Thomas Crow, André Fermigier, Walter Robinson, Brook Adams, Paul Tucker, and Lynne Tillman. 1986. "Renoir: A Symposium." *Art in America*: 103–24.

Norman Rockwell: Painting America. 2002. Retrieved February 18, 2002, from http://www.drjohnholleman.com/bs/normrock.html.

"Not Here, O Apollo." 1982. In *T. S. Eliot: The Critical Heritage.* London: Routledge and Kegan Paul. First published in *Times Literary Supplement* 908 (June 1919): 322.

Novitz, David. 1997. "The Anaesthetics of Emotion." In *Emotion and the Arts*, edited by Mette Hjort and Sue Laver (246–62). New York and Oxford: Oxford University Press.

Noyes, Alfred. 1970. "Rottenness in Literature." In *James Joyce: The Critical Heritage* (274–75). London: Routledge and Kegan Paul. First published in *Sunday Chronicle* (October 29, 1922): 2.

Nystrand, Martin. 1991. "Making It Hard: Curriculum and Instruction as Factors in the Difficulty of Literature." In *The Idea of Difficulty in Literature*, edited by Alan C. Purves (141–56). Albany: State University of New York Press.

Oatley, Keith. 1992. *Best Laid Schemes: The Psychology of Emotions, Studies in Emotion and Social Interaction.* Cambridge and New York: Cambridge University Press; Paris: Editions de la Maison des Science de l'Homme.

O'Brian, John. 1996. "Introduction: Bruising the Public Eye." In *Voices of Fire: Art, Rage, Power, and the State*, edited by Bruce Barber, Serge Guilbaut, and John O'Brian (3–21). Toronto: University of Toronto Press.

O'Brien, Sharon. 1984. "The Thing Not Named: Willa Cather as a Lesbian Writer." *Signs* 9, no. 4: 576–99.

———. 1988. "Becoming Noncanonical: The Case against Willa Cather." *American Quarterly* 40, no. 1: 110–25.

O'Connor, William Van. 1945. "This Alexandrian Criticism." *The American Scholar* (Summer): 357–61.

———. 1948. "Forms of Obscurity." In *Sense and Sensibility in Modern Poetry* (227–39). Chicago: University of Chicago Press.

O'Donnell, George Marion. 1995. "Mr. Faulkner Flirts with Failure." In *William Faulkner: The Contemporary Reviews* (142–44). Cambridge: Cambridge University Press. First published in Nashville *Banner* (October 25, 1936): Magazine section, 8.

O'Hara, Daniel T. 1988. *Lionel Trilling: The Work of Liberation*. Madison: University of Wisconsin Press.

Öhman, Arne. 1993. "Fear and Anxiety as Emotional Phenomena: Clinical Phenomenology, Evolutionary Perspectives, and Information-Processing Mechanisms." In *Handbook of Emotions*, edited by Michael Lewis and Jeannette M. Haviland (511–36). New York: Guilford.

Orton, Fred. 1985. "Reactions to Renoir Keep Changing." *Oxford Art Journal* 8, no. 2: 28–35.

Pach, Walter. 1960 [1951]. "Pierre Auguste Renoir." In *Pierre Auguste Renoir* (11–30). New York: Abrams.

Palgrave, Francis Turner. 1861. *Palgrave's Golden Treasury of Poems and Songs*. Revised and enlarged ed. New York: Thomas Y. Crowell,.

Palmer, Herbert. 1931. *Cinder Thursday*. London: Ernest Benn.

———. 1938. *Post-Victorian Poetry*. London: J. M. Dent and Sons.

Parkes, Henry Bamford. 1972. "Two Pounds of Poetry." In *Ezra Pound: The Critical Heritage* (239–42). London: Routledge and Kegan Paul. First published in *New English Weekly* 2 (December 22, 1932): 227–28.

Parsons, I. M. 1936. "Introduction." In *The Progress of Poetry: An Anthology of Verse from Hardy to the Present Day*, edited by I. M. Parsons (xi–xl). London: Chatto and Windus.

Payne, William Morton. 1977. Review of *A Boy's Will*. In *Robert Frost: The Critical Reception* (4–5). New York: Burt Franklin. First published in *Dial* 55 (September 16, 1913): 211–12.

Pearson, John. 1978. *Façades: Edith, Osbert, and Sacheverall Sitwell*. London: Macmillan.

Peck, Demaree C. 1996. *The Imaginative Claims of the Artist in Willa Cather's Fiction*. Danvers: Associated University Presses.

Pelorson, Georges. 1970. "*Finnegans Wake* of James Joyce, or the Book of Man." In *James Joyce: The Critical Heritage* (Vol. 2, 680–83). London: Routledge and Kegan Paul. First published in *Aux Ecoutes* 23, no. 1096 (May 20, 1939): 29.

Perelman, Bob. 1994. *The Trouble with Genius: Reading Pound, Joyce, Stein, and Zukofsky*. Berkeley and Los Angeles: University of California Press.

Perin, Constance. 1994. "The Reception of New, Unusual, and Difficult Art." In *The Artist Outsider: Creativity and the Boundaries of Culture*, edited by Michael D. Hall and Eugene W. Metcalf (172–97). Washington: Smithsonian Institution Press.

Perloff, Marjorie. 1985. *The Dance of the Intellect: Studies in the Poetry of the Pound Tradition*. Cambridge: Cambridge University Press.

Peschmann, Hermann. 1950. "Introduction." In *The Voice of Poetry (1930–1950)*, edited by Hermann Peschmann (xxv–xliii). London: Evans Brothers Limited.

Phillips, Patricia C. 1985. "Forum: Something There Is That Doesn't Love a Wall." *Artforum* 23: 100–1.

Pierce, Frederick E. 1977. "Three Poets Against Philistis." In *Robert Frost: The Critical Reception* (70). New York: Burt Franklin. First published in *Yale Review* 18 (December 1928): 365–66.

Pinto, Vivian de Sola. 1951. *Crisis in English Poetry: 1880–1940*. London: Hutchinson House.

"The Play's the Thing . . . " 1957. *San Quentin News* (November 28): 2.

Poirier, Richard. 1977. *Robert Frost: The Work of Knowing*. New York: Oxford University Press.

———. 1992. "The Difficulties of Modernism and the Modernism of Difficulty." In *Critical Essays on American Modernism* (104–14). New York: G.K. Hall. First published in *Humanities in Society* 1 (1978): 271–82.

Pomeroy, Wardell Baxter. 1968. *Boys and Sex*. New York: Delacorte Press.

Pool, Phoebe. 1967. *Impressionism*. London: Thames and Hudson.

Pound, Ezra. 1914. "The Audience." *Poetry* 5: 29–30.

———. 1917. "A Letter from Remy De Gourmont." *Little Review* 9: 6–7.

———. 1918. "A List of Books." *Little Review* (March): 54–58.

———. 1921. "Review of *Poesies*, by Jean Cocteau." *Dial* (January): 110.

———. 1934. *ABC of Reading*. New York: New Directions.

———. 1952 [1910]. *The Spirit of Romance*. Norfolk, Conn.: New Directions.

———. 1954a. "Dubliners and Mr James Joyce." Review of *Dubliners* by James Joyce. In *Literary Essays of Ezra Pound* (399–402). New York: New Directions. First published in *Egoist* 1, no. 14 (July 15, 1914).

———. 1954b. "Lionel Johnson." In *Literary Essays of Ezra Pound* (361–70). New York: New Directions. First published in Preface to *The Poetical Works of Lionel Johnson*, London: Elkin Mathews, 1915.

———. 1954c. Review of *North of Boston* by Robert Frost. In *Literary Essays of Ezra Pound* (384–86). New York: New Directions. First published in *Poetry* 5, no. 3 (December 1914).

———. 1954d. "The Serious Artist." In *Literary Essays of Ezra Pound* (41–57). New York: New Directions. First published in *The Egoist* (1913).

———. 1970. "James Joyce et Pécuchet." In *James Joyce: The Critical Heritage* (263–67). London: Routledge and Kegan Paul. First published in *Mercure de France* 156 (June 1922): 307–20.

———. 1973. "Affirmations: As for Imagisme." In *Selected Prose 1909–1965* (374–77). New York: New Directions. First published in *The New Age* (January 28, 1915).

———. 1977. "*A Boy's Will*." In *Robert Frost: The Critical Reception* (1–2). New York: Burt Franklin. First published in *Poetry* 2 (May 1913): 72–74.

———. 1982. T. S. Eliot In *T. S. Eliot: The Critical Heritage* (75–80). London: Routledge and Kegan Paul. First published in *Poetry* 10 (August 1917): 264–71.

Powell, Charles. 1982. Review of *The Waste Land*. In *T. S. Eliot: The Critical Heritage* (Vol. 1, 194–95). London: Routledge and Kegan Paul. First published in *Manchester Guardian* (October 31, 1923): 7.

Powell, Dilys. 1934. *Descent from Parnassus*. London: Cresset.

Powys, John Cooper. 1929. "Edgar Lee Masters." *Bookman* 69: 650–56.

"Preludes to a Mood." 1977. In *Ernest Hemingway: The Critical Reception* (7–8). Greensboro: Burt Franklin. First published in *New York Times Book Review* (October 18, 1925): 8.

Princenthal, Nancy. 1997. "The Arrogance of Pleasure." *Art in America* 85, no. 10: 106–9.

Pritchard, William H. 1984. *Frost: A Literary Life Reconsidered*. Oxford: Oxford University Press.

"Procession of the Muses." 1977. Review of *A Boy's Will*. In *Robert Frost: The Critical Reception* (5) New York: Burt Franklin. First published in *Academy* 85 (September 20, 1913): 360.

"Professionalism in Art." 1918. *Times Literary Supplement* (January 31): 49–50.

Publicity brochure. 1914. New York: Claire Marie.

Purves, Alan C. 1991a. "Indeterminate Texts, Responsive Readers, and the Idea of Difficulty in Literature." In *The Idea of Difficulty in Literature*, edited by Alan C. Purves (157–70). Albany: State University of New York Press.

———. 1991b. "Introduction." In *The Idea of Difficulty in Literature*, edited by Alan C. Purves (1–4). Albany: State University of New York Press.

Purves, Alan C., ed. 1991. *The Idea of Difficulty in Literature*. Albany: State University of New York Press.

"Pushcarts and Other Poetic Things." 1922. *New York Times Book Review* (December 17): 2.

Rahv, Philip. 1937. "The Taste of Nothing." Review of *Nightwood*, by Djuna Barnes. *The New Masses* 23, no. 1: 32–33.

Rainey, Lawrence S. 1998. *Institutions of Modernism: Literary Elites and Public Culture*. Henry McBride Series in Modernism and Modernity. New Haven: Yale University Press.

Ransom, John Crowe. 1938. *The World's Body*. New York: Charles Scribner's Sons.

———. 1982. "Waste Lands." In *T. S. Eliot: The Critical Heritage* (Vol. 1, 172–79). London: Routledge and Kegan Paul. First published in *New York Evening Post Literary Review* 3 (July 14, 1923): 825–26.

———. 1984. "Poetry: I, The Formal Analysis." In *Selected Essays of John Crowe Ransom* (192–212). Baton Rouge: Louisiana State University Press. First published in *Kenyon Review* 9 (Summer 1947): 436–56.

Read, Herbert. 1938a."The Nature of Metaphysical Poetry." In *Collected Essays in Literary Criticism* (69–88). London: Faber and Faber.

———. 1938b. "Obscurity in Poetry." In *Collected Essays in Literary Criticism* (89–100). London: Faber and Faber.

———. 1964. "The Modern Epoch in Art." In *The Philosophy of Modern Art* (17–43). London: Faber and Faber.

Recht, Harold W. 1995. "Southern Family Sinks into Dark Mental Decadence." In *William Faulkner: The Contemporary Reviews* (34–35). Cambridge: Cambridge University Press. First published in Philadelphia *Record* (September 29, 1929).

Reeves, James. 1962. *Georgian Poetry*. Penguin Poets. Harmondsworth, Middlesex, Eng.: Penguin.

Rehm, George. 1970. Review of *Ulysses*. In *James Joyce: The Critical Heritage* (Vol. 1, 212–13). London: Routledge and Kegan Paul. First published in *Chicago Tribune* 13 February 1922: 2.

Review of *Harmonium*, by Wallace Stevens. *Bookman*, October 1931, 207–8.

Review of *Prufrock and Other Observations*. 1982a. In *T. S. Eliot: The Critical Heritage* (Vol. 1, 74). London: Routledge and Kegan Paul. First published in *Literary World* (July 5, 1917): 107.

Review of *Prufrock and Other Observations*. 1982b. In *T. S. Eliot: The Critical Heritage* (Vol. 1, 75). New York: Routledge and Kegan Paul. First published in *New Statesman* 40 (August 1917): 477.

Review of *The Waste Land*. 1982. In *T.S. Eliot: The Critical Heritage* (Vol. 1, 134–35). London: Routledge and Kegan Paul. First published in *Times Literary Supplement* (October 26, 1922): 690.

Review of *The Winding Stair* by William Butler Yeats. 1977. In *W. B. Yeats: The Critical Heritage* (299–301). London: Routledge and Kegan Paul. First published in *Times Literary Supplement* (November 6, 1930).

Reynolds, Frank. 1910. "Post-Impressionist Expressions." *Illustrated London News* (December 3): 883.

Richards, I. A. 1960 [1935]. *Coleridge on Imagination*. Bloomington: Indiana University Press.

Riding, Laura. 1980 [1933]. *The Poems of Laura Riding: A New Edition of the 1938 Collection*. Manchester: Carcanet New Press.

Riding, Laura, and Robert Graves. 1927. *A Survey of Modernist Poetry*. London: Heinemann.

Rifkin, Ned. 1999. "Why Norman Rockwell, Why Now?" In *Norman Rockwell: Pictures for the American People*, edited by Ned Rifkin and Laurie Norton Moffatt (17–20). New York: Harry N. Abrams.

Robbins, Bruce. 1993. *Secular Vocations: Intellectuals, Professionalism, Culture*. London and New York: Verso.

Robbins, Rossell Hope. 1951. *The T. S. Eliot Myth*. New York: Henry Schuman.

Roberts, Frank Cecil. 1979. *Obituaries from the Times, 1951–1960: Including an Index to All Obituaries and Tributes Appearing in the Times During the Years 1951–1960*. Reading, Eng. and Westport, Conn.: Newspaper Archive Developments; distributed in North and South America by Meckler Books.

Roberts, Michael. 1932. "Preface." In *New Signatures: Poems by Several Hands*, edited by Michael Roberts (7–20). London: Hogarth Press.

———. 1936. "Introduction." In *The Faber Book of Modern Verse*, edited by Michael Roberts (1–35). London: Faber and Faber.

Robertson, D. W., Jr. 1958. "Translator's Introduction." In *On Christian Doctrine*, edited by D. W. Robertson. Indianapolis: Bobbs-Merrill.

Robinson, Lillian S. 1997 [1983]. "Treason Our Text: Feminist Challenges to the Literary Canon." In *Feminisms: An Anthology of Literary Theory and Criticism*, edited by Robyn R. Warhol and Diane Price Herndi (115–28). New Brunswick, N.J.: Rutgers.

Robinson, Ted. 1995. "Faulkner's New Book Engrossing." In *William Faulkner: The Contemporary Reviews* (46). Cambridge: Cambridge University Press. First published in Cleveland *Plain Dealer* (October 12, 1930): Amusement section, 17.

Rockwell, Norman. 1960. *Norman Rockwell: My Adventures as an Illustrator*. New York: Doubleday.

Rodman, Selden. 1938. "Introduction." In *A New Anthology of Modern Poetry*, edited by Selden Rodman (21–46). New York: Random House.

———. 1946. "Introduction." In *A New Anthology of Modern Poetry*, edited by Selden Rodman (xxvii–xlvi). New York: Modern Library.

———. 1949. "Introduction." In *100 Modern Poems*, edited by Selden Rodman (vi–xxx). New York: Pellegrini and Cudahy.

Rogers, Robert E. 1986. "*Tender Buttons*, Curious Experiment of Gertrude Stein in Literary Anarchy." In *Critical Essays on Gertrude Stein* (31–33). Boston: G. K. Hall. First published in *Boston Evening Transcript* (July 11, 1914): 12.

Roosevelt, Theodore. 1913. "A Layman's View of an Art Exhibition." *The Outlook* 103: 718–20.

Root, E. Merrill. 1977. "Encore for the Morning Stars!" In *Robert Frost: The Critical Reception* (74–75). New York: Burt Franklin. First published in *The Christian Century*, 46 (January 3, 1929): 19–20.

Rosen, Charles. 1998. "Classical Music in Twilight." *Harper's* (March): 52–58.

Rosenberg, Harold. 1975. "The Cubist Epoch." In *Art on the Edge: Creators and Situations* (162–72). New York: Macmillan.

Rosenfeld, Paul. 1980 [1924.] "Fleeting Patterns." *Port of New York*. In *William Carlos Williams: The Critical Heritage* (76–82). London: Routledge and Kegan Paul.

Rosten, Norman. 1959. "Letter to the Editor." *New York Times Book Review* (May 3).

Rothschild, Edward F. 1972 [1934]. "The Meaning of Unintelligibility in Modern Art." In *Studies of Meaning in Art*. New York: Arno.

Rumelhart, David E. 1980. "Schemata: The Building Blocks of Cognition." In *Theoretical Issues in Reading Comprehension: Perspectives from Cognitive Psychology, Linguistics, Artificial Intelligence, and Education*, edited by Rand J. Spiro, Bertram C. Bruce, and William F. Brewer (33–58). Hillsdale, N.J.: Lawrence Erlbaum Associates.

Russell, Francis. 1954. *Three Studies in Twentieth Century Obscurity*. London: Hand and Flower Press.

Rybert, Walter. 1970. "How to Read *Finnegans Wake*." In *James Joyce: The Critical Heritage* (Vol. 2, 731–36). London: Routledge and Kegan Paul. First published in *New Horizons* 3 (November–December 1940): 14–19, 31.

Saint-Saëns, Camille. 1956 [1913]. *École buisonnière*. In *Composers on Music: An Anthology of Composers' Writings from Palestrina to Copland* (228–29). New York: Pantheon.

Sandburg, Carl. 1972. "The Work of Ezra Pound." In *Ezra Pound: The Critical Heritage* (112–17). London: Routledge and Kegan Paul. First published in *Poetry* 7 (February 1916): 249–57.

Sayler, Oliver M. 1930. "The Implications of Revolt." In *Revolt in the Arts: A Survey of the Creation, Distribution and Appreciation of Art in America*, edited by Oliver M. Sayler (55–172). New York: Brentano's.

Schlauch, Margaret. 1970. "The Language of James Joyce." In *James Joyce: The Critical Heritage* (Vol. 2, 722–24). London: Routledge and Kegan Paul. First published in *Science and Society, A Marxian Quarterly* 3, No. 4 (Fall 1939): 482–97.

Schneider, Alan. 1993. "Waiting for Beckett." In *Critical Essays on Samuel Beckett* (69–83). Aldershot Eng.: Scolar Press. First published in *Chelsea Review* (Autumn 1958): 3–13, 15–20.

Schoenberg, Arnold. 1950. *Style and Idea*. New York: Philosophical Library.

———. 1975 [1937]. "How One Becomes Lonely." In *Style and Idea* (30–53) edited by Leonard Stein. Berkeley: University of California Press.

Scorsese, Martin. 1993. "Letter to the Editor: Why Make Fellini the Scapegoat for New Cultural Intolerance?" *New York Times* (November 25): A26:4.

Searle, Leroy F. 1994. "New Criticism." In *The Johns Hopkins Guide to Literary Theory and Criticism*, edited by Michael Groden and Martin Kreisworth (528–34). Baltimore: Johns Hopkins University Press.

Seiffert, Marjorie Allen. 1923. "The Intellectual Tropics." *Poetry* 23, no. 3 (December): 154–60.

Seldes, Gilbert. 1982. "T. S. Eliot." In *T. S. Eliot: The Critical Heritage* (Vol. 1, 144–51). London: Routledge and Kegan Paul. First published in *Nation* (December 6, 1922): cxv, 614–16.

Senie, Harriet. 1989. "Richard Serra's "Tilted Arc": Art and Non-Art Issues." *Art Journal* 48: 298–302.

Sergeant, Elizabeth Shepley. 1927. *Fire under the Andes: A Group of Literary Portraits*. Port Washington: Kennikat.

Serra, Richard. 1980. "Interview with Douglas Crimp." In *Richard Serra: Interviews, Etc., 1970–1980*, edited by Richard Serra and Clara Weyergraf. Yonkers: Hudson River Museum.

———. 1989. "'Tilted Arc' Destroyed." *Art in America* 77 (May): 35–47.

Serra, Richard, and Clara Weyergraf. 1980. *Richard Serra: Interviews, Etc., 1970–1980*. Yonkers: Hudson River Museum.

Sessions, Roger. 1950. *The Musical Experience of Composer, Performer, Listener*. Princeton, N.J.: Princeton University Press.

Sessions, Roger. 1979. *Roger Sessions on Music: Collected Essays*. Edited by Edward T. Cone. Princeton, N.J.: Princeton University Press.

Shakespeare, William. 1972. *The Complete Signet Classic Shakespeare*. Edited by Sylvan Barnet. New York: Harcourt Brace Jovanovich.

"Shakespeare for Mere Mortals." 1993. *New York Times* (September 3): A22.

"Shantih, Shantih, Shantih: Has the Reader Any Rights before the Bar of Literature?" *Time* 1, no. 1 (1923): 12.

Sharp, Robert Lathrop. 1934. "Some Light on Metaphysical Obscurity and Roughness." *Studies in Philology* 31: 497–518.
Shetley, Vernon. 1993. *After the Death of Poetry: Poet and Audience in Contemporary America*. Durham and London: Duke University Press.
Shipp, Cameron. 1995. "Confederacy's Hamlet: Faulkner's New Novel." In *William Faulkner: The Contemporary Reviews* (150–51). Cambridge: Cambridge University Press. First published in Charlotte *News* (November 1, 1936): 8–B.
Shklovsky, Victor. 1965. "Art as Technique." In *Russian Formalist Criticism: Four Essays* (3–24). Lincoln: University of Nebraska Press. First published in *Sborniki* 2 (1917).
Shrdlu, Etaoin. 1957. "Bastille by the Bay." *News* (November 28): 2.
Silver, Kenneth E. 1998. "An Invented Paradise." *Art in America* 86, no. 3 (March): 78–87.
Simpson, J. A., and E. S. C. Weiner. 1989. *The Oxford English Dictionary*. 2nd ed. Oxford and New York: Oxford University Press.
Sinclair, Lister. 1997. *Ideas*. CBC Radio.
Sinclair, May. 1982. "'Prufrock and Other Observations': A Criticism." In *T. S. Eliot: The Critical Heritage* (Vol. 1, 83–88). London: Routledge and Kegan Paul. First published in *Little Review* 4 (December 1917): 8–14.
Sitwell, Edith. 1926. *Poetry and Criticism*. New York: Henry Holt and Company.
———. 1934. *Aspects of Modern Poetry*. London: Duckworth.
Smith, A. J., ed. 1975. *John Donne: The Critical Heritage*. London and Boston: Routledge and Kegan Paul.
Smith, J. C. 1925. "Preface." In *A Book of Modern Verse*, edited by J. C. Smith (iii–vi). Oxford: Clarendon Press.
Smith, Paul Jordan. 1969 [1934]. *A Key to the Ulysses of James Joyce*. New York: Haskell House.
Soupault, Philipe. 1970. "Autour de James Joyce." In *James Joyce: The Critical Heritage* (Vol. 2, 523–26). London: Routledge and Kegan Paul. First published in *Bravo* (September 1930): 16–17.
Sparrow, John. 1934. *Sense and Poetry: Essays on the Place of Meaning in Contemporary Verse*. London: Constable and Company.
Spencer, Theodore. 1931a. "Donne and His Age." In *A Garland for John Donne*, edited by Theodore Spencer (179–202). Cambridge and London: Harvard and Humphrey Milford.
———, ed. 1931b. *A Garland for John Donne*. Cambridge: Harvard University Press.
Spiller, Robert. 1955. *The Cycle of American Literature*. New York: Macmillan.
Squire, J. C. 1919. "Editorial Notes." *London Mercury* (November): 1–6.
———. 1920. "Editorial Notes." *London Mercury* (February): 385–90.
———. 1922. "An Introductory Note on Eighteenth-Century Poetry." In *By-Ways Round Helicon: A Kind of Anthology*, edited by Iola A. Williams (vii–xxiv). London: William Heinemann.
———. 1923. "Poetry." *London Mercury* (October): 655–56.
———. 1924. "The Man Who Wrote Free Verse." *London Mercury* (June): 121–37.

———. 1928. "Editorial Notes." *London Mercury* (August): 337–46.
Squire, J. C. [Affable Hawk, pseud.]. 1923. Review of *Ulysses*, by James Joyce. *New Statesman* (April 7): 775.
Stafford, Barbara Maria. 1998. "Coldness." *Art Issues* 52 (March–April): 24–27.
Stauffer, Donald A. 1946. *The Nature of Poetry*. New York: W. W. Norton and Company.
Stegner, W. E. 1995. "New Technique in Novel Introduced." In *William Faulkner: The Contemporary Reviews* (153–55). Cambridge: Cambridge University Press. First published in Salt Lake City *Tribune* (November 29, 1936): 13–D.
Stein, Arnold. 1946. "Donne's Obscurity and the Elizabethan Tradition." *ELH:* 98–118.
Stein, Gertrude. 1934a. "Interview with Gertrude Stein." *Times* (January 3).
———. 1934b. "Interview by William Lundell." *Paris Review* (Fall). 1990.
———. 1962. *Selected Writings*. New York: Random House.
———. 1971. A Transatlantic Interview 1946. In *A Primer for the Gradual Understanding of Gertrude Stein* (15–35). Los Angeles: Black Sparrow.
Steiner, George. 1978. "On Difficulty." In *On Difficulty and Other Essays* (18–47). Oxford: Oxford University Press.
Steiner, Wendy. 1995. *The Scandal of Pleasure*. Chicago: University of Chicago Press.
Stevens, Wallace. 1989. Untitled Comment, *Explicator* (November 1948). In *Opus Posthumous* (249–50). New York: Knopf.
Stewart, D. H. 1966. "Cather's Mortal Comedy." *Queen's Quarterly* 73, no. 2: 244–59.
Stock, Noel. 1974 [1970]. *The Life of Ezra Pound*. New York: Random House.
Stonier, G. W. "Mr. James Joyce in Progress." In *James Joyce: The Critical Heritage* (Vol. 1, 408–10). London: Routledge and Kegan Paul. First published in *New Statesman* 35, no. 896 (June 28, 1930).
Stork, Charles Wharton. 1923. "Introduction." In S*econd Contemporary Verse Anthology*, edited by Charles Wharton Stork (xix–xxvii). New York: E. P. Dutton.
Storr, Robert. 1985. "'Tilted Arc': Enemy of the People?" *Art in America* 73 (September): 90–97.
Strobel, Marion. 1922. "A Symposium on Marianne Moore." *Poetry* 19, no. 4 (January): 208–17.
———. 1980. Review of *Spring and All*, by William Carlos Williams. In *William Carlos Williams: The Critical Heritage* (75–76). London: Routledge and Kegan Paul. First published in *Poetry* 23, no. 2 (November 1923): 103–5.
———. 1982. "Perilous Leaping." In *T. S. Eliot: The Critical Heritage* (Vol. 1, 119–21). London: Routledge and Kegan Paul. First published in *Poetry* 16 (June 1920): 157–59.
Strong, L. A. G. 1931. *Common Sense about Poetry*. London: Victor Gollancz.
Strychacz, Thomas. 1993. *Modernism, Mass Culture and Professionalism*. Cambridge: Cambridge University Press.
Sturgeon, Mary C. 1916. *Studies of Contemporary Poets*. London: Harrap.
Sudjic, Deyan. 1995. "Art Attack." In *Rachel Whiteread: House*. London: Phaedon. First published in Manchester *Guardian* (November 25, 1993).

Surette, Leon. 1993. *Birth of Modernism: Ezra Pound, T. S. Eliot, W. B. Yeats and the Occult.* Montréal and Buffalo: McGill-Queen's University Press.
Sutton, Denys. 1985. "Renoir's Kingdom." *Apollo* 121: 243–47.
Tate, Allen. 1922. "Whose Ox." *The Fugitive* 1, no. 4: 99–100.
———. 1959. "Understanding Modern Poetry." In *Collected Essays* (115–28). Denver: Allan Swallow. First published in *College English* 1 (April 1940): 561–72; *English Journal* 29 (April 1940): 263–74.
Taylor, Rev. Harry. 1949. "Letter to the Editor." *Saturday Review* (April 16): 31.
Taylor, John R. 1995. *Linguistic Categorization: Prototypes in Linguistic Theory.* 2nd ed. Oxford and New York: Clarendon Press and Oxford University Press.
Taylor, Rachel A. 1975. Review of *To the Lighthouse.* In *Virginia Woolf: The Critical Heritage* (198–200). London: Routledge and Kegan Paul. First published in *Spectator* (May 14, 1927): 871.
Thayer, Scofield. 1919. "Casual Comment." *Dial* (November 29): 484–86.
Theobald, Lewis. 1740. "Preface." In *The Works of Shakespeare*, edited by Lewis Theobald. London.
Thomas, Edward. 1972. "The Newest Poet." In *Ezra Pound: The Critical Heritage* (61–62). London: Routledge and Kegan Paul. First published in *Daily Chronicle* (November 23, 1909): 3.
Thomas, Wright, and Stuart Gerry Brown. 1941. *Reading Poems: An Introduction to Critical Study.* New York: Oxford University Press.
Thomson, Virgil. 1981 [1939]. "Our Island Home: Or What It Feels Like to Be a Musician." In *A Virgil Thomson Reader* (88–93). New York: E. P. Dutton.
Tietjens, Eunice. 1923a. "The Lyric in Poetry." *Poetry* 22, no. 3 (July): 148–53.
———. 1923b. "A Plea for a Revaluation of the Trite." *Poetry* 22, no. 6 (September): 321–25.
"'Tilted Arc' Hearing." 1985. *Artforum* (September): 98–99.
Touponce, William. 1991. "Literary Theory and the Notion of Difficulty." In *The Idea of Difficulty in Literature*, edited by Alan C. Purves (51–71). Albany: State University of New York Press.
Towne, Charles Hanson. 1923. "Introduction." In *Verse of Our Day: An Anthology of Modern American and British Poetry*, edited by Margery Gordon and Marie B. King (vii–ix). New York: D. Appleton and Company.
Travis, Molly Abel. 1998. *Reading Cultures: The Construction of Readers in the Twentieth Century.* Carbondale, Ill.: Southern Illinois University Press.
Trench, Herbert. 1907. *New Poems.* London: Methuen.
Trilling, Lionel. 1936. "Willa Cather." In *After the Genteel Tradition: American Writers 1910–1930*, edited by Malcolm Cowley (48–56). Carbondale: Southern Illinois University Press.
———. 1959. "A Speech of Robert Frost: A Cultural Episode." *Partisan Review* 26: 449–52.
Troy, William. 1970. "Notes on *Finnegans Wake.*" In *James Joyce: The Critical Heritage* (Vol. 2, 704–7). London: Routledge and Kegan Paul. First published in *Partisan Review* 6 (Summer 1939): 97–110.

Tryphonopoulos, Demetres P. 1992. *The Celestial Tradition: A Study of Ezra Pound's The Cantos*. Waterloo, Ont.: Wilfrid Laurier University Press.

Turner, Mark. 1991. *Reading Minds: The Study of English in the Age of Cognitive Science*. Princeton, N.J.: Princeton University Press.

———. 1996. *The Literary Mind*. New York and Oxford: Oxford University Press.

Turner, W. J. 1917. "Romance." In *Georgian Poetry 1916–1917* (3–4). London: The Poetry Bookshop.

Tzara, Tristan. 1977. *Seven Dada Manifestos and Lampisteries* (39). London: John Calder.

"Ulysses Lands." 1934. *Time* (January 29): 49–51.

Untermeyer, Louis. 1919a. "An Introduction." In *Modern American Poetry: An Introduction*, edited by Louis Untermeyer (vii–xi). New York: Harcourt, Brace and Howe.

———. 1919b. *The New Era in American Poetry*. New York: Henry Holt and Company.

———. 1920. "Irony De Luxe." *Freeman* 1 (June 30): 381–82.

———. 1924. *American Poetry since 1900*. London: Richards.

———. 1925. "Preface." In *Modern British Poetry*, edited by Louis Untermeyer (3–19). New York: Harcourt, Brace and Company.

———. 1930. "Preface." In *Modern American Poetry: A Critical Anthology*, edited by Louis Untermeyer (3–34). New York: Harcourt, Brace and Company.

———. 1935. "Einstein among the Coffee-Cups." In *Selected Poems and Parodies of Louis Untermeyer* (363). New York: Harcourt, Brace and Company.

———. 1938. *Doorways to Poetry*. New York: Harcourt, Brace and Company.

———. 1972. "China, Provence, and Points Adjacent." In *Ezra Pound: The Critical Heritage* (128–31). London: Routledge and Kegan Paul. First published in *Dial* 63 (December 1920): 634–35.

———. 1977. Robert Frost's 'New Hampshire.' In *Robert Frost: The Critical Reception* (62–65) New York: Burt Franklin. First published in *Bookman* 58 (January 1924): 578–80.

———. 1982. "Disillusion vs. Dogma." In *T. S. Eliot: The Critical Heritage* (Vol. 1, 151–53) London: Routledge and Kegan Paul. First published in *Freeman* 6 (January 17, 1923): 453.

Van Doren, Carl. 1940. *The American Novel: 1789–1939*. New York: Macmillan.

Van Doren, Mark. 1930a. "Introduction." In *Prize Poems 1913–1929*, edited by Charles A. Wagner (5–20). New York: Charles Boni.

———. 1930b. "The Poetry of Hart Crane." *Theatre Guild Magazine* (June): 50, 59.

———. 1942. *The Private Reader: Selected Articles and Reviews*. New York: Henry Holt.

Van Spanckeren, Kathryn. 2002. *Outline of American Literature* [website]. U.S. Department of State. Retrieved February 18, 2002, from http://usinfo.state.gov/products/pubs/oal/lit6.htm.

Van Vechten, Carl. 1916. *Music and Bad Manners*. New York: A. A. Knopf.

———. 1986. In *Critical Essays on Gertrude Stein* (34–37). Boston: G. K. Hall. First published in *Trend* 5 (August 1914): 553–57.

van Zuylen, Marina. 1994. *Difficulty as an Aesthetic Principle: Realism and Unreadability in Stifter, Melville, and Flaubert.* Edited by Michael Kenneally and Wolfgang Zach. Vol. 9, *Studies in English and Comparative Literature.* Tübingen: Gunter Narr Verlag.

———. 1998. "Difficulty, Aesthetics of." In *Encyclopedia of Aesthetics,* edited by Michael Kelly (43–47). New York: Oxford University Press.

Vanderham, Paul. 1998. *James Joyce and Censorship: The Trials of Ulysses.* Washington Square, N.Y.: New York University Press.

Vern, David. 1995. Review of *Absalom, Absalom!,* by William Faulkner. In *William Faulkner: The Contemporary Reviews* (155–56). Cambridge: Cambridge University Press. First published in *Washington Square Review* (December 1936): 8, 23.

Walton, Eda Lou. 1972. "Obscurity in Modern Poetry: Ezra Pound's Cantos Provide an example of the Type which Demands Scholarly Equipment on the Part of the Reader." In *Ezra Pound: The Critical Heritage* (256–59). London: Routledge and Kegan Paul. First published in *New York Times Book Review* (April 2, 1933): 5:2.

Warner, Michael. 1985. "Professionalization and the Rewards of Literature: 1875–1900." *Criticism* 27, no. 1: 1–28.

Waugh, Arthur. 1919. *Tradition and Change: Studies in Contemporary Literature.* London: Chapman and Hall.

Waugh, Evelyn. 1945. *Brideshead Revisited: The Sacred and Profane Memories of Captain Charles Ryder, a Novel.* London: Chapman and Hall.

Weber, Bruce. 1993. "Excuse Me; I Must Have Missed Part of the Movie." *New York Times* (November 7): IV 2:1.

Weber, Samuel. 1982. "The Limits of Professionalism." *The Oxford Literary Review* 5, no. 1–2: 59–74.

———. 1990. "The Vaulted Eye: Remarks on Knowledge and Professionalism." *Yale French Studies* 77: 44–60.

Weirick, Bruce. 1930. *From Whitman to Sandburg in American Poetry: A Critical Survey.* New York: Macmillan.

West, Rebecca. 1928. *The Strange Necessity.* New York: Doubleday.

Wetherell, J. E. 1922. *Later English Poems 1901–1922.* Edited by J. E. Wetherell. Toronto: McClelland and Stewart.

Weyergraf-Serra, Clara, and Martha Buskirk. 1988. *Richard Serra's Tilted Arc.* Eindhoven: Van Abbemuseum.

White, Allon. 1981. *The Uses of Obscurity: The Fiction of Early Modernism.* London: Routledge and Kegan Paul.

White, Barbara Ehrlich. 1984. *Renoir: His Life, Art, and Letters.* New York: Harry Abrams.

White, E. B. 1980 [1952]. *Charlotte's Web.* New York: HarperCollins.

Whiteley, Linda. 1998. "Renoir's Portraits." *Apollo* 147 (February): 51–52.

Wilhelm, James J. 1982. *Il Miglior Fabbro: The Cult of the Difficult in Daniel, Dante, and Pound.* Orono, Maine: National Poetry Foundation University of Maine at Orono.

Wilkin, Karen. 1996. "The Trouble with Renoir." *New Criterion* 15 (October): 46–50.

Wilkinson, Bonaro. 1931. *The Poetic Way of Release.* New York: Alfred A. Knopf.

Wilkinson, Marguerite. 1919. "New Voices: The Reader's Approach to Contemporary Poetry." In *New Voices: An Introduction to Contemporary Poetry* (1–14). New York: Macmillan.

———. 1923. "An Introduction." In *Contemporary Poetry*, edited by Marguerite Wilkinson (3–30). New York: Macmillan.

———. 1929. *New Voices: An Introduction to Contemporary Poetry*. New York: Macmillan.

Williams, Oscar. 1946. "Introduction." In *A Little Treasury of Modern Poetry, English and American*, edited by Oscar Williams (21–44). New York: Charles Scribner's Sons.

Williams, William Carlos. 1929. "For a New Magazine." *Blues* (May): 30–32.

———. 1967 [1951]. *The Autobiography of William Carlos Williams*. New York: New Directions.

———. 1969. A 1 Pound Stein. In *Selected Essays* (162–66). New York: New Directions.

———. 1969 [1927]. "Notes in Diary Form." In *Selected Essays* (62–74). New York: New Directions.

———. 1970. "Kora in Hell: Improvisations, 1920." In *Imaginations* (6–82). New York: New Directions.

———. 1986a [1935]. *Poems 1929–1935*. In *The Collected Poems of William Carlos Williams* (Vol. 1, 1909–1939, 319–74) New York: New Directions.

———. 1986b [1923]. *Spring and All*. In *The Collected Poems of William Carlos Williams* (Vol. 1, 1909–1939, 175–236). New York: New Directions.

Williamson, Alan. 1995. "A Valediction: On Difficulty." *The American Poetry Review* (September–October): 51–55.

Williamson, George. 1927. "The Talent of T.S. Eliot." *Sewanee Review* 35: 284–95.

———. 1931. "Donne and the Poetry of Today." In *A Garland for John Donne*, edited by Theodore Spencer (155–76). Cambridge and London: Harvard and Humphrey Milford.

Williamson, Hugh Ross. 1933. *The Poetry of T. S. Eliot*. New York: G. P. Putnam's Sons.

Wilson, Edmund. 1924. "Wallace Stevens and e. e. cummings." *New Republic* (March 19): 102–3.

———. 1970. "*Ulysses*." In *James Joyce: The Critical Heritage* (Vol. 1, 227–31). London: Routledge and Kegan Paul. First published in *New Republic* 31: 396 (July 5, 1922): 164–66.

———. 1982. "The Poetry of Drouth." In *T. S. Eliot: The Critical Heritage* (Vol. 1, 138–44). London: Routledge and Kegan Paul. First published in *Dial* 73 (December 1922): 611–16.

———. 1986. From *Axel's Castle*. In *Critical Essays on Gertrude Stein* (58–62). Boston: G. K. Hall.

Winters, Yvor. 1937. *Primitivism and Decadence: A Study of American Experimental Poetry*. New York: Arrow Editions.

———. 1943. *The Anatomy of Nonsense*. Norfolk, Conn.: New Directions.

———. 1947. *In Defense of Reason*. New York: Swallow Press and W. Morrow and Company.

Wolfe, Humbert. 1931. *Signpost to Poetry: An Introduction to the Study of Verse*. London: Cassell and Company.

———. 1982. "Waste Land and Waste Paper." Review of *The Waste Land*. In *T. S. Eliot: The Critical Heritage* (Vol. 1, 200–3). London: Routledge and Kegan Paul. First published in *Weekly Westminster* (November 17, 1923): i, 94.

Wolfe, Thomas. 1970. Letter to Maxwell E. Perkins (15 December 1936). In *James Joyce: The Critical Heritage* (Vol. 2, 642). London: Routledge and Kegan Paul. First published in *The Letters of Thomas Wolfe* (1956), ed. Elizabeth Nowell (585–86).

Woolf, Leonard. 1982. "'Jug Jug to Dirty Ears." In *T. S. Eliot: The Critical Heritage* (Vol. 1, 213–15). London: Routledge and Kegan Paul. First published in *Nation and Athenaeum* 38 (December 1925): 354.

Woolf, Virginia. 1925. "Modern Fiction." In *The Common Reader* (184–95). London: Hogarth Press.

———. 1966. "Mr. Bennett and Mrs. Brown." In *Virginia Woolf: Selections from Her Essays* (95–115). London: Chatto and Windus.

Wordsworth, William. 1974. "Essay, Supplementary to Preface." In *Wordsworth's Literary Criticism*, edited by W. J. B. Owen. London and Boston: Routledge and Kegan Paul.

"Workshop Players Score Hit Here." 1957. *San Quentin News* (November 28): 1, 3.

Wright, Richard. 1945. Review of *Wars I Have Seen*, by Gertrude Stein. *PM* (March 11).

Wylie, Elinor. 1982. "Mr. Eliot's Slug-horn." In *T. S. Eliot: The Critical Heritage* (Vol. 1, 153–56). London: Routledge and Kegan Paul. First published in *New York Evening Post Literary Review* (January 20, 1923): 396.

Yust, Walter. 1995. "Of Making Many Books." In *William Faulkner: The Contemporary Reviews* (35–36). Cambridge: Cambridge University Press. First published in Philadelphia *Public Ledger* (October 4, 1929).

Zabel, Morton Dauwen. 1931. "A Poetry of Ideas." *Poetry* 37, no. 3 (January): 225–31.

Index

Abbott, Craig 185, 249, 264, 270, 273
Abercrombie, Lascelles 111, 209–10; "Hymn to Love" 209
academia xiv, 17, 29, 162, 186, 202, 203, 204, 205, 207, 208, 210, 212, 219, 224, 225–27, 241, 244, 246, 262, 270, 274
Acocella, Joan 273
Adamov, Arthur 92
Adams, J. Donald 160, 204–5
Adams, Marilyn Jager 257
Addison, Joseph 28
Adler, Jonathan 228
Adorno, Theodor 118–19, 120, 121, 239, 266, 267, 271
affect xiv–xv, 64–84, 118, 120, 144, 145, 150, 237, 244, 266; see also viscerality
Aiken, Conrad 62, 63, 107, 128–29, 134, 147, 198, 238, 252, 263, 274
Aimone, Joseph 178, 245, 275
Alexandrianism 21–22, 29, 47, 248, 250
Aldington, Richard 25, 47, 83, 160, 163–64, 166, 252, 261
Alington, Rev. Cyril 71, 97–98, 179, 180. 185, 195, 201, 205–6
Althusser, Louis 196
amateurism 97, 99, 102, 103, 206; see also professionalism, love
ambition 66, 75–76, 82, 111, 125, 161, 174–75, 192–93, 224, 228
American Scholar 100, 128, 221, 246
Amis, Martin 197
anarchy 113, 116, 117, 141, 266
Anderson, Laurie 233
Anderson, Sherwood 71, 122, 147
André, Albert 217
André, Carl x
anger xiv–xv, 17, 36, 45, 64–84, 85, 88, 121, 138, 143–44, 150, 122, 215, 216, 224

ANGER IS HEAT 255
anxiety xi, xiv, 10, 17, 44–45, 64–84, 116, 133, 144, 145, 146, 150, 170, 171, 172–73, 206, 207, 208, 210, 214, 221, 222, 225, 230, 231, 236, 237, 244, 247, 256, 258, 267, 268
Aristotle xiii, 31, 251, 256, 268
Armory Show x, 17–18, 35, 45, 52–53, 66–69, 75, 81, 86, 215, 247
Arnold, Matthew 180
Art Institute of Chicago 68
art, visual 7, 17–18, 39–42, 62, 74–75, 114, 117, 159, 247, 260
Artaud, Antonin 176
Arts and Decoration 17
Ashbery, John 93
amazement, wonder 126, 235, 256, 258, 268; see also Aristotle, sublime
Athenaeum 12
Atkins, Elizabeth 16, 83, 134
Atlantic Monthly 160
Atwood, Margaret 225
Auden, W. H. 155, 197, 229, 247, 260
Augustine, St. 256, 266–67
authenticity 32, 37, 91, 92–94, 95, 108, 109, 111, 127, 131, 133, 134, 166, 177, 185, 188, 192, 240, 250
avant-garde 4, 7, 102, 115, 236, 240, 241, 260

Babbitt, Milton 96
Bach, J. S. 153, 268
Bailey, Colin 219
Baldick, Chris 275
Ballet Russes 65, 256
Barker, Ronald 88
Barnes, Djuna 80; *Nightwood* 80
Barthes, Roland 267
Bataille, Georges 176
Baudelaire, Charles 250

beauty 97, 98, 104, 131, 141, 145, 150, 158, 170, 179, 180, 191, 192, 206, 210, 269, 274; *see also* simplicity
Beckett, Samuel 88–94, 229, 261; *Waiting for Godot* 88–94, 131, 137, 261
Beethoven, Ludwig van 161
Bell, Clive 83, 156, 263
Bell, Julian 239
Bénet, William Rose
Benlowes, Edward 133
Bennett, Arnold 82, 123
Bentley, Eric 89, 262
Berg, Alban 233
Berlyne, D. E. 76–77, 83, 258
Bernstein, Charles 252
Bettany, Lewis 152
Binyon, Luarence 12, 103
Birch-Bartlett, Helen 209
Birkerts, Sven 270
Bishop, John Peale 130, 131
Blackmur, R. P. 192
Blake, William 22, 23, 29, 31, 34, 59, 166, 242, 250
Blau, Herbert 89, 90
Bledstein, Burton 96, 262
Bloom, Edward 194, 201
Bloom, Lillian 194, 201
Bodenheim, Maxwell 75, 106
bolshevism 4, 7, 8, 116, 117, 251
Bookman, The 29, 32, 146
boredom 9, 76, 77, 78, 81, 121, 243
Bosanquet, Bernard 163, 251, 260
Bottrall, Ronald 149
Bourdieu, Pierre 261–62, 263
Bowie, Malcolm 245
Brancusi, Constantin 17, 158, 211
Braque, Georges 158
Brecht, Bertolt 118
Brickell, Hershell 191
Brooker, Jewel Spears 262
Brooks, Cleanth 15, 16, 28, 32, 33, 43, 105, 109, 136, 162, 166, 176, 193, 229, 246, 248, 270, 274
Brooks, Van Wyck 100, 102
Broom 147
Browne, George 190–91, 273
Brown, Oliver 78
Brown, Sharon 111, 264
Brown, Stuart Gerry 198
Browning, Robert 23, 26, 27, 47, 99, 132, 133, 250; "Sordello" 26
Bryher, Winifred 166
Buchloh, Benjamin 141, 143
Bull, Peter 88
Bürger, Peter 118
Burke, Kenneth 57
Burke, Edmund 258–59
Burns, Robert 27

Burnshaw, Stanley 274
Bush, Douglas 29–30
Buskirk, Martha 270
Bynner, Witter 16

Cage, John 230
canon xii, xiv, 2, 3, 13, 15–16, 17, 22–35, 45, 83, 84, 91, 94, 95, 109, 134, 155, 163, 172, 174, 175, 178–220, 221, 223, 225, 226, 229, 231, 232, 233, 241–42, 247, 253, 264, 270, 273, 275
Caputo, John 175–77, 240
Cardon Émile 216
Carey, John 263
Carter, Elliott 238–39
Caruso, Enrico 66
Castelli, Leo 139
categorization 53–57, 252; and radial categories 54–57, 253–54
Cather, Willa xii, 183, 188–204, 217, 228, 273, 274; *Death Comes for the Archbishop* 195
Catholic Anthology 12
Cervantes 30
Cézanne, Paul 66
Chapbook, The 23, 65, 99
Chapman, John 26
Child, Harold 72
Christie, William 245
Ciardi, John 195, 196
Cinna 22
Clark, J. F. 193
Coffin, Tristram 87
cognitive dissonance 73
Coleman, David 228
Coleman, Robert 89
Coleridge, Hartley 24
Coleridge, S. T. 23, 31, 32–33, 34, 126, 149, 155, 251, 268
Collins, Joseph 80, 106, 259
Colum, Mary 135
concision 57, 80, 114, 134, 169–70
Conkling, Grace Hazard 213; "Tampico" 213
Conrad, Joseph xiii
Copland, Aaron 17
coterie 10, 11, 16, 19, 31, 39, 183; *see also* elitism
Courbet, Gustave 215
Courtney, W. L. 271
Cowley, Abraham 79
Cox, Kenyon 267
Crane, Hart 108, 210
Crimp, Douglas 143
crisis 2, 12–13, 19, 34, 35, 78–79, 96, 102, 110, 195, 198, 199, 206, 210, 224, 228, 231, 257, 265
critics 21–22, 29, 30, 36, 38, 47, 55, 70, 72, 74, 80, 91, 92, 100, 125, 132, 136, 137, 145, 150, 206, 248; *see also* professionalism

crossword puzzles 20, 74, 134, 145, 157, 158, 175, 234, 271
cubism 4, 7, 11, 12, 17, 21, 37, 46, 68, 69, 79, 81, 83, 113, 116, 121, 125, 158, 165, 224, 247
cult 16, 18–20, 36, 80, 83, 88, 103, 134, 248; *see also* fashion, imitation
culture, contemporary xii, xiv, xv, 35, 84–86, 118, 137–44, 174, 222–23, 227–33, 236, 241; *see also* postmodernism
cummings, e. e. 26, 210
Cunningham, J. V. 268
Curie, Marie 31
Curtius, Ernst R. 210, 267

Dada 73, 159
Daiches, David 98, 134, 151, 157, 162, 166, 193, 261
Dante xiii, 22–23, 31, 106, 126, 128, 130, 131, 134, 248, 269
Davies, John 26
Day Lewis, Cecil 94, 252, 261, 270
DEATH IS DEPARTURE 61
de Born, Bertrans 269
decadence 9, 10, 26, 38, 92
deconstruction 267
defamiliarization 117, 118, 212–13, 268
Degas, Edgar 220
Delage, Maurice 66
de la Mare, Walter 12
Dell, Floyd 71, 161
De Man, Paul 119, 267
depth *see* surface and depth
Derleth, August 205
Derrida, Jacques 119, 175–76
Deutsch, Babette 108, 109, 128, 210, 261
development, aesthetic xi, 9, 24, 99, 101, 102–3, 104, 105, 114–15, 265; *see also* experimentation, newness
De Voto, Bernard 127
Dial, The 12, 146, 245, 273
Diamond, William 139, 141, 144
dichotomies, in argument xv, 1–2, 12–13, 82, 215, 236, 246
Dickens, Charles 61
Dickinson, Emily 29, 61
Diepeveen, Leonard 257, 275
DIFFICULTIES ARE IMPEDIMENTS TO MOTION 254
difficulty, category of 48–50, 53–57, 253–4; conceptualizing of 43–44, 45–64; defined x–xi, 49–53; deliberate ix, 7, 11, 19–20, 23, 31, 38, 55, 83, 87, 94–95, 98, 111–12, 114, 119, 120, 123, 134, 151, 182, 183, 248, 260, 261, 265; distinctions between forms of 83; inherent properties of 43–45, 72–76, 81; of language 27–28; lexical terms for 47–48, 50, 54–57, 79, 83; necessity for 14, 16, 19, 87, 94–96, 100, 101, 109, 111, 114, 124, 131, 136, 231, 265; prevalence of ix, x, xi, xiii–xiv, 3, 10–20, 35, 43, 87, 114, 221, 245, 247–48; relationship, difficulty as 62–63, 163; transitory xv, 22, 26, 27, 82, 109, 122–25, 127, 142, 219–20, 238–39, 250, 268; universal xv, 1, 25, 27–30, 44, 94, 95, 114, 115, 118, 135–37, 177, 198, 199, 225, 227–78, 236, 250
directness 56, 95, 108, 157, 166, 178, 181, 182, 183, 185, 190
Dobrée, Bonamy 114, 131, 149, 169
Dodge, Mabel 17, 94, 95, 106, 155, 169
Donne, John 23, 25, 26, 28–30, 31, 33, 34, 79, 106, 109, 110, 127, 131, 136, 167, 171, 249, 250, 254–55, 259, 263, 264, 267
Dos Passos, John 36, 191
Dreiser, Theodore 199
Drew, Elizabeth 27, 135, 163, 252, 270
Drinkwater, John 185
Dryden, John 24, 28
Duchamp, Marcel 52, 66, 210; *Nude Descending a Staircase* 18, 52, 68, 71
Dudley, Dorothy 14, 247
Duncan, Carol 272
Dunlop, Ian 72
Dupee, F. W. 156, 221
Duykinck, Evert 79, 259

Eagleton, Terry 231
Eastman, Max 16, 18, 19, 36, 72, 83, 98, 157
Edison, Thomas A. 148
Ehrmann, Jacques 252
Eksteins, Modris 256
Eighteenth century literature 24, 28
Elam, Helen 266
El Greco 249
Eliot, T. S. xi, xii, 5, 7, 9, 12, 16, 22, 23–24, 26, 27, 29, 45, 47, 48, 50, 51–52, 55, 57, 58, 62, 80, 82, 83, 87, 93, 95, 98, 99, 100, 101, 103, 105, 106, 107, 109, 110, 114, 116, 119, 126, 127, 128, 129, 130–31, 132, 133, 134, 146–9, 150, 152, 154, 155, 158–59, 160, 161, 162, 163, 166, 169, 170, 174, 176, 177, 178, 187, 188, 201, 202, 206, 207, 208, 210, 212, 214, 223, 225, 242, 244, 246, 247, 248, 249, 250, 251, 252, 255, 256, 260, 262, 264, 268–69, 269–70, 272, 275; "Ash Wednesday" 11; "Boston Evening Transcript" 169, 272; "Burnt Norton" 28; "Gerontion" 156, 171; "Love Song of J. Alfred Prufrock" 12, 21, 35, 99, 107, 116, 158–59, 169, 251, 272; "The Metaphysical Poets" xi, 1, 14, 48, 95, 110, 169, 176, 245–46, 253, 264, 265; *Poems 1909–1925* 47; *Prufrock and Other Observations* 116, 119, 149; "Sweeney Among the Nightingales" 5–6; "Sweeney Erect" 53;

Eliot, T. S. (cont.) *The Waste Land* 11, 14, 21–2, 24, 29, 35, 36, 43, 47–8, 49, 55, 56, 57, 59, 60, 65, 73, 99, 105, 108, 112, 113, 117, 128, 129, 131, 132, 133, 134, 135, 146, 147, 149, 151, 155, 147, 176, 187, 195, 197, 198, 200, 206, 208, 212, 227, 235, 247, 255, 264, 269–70, 274; influence of 20, 24, 29, 80, 83, 146, 245–46, 270
elitism xiv, 9–10, 16, 20, 35, 91, 92, 101–2, 103, 119, 123, 126, 131, 132, 142, 157, 158, 166, 203, 204, 227, 238, 244, 250, 266; see also coterie
Elizabethan literature 23, 24, 28, 248
Elkins, James 245, 271, 273
Elton, Lord 104, 159
emotional expression x, 4, 25, 37, 128, 131, 135, 136, 156, 157, 158, 159, 180, 181, 206, 269
Empson, William 16, 260, 270, 271
entanglement 58, 60, 79, 83, 169–70, 171, 183, 185, 195, 249
entrenchment 49, 74, 170–71, 212, 253
Epstein, Jacob 211, 246
Ernst, Max 77
Esquire 29, 246
Esslin, Martin 90–94, 100, 210, 238, 261
ethics 70, 72, 73, 75–76, 77–81, 82, 119–21, 144, 149, 161, 163, 165–68, 172, 173, 175–77, 216, 229, 231, 236, 240–41, 256, 260, 267, 272
Euphues, euphuism 22, 147
excess, difficulty as 55–56, 151–53, 169, 181, 183, 244
experimentation 26, 98–99, 116, 191, 193, 215; see also development
evaluation 34, 37–38, 43, 53, 85–86
Evans, M. 264

Fadiman, Clifton 80
Farge, Léon-Paul 66
fashion 3, 7, 8, 10, 14, 19–20, 25, 29, 34, 36, 37, 39, 94, 97, 102, 104, 114, 115, 137, 157, 174, 190, 191, 231, 245, 249, 250, 252, 271; see also difficulty, prevalence of
Faulkner, William xi, xii, 17, 58, 127, 170, 247, 248; *Absalom, Absalom!* 35, 99, 127, 162, 170, 195, 199, 247, 248, 257; *As I Lay Dying* 48; *The Sound and the Fury* 36, 58, 103
Fausset, Hugh l'Anson 29, 32, 106
Feaver, William 218, 220
Feger, Lois 194
Fellini, Federico 229–30
Firkins, O. W. 159–60
Fish, Stanley 212, 222, 262
Fitts, Dudley 131, 156, 257, 269–70
Flam, Jack 216
Fletcher, John Gould 58
Flint, F. S. 190
Ford, Ford Madox 250

formalism 85–86, 98, 118, 126, 127, 172, 266, 268
Foucault, Michel 44–45, 62
Fraser, G. S. 229–30
Frasier 234
Freeman, John 12
Freud, Sigmund 105
Fried, Michael 218
Friedlaender, Marc 128, 268
Frijda, Nico 75
Fromm, Harold 70
Frost, Robert xii, 64, 153, 154, 159, 168, 174, 178, 181, 186–87, 188–214, 217, 228, 235, 242, 263, 273, 274; *A Boy's Will* 159, 186, 189, 190; "Flower-gathering" 186–87, 209; *New Hampshire* 191; *North of Boston* 190; "Nothing Gold Can Stay" 235; "Storm Fear" 189
Fry, Roger 66, 114
Futurism 7, 11, 38, 68, 69, 81, 165

Gablik, Suzi 121
game, art as 1, 4, 11, 20, 47, 80, 95, 136, 150, 156, 157, 175, 183, 271; see also crossword puzzles
Ganz, Victor 142
Gardner, Helen 217
Gardner, Howard 257
Gascoigne, George 251
gatekeeper, difficulty as xv, 10, 42, 45, 81–82, 83, 91, 222–23, 224, 226
Gaunt, William 216
Geismar, Maxwell 194
General Services Administration 137–38, 139, 141, 143, 144
genius 22, 23, 25, 38, 114
Georgians 162, 164, 223
Georgian Poetry 12, 13, 23, 30, 206, 245
Gertsfelde, V. 265–66
Gesner, Clark 235
Gibbs, Raymond 255
Gilbert, Stuart 127–28
Gilbert, W. S. 39
Gilbert-Rolfe, Jeremy 120, 245
Gilfillan, George 79
Gillet, Louis 123
Glass, Philip 139
Goethe, Johann Wolfgang von 251
Gogarty, Oliver 158
Gold, Joseph 205
Goldin, Nan 260
Golding, Alan 264, 270, 275
Goldstein, Paul 140
Gongora 26
Gordon, Margery 112
Gorman, Herbert 25
Gosse, Edmund 12

government 137–44; committees of inquiry 81, 85, 139–44; *see also* General Services Administration, law, National Endowment for the Arts
Graff, Gerald 226, 227, 262, 270
Grant, Duncan 72
Granville, Charles 80
Graves, Robert 43, 157, 166, 188, 224, 246, 252, 270
Gray, Jeffrey 75, 257
Greenberg, Clement 127, 217, 251, 275
Gregory 255
Grierson, Herbert 109, 110
Grigson, Geoffrey 166
Gross, Valentine 66
Guerin, T. M. 205
Guillory, John 225, 227, 246, 263, 270, 275

habitualization 77, 118, 125, 172, 173, 219, 227, 230, 232; *see also* defamiliarization; difficulty, as transitory
Harmon-Jones, Eddie 257
Harper's 246
Hauser, Arnold 267
Hawthorne, Nathaniel 199; *The Scarlet Letter* 201
Hayes, Colin 216
H. D. (Hilda Doolittle) 6, 267
health 58, 59, 79–80, 83, 163, 166, 168, 170, 240, 252
Heidegger, Martin 176
Hegel, G. W. F. xiii
Hemingway, Ernest 164, 191, 199, 214; *The Sun Also Rises* 147
Herrick, Robert 27
high art 34, 76, 93, 96, 212, 223, 232, 243, 249, 267, 268
history xi, xiii, 19–35, 43, 79, 115, 124, 136–7, 165–66, 245, 249–50, 250, 251
hoax 4–10, 11, 14, 16, 35–39, 53, 69, 71, 73, 80, 85, 88, 89, 158, 166, 184, 251, 252
Hobson, Harold 88
Holmes, Oliver Wendell 141–42
Holtmann, Felix 85
Homer 79, 99, 106
Hopkins, Gerard Manley 23, 31, 163, 250
Horkheimer, Max 120
Horowitz, Gregg 143
Housman, A. E. 154, 187, 188, 196–97, 214
Huggins, A. W. F. 257
Hurston, Zora Neale 214
Huxley, Aldous 103
Huyssen, Andreas 272

Ibsch, Elrud 77, 258
Illustrated London News 66, 67
Imagism 11, 153, 156, 190

imitation 23–25, 35, 50, 78, 99, 223, 248
inexhaustibility 56, 57, 64, 195–96, 233, 273
influence *see* imitation
Ingres, J. A. D. 68
intellectual art 90, 91, 104, 145, 146, 154, 158, 163, 166, 181, 183, 184, 192, 218, 234, 260
intellectuals 82, 88, 89, 92, 102, 111, 115, 146, 152, 156, 193, 194, 202, 210, 217, 248
interpretation 103, 153, 155, 225; simplicity and 184–88, 198; *see also* literary criticism, academia
Ionesco, Eugène 92

Jackson, Holbrook 76
Jacobean literature 28, 248
Jacoby, Russell 244
Jacquette, Dale 260
Jaffé, Hans 216
James, Caryn 229–30
James, Henry 23, 249, 250
James, William 73
Jameson, Frederic 120–21
Jarrell, Randall ix–x, 193–94, 242–43, 246, 249–50, 273
Jarvis, Simon 266
Jauss, Hans Robert 125, 220, 265
Javits, Marion 141
Javits, Senator Jacob K. 141
jazz 7, 89, 113, 162
Jeromack, Paul 219
Johnson, Samuel 28, 31–32, 34, 79, 251
Jolas, Eugene 115
Joyce, James xi, 16, 25, 26, 45, 56, 73, 78, 89, 99, 105, 106, 109, 128, 158, 160, 167, 176, 207, 212, 214, 235, 241, 247, 248, 262, 263, 266; *Dubliners* 160; *Finnegans Wake* (*Work in Progress*) x, 35, 56, 73, 81, 105, 122, 123, 127, 151, 155, 160–61, 260, 262, 263, 266, 270; *A Portrait of the Artist as a Young Man* 160; *Ulysses* x, 11, 14, 18, 35, 48, 55, 71, 76, 77, 78, 99, 101, 105, 106, 110, 113, 123, 124, 127, 132, 146, 158, 160, 167, 173, 187, 200, 226, 234, 241, 248, 250, 251, 259–60, 262, 263, 266
Judd, Donald 139
Jung, C. G. 78

Kant, Immanuel xiii, 266, 271
Kazin, Alfred 183, 191, 193
Keats, John 27
Kilmer, Joyce 274
King, Marie 112
Kipling, Rudyard 190
knowledge 51, 55, 56, 62, 94, 126, 129–35, 152, 153, 157, 198, 262, 269–70
Knowles, F. L. 272
Knowlson, James 261

Kövecses, Zoltan 254, 255
Krauss, Rosalind 139
Krenek, Ernst 157
Kreymborg, Alfred 147
Kronenberger, Louis 57, 58

Lacan, Jacques 119
lack 151, 153; difficulty as 55, 56–57; simplicity as 185
Lakoff, George 49, 54, 60–61, 253, 254
Larbaud, Valéry 259–60
Larson, Magali Sarfatti 96, 262
Last Year at Marienbad 230
laughter xiv, 17, 36, 43, 45, 52–53, 64–84, 85, 121, 215, 219–20, 224, 256
law, difficulty and the 11, 68, 81, 137–44, 211, 259–60
Lawrence, D. H. 204, 205
Lawson, K. C. 264
Leavis, F. R. 16, 29, 33, 36, 57, 99, 101, 113, 145, 149, 183, 251, 252, 273
Leavis, Q. D. 162
Lentricchia, Frank 168, 199, 204, 272, 273
Leslie, Shane 55, 106
Lewis, Sinclair 29, 194, 198, 246
Lewis, Wyndham 152
Lindsay, Vachel 153, 184
Lipman, Samuel 70
Loeb, Harold 147
Lodge, David 162
Logical meaning x, 52, 75, 126, 128, 129–30, 269
London Mercury xii, 2, 9, 10–12, 38
Longfellow, Henry Wadsworth 194, 257
love 97, 98, 180, 205–6; *see also* amateurism, simplicity
Lowell, Amy 147, 190, 243
Lowell, James Russell 243
Lowell, Robert 243
Loy, Mina 120, 247, 264
Lucas, F. L. 21, 29, 197, 248
Lyall, Mary Mills 37, 68, 121, 158, 165
Lycophron 22, 250
Lyly, John *see* Euphues
Lynd, Robert 12, 36

MacDougall, Curtis D. 74
machismo xiv, 35, 82, 98, 115, 116, 120, 138, 145, 146, 149–50, 154, 161–77, 182, 183, 190, 192–3, 198, 210, 216, 229, 231, 236, 239–40, 271, 272
MacNiece, Louis 267
madness 59, 78–80, 81, 83, 106, 140, 166, 250, 252; *see also* health, perversion
Mahoney, Eva 191
Mallarmé, Stéphane 38, 176, 250, 272
Malley, Ern 184
Malory, Sir Thomas 269

Manet, Edouard 220
Mannes, Marya 88
Man Ray 147
Mansfield, Katherine 12
Mapplethorpe, Robert 235, 260
Marcuse, Herbert 118
Marinetti, Filippo Tommaso 38
marketing *see* publicity
Marsh, Edward 206
Martin, Jane 86
Martindale, Colin 258
Marvell, Andrew 25, 29
Marxism 10, 16, 92, 117, 165; *see also* bolshevism
Mason, William 79
mass culture 31, 91–92, 116, 119, 200, 238, 249, 267, 272; *see also* reader, common; general public
Massinger, Philip 107
Masters, Edgar Lee 181
Matisse, Henri 17, 66, 68, 147, 239
Matthiessen, F. O. 109
Mayer, Richard 257, 258
Mayne, Jasper 254
Mays, John Bentley 86
McCallum, Pamela 245
McCarthy, Desmond 66, 133
McClary, Susan 241, 245
McDonald, Gail 224, 227, 270, 275
McDowall, A. S. 107
McGann, Jerome 252, 274
McGreevy, Thomas 250
meaning beyond language 24, 32, 126–35, 136, 238, 268
Mégroz, R. L. 20
Mellers, Wilfrid 103
Menand, Louis 96, 262
Meredith, George xiii, 17, 23, 249
metaphor 29, 32, 50, 51–52, 108, 114, 136, 169–70, 196; conceptual metaphor 54, 55, 58–64, 74, 75, 108, 168–69, 172, 240–41, 255, 272
metaphysical poetry ix, 23, 28, 29, 79, 80, 127, 166, 169
Meyers, Jeffrey 194, 204, 274
Middleton, Jo Ann 195, 273
Millay, Edna St. Vincent 16, 134, 174, 188, 214
Milton, John 145, 183, 190, 243
mimesis, cultural xi, xv, 4, 13, 86, 95, 104, 106, 108–13, 117, 167, 182, 230, 235, 244, 252, 264; psychological xv, 95, 104, 105–8, 112, 128, 235, 250, 263
Mitchison, G. R. 155
modernism, defined xiv, xv–xvi, 245
Modern Quarterly 25
Molière 30
Mondale, Joan 142

Index

Mondrian, Piet 219
Monet, Claude 215, 216, 220
Monro, Harold 12, 23, 65, 73, 154, 182, 245
Monroe, Harriet xii, xvi, 30, 52, 112, 113, 146, 148, 154, 180, 185, 188, 210, 245, 248, 249, 264; *see also Poetry*
Moore, Marianne xi, xii, 52, 107, 120, 126, 133, 149, 166, 167, 170, 174, 240, 247, 264, 268
Morgan, Louise 47
Morley, Christopher 29
Morrell, Lady Ottoline 7
Morris, William 268
Morton, David 146
Mosher, Thomas 191
movements, aesthetic 4, 7, 11, 19–20, 25, 74, 100, 103, 114, 249, 263
Munson, Gorham 31, 56, 107, 269
Muir, Edwin 58–59, 80, 259
Murphy, John 194–95
Murry, J. Middleton 12–13, 151, 165–66, 265
music xii, 17, 18, 52, 62, 70, 76, 103, 110, 112–13, 153, 157, 247

Nabokov, Vladimir 95
Nation, The 246
National Endowment for the Arts 144
National Gallery of Canada 85–86, 219
Neff, Emory 205
Neo-classical literature (Augustan) 28, 29
New Age 10, 82
Newcomb, John Timberman 270
New Criticism 103, 115, 118, 126, 130, 131, 135, 136, 137, 175, 187, 205, 206, 223, 224–26, 228, 246, 250, 270, 274
Newman, Barnett 85–86; *Voice of Fire* 85–86, 232
Newman, J. K. 248
New Masses 80
newness xv, 11, 23, 27, 32, 75, 77, 113–25, 165, 182, 258, 262, 265; *see also* difficulty, transitory
New Republic 127
New Statesman 10, 21, 272
New York *Herald Tribune* 94
New York Times 138, 160, 207, 229, 230
New York Times Book Review 80, 146, 204
Nichols, Robert 30, 36, 134–35, 269, 271
Nietzsche, Friedrich 119, 266, 267
Nineteenth Century Literature 15, 21, 28, 33, 34, 104, 105, 136, 166, 256
North American Review 191
Novitz, David 76
Noyes, Alfred 251

Oatley, Keith 75
obscenity 77, 80–81, 123, 259–60
O'Brian, John 261

O'Brien, Sharon 195, 199, 201, 273
O'Connor, William Van 100, 136, 267–68
O'Donnell, George 197
O'Dougherty, Vicki 143
O'Hara, Daniel 274
Öhman, Arne 257
Ohmann, Richard 262
Oldenburg, Claes 141
originality *see* newness
Orton, Fred 275

Pach, Walter 215–16
Palgrave, Francis Turner 179–80, 236, 272, 273
Palmer, Herbert 50–51, 59, 248; *Cinder Thursday* 50–51, 59, 117
paraphrase 136
Parkes, Henry 156
parodies 2–10, 24, 25, 37, 50–53, 117, 243; *see also* hoax
Parsons, I. M. 106
passivity 25, 126, 146, 153–55, 161, 163, 166, 267, 271
Payne, William 154, 186–87, 188, 209
Peck, Demaree 202, 204, 274
Pelorson, Georges 155
Perelman, Bob 245, 273
Perin, Constance 74–75, 245
Perloff, Marjorie 272
perversion 79–80, 168, 170; *see also* twisting, entanglement, health
Perveslin, Hank 141
Peschmann, Hermann 154
Petrarch 255–56
Phillips, Patricia 139, 143
Piaget, Jean 258
Picabia, Francis 165
Picasso, Pablo 17, 106, 147, 155, 165, 256
Pierce, Frederick 192
Pinter, Harold 92
Pisarro, Camille 220
pleasure x, xii, xv, 2, 25, 33, 37, 49, 53, 76–77, 95, 104, 169, 172, 173–4, 175, 180, 185, 186, 198, 206, 217, 219, 223, 224, 229, 234–35, 236, 239–40, 243, 244, 256, 258, 267, 268, 271, 272, 273, 275; levels of 155–61
Plotinus 256
Poetry xii, 15, 30, 52, 64, 103, 104, 149, 159, 180, 181, 245
Poirier, Richard 146, 202, 204, 245, 273, 274
Pollock, Jackson 39–42, 251
Pomeroy, Wardell B. 222
Pool, Phoebe 219–20
Pope, Alexander 27
Post-Impressionist Exhibition, 1910 17, 45, 66, 69, 70, 71–72, 75, 78, 82, 103, 123
postmodernism xiv, 175–7, 229, 239–40; *see also* culture, contemporary

Pound, Ezra xi, xii, xvi, 7, 17, 23, 27, 30–31, 58, 62, 71, 79, 99, 100–1, 102, 103, 106, 111, 120, 123, 130, 131, 133, 134–35, 161, 163, 179, 190, 191, 201, 202, 210, 214, 223, 243, 246, 249, 252, 259, 262, 264, 265, 267, 268–69; *The Cantos* 30, 75, 126, 130, 131, 134–35, 156, 157, 166, 257; *Hugh Selwyn Mauberley* 36, 259; *Instigations* 100; *Lustra* 133; *Provença* 71; *Ripostes* 72
Powell, Charles 146, 269
Powell, Dilys 253
Powys, John Cooper 187
Princenthal, Nancy 239
Pritchard, William H. 188–9, 193, 273
professionalism xii, xv, 2, 9–10, 22, 23, 24, 31, 35, 36, 38, 70, 77, 85, 87, 91, 94, 96–104, 105, 108, 109, 111, 113, 114–15, 125, 126, 129, 130, 135, 136, 138, 140, 144, 157, 168, 174, 175, 179, 186, 198, 199, 206, 208, 214, 215, 216, 217, 224, 225, 226, 228, 229, 230, 231, 236, 238, 241, 244, 251, 259, 260–61, 262, 268, 270, 272; defined 96–97; *see also* amateurism
Propertius 22
Proust, Marcel 45, 109
public, general *see* reader, common
publicity 3–4, 8, 9, 11, 14, 38,68, 71, 88–89, 116, 117, 130, 132, 196, 238
Puccini, Giacomo 70
Purves, Alan 245, 274
Pynchon, Thomas 230

Quarterly Review 55
Quinn, John 12
quotation 46
quotation marks 14, 45–47, 86, 128, 189, 252

Rahv, Philip 80
Rainey, Lawrence 263, 267
Ransom, John Crowe 16, 29, 55, 60, 61, 136, 225–26
Ratcliff, Carter 218
Ravel, Maurice 66
Re, Judge Edward D. 139, 143
Read, Herbert 108, 167, 215, 263
reader, common (general public) 8–9, 10, 27, 28, 30–31, 36, 46, 77, 93, 96, 101, 104, 132, 140, 141, 144, 157, 162, 166, 173, 180, 182, 190, 202, 204, 205, 206, 207–8, 217, 218, 223, 237–38, 243, 250, 251, 256, 259, 262, 270; educated 156, 268, 269; lazy 25, 26, 47, 82, 115, 120, 141, 149, 159, 162–63, 171, 172, 175, 272
Recht, Harold 103
Reeves, James 223
Reger, Max 239
Rehm, George 248

Renoir, Auguste 214–20, 238, 275
revolution 4, 8, 38, 92, 115–21, 143, 164, 216, 240, 265–66; *see also* social change
Reynolds, Frank 67, 69, 76
Richards, I. A. 16, 32, 268, 270
Riding, Laura 43, 46, 157, 166, 188, 210, 224, 247, 252, 270
Rifkin, Ned 232
Rimbaud, Arthur 250
Rittenhouse, Jessie Belle 272
Robbins, Bruce 262, 272
Roberts, Michael 52, 101, 111, 113, 114–15, 252
Robinson, E. A. 184
Robinson, Lillian 229
Robinson, Ted 58
Robinson, Walter 218–19
Rockwell, Norman 39–42, 65, 202, 218, 232; *The Conoisseur* 39–42; *40*
Rodman, Selden 29, 31, 109, 251, 261
Rogers, Robert E. 80
romanticism ix, xv, 22, 23, 27, 29, 31, 32, 33, 87, 105, 108, 111, 114, 125, 126, 128, 129, 136, 145, 161, 163, 166, 175, 206, 224, 228, 229, 236, 246, 251, 258, 260–61, 262, 268
Roosevelt, Theodore 66, 243, 271
Root, E. Merrill 192
Rosenfeld, Paul 171
Rosenthal, M. L. 274
Rosten, Norman 205
Rothschild, Edward 168, 263, 271
Rosenberg, Harold 223–24
Rosenberg, Isaac 106
Ross, Trevor 173
Rubin, William 142
Rumelhart, David 257
Russell, Francis 248
Rybert, Walter 151, 161

Saint-Saëns, Camille 153
Salon des Refusés 256–57
Sandburg, Carl 123, 153, 184, 188, 209, 214, 262
San Quentin 88–94, 127, 131, 210, 238, 261
Santayana, George 274
Saturday Evening Post 39, 41, 251
Sarett, Lew 146–49, 150, 165, 184; *The Box of God* 150, 165, 184
Sayler, Oliver 94, 122
Schiele, Egon 218
Schjeldahl, Peter 121, 218
Schlauch, Margaret 81
Schneeman, Carolee 235
Schneider, Alan 88–89, 261
Schoenberg, Arnold 170, 233, 239, 240, 268
Schubert, Franz 268
science 25, 99, 100, 101, 112, 262, 263

Scorsese, Martin 230
Searle, Leroy 270
Seiffert, Marjorie 64
Seldes, Gilbert 269, 270
Senie, Harriet 143
Sergeant, Elizabeth 191
seriousness 96, 100–1, 102, 103, 104, 120, 141, 149, 163, 168, 174, 185, 202, 218, 219, 221, 224, 232, 238, 243, 244, 267, 274
Serra, Richard 137–44; *Tilted Arc* 137–44, 175, 232
Seurat, Georges 219
Sessions, Roger 70, 94–95, 110, 122, 124, 163
Shakespeare, William 22, 27, 30, 79, 106, 207, 242, 251, 259, 270
Shanks, Edward 12
Sharp, Robert Lathrop 264
Shaw, George Bernard 102
Shelley, Percy Bysshe 27, 38, 251
Shetley, Vernon 245, 273, 275
Shipp, Cameron 247, 257
Shklovsky, Victor 118, 266
Sickert, Walter 66
Sidney, Sir Philip 27
Silver, Kenneth 174
simplicity xv, 27, 28, 32, 33, 58, 64, 79, 97, 98, 116, 122, 133, 135, 145, 150, 152, 157, 163, 174, 178–220, 225, 226, 231, 232, 259, 273, 274; actual, of difficulty xv, 25, 46, 47, 83, 131; as argumentation 183–88, 243; deceptive 27, 64, 85, 135, 189, 193–95, 197, 199, 202, 204, 205, 220, 232, 234, 235
sincerity 83, 95, 108, 147, 154, 166, 178, 180, 184, 185, 188, 191, 192
Sinclair, May 105, 107, 119, 169, 170
Sitwell, Edith 7, 27, 58, 62, 106, 163, 164, 197, 246
Sitwell, Osbert 7, 58, 164
Sitwell, Sacheverell 7, 58, 164
Smith, Brydon 86
Smith, J. C. 183
Smith, Paul Jordan 73–74, 78
Smith, Roberta 142
social context, of difficulty ix–x, xi, xiii, xv, 9, 10, 19, 22, 23, 30–31, 35, 38–39, 41–42, 43, 56, 71, 76, 77, 81–82, 86, 98, 117–21, 125, 137, 139, 162, 168, 103, 204, 225, 229, 236, 239, 250, 261, 267, 271
social change xv, 142, 143; *see also* revolution
Soupault, Philippe 122
Sparrow, John 36, 45, 83, 154, 248, 272
specialization 96, 97, 99–100, 101, 102, 103, 132, 134, 141, 148, 158, 160, 181, 250, 251, 269
Spencer, Theodore 264
Spiller, Robert 194
Squire, J. C. xii, 1, 2, 9–13, 16, 18, 19, 20, 24, 27, 35, 36, 37–8, 51, 56, 82, 105, 117, 125, 187, 197, 200, 236, 246, 248, 249, 263; "The Man Who Wrote Free Verse" 2–10, 20, 27, 35, 37, 39, 43, 51, 56, 116, 16; "Piebald Unicorn" 51; *see also London Mercury*
Stafford, Barbara 275
Stauffer, Donald 27, 135, 136, 196–7, 260
Stegner, W. E. 99
Stein, Arnold 251
Stein, Gertrude xi, xii, 16, 17, 26, 45, 52, 53, 57, 65, 68, 71, 72, 81, 92, 94, 95, 106, 108, 122, 127, 128, 151, 152, 157, 169, 174, 201, 214, 234, 237, 240, 241, 247, 248, 265; *The Making of Americans* 48; *Melanctha* 92; "Portrait of Mabel Dodge" 108, 247; *Tender Buttons* 18, 35, 64–65, 71, 81, 116
Steinbeck, John 188, 214
Steiner, George 51, 52, 245, 274
Steiner, Wendy 267
Steinlauf, Norman 140
Stella, Frank 139
Sterling, George 184
Stevens, Wallace 58, 137, 147, 168, 181–82, 247; *Harmonium* 64, 181–82
Stewart, D. H. 195, 196, 273
Stieglitz, Alfred 241
Stifter, Adalbert 274
Stonier, G. W. 56
Stork, Charles Wharton 180, 182
Storr, Robert 138, 142
Stravinsky, Igor 52, 256; *Sacre du printemps* x, 35, 45, 65–66, 75, 124, 156, 256, 264
Strobel, Marion 133, 164, 169, 170, 171
Strong, L. A. G. 106, 122, 171, 270, 272
Strychacz, Thomas 96, 262, 270
Sturgeon, Mary 111
sublime 23, 32, 86, 128, 130, 155, 156, 161, 171, 172, 228, 235, 236, 251, 256, 258–59, 261–62, 268
Sudjic, Deyan 236
Surette, Leon 267
surface and depth 60, 62, 63–64, 108, 192, 193, 194, 195–99, 233, 236, 254, 273, 274
Sutton, Denys 217–18
Swinburne, Algernon 190, 257
Symbolism 22, 23, 129

Tate, Allen 16, 25, 264, 270
Taylor, John 252
Taylor, Rachel 263
Taylor, Rev. Harry 137
Tchaikovsky, Peter 238
Teasdale, Sara 159, 181, 184
technique 11, 20, 22, 24, 25, 35, 80, 98, 103, 113, 159, 191, 216, 250, 265
Tennyson, Alfred Lord 27, 131, 179, 236, 250, 251, 257, 269
Thayer, Scofield 99

Index

Theobald, Lewis 259
theory, difficulty's relation to xii–xiii, 14, 31–34, 44–49, 64, 104
Thomas, Dylan 192
Thomas, Wright 198
Thomas, Edward 58
Thompson, Francis 129
Thomson, Shirley 86
Tietjens, Eunice 62, 103, 104, 159, 185, 172–73
Time 14, 17, 106, 146
Times Literary Supplement 72, 98, 107, 132, 245, 249
Tolstoy, Leo 200
Towne, Charles Hanson 251
transition 115, 152, 154
Travis, Molly 275
Trench, Herbert 2, 3
Trilling, Lionel 194, 201, 204–5, 273
Troy, William 124
Tryphonopoulos, Demetres 267
Tucker, Paul 218
Turner, W.J. 13
Turner, Mark 49, 61, 253, 254, 257
twisting 29, 79–80, 152, 159, 169–70; *see also* perversion, madness
Tynan, Kenneth 88
Tzara, Tristan 15

understanding x, 59–60, 61–64, 74, 108, 126, 160, 229, 236; defined 49–53
UNDERSTANDING IS FOLLOWING 62, 108, 109
UNDERSTANDING IS GRASPING 62
UNDERSTANDING IS SEEING 61, 63
Untermeyer, Louis 16, 24–25, 51–52, 58, 126, 132, 133, 135, 150, 153, 157, 164, 178, 180–81, 182, 185, 191, 201, 202, 208, 243, 248, 249, 270, 271; "Einstein Among the Coffee-cups" 51–52; on T. S. Eliot 51–52, 132, 135, 152, 157, 248, 249

Valéry, Paul 58
Vanderham, Paul 259
Van Doren, Carl 191
Van Doren, Mark 27, 108, 124–25,149, 150, 164, 232–33, 257
Van Spanckeren, Kathryn 194
Van Vechten, Carl 65–66, 127, 129
van Zuylen, Marina 119, 245, 273–74
Vern, David 271
Victorian literature 29, 104, 105, 146, 166, 257
Virgil 106
viscerality 18, 22, 35, 44–45, 61, 64–84, 145, 165, 170–73, 214, 232, 234, 240, 243–44, 253, 255, 256–57, 258
Vonnegut, Kurt 221; *Slaughterhouse-Five* 221–23
Vorticism 11

Warhol, Andy 230
Warner, Michael 262
Warren, Robert Penn 16, 274
Waugh, Arthur 12, 20, 21, 116, 271
Waugh, Evelyn 12, 21; *Brideshead Revisited* 21
Weber, Bruce 230
Weber, Samuel 262
Webern, Anton 239
Weireck, Bruce 147
Weiss, Ted 140, 141
Weston, Jessie L. 270
Wetherell, J. E. 10
West, Rebecca 192–93
Weyergraf-Serra, Clara 270
Wharton, Edith 228
White, Allon 196, 245
White, E. B. 231
Whiteley, Linda 217
Whitman, Walt 29, 30, 182
Wilhelm, James 245
Wilkin, Karen 275
Wilkinson, Bonaro 252
Wilkinson, Marguerite 145, 153, 156, 158, 160, 178, 182, 184–85, 188, 200, 201, 206, 214, 249, 273
Williams, William Carlos 15, 26, 63, 107, 110, 164, 167, 170, 171, 209, 210, 211, 212, 247, 264, 265, 274; Poem (As the cat) 209; *Spring and All* 164, 167
Williamson, Alan 252
Williamson, George 127, 167
Williamson, Hugh Ross 27, 29, 45, 163
Wilson, Arthur 254–55
Wilson, Edmund 16, 57, 108, 131, 146, 269
Winters, Yvor 16, 210, 246, 253, 264, 268
Wolfe, Humbert 20
Wolfe, Thomas 113, 123, 124
Wolff, Albert 215
Woolf, Leonard 155
Woolf, Virginia xi, xii, 1, 17, 82, 155, 156, 167, 174, 214, 261, 265; *Jacob's Room* 107, 152; *Mrs. Dalloway* x; *To the Lighthouse* 57, 58–59, 193
Wordsworth, William 23, 27, 33, 149, 259
Wright, Richard 92
Wylie, Elinor 23, 29

Xenophobia 55, 82, 103, 104, 148, 230

Yeats, William Butler 23, 105, 149, 154, 176, 210, 249, 260, 267; *The Winding Stair* 249
Young, Marguerite 198
Yust, Walter 271

Zabel, Morton Dauwen 57
Zorach, William 66
Zukofsky, Louis 197